PRAISE FOR

'An important new perspecti putting the women who suppo centre stage ... also a damn goo

Mensun Bound, Directo ion of Endurance22, and author of *The Ship Beneath the Ice*

'The human story behind the well-known heroism is beautifully told. After more than a century in the shadows, the wives left behind by the Scott expedition are brought vividly, poignantly to life. A compelling, unforgettable book.'

Dr Tracy Borman

'This is the most mesmerising book! I wanted to follow these women's lives – their highs and lows – and couldn't turn the pages quickly enough. Their unique personalities leap out through Anne's expressive writing, and they appear so three-dimensional against such carefully constructed backdrops. This is social history at its best.'

Dr Janina Ramirez

'By avoiding reducing women's history to the cliché that "behind every great man is a great woman", [*Widows of the Ice* shows] that history in the making is not only experienced but felt, poignantly and painfully.'

Times Literary Supplement

'*Widows of the Ice* explores materials drawn from an impressively wide range of sources in both public archives and private collections ... Historians and polar enthusiasts alike will find much in here to mull over, as the book helps to uncover hidden histories of the Heroic Era.'

Polar Journal

'A fascinating book that lifts the veil on an untold chapter of polar history.'

Michael Smith, author of *An Unsung Hero: Tom Crean* and *Shackleton: By Endurance we Conquer*

[illegible] WIDOWS OF THE ICE

"[illegible] perspective on our polar heroes achieved by [illegible] who supported, and sometimes drove them, at [illegible] read."

—[illegible] of Exploration [illegible]

[illegible]

WIDOWS OF THE ICE

THE WOMEN THAT SCOTT'S ANTARCTIC EXPEDITION LEFT BEHIND

To Philippa
Happy birthday!
Anne Fletcher

ANNE FLETCHER

AMBERLEY

For my mother, Pauline Fletcher,
the most formidable widow I know.
With love and gratitude.

This edition published 2023

Amberley Publishing
The Hill, Stroud
Gloucestershire, GL5 4EP

www.amberley-books.com

British Library Cataloguing in Publication Data.
A catalogue record for this book is available from the British Library.

ISBN 978 1 3981 1731 0 (paperback)
ISBN 978 1 4456 9377 4 (ebook)

1 2 3 4 5 6 7 8 9 10

Typesetting by SJmagic DESIGN SERVICES, India.
Printed in India.

Contents

A Note on Names

Robert Falcon Scott led two British expeditions to the Antarctic. The first, from 1901 to 1904, was called *Discovery*, after the ship that took the men and their supplies via New Zealand to Antarctica. For his second expedition, Scott used a different ship which again gave its name to the venture. The *Terra Nova* expedition lasted from 1910 to 1913, but Scott did not return.

The men of the *Terra Nova* expedition gave each other nicknames. Captain Robert Falcon Scott was 'The Owner', Dr Edward Wilson was 'Bill' or 'Uncle Bill', and Petty Officer Edgar Evans was 'Taff'. Because this book is about their wives, however, I have chosen instead to call their husbands by the names that they used.

Kathleen Scott called her husband Con, an abbreviation of his middle name, Falcon, and the name also used by his mother. Because his name is famous throughout the world and is synonymous with the Antarctic, I have called him Scott when talking about the expedition and wider national matters.

Oriana Wilson called her husband Ted in private and so that is how I refer to him. When corresponding with his *Terra Nova* colleagues, however, Oriana did use their name for him, Bill or Uncle Bill. I have also called him Wilson when talking about expedition matters as with Scott, primarily to distinguish him from Lieutenant Edward Evans (later Admiral Lord Mountevans) who was known as Teddy Evans.

There are no surviving letters between Lois Evans and her husband Edgar and so we do not know what she called him. I can't imagine it to have been anything other than Edgar, however, so I have chosen to refer to him as that. Calling him Edgar throughout also helps to distinguish him from the other Evans on the expedition, whom I have tried to consistently call Teddy Evans for clarity.

Prologue

Ten thousand miles from home, in the Antarctic waste, three bodies float in the ice for all eternity. Entombed in the Ross Ice Shelf, they lie where they died, inside their tent: Robert Falcon Scott, Edward Wilson and Henry Bowers, the last survivors of the five-man team that had reached the South Pole on 17 January 1912 only to find that a Norwegian team led by Roald Amundsen had beaten them by a month. All five had died on the way home. Edgar Evans had perished first, and his body lay somewhere at the foot of the Beardmore Glacier. One month later, Lawrence Oates had walked out of the tent into a blizzard, telling his comrades, 'I am just going outside and may be some time.' The surviving three walked on, but when they pitched their tent for the final time a vicious storm prevented them going any further. It raged for nine days. As food and fuel ran out, Scott, Wilson and Bowers prepared for death and Scott wrote for the last time in his diary on 29 March. With their last thoughts for their loved ones, Scott and his comrades passed into immortality, their deaths a formative moment in the life of the nation and its history.

When Scott's 'Message to the Public' was printed, his final words fuelled an outpouring of both grief and pride:

> I do not regret this journey, which has shown that Englishmen can endure hardships, help one another, and meet death with as great a fortitude as ever in the past ... Had we lived, I should have had a tale to tell of the hardihood, endurance and courage of my companions which would have stirred the heart of every Englishman. These rough notes and our dead bodies must tell the tale...[1]

Their heroic failure catapulted the polar five into popular culture, forever a proud symbol of British courage, duty and determination to fight against even the toughest of odds. The newspapers, which only ten months before had seen their circulation figures rocket thanks to stories about *Titanic*, saw another opportunity for sales. Their coverage of the *Terra Nova* expedition lasted weeks and transformed Scott and his men into international heroes.

The account of the expedition and the death of its Polar Party was built up from the final words of a group of very courageous men and translated into a story of derring-do for public consumption, and the public reaction to it illuminates a world where duty and sacrifice were seen as essential tenets of Britishness. Less than eighteen months later, thousands of young men would volunteer to fight at the outbreak of the First World War, excited by the chance to do their duty and possibly to sacrifice themselves for their country in the heroic manner of Scott and his company. But behind this inspiring story of 'Scott of the Antarctic' is another version. It is the story of those left behind by this bravery, and the terrible loss with which they had to come to terms. While their loved ones were lionised by the public for their courage, they were tortured by the horror that this entailed; suffering from exhaustion and hypothermia, and without water or food, they had starved to death. These men were sons, brothers and most importantly husbands, and their heroism left behind women with broken lives. Scott and his men knew this. Their last letters were to the women they loved, and Scott's last diary entry put the future of the families of those who died with him into the hands of the nation: 'For God's sake look after our people.'

Of the five men in the Polar Party, three were married: Scott, Wilson and Evans. Bowers and Oates had devoted mothers, but it was the three wives, widowed together in the early months of 1912, whose lives were most dramatically changed. It was these women – Oriana Wilson, Kathleen Scott and Lois Evans – who would have to live the rest of their lives without the men they loved. Their lives have mostly been obscured by those of their husbands, relegating them to the supporting roles Edwardian wives were expected to take. This has been compounded to varying degrees by the paper trail that each left behind. It was a time of voluminous correspondence, and these couples were apart for long periods of time, so they filled that time by writing to each other. Scott was a wonderful writer, expressive and full of emotion. Ted Wilson wrote often and freely, as did Edgar Evans, sending colourful and fascinating accounts of his time away. The letters written by their wives show their passion, doubts, fears and tensions, but unfortunately they have not all survived. Some, too intimate to share, were kept private; some were edited or lost; others were destroyed. This fractured record, together with the enormous interest in their husbands, has meant that Kathleen, Oriana and

Lois have primarily been glimpsed throught the letters and diaries of their men. But these women played a central role not only in their husbands' private lives but also in the Antarctic story.

This book is about three women with very little in common except the traumatic experience that they shared. Their husbands died together, and for a few months in 1913 they were thrown together to grieve in the limelight as people all over the world held their men up as heroes. Although they met together only on a few occasions, and probably would never have met under normal circumstances, this was a shared experience that was to shape the rest of their lives as they fiercely and loyally defended their husbands' legacies. This is not the story of famous women but of forgotten wives, whose love and support helped to shape one of the most famous stories in British history. Putting them back into it gives a new perspective to those events. It is a story of imperialistic dreams, misogyny and classism, but also of enormous courage, high ideals, duty – and, of course, love.

PART 1

Wives

You from the first have always been different …
and I am the man you have blessed above all.

Ted to Oriana

Oriana

When Oriana Fanny Souper was born on 19 September 1874 the stars seemingly aligned to make her the wife of an explorer. Ernest Shackleton, the man who would lead three British Antarctic expeditions, was born the same year, as was Howard Carter, who unearthed Tutankhamun's tomb and all its treasures. Five months before her birth, the body of missionary and explorer David Livingstone was brought home to be interred in Westminster Abbey. The stories of his travels into Africa, his disappearance and his eventual death had made him a national hero. But Oriana did not take the adventurous path. She would choose for her husband a doctor, naturalist and devout Christian. Perhaps it was a trick of fate that took this most unassuming of men and turned him into a polar explorer.

Oriana was the product of a family which had nurtured lawyers, doctors, artists and clergymen, and in which the tradition of public service was embedded. Dr Philip Dottin Souper, her grandfather, had spent significant time in Trinidad as colonial secretary and Clerk of the Council to the Governor, living the life expected of such a man, including owning a slave.[1] When he returned to England in the 1830s, he worked as Company Secretary to some of the newly emerging railway companies but concluded his career as he began it, in the colonies, taking on various administrative roles in Mauritius. Fortunately, his reputation as a public servant was not marred by the career of his father, William Souper, a British Army officer who had been found guilty of murder. On 13 April 1814, in Lymington, William shot and killed a fellow officer in a duel. According to a witness report, the other man had fired first and missed. The judge brought down the full weight of the law on William to deter other officers from duelling, and he was sentenced to death at Winchester assizes.[2] An execution date was set but he was pardoned after his fellow officers organised five signed petitions.

Oriana's family also had a very strong creative streak which ran through its Reinagle branch. Philip Reinagle was a famous artist and member of the Royal Academy of Arts. He worked alongside Allan Ramsay on his official portraits of George III and Queen Charlotte, and after many years of portraiture began to paint animals, botanical subjects and landscapes. His wife Jane was an artist too, and their passion flowed down through their nine daughters and two sons. Charlotte, Oriana Georgiana, Maria, Jane and Harriet were all amateur artists, some of whom exhibited at the Royal Academy and the British Institution. As women they could not be elected to either, but this privilege was enjoyed by their brother Ramsay Richard Reinagle, who was elected to the Academy in 1823. Almost certainly named for his father's mentor, Ramsay studied under his father and followed his style, specialising in landscapes. Inexplicably in 1848, he sent a painting to be exhibited at the Royal Academy only for it to be revealed as the work of another artist which Ramsay had bought, made a few alterations to, and submitted under his own name. The deception was discovered, and he was forced to resign from the Royal Academy, eventually dying in poverty. Ramsay's daughter Oriana Jane Reinagle married her cousin Philip Dottin Souper in 1827, uniting the two sides of the family. Their son the Reverend Francis Abraham Souper would be Oriana's father.

Francis did not follow his grandfather William into military service or his father Philip into colonial office, nor did he take up a paintbrush as his great-grandfather Reinagle and his children had. Francis Souper's calling was to be a clergyman and a teacher. After graduating from St John's College, Cambridge, he was ordained into the church when he was twenty-five. He had been teaching for a few years at Bradfield College in Berkshire where he had been a pupil then in 1871 moved to Scotland to take up a post at Glenalmond College in Perth.[3] But after only a year, Francis returned to England because he'd been offered an unmissable opportunity: he became Headmaster of Bradfield.[4] The appointment was a significant step up in his career and the security gave him the confidence to change his life in another, even more important way because the following year he married Fanny Emmeline Beaumont.

Fanny came from a family of lawyers with very strong links to the City of London. They were respectable, professional and class conscious and her father, James Beaumont, was a solicitor. His wife, Eliza Charlotte Fisher, also came from a London legal family and was only sixteen years old when she married him. They moved to Highgate, then a village to the north of London, and into one of the grand houses in The Grove, where they had four servants: a cook, a nurse and two maids.[5] James's profession made the family welcome members of what would have been regarded at the time as a very respectable social circle. Eliza gave birth to nine children, including Oriana's mother, Fanny, in 1848. At least three of her sons became lawyers like their father and grandfather; both William Coppard Beaumont and Edward Beaumont were based at Lincoln's Inn as James had been, and William also followed his father by being made a Freeman of the City of London in 1863.[6]

The family moved to south London at some point in the 1860s, eventually choosing Arundel House in the village of Lee in Kent. Close to Greenwich and Blackheath, this area is now in the London borough of Lewisham, but when James and Eliza moved there it was outside the city. Merchants and wealthy families were establishing themselves there in new villas and ornate cottages that were close enough to work in London but offered a cleaner and more picturesque setting. Fanny was living at Arundel House with her parents when she met Francis Souper, whom she married in August 1873 when she was twenty-four and he was twenty-eight. The wedding took place at St Margaret's Church in Lee and the vicar was assisted by the rector and warden of Bradfield College, where Francis was already headmaster.[7] After the ceremony, Fanny moved with her new husband to Bedfordshire to begin their married life at the school. They were to have eight children, and the names that they chose for them resonated with those of their ancestors. Among them would be James Francis Dottin Souper, Noel Beaumont Souper and Edward Reinagle Souper. Their first child, and eldest daughter, born at Bradfield on 19 September 1874, was given the names of both her grandmother and her mother: Oriana Fanny Souper. Her childhood was typical of a well-to do Victorian girl and she spent the first three years of her life at the school, joined when she was two by her brother James.

Bradfield had been founded by the Reverend Thomas Stevens, and it was he who had appointed Francis as headmaster, the first former pupil to take that role. Unfortunately, his five-year tenure as headmaster was not a success. Francis had gained experience of how other schools operated during his time at Glenalmond and now had ideas of his own about education. This caused friction with the founder of the school, who'd chosen him because he thought he'd toe the line. Perhaps it was these new ideas that caused a contemporary to describe Francis as 'a pronounced faddist of the most irritating kind'.[8] These problems were compounded by financial difficulties. Salaries were paid irregularly, and as a result the college lost some of its talented senior staff. Even

Francis was asked by Stevens if he wouldn't mind a delay in receiving his payments.[9] It's impossible to say if Francis Souper would have made a better headmaster of Bradfield under different circumstances, but he certainly left the school disappointed and regarded as a failure. He did not give up, however. He relocated his young family to the south coast and embarked on a new venture where he could put his own ideas into practice.

The village of Meads in East Sussex lay near the sea and the chalky South Downs. Agriculture was the main industry in the area, but the hills supported the other major source of employment. The chalk that was mined from them was burnt in kilns to produce lime, used as a fertiliser on farmland and, since Roman times, in cement and whitewash. Lime quarries and kilns broke up the grassy landscape, which was otherwise barren from the chalky soil and the wind that came off the cliffs. There were no trees to interrupt the view one way towards the seaside town of Eastbourne and the other to the towering chalk cliffs of Beachy Head.

Meads was a tiny settlement. There were one or two large houses, including the All Saints Convalescent Home that dominated the area, but it mainly comprised small fishermen's cottages clustered around Colstocks Farm. It was here that Francis Souper brought Fanny and their two young children, Oriana and James, in 1877. The farm had been converted into a school twelve years before and although Eastbourne had over seventy schools, there was very little competition in Meads.[10]

This small village school on the south coast, which Francis eventually renamed St Andrew's, was Oriana's home for thirteen years. Because Francis owned it, he could set about creating a prep school that reflected his own educational philosophy. His liberal attitude seems to have been ahead of his time. He didn't believe in cramming children for exams and resented having to teach subjects solely to pass entry exams for schools such as Winchester. He insisted on the importance of fresh air and health; his choice of this little school on the top of a cliff, blustery with sea air, was part of this philosophy. In his correspondence with parents there is evidence that many of his boys suffered from poor health, and that is perhaps why they chose his school and its healthy environment. Pupils studied a range of subjects including drawing, singing and shorthand, and plenty of time was made for outdoor recreation. Cricket and football were played on the school field and boys were led on rambles across the South Downs. Francis taught many of the classes himself, and to fit in as much as possible it was a long school day, starting with half an hour of religious instruction and ending as late as half-past eight in the evening.[11]

The remote and bracing environment of Meads must have been a wonderful place for Oriana to grow up. She was three when the family moved there, and because her father was fully occupied with his pupils and running the school much of her time would have been spent with her mother Fanny and her baby brother James. She grew up enjoying the South Downs, the nearby cliffs at Beachy Head, the seashore, and the lively atmosphere of the school.

Because of her father's position as headmaster of St Andrew's, the family had a certain status in the area. When the Duchess of Albany visited Eastbourne in 1889 to lay the hospital's foundation stone, he attended with local dignitaries and later that year he was one of the great and the good who dined at the mayoral banquet in the town.[12] Francis was also involved in local politics as a Liberal, and he was often vocal in the local press, particularly on church matters and the evils of drink. Consequently, Oriana would have been encouraged to acquire the accomplishments expected of a Victorian young lady: to play the piano, to sew and to dress well. Music was very important at her father's school; every boy learnt to play the piano and the choir often stood in at services in the local church.[13] Oriana learnt to play the piano beautifully and music was a great pleasure to her for the rest of her life. Girls of her class would expect to attend a boarding school or, if poorer, have a governess or go to a local dame school, but growing up in a school meant that Oriana was educated at home. Her father's attitude to rearing children, which sought to develop the whole child, must surely have been applied to her too. The strong faith, sense of duty and responsibility that would characterise her life can be traced to her parents, but so too, perhaps, can her streak of independence.

Shortly after Francis and Fanny arrived at Meads, Noel Beaumont Souper was born. Two years later came Constance Mary. Their fifth child, aptly named Quintus Meads, was born in 1881, and within two years was followed by Woodford Nowell and Edward Reinagle Souper. But this story of a thriving family hides a tragedy. In the spring of 1888, Fanny was pregnant with her eighth child. Settled in the home where she had already given birth to five children, she must have been awaiting her delivery with some confidence. Childbirth in Victorian England was never without risk, however, even for those women who'd safely delivered several babies. Fanny died soon after the birth, on 2 April 1888, aged only thirty-nine.

Before the family had been able to come to terms with their loss, just weeks after her death, tragedy struck the Soupers again. Oriana's oldest brother, eleven-year-old James, was playing with his nine-year-old sister Constance and one of his younger brothers. They had walked from the school to the cliff edge at nearby Holywell, close to Beachy Head, to gather wildflowers. What happened to James next was reported in newspapers all over the country:

> ... he fell down the cliff on the beach, a distance of fifty feet. The screams of his brother and sister brought assistance to the spot, and medical aid was at once obtained, but the boy's skull was fractured. The lad died in less than an hour. The greatest sympathy is expressed in the town for Mr Souper, who only four weeks ago was bereaved of his wife.[14]

It is hard to imagine a greater trauma. With two swift blows the family lost both Fanny and James, and gained a baby, Adrian Wilfred James, who would never know his mother. The effect on Francis was shown clearly in his work. His grip on the school, and particularly on its finances, began to loosen and life at St Andrew's began to fall apart. Keeping up student numbers – and therefore revenue – had been a problem for some time. In 1880 he had thirty pupils, six years later there were twenty, and by 1890 numbers had dropped to a perilous twelve. One of Francis's solutions to dwindling numbers was to keep places filled by being flexible about leaving ages, as shown by this letter to a parent in 1886:

> You will understand, I'm sure, that – as this professes to be a Preparatory School – it is practically impossible for me to keep Ernest any longer, now that he is seventeen years of age. The transparent pretence that he is some sort of Master would not serve...[15]

After Fanny and James died, Francis's accounts fell into even more of a muddle. Grieving and left to manage the school and a young family, it all became too much and in 1890 Francis was forced to sell his school. Aged just forty-six, his departure marked the end of a teaching career that had been marked by disappointment and financial difficulties.

Oriana was thirteen when her mother and brother died. As the eldest child and the eldest daughter, she took on many of her mother's duties including looking after her younger siblings and a brand-new baby as her father oversaw his struggling school. This period of her life lasted three years, until her father married again in 1891, and his children and new wife, Henrietta, moved with him as he took up a succession of posts. For four years they lived in Devon, where Francis was chaplain and secretary to the British Seamen's Orphan Boys' Home in Brixham. He then took up several church posts, and Oriana moved with him from Devon to Hampshire and then to Dorset.[16]

The tragic events of Oriana's early life, and the impact that they had on her childhood, helped to form the woman that she became. She adopted the role of nurturer and supporter at a young age as she stepped into the void in her family left by her mother, and she began to develop the resilience on which she would need to draw for the rest of life.

Ted

Edward Wilson, a gentle, devout, dutiful, hard-working and creative man, was the perfect choice for a girl of Oriana's respectable and genteel upbringing. They were introduced on 4 April 1897 in Battersea in south London. Oriana was there to visit her stepmother's sister Emily, who had recently married the Reverend William Bonner Leighton Hopkins. Emily and Henrietta Escreet, Oriana's stepmother, had family ties with the great social reformer Charles Booth, and both women made a point of working with the most disadvantaged in society. It was Henrietta who had persuaded Oriana's father to leave the school system and move to Devon to work for the British Seamen's Orphan Boys' Home in Brixham after they married. Emily, meanwhile, actively supported her husband in his work in the slums of Battersea, where he had been running Caius House for six years when Emily married him in the nearby church of St Mary's.[1]

Established as a joint venture between St Mary's and Gonville & Caius College in Cambridge, Caius House was the centre of a mission to improve the lives of those who lived in the slums around it, the children in particular.[2] The initiative was part of a wider philanthropic drive called the Settlement Movement, founded by Canon Barnett in the 1880s and the earliest example of social work in Britain. Men like the Reverend Hopkins, Oriana's step-uncle, had a new attitude to the poor. Rather than blaming poverty on weak character, the Settlement Movement believed that social conditions were its cause. Their solution was to recruit educated people to form relationships with those in socially deprived areas and encourage them to see not only the importance of education but a broader view of the world.

The Settlement ethos resonated with those among the middle classes, particularly those studying at Oxford and Cambridge, who felt a duty to help those who were less fortunate. Because the idea would only work if they were living among the people they were trying to help, settlement houses sprung up in some of the poorest parts of the country.[3] Caius House ran activities and clubs and offered support and advice, and Reverend Hopkins had students from Cambridge University staying with him to help. Edward Wilson, or Ted as he was known, was one of these 'settlers'. It was a role that suited him in several ways. He had a place to live just a short walk from St George's Hospital, where he was working as part of his Cambridge medical degree, and he had the opportunity to work in the nearby slum, helping with health issues and with the mission's social work.[4]

On that evening in April, Oriana was sitting chatting with Emily Hopkins when she heard the front door open. She looked up to see a red-headed young man with bright blue eyes and freckles standing rather shyly in front of her. To escape the awkwardness of the moment, Ted thrust into his landlady's hand the small bunch of bright yellow spring narcissi that he had picked on his way home from the hospital. For Ted it was love at first sight. He wrote later, 'Nothing is more extraordinary, I think, than the feeling one has of loving people at first sight, and without a word being spoken. *You* know what I mean by love in this way.'[5] He was so smitten with the tall, blue-eyed, brown-haired twenty-two-year-old Oriana that after going to bed he slipped back downstairs just to hear her sing. Two days later their hosts returned from dinner and were surprised to find the young couple sitting and talking together; they were so engrossed with each other that they hadn't noticed that the fire had gone out.[6]

But all was not as it seemed with this energetic young man. Ted was suffering from an illness that was diagnosed the following spring as pulmonary tuberculosis.

Ted's illness had been exacerbated by his ascetic lifestyle. His profound Christian faith had led him to a belief that only a life of self-control and self-deprivation would do, as he wrote to his sister Polly in 1893:

> I've decided that if I once got hold of that perfect self-control, then a higher ideal than a monk's life would be open to one, ... you might get into a state so much wrapped up in the welfare of others that your own never crossed your mind ... This is the most fascinating ideal I think I have ever imagined to become entirely careless of your own soul and body in looking after the welfare of others.[7]

During his three years at Cambridge Ted had put this philosophy into practice, testing his physical endurance through rowing and other sports and living very frugally despite his father's generous provisions. In 1895, when he began the three years of clinical work at St George's required by his degree, he continued to overstretch himself. In addition to his studies and work at the hospital he ran a youth club twice a week and a children's service and Bible class on Sundays at the Caius Mission. He regularly skipped meals, racing around London to visit art galleries and lectures. Drawing was central to his life, and he fitted in frequent trips to sketch at London Zoo, the National Gallery and the Natural History Museum. Every morning before work he read and annotated the New Testament. This gruelling schedule had finally caught up with him.

When Ted was diagnosed with pulmonary tuberculosis, it was understood that there was no cure. Patients were advised to rest and take fresh air, and so Ted left the polluted London streets and returned to his family home in Gloucestershire, quite possibly to die. Oriana knew none of this. She had returned home to her father's house in Dorset and had heard nothing from the young medical student who had so enchanted her at the Mission.

Nearly a year after their fireside chat in Battersea, Oriana arrived in Ted's home town, Cheltenham, to take up a job. She was now twenty-four years old and had to earn her own living in one of the few ways open to a genteel, middle-class, unmarried woman of limited funds. She had grown up in public schools, and her sense of duty and experience in helping to run a home and look after her siblings – as well as the boys at the orphanage – equipped her well for a role as a school matron. She took a job at Suffolk Hall Preparatory School in Cheltenham.[8] She lived at the school and helped to look after seventeen boys, aged six to twelve, who had come from all over the world to board there.

Oriana's choice of a school in Cheltenham rather than in Dorset must surely have had something to do with Ted. Suffolk Hall was in the fashionable Montpellier area, only a short walk from Westal, the Wilson family home on Montpellier Parade. Her great-nephew David Wilson says that she was unaware of the connection and that it was her step-uncle and aunt, Revd and Mrs Hopkins, from Caius House, who told Ted that Oriana was in Cheltenham.

Whether she had taken up the post to meet with Ted again or had been an unknowing pawn in a matchmaking exercise by her relatives, the attraction was mutual. Oriana could not know it but Ted, confined to his sickbed, was yearning for a soulmate. Just two days before they met again, he wrote in his diary:

> If there was one whom I could trust and love and be so bound up with that he or she could share with me and understand my joys and my love, and my passion for beauty, for colour, for form, for pure joy of

> nature, – if he or she could enter into my thoughts and feel with me ... But it is only now and again and for years the heart hungers in between.[9]

Ted had told his family about Ory, as he called Oriana, and his sisters were keen to find out more. She was invited to Westal for the first time on 12 March 1898.[10] It was a large, detached white Regency-style house with four reception rooms, ten bedrooms and a nursery, set in beautiful gardens with greenhouses, stables and a fernery. The family had five servants: a cook, a housemaid, a parlour maid, a kitchen maid and, when the children were young, a German governess.[11] It was just the sort of home that a successful physician like Ted's father would purchase for his family. It was also a home that encouraged Ted's interests and independence. When he brought a buzzard home it was happily accommodated, even after it stood in a plate of sliced tomatoes at supper before falling asleep on Ted's knee.[12]

Ory walked the five minutes from Suffolk Hall up the private carriage sweep and rang the doorbell. If she was nervous when she sat down with Ted and his sisters for tea and cake, she soon forgot about it as she noticed that he was not well. He didn't have the energy that he'd had in London, and he had a very troublesome cough. When Ted told her of his illness, he seemed resigned to it; his faith in God and the afterlife meant that he did not fear death. Ory, however, was determined that he would live. Nurturing and supporting others had been her way of life since she was thirteen, and so she rolled up her sleeves to help look after him. When he'd written to his parents about her earlier in the year, Ted had said that Ory was going to be a 'Useful Help' at the school in Cheltenham, and very soon the Wilson family began to refer to her as 'the UH'.

Ted did grow stronger in the home and countryside that he loved. His sister Polly stayed with him most of the time and Ory was a regular visitor. Still, his health had not fully returned when in May he decided to travel to Norway. He'd been invited to stay by friends, and his doctor believed that the climate would be good for his health. He would be away for three months, the first of many separations Ory would have to endure. Their reunion in Cheltenham had set a pattern that was to shape their life together; Ory would nurse the man she adored while he would be forced away from her frequently by his search for a mission and a meaning for his life.

Ory saw Ted again in August at Westal. They also spent a great deal of time at Crippetts, his family's rented farmhouse 3 miles outside Cheltenham, which was one of his favourite places. There he introduced Ory to two of his greatest passions: observing and painting nature, particularly birds. They spent happy days in the summer of 1898 exploring the countryside that had inspired his love of nature and his desire to be a naturalist. She and Polly walked across the countryside with him and stopped to sketch as he wished. But Ted was still far from well and it was decided that he should spend the winter at the sanitorium in Davos in Switzerland to try to get better. Ory could do nothing but hope and pray for his recovery and endure another separation, this time of seven months. They had agreed to write to each other before he left, and over the next few months she received regular letters from Ted as their relationship deepened.

Ory had found a free-thinking, artistic, sensitive young man whose deep faith matched her own. She could listen sympathetically and enthusiastically to his view of a world guided by God in which one's own interests were never paramount. It was a belief that she shared but which was to be tested many times during their relationship, and perhaps for the first time when Ted returned briefly to England in May 1899, still coughing up blood and too unwell to work or complete his degree. She and Ted had been writing for months, but she was still unsure of his intentions. He had embarked on a medical career, but he talked of his loathing of domestic routine and his yearning for adventure. Ory could see that this was not a man who seemed likely to settle down to married life. His parents, witnessing their son's relationship at close quarters, were equally concerned. Ted's mother wrote to him to ask if he was going to marry Ory and he replied quite firmly, 'I am not engaged to Ory or anyone else nor do I ever intend to be.'[13] Perhaps Ted believed his own protests, or perhaps he was protesting too much because he knew that he had little to offer Ory. His health and ability to work were so uncertain; how could he commit to a life with her when he might not be able to provide for her? He was too ill to finish his degree, he had no income, and his prognosis was poor. He did not expect to have a future.

Ted travelled to Norway again in the summer, this time staying for two months, but when he returned to Cheltenham he had put his doubts aside and on 19 October 1899, exactly one month after Ory's twenty-fifth birthday, he proposed. She gladly accepted. She'd instantly fallen in love with the red-haired, exuberant Ted and her two-year wait for him was at last over.

Ory's expectations might well have been of marriage to a doctor, probably based at a general practice in Cheltenham, but Ted's thoughts were now diverging from the expected path. The freedom that he'd enjoyed in his travels made him reluctant to settle into the life of a doctor.[14] Lingering inflammation in his lungs rendered missionary work in Africa impossible, and he needed to acquire much more practical experience before he could take on any sort of medical specialism. The answer to his dilemma appeared quite out of the blue, and must have been an astonishing surprise to Ory.

A Scientist's Wife

As the first year of a new century dawned, the world changed irrevocably. On 22 January 1901, the diminutive queen who had ruled Britain for sixty-three years passed away. Victoria was escorted to her grave by five reigning monarchs and seven grand princes, most of whom were her relatives. For the last forty years she had isolated herself, immured in her grief and her widow's weeds and out of the public eye for much of the time, and so the accession of her son as King Edward VII marked the start of a new age. With his beautiful Danish wife Alexandra and their mutual love of fashion, sport and entertaining, the new king dusted down the old reign, threw open the windows and brought a glamorous, glittering shine to the monarchy. He inherited the world's leading industrial nation and an empire covering a fifth of the globe and a quarter of its population. The promise of a new Edwardian age and a fresh start was reflected very clearly in Ory's life.

Ted went back to his studies as soon as Ory accepted him. He needed a job if he was to marry, so the immediate priority was to complete his medical degree. Ory helped him find accommodation in Stanmore, close enough to London for his work but far enough for him to breathe cleaner air. Stanmore had the added benefit of a common rich in birdlife. Owls, coots, herons, jays, kestrels, nuthatches and woodpeckers swooped around it, and Ory soon became as eager to watch them as Ted. His love of ornithology was infectious. His friend John Fraser described how Ted loved to sleep in the woods listening for bird and animal noises and could tell not only what bird it was but also what the bird was doing.[1] Ory developed a love of 'earbirding', writing down the calls of individual birds almost as she would a musical score, recording the pitch, the repeated notes and the words that they resembled.[2]

Ory returned to work in Cheltenham but wrote encouraging letters as Ted worked and revised and crammed to catch up on the eighteen months he had missed through illness. He was due to take his final exams at Cambridge in December. Ory's father had moved his family to Cambridgeshire a year earlier when he became vicar of Hilton, so during the Christmas holidays and between exams Ted and Ory were reunited at the vicarage. It was the first time that Frances Souper had met his daughter's fiancé, and he approved. He saw that Ted's natural tolerance would be a perfect balance for Ory's critical tendencies. She struggled to control this side of her temperament, and to remind her to think before commenting she kept on her mantlepiece the words, 'Is it Kind? Is it True? Is it Necessary?'[3] Ted passed his exams, and after completing his dissertation on 'Yellow Atrophy of the Liver' was awarded his degree on 7 June 1900. He had missed Ory terribly during the slog to become a doctor, but finally he had career prospects. He was thrilled to announce to his family that he was now 'a ginger-headed copper-knob named Ted, M.B.'[4]

Just as the course of their life seemed set, a letter arrived. During his convalescence Ted had worked on developing his artistic skills, and a family friend, Dr Philip Sclater, had taken him under his wing as his talents as a painter emerged. Impressed by his work, Sclater, who was Secretary of the Zoological Society of London, granted Ted access to London Zoo and its library for sketching. He also invited Ted to the British Ornithological Union, where he met many influential bird artists and was eventually proposed as a member. Ted had progressed from a hobbyist to an artist respected by other ornithologists.

In the early summer of 1900, Sclater wrote to his young protégé, urging him to apply for the post of junior surgeon and zoologist on the *Discovery* expedition to Antarctica. Antarctica, unoccupied and unmapped, was the last great frontier on Earth. It was by no means certain that there was a continent in the blank space that appeared on every chart; only small areas of coastline and the peaks of mountains protruded from a permanent sheet of ice, which was in places 2 miles thick. But the possibilities were tantalising.

Attempts to reach Antarctica – or *Terra Australis Incognita*, the Unknown Southern Land – had been dominated by the British Navy. In 1773 Captain James Cook became the first recorded navigator to cross the Antarctic Circle, but land was not sighted for another fifty years. Captain James Clark Ross, who had reached the Magnetic North Pole in 1831, was then sent to try to find the Magnetic South Pole. His expedition, which endured from 1839 to 1843, failed in this objective but his fleet did sail along the Antarctic coastline, discovering and naming many of the features that would be central to the stories of later explorations. Among them were McMurdo Sound, an area which he named Victoria Land after his queen, and Ross Island, whose twin peaks he named after his ships *Erebus* and *Terror*. Any attempt to explore further was blocked by an enormous cliff of ice that he named the Great Ice Barrier.[5]

In 1895, the 6th International Geographical Congress passed a resolution that 'the exploration of the Antarctic Regions is the greatest piece of geographical exploration still to be undertaken' and that, in light of the advances to be made there in almost every branch of science, scientific societies throughout the world should encourage it. Expeditions were launched by several European countries to explore different areas of the Antarctic coast and share their discoveries. Belgium sent *Belgica* south in 1898, and the ship and its crew, including a young Roald Amundsen, were the first to endure an Antarctic winter after getting stuck in the ice. German and Swedish teams would set out next, and their departure would be followed by the British National Antarctic Expedition, also known as *Discovery*. The origins of the *Discovery* expedition lay with Sir Clements Markham, secretary and then president of the Royal Geographical Society, whose passionate pursuit of geographical discovery and the advancement of science shaped the progress of British polar exploration. Under his leadership, the society's objectives shifted. No longer could the heroic explorer bring back mere tales of adventure; he must measure the world too, recording scientific observations and providing the geographical information necessary for the empire to prosper.[6] The pursuit of knowledge was an important part of *Discovery*'s mission, which included sailing to Victoria Land to undertake a full magnetic survey, and travelling as far south as possible to conduct a scientific survey of botanical and geological material.

Ted was uncertain at first about applying to join the expedition. He was still recovering from tuberculosis, he'd only just qualified as a doctor, he still doubted his abilities as a painter, and, of course, he had just become engaged. Pulling against these constraints was his childhood dream of becoming a naturalist, which was still burning bright, as were the tales of empire and exploration that had inspired him throughout his youth. He came from a family of enthusiasts, original thinkers and explorers. Typically for a Victorian middle-class boy, Ted was a 'Child of the Empire', proud to be British and keen to serve God, monarch and country. The joy that he had found in his travels to Norway opened him up to the glorious possibilities of the world, and he had thrilled at the tales of polar exploration shared by Norwegian explorer Fridtjof Nansen on his lecture tour in 1897.[7]

Four years before, Nansen's *Fram* expedition had set out to reach the North Pole. When his ship could go no further, Nansen and one of his team had attempted to make it overland using sledges and dogs.

Although they hadn't succeeded, his lecture series celebrated the scientific knowledge that the expedition had gathered. The first, held on 8 February at the Albert Hall in London, was hosted by the Royal Geographical Society and about 7,000 Fellows and their friends came to watch the lecture. Nansen had illustrated his talk with his own photographs and coloured sketches, which must have thrilled Ted.[8] Here were combined all of his passions: art, science and exploration.

Perhaps Ted remembered this when the letter arrived in the early summer of 1900 suggesting he go to Antarctica. He told his father, 'I am going for it for all I know because it is obviously a golden opportunity.'[9] Ted was certain the climate would be good for his lungs, but more importantly he had been adrift, unwilling to do what was expected but uncertain of the alternative. Now he had a purpose. He sent in his provisional acceptance, and his name was proposed by his uncle Charlie, who talked up his nephew's abilities at the Royal Geographical Society, handing out examples of Ted's drawings and painting as he did so.

But what about Ory?

Having been engaged for only eight months, she was faced with the immediate prospect of her beloved Ted sailing into the unknown to disembark on the ice for two years. Communication would be sparse until he returned – if he returned at all. In the three years that she had known him she had become used to months of separation, but this was something that she had not expected to be asked to endure. When he came to see her in Cheltenham to talk to her about their future, she no longer saw a young doctor or a recovering invalid but a man who had found a mission. He told her that he could take on the two-year position at St George's that he'd been offered, and they could set up home on his salary, or he could go to Antarctica, which paid a salary too. She could see that his heart was set on scientific discovery and exploration with a passion that would put it before her and the life that they might share together. Birthdays, anniversaries and even honeymoons would have to flounder in its wake. And Ted was prepared to risk his life for it.

Ory did not feel the same. Ted knew the sacrifice that he was asking her to make, and he may have felt guilty, but his mind was made up and the odds were stacked in his favour. Even if they married, Ory's wishes would be steered by her husband's because promising to obey Ted, as she would in the wedding service, meant something. And besides, Ted had God on his side. He believed in divine providence, and it was his obligation to follow. Joining the *Discovery* expedition was God's will, and how could Oriana argue with that?

At the end of their conversation, Ted asked Ory to sign a letter acknowledging that the decision to join the Antarctica expedition had been a mutual one. It was an unusual prenuptial agreement, one that meant Ory was signing away her right to bear any resentment or to blame Ted for whatever might happen. It was odd that he should ask her to sign such a document, but perhaps not odd that she would do so. Ory loved Ted. How could their relationship survive if she stood in the way of what he believed God wanted for him? With great reluctance, she gave her written consent. Ted was overjoyed and wrote to her that she had removed all the thorns from his path.[10]

The *Discovery* Expedition

Sir Clements Markham had appointed a young Navy officer, Robert Falcon Scott, to lead the *Discovery* expedition. They had first met in 1887 when Scott was serving on HMS *Rover* and Sir Clements described him as a charming boy. After meeting up at various points over the following years, it was at Sir Clements' house in Eccleston Square in June 1899 that Scott, then a torpedo officer on *Majestic*, volunteered to command the Antarctic expedition. Markham accepted and Scott was promoted to commander for the purpose.

Ted had to impress Scott in order to join *Discovery*, and so travelled down to London to meet him. He was 'practically appointed' on the spot. Scott recommended a move to London as soon as possible, and later that month Ory helped Ted to find rooms in Pinner. His expedition medical was now due, but he'd been seriously ill for a couple of months with an infected abscess in his armpit. His sister Polly went with him to London, and despite feeling very ill and suffering from a bad headache, Ted passed provisionally in January 1901 and was given three months for his arm to heal.[1] In fact, the head of the scientific staff accepted his appointment regardless as long as he went at his own risk. On 13 July, however, a fully recovered Ted told the Admiralty Medical Board about his tuberculosis. They promptly failed him, ruling that the scar tissue on his lungs rendered him unfit. Scott was nonetheless adamant that Ted should come, insisting that the medical made no difference given that he had already agreed to go at his own risk. He prevailed. A delighted Ted had secured his place:

> I am going … they accept me in spite of everything if I will go at my own risks. I don't care in the least if I live or die – all is right and I am going; it will be the making of me.[2]

For a young man in love and engaged to be married to say that he does not care if he lives or dies seems peculiar. Ted was passionately in love with Ory, but his Antarctic mission overwhelmed him to the extent that he was unsure whether he should get married.

Even before he officially secured his place, Ted was involved in expedition planning, travelling to Dundee to see the ship, studying birds and taxidermy at the Natural History Museum, attending dinners and functions, and meeting his expedition mates. Ory was working at the school in Cheltenham and only managed to see him on those weekends when he was able to come home. Her break from school for the Easter holidays gave her a precious opportunity to spend time with him, and he joined her at Westal for the Easter celebrations. They travelled to Westerham in Kent to stay with the Hopkinses, who'd recently moved there after leaving Battersea,[3] with Ted commuting back to London daily for work. A final visit to Eastbourne to see Ory's stepmother marked the end of this precious time with Ted.

When the expedition ship *Discovery* arrived in London in May, Ted had hardly any free time. He desperately wanted Ory to be his wife, but he didn't know if it was fair to ask so much of her. Ted's mother certainly didn't think they should marry. Waiting was a prerequisite for a chaste young woman, and for many wives of the time separation was the norm. The expansion of the empire and the war in South Africa meant many wives of soldiers or civil servants were kept from their spouses for a very long time. Togetherness, then, was not an expectation of marriage, but children were, and Ted's mother did not want such a responsibility for her son, who had already been weakened by illness. She wanted him to be free to concentrate on his work and not to worry about a wife and children at home.[4]

On 13 July 1901, Ory received a telegram from Ted telling her that his place on the expedition was confirmed and, putting all his worries aside, that they should begin planning their wedding. Three days later they were married at the Church of St Mary Magdalene in Hilton, Cambridgeshire, where Oriana's father was the vicar. Oriana was twenty-six and her new husband twenty-nine.

> The bride looked charming in dress of white satin trimmed with chiffon and lace, and she wore tulle veil with a wreath of real orange blossoms. She also carried a bunch of white trumpet lilies ... There was a large number of villagers and others to witness the happy ceremony...[5]

Summer was glorious that year, and on this beautiful day the church was filled with white flowers and music. It was a very happy family occasion.

Ory's sister Connie and Ted's sister Polly were the bridesmaids, carrying bouquets of rosebuds and wearing large black hats and long dresses of soft white silk trimmed with lace.[6] Each had a long black ribbon attached to their left shoulder in memory of Queen Victoria. Oriana's father Francis gave her away, and the ceremony was conducted by the Reverend Hopkins, who had introduced the young couple four years before at his mission in Battersea. Ted's brother Bernard, newly returned from the South African War, was best man while Oriana's thirteen-year-old brother Adrian played the organ.[7] The wedding reception was held at her father's vicarage in Hilton, and afterwards Ory, who always wore elegant brimmed hats and beautiful shoes and loved to wear blue, changed into her going-away outfit.[8] Dressed in 'blue grey cloth trimmed with guipure lace, and a hat trimmed with white ostrich plumes', the new Mrs Ted Wilson travelled with her husband to his lodgings in Pinner to begin married life.[9]

Among their wedding presents was a beautiful triple dessert stand inscribed, 'Presented to E. A. Wilson on his marriage with Miss O. F. Souper, Sir Clements Markham, K.C.B., and the Commander. Officers, and Scientific Staff of the S.S. *Discovery*, 16th July.'[10] This reminder of what lay ahead must have been compounded in Oriana's mind when her young husband wrote his will just nine days after they married.[11] They had only two weeks until he had to leave, and they spent what should have been their honeymoon preparing for their long separation and saying goodbye to relatives. Oriana embraced the challenge with gusto equal to her love for Ted. She threw herself into helping him in his preparations, sewing and embroidering his sledging flag as did all polar wives of her class; the design incorporated his own crest, coat of arms and motto. She knitted woollen vests for him too, while Polly knitted helmets and she made treats of butterscotch and ginger for him to take on his journey.[12]

The day after the wedding Oriana was given her first look at *Discovery*, the ship that would take her husband to the Antarctic. It had sailed from Dundee to the East India Dock in London, where it was being fitted out and loaded with coal, provisions and scientific equipment. This work was being done around visits to the ship by dignitaries and amid a great deal of public attention. Ory met many of the men with whom her husband would be sailing, and for the first time she got a sense of how he would be living for the first few years of their marriage. A few days later she proudly guided twenty of her relatives around the ship.

On 31 July, *Discovery* left London. As it sailed down the Thames and around the south coast, it was met with cheers and hoots as excitement about the expedition grew. For Oriana, the departure meant that she had Ted to herself for a few precious days as he was given special permission to spend time with her at their home in Pinner.[13] Ory and Ted were blissfully happy, and very well suited. They were extremely loyal to each other, and although he was much better educated, Ory was clever and could help Ted with his work. He wrote to his friend John Fraser that he was 'as happy as it is given to mortals ever to be on this earth'.[14]

The ship made a stop at Cowes on the Isle of Wight where the expedition's patron, the new king Edward VII, was on his royal yacht for the annual regatta. Ted was due to meet up with it there, so on 3 August Ory helped him to pack up their possessions at Pinner and put aside all the memories of those few days together in their first home. Those memories would have to last them years. Ted wrote in his diary:

> It was very very difficult to pretend to be cheerful ... Alas, there was a sound of weeping and woe ... It was very sad though leaving the place where we had both had the very cream of this life's happiness, I could believe of the next life's too. Goodness me. We were happy there![15]

Their last night together was spent at the Grosvenor Hotel in Southsea. It followed the pattern that their married life would take: Ted working flat out to try to finish his report on seals for the Natural History Museum, with Ory at his side supporting his efforts and making copies. On 5 August, King Edward VII and Queen Alexandra boarded *Discovery* and were met by Sir Clements Markham to inspect the ship and meet the crew.[16] As soon as the royal party had gone, the relations and friends of the expedition were allowed to come aboard. Ory left Ted on the ship after lunch, taking the launch back to the mainland with the other relatives to spend the night in the hotel. She had had a terrible headache all day, quite possibly from the strain of knowing that this was almost their last day together and that the final goodbye was imminent. That night she slept alone – she would have to get used to it.

The next morning, 6 August 1901, Ory and her sister Constance travelled to *Discovery* to say their goodbyes to Ted. Dressed in a grey dress and black hat, she stood on the deck with him in the brilliant sunshine as the ship set sail from Cowes and thousands of people waved and cheered from the shore and myriad small boats hooted from the water. Family and friends stayed on board for as long as possible. Ory and Ted sailed together all morning while the ship made its way to Yarmouth, where she would be forced to disembark. She pressed into Ted's hands a small icon. He promised to carry it on him until he returned, and he would be true to his promise, even keeping it in his pyjama pocket.[17]

Ory made a supreme effort to be brave as she prepared herself to say goodbye to her husband of only three weeks. There were a few tears, and the parting was 'painful but happy … she smiling to the last was just as brave as could possibly be'.[18] In her farewell Ory did her husband a great service. She sent him on his way with a smile and her total support, leaving him free of worry and able to commit to the great challenge ahead. What it cost her to wave Ted away with such a cheery smile can only be imagined.

Reunited

While Ted was away Ory made her home with his parents at Westal so that she could finish the term at Suffolk House, returning to her father's home in Hilton during the school holidays. She and her new in-laws wrote letters to every port where Ted would dock, and they received regular letters from him. Unfortunately, they often overlapped and so it was difficult to keep up to date with news.

Regular updates in the form of carbon copies of Ted's diary entries arrived at Westal, however. 'Written primarily for my Wife', these pages allowed the family to read about his adventure and share his wonder at the plants, trees, animals and birds that he was encountering. They also reassured Ory that she was always with Ted in spirit. He recorded every birthday and every wedding and engagement anniversary that he missed – 'Ory's birthday – the third that I have missed since we were married. What a husband, poor girl!'[1] – and he frequently took himself off on his own to spend time alone with his thoughts of her, touchingly describing these times as being given up 'entirely to Ory' or 'in the evening I devoted myself to Ory'.[2]

Ory had decided that she would not wait for Ted to return home but would shorten their time apart by meeting him in New Zealand, where the ship would dock after leaving Antarctica. She had already booked her passage. It was probably best that the stay at Westal would be short as it was rather a strain. Ted's parents were a formidable couple. Mary Agnes Wilson had been born in St Petersburg into an English expat family which ran a successful trading company in Russia. Although she had moved to Cheltenham as a child, her family travelled back and forth to the land of her birth and those who had stayed in Russia came to Cheltenham to visit. Mary Agnes was artistic, with a fond curiosity for nature. She rented Crippetts, the farm that Ted so loved, so that she could experiment with raising poultry and she became an authority on breeding them, writing a book, *The ABC Poultry Book*. She was also deeply religious. Her husband, Edward Thomas Wilson, was a doctor and worked at Cheltenham General Hospital for over thirty years. His concern for the poor of the town drew him to the slums and to work tirelessly in support of public health measures. He'd passed his social conscience on to Ted and also to his brother Jim, a socialist who was concerned about working conditions.

Oriana had a great deal in common with this couple, whose Christian beliefs directed their life and work, and who also loved nature and had an artistic bent. They all loved Ted with a passion. Edward Wilson was deeply attached to his son, and Mary Agnes described him as the pride of the bunch, the brightest and jolliest of her babies.[3] But they had not known Ory for very long before she came to live with them, and Mary Agnes had certainly been reluctant for her son to take on the responsibility of a wife before he left. Now that responsibility had fallen upon her and her family, and it was not without its tensions. Ory was a no-nonsense sort of woman and could tend towards criticism. There must have been times when she struggled to hold her tongue. Jealousy flared in Mary Agnes when her treasured son first shared news with his young wife. The situation was not helped when Mary Agnes opened Ted's letters to Ory by mistake because she was Mrs E. Wilson too.[4] Ted was aware of the situation, and in letters to his favourite sister Polly he asked her to help:

> ... do your best to smooth down jealousies between the family and my Ory, over things I am sending home. I know I am sending everything to her, but then she is my wife & has a right to me, first right above everyone else alive, to me & all I do, and I love her as I have never loved anyone, and she loves me too as she has never loved anyone, and it's an awful thing this separation that God has put on us and I must do all I can to help her in it.[5]

Ted's letters to his family show his great love for his new wife and his admiration for the strength she was demonstrating in his absence:

> However much I trusted her, I never quite expected that her love could overcome her self in this way and how I admire her for it you can guess. I miss her badly sometimes of course and there's a chronic undercurrent of a bad want...[6]

It was Ory's strength and support that were sustaining him and making the challenges that he had to face so much easier for him. 'I feel as fit and as happy as can be, how can I help it, when my Ory is such a brick,' he wrote.[7] Ted's parents must soon have come to realise just how important a role their new daughter-in-law was playing in their son's great adventure. In her determination not to show her sadness and fear, Ory displayed all the essential characteristics of a polar wife. Although her bravery came from her total devotion to her husband and her deep Christian faith in his mission, the resilience and stoicism that resulted were exactly the qualities she needed to survive, and to support the rest of the family. Ted held a firm belief that his mission was sent by God and that their separation would end in a happy future together, but he could also sound fatalistic and some of his letters must have been hard to read.

Ory needed all her strength and faith to keep positive during their long separation, especially after *Discovery* sailed away from New Zealand on Christmas Eve 1901. The Eastern Extension Telegraph Co. allowed all crew members to send their final farewell messages to their families free of charge before all communication with the ship was lost.[8] Ory would now be cut off from any news of Ted for at least a year. Not until the relief ship *Morning* sailed to Antarctica to meet up with *Discovery* and bring the crew's letters back to New Zealand would she hear from him again. Ory hoped that Ted would come back too; if he did, she would be there to meet him.

In January 1903, she set sail for the seventy-five-day journey to New Zealand with her sister Connie, who had taken a job as a teacher at a mission school on the North Island. After visiting their brother Woodford, who was already teaching at a school in Marton, they travelled by train to the South Island and the city of Christchurch.[9] This was the *Discovery* expedition's base in New Zealand, and it was to nearby Lyttelton Harbour that the ship would return from Antarctica. Shipping magnate Joseph Kinsey, the expedition's agent in New Zealand, welcomed Ory into Warrimoo, his family home in the city to wait for *Discovery*'s return. On 25 March, a ship was sighted coming into harbour. Ory rushed to greet it, but soon discovered that it was the relief ship *Morning*. Greater disappointment was to come. The crew carried the news that *Discovery* was to remain in the Antarctic for the winter. Ted was not coming home.

It was a crushing blow. Ory had known that this was a possibility but had travelled to New Zealand hoping that it would be otherwise. Now she had to gird herself for another year without Ted. *Morning* had brought her his letters and his diary and also a message from Scott. Realising how shocked and disappointed she would be to hear that Ted was not coming home, he sought to soften the blow by telling her how invaluable her husband was to the expedition:

> We had some trying times, and if such come my way again I hope I may have such a man as your husband by me ... I feel confident he will get home safe and in better health than when we started, and I trust it may comfort you in your disappointment to know how well he is and how much we all esteem him.[10]

As Ory read Ted's diary and letters she came to understand what Scott meant by 'trying times'. On 2 November 1902, Scott had led Ted and fellow expedition member Ernest Shackleton on an attempt to travel as far south as they could, to the Pole if possible, or at least to some new land. In what became known as the Southern Journey, the three men pulled sledges for ninety-three days over a distance covering 1,540 kilometres, battling through scurvy, starvation and adverse weather. It had been dangerous and difficult. Despite leaving the seriously ill Shackleton behind to guard the camp while they pressed further, Scott and Wilson could not reach the pole. They did, however, set a new record for 'furthest south'. On the way home, Shackleton, suffering badly from scurvy, had to be pulled on a sledge for some of the journey. When they returned safely to base, Scott sent him back on *Morning*, believing he was too ill to endure another winter in Antarctica. Ted had been bedridden for a month, but had stayed, and now he would be looking forward to the prospect of more discovery and exploration. For Ory, there was no option but to be proud and patient.

Ory was the most senior *Discovery* wife present, and with the *Morning*'s return generating local excitement about the expedition, attention focussed on her. Shackleton also became something of a star for surviving the 'furthest south' journey, and the pair were invited as guests of honour to garden parties and social occasions among the elite of Christchurch. Not having known quite what to expect as an explorer's wife, fortunately Ory had packed a chiffon tea gown and her wedding dress as well as more practical daytime outfits in case there were social events to attend. She enjoyed this social whirl a great deal, writing to Ted's brother Jim, 'There is nothing like being married to a *Discovery* man, there is quite a glamour of romance over one & I am having a splendid time.'[11]

Ory had promised not to be sad when Ted had first set out, and so she tried to stay positive. Rather than return home, she decided to stay in New Zealand. She had a growing group of friends, in particular Sir Clements Markham's sister Lady Bowen, who lived near Christchurch, and she had the time to explore the country with Connie, using the free travel passes that the New Zealand government had given them. But when her sister had to leave to begin her teaching job, Ory began to feel very lonely.

During her year of waiting, she had too much time to think about the future. There was the anticipation of a wonderful reunion, but she was also plagued by uncertainty about what would come next. Without Ted there to talk to, her mind raced. The arrival of the New Zealand winter brought even greater isolation, so much so that Ory booked onto a ship that would take her home for Christmas, only changing her mind at the very last moment and disembarking. To keep herself busy, she took up the post of matron at the school where her brother Woodford was teaching. When term ended, she made cups of tea and plates of food at a café in Palmerston North.

While Ory worked hard to distract herself, Connie had a nervous breakdown from overwork, prompting their aunt Constance to travel to New Zealand to scoop up her nieces and settle them in a rented house with her in Sumner. There Ory waited for Ted, cut off from regular news and climbing up the hills to look out for his ship in Lyttelton Harbour below.[12]

Bright and early on 1 April 1904, Good Friday morning, Ory was awakened with the news that *Discovery* was sailing in.[13] It would be in port in an hour. In a letter written to the family back home in Westal, she wrote,

> You can imagine how quickly we huddled on clothes and tore off on the road over the Port Hills to Lyttelton. We did the walk of four miles in record time; but when we reached the top there was no sign of any of the ships. By a piece of great luck, we found the Harbour Master, Capt. Clarke, who said he would take me out with him before any of the Harbour Board got down … The Pilot's daughters were there; they had gone early with the Pilot boat. I asked them whether they had any news of Ted and imagine my joy when they said they had seen him on the bridge with Captain Scott! … Presently the Mayor, Mr Wigram, came up and said that he had been deputed to see that I was the first to be put on board the *Discovery*. When Ted at last appeared beaming, and I was helped on board, then indeed all was well.[14]

Ted was delighted to be reunited with his wife, who didn't look a day older than when they parted and yet far more beautiful. For him their reunion 'beats a wedding hollow'.[15] He recorded in his diary, 'What a day it was, a brilliant sunshine and as still as possible. What a day, indeed! We both felt that.'[16] There was so much to catch up on, not just about Antarctica but also Ory's year in New Zealand. She had waved him off with a smile and a promise to be cheerful, but the wait had been long and punctuated by the terrible shock of finding that their separation would last another year. Ted had worried about what he would be asking of Ory when they parted, but it was only now that they were reunited that he realised just what a good job she had done of keeping the challenges to herself. He was grateful to her and to those who had supported her, particularly the Kinseys, who had provided a home from home.

Over the next few weeks, Ory supported Ted as she had always wanted to do. He had social duties to perform in New Zealand as a *Discovery* officer and they were made much more bearable by her presence. The couple spent many hours together in Christchurch museum labelling, drying and recording specimens that he had brought back or spotting emus, pukekos, waxeyes and paradise ducks as they walked around the city.[17] Ted was granted leave and he was able to take Ory on a proper honeymoon where she could share with him the New Zealand that she had discovered in his absence. This precious time together forged in them a mutual love of the country, its wildlife, trees and plants, and sowed in their minds the idea of a future life there, cataloguing the indigenous plants that were already being destroyed as the island was developed.[18]

With their passionate attachment to each other and a mutual love of natural history, Ory could imagine a life supporting Ted in the field as naturalists. Ted felt that if he could write and illustrate books on the animals of the South Polar region and New Zealand, his life would have been worth living. He told his father that 'in a century or less, all or most of this unique flora and fauna will be extinct – they are dying out before one's eyes. I could spend a few years here with advantage on a really classic piece of work.'[19] Ted and Ory hoped that he would be funded to stay in New Zealand, but no job was forthcoming and reluctantly they accepted they would have to leave, at least for now.[20] But first Ory had a very important duty to perform.

The expedition threw a ball for the people of Christchurch on 1 June, and Ory decorated the hall, bringing in lush foliage to represent their host country and installing an expedition sledge piled high with equipment and crowned by two men in furs.[21] As Scott was unmarried, Ory stood beside him to receive guests on behalf of *Discovery*.[22] The newly married Hilda Evans, meanwhile, took on the role for the guests of the *Morning*.

Twenty-year-old Hilda Russell had married twenty-three-year-old Lieutenant Edward 'Teddy' Evans, the second officer of the relief ship *Morning*, on 13 April. Ory and Ted had attended the ceremony in which the beautiful young New Zealander married her English sailor. It was a fashionable naval wedding, held at St Barnabas Church in Christchurch with a reception afterwards at Hilda's family home.[23] As the *Discovery* ball was Ory's first as a married woman and it was Hilda's too, they both wore their wedding dresses as was the tradition.[24] The ball was a huge success, and Ted observed it all proudly: 'I could only stand in the crowd and admire her, and wonder how the deuce such a girl came to give herself to me ... She behaved as though she had done that sort of thing all her life – and she looked so tall and graceful.'[25] The three hundred and fifty guests drank, dined and danced until four in the morning.

When the time came to return to England, Ted and Ory sailed back separately, he on *Discovery* to continue his work and she with Connie on the *Tongariro*. Hilda Evans was on board with her mother, travelling to her new homeland.[26] The long voyage gave Ory the chance to get to know her better and the two wives became friends. Talking to Hilda about her new love, her wedding and her excitement about her new married life must have made Ory's pain sharper when on 16 July she passed her third wedding anniversary without her husband. She and Ted had been apart for all their anniversaries and during their marriage had spent only thirteen weeks together, but they were nearly home now and could finally look forward to a shared life.

Ted and Ory settled into married life in Bushey, which satisfied Ted's usual requirements of proximity to both city and countryside. They eventually moved into a small house called Tynecote, which had a studio for Ted at the bottom of the garden. Just a few minutes' walk down the lane there were copses and marshy hollows full of the natural wonders that they both loved, and Ted's favourite sister Polly lived close by with her family. Ted busied himself illustrating Scott's book *Voyage of the Discovery* and copying his Antarctic pictures, along with lecturing, writing his scientific reports for publication, attending social events and preparing for an exhibition of his paintings in London. He was also commissioned to illustrate a new book, *The History of British Mammals*. Oriana found herself immersed in Ted's passion for the natural world. She was a willing and able assistant, on one occasion helping him to collect a rare and precious type of flea. He'd been hunting bats and brought twenty of them home. While sketching one, he adjusted the fur with his pencil and a flea crawled out and on to it. Recognising it as an important specimen, Ted called for Ory, who prevented the flea from escaping while her husband raced off to fetch preserving fluid.

A couple of their status would be expected to have servants, as Ted's parents did at Westal, but they made the highly unusual decision to run their home themselves. Ory did all the cooking and house cleaning, and Ted cleaned the flue, lit the fire and cleaned the kitchen grate. Since Mrs Beeton had written her *Book of Household Management* in 1861, the status quo had been set. An income of £150 a year or more warranted a general servant girl at the very least, and no self-respecting, socially aspiring woman could afford to flout the rules. When Ory and Ted married, two out of every five women in employment in England and Wales (approximately 1.7 million) worked as domestic servants.[27] But Ory had seen many households run perfectly well without servants in New Zealand, and Ted valued time much more than money and felt that anyone buying time from another should ask themselves,

> Am I getting good enough out of this book to warrant my getting others to do my drudgery while I read it? ... If not, I am not fulfilling my side of the bargain, and I shall not be responsible to them for the time they have given me.[28]

Tragedy struck at the end of the year when Ory heard that her younger brother Woodford, who was studying at St John's College near Auckland, had been found dead at the foot of a tree. Unable to get to New Zealand in time for the funeral, she may have thought again how much she wished that Ted had found work out there. Instead, she and Ted joined the rest of her family at her father and stepmother's home at Hilton to grieve.[29] Oriana had now lost two brothers in fatal falls, but this time she had Ted's love and support to help her endure the tragedy.

Ted adored Ory. They were lovers, friends, companions and soulmates. He wrote of their marriage, 'For real happiness our marriage would be hard to beat, and our married life hard to improve upon.'[30] Intensely private and wrapped up in each other and in Ted's work, they didn't need anyone else. As Ted was praising the unbeatable joy of his marriage, Ory was finally able to look forward to a lifelong partnership of work and domestic bliss.

Lois

Excitement about *Discovery* had spread nationwide, and as Ory was reunited with Ted the remote Welsh parish of Rhossili was agog with anticipation as it awaited the return of its own Antarctic hero. But there was one person in the close-knit community who was more excited than anyone else: Lois Beynon, who harboured a hope that the local hero might favour her above all when he returned.

At the very tip of the Gower Peninsula, 18 miles from Swansea, Rhossili was a small rural area comprising the villages and hamlets of Rhossili, Middleton, Pitton and Pilton and the isolated farms and cottages that dotted the landscape around them. It was a very close community from which people seldom strayed very far because it was virtually cut off from the rest of the country until well into the nineteenth century. Even when a road was built from Swansea out to Gower, it stopped at Pitton Cross. A muddy track, squeezed on both sides by high hedges and just wide enough for a horse and cart, ran the rest of the way through Middleton and on to Rhossili.

Perhaps because of its isolated nature, this part of Gower had hardly changed in centuries. It had been settled by the Normans in about 1100, and the earls of Warwick had established an English colony in the south and west. Welsh was spoken in the rest of Gower, but in Rhossili the language was English, and the system of land tenure set up by the Normans had continued. Most of the land, and the homes and farms on it, was owned by the Penrice estate, effectively the Lords of the Manor. Many of the families had lived in Gower for generations, including the Beynons, Tuckers and Bevans, and had become intertwined over the centuries through marriage. There were approximately seventy households and fewer than three hundred people in the entire parish, and over half of the populace were farmers. Those with smaller holdings of land also worked as stonemasons, coastguards, butchers, blacksmiths and shoemakers, but this was principally a farming community.

The families that lived in Gower were focused on the land for their livelihood, but the sea was never far from view. It surrounded their limestone plateau, which looked out towards the Bristol Channel. There were seafaring families and fishermen in Rhossili, and the sea lanes off Gower were crowded with shipping, some even dropping anchor in Rhossili Bay to await more favourable winds. It was a dangerous coast, and ships that ran aground often found themselves washed up on the isolated beaches. Crews were rescued by the 'rocket apparatus' kept near Rhossili Bay, hauled ashore one by one via the long line that was shot out to them from the beach. When they couldn't be saved, drowned seafarers were buried in the churchyard. Wrecks were a source of booty for locals, who found ivory, timber, oranges, wine barrels and all manner of exotic goods scattered on the sand. Smuggling had been eradicated in the 1820s, but prior to that it was an organised night-time industry in Gower, involving many local people transporting goods, particularly French brandy, that was deposited on the isolated beaches and then hidden in the many caves and potholes along the coast.

The sea affected all of the locals in one way or another. It's uncertain where the name of the parish came from, but it may have had its roots in the Welsh words *rhos* (moor) and *heli* (salt water), which is fitting. The smell of the sea blew in with the wind, and the landscape was punctuated with dry stone walls, hedges and banks to protect crops and livestock from its bluster. The very first village of Rhossili was almost certainly lost to coastal erosion and buried by sand, forcing the inhabitants to move up to the relative safety of the clifftop, but even there the Atlantic storms lashed the land and cloud often obscured the view. Only one tree thrived in the new village of Rhossili, an ash tree that grew horizontally because of the relentless battering of the salt-soaked wind. It stood near the parish church of St Mary's, where the rector, Reverend Lewis Hughes, guided the spiritual life of the parish for over twenty years.[1]

Middleton, where Lois lived, was just a short walk from the tiny settlement of Rhossili. It was a hamlet of ten to twelve two-storey whitewashed cottages with small square windows and, in most cases, thatched roofs. There was a shop, a post office and a forge, and there was also a pub called the Ship Inn. It had been run by Lois's family for much of the nineteenth century. Her grandfather was a farmer who had once cultivated approximately 30 acres but in late middle age had reduced his acreage and taken on the running of the pub too.[2] This wasn't unusual, because there were not that many full-time farmers in Rhossili; the land on which they were tenants often didn't bring in enough money to pay rent and to be self-sufficient in food, so most men had other jobs too and many women helped.[3]

When Lois's grandmother died, her grandfather was supported by his daughter Eliza, who went on to run the pub herself for nearly twenty years, although the licence was held for most of that time by one of her three husbands. Aunt Eliza ran a good pub, but some of the hard drinking that went on there shocked a number of the locals. She also had a tragic life, outliving all of her husbands and nearly all of her children, including three who died of typhoid in 1880. After her death in 1893, the pub licence passed to her brother William Beynon, Lois's father.[4]

Lois had spent the first fourteen years of her life in Swansea, where she was born at home on 4 March 1879. Her father had moved to the city from Gower with his wife Jane, and they ran a greengrocers' shop there.[5] Jane gave birth to ten children, but like many women of the time she suffered a great deal of loss. Only five of her brood survived to adulthood: Lois, her sisters Jane and Beatrice, and her brothers Enoch and Stanley.[6]

The Welsh name for Swansea, Abertawe, means 'the mouth of the river Tawe' and gives a clue to the source of the area's industrial success. The Tawe provided power and a water supply for a metalworking industry until steam took over, and then the local coalfields fuelled it. At first zinc and copper were smelted in huge quantities, but by the late nineteenth century it was the tinplate industry that was booming, and its products were exported all over the world via Swansea's docks. Like all thriving industrial towns in the Victorian era, this success came with an appalling set of consequences. Swansea was dirty and overcrowded. The polluted water of the Tawe and the unsanitary conditions in which many people had to live contributed to several devastating epidemics of cholera. In the outbreak of 1849, over one hundred and fifty people died.

The prospect of healthier living conditions and a job and home at the Ship Inn may well have contributed to the decision made by Lois's parents to return to Gower. William came from a large family and had at least eight older sisters, but in his mid-forties, he was the youngest and perhaps best placed to take over the pub. Most of his siblings lived very nearby and so Lois and her brothers and sisters found themselves in a large extended family of aunts, uncles and cousins, as well as a wider group of friends and neighbours. Lois became very well known in the small community, not just because she came from an established local family but because she had a beautiful voice. She joined the congregation of St Mary's and sang in the church choir and in local concerts.[7] She was also a well-known face at the Ship Inn, where she was working to help her parents, when *Discovery* docked at distant Portsmouth on 10 September 1904.[8] Aboard was her cousin Edgar Evans, who had left to join the Royal Navy in 1891 when he was just fifteen.

Edgar

Edgar was the son of a seaman and had grown up on the coast. He was born in Middleton, just a short walk from the Ship Inn, and then moved to Swansea with his parents when he was about six years old.[1] Their house in Hoskins Place was a ten-minute walk from Lois's home in Catherine Street, and her father must have welcomed his sister Sarah and her young family of five to the city. Lois and Edgar were only three years apart in age and theirs was a close and interconnected family. They must surely have spent time together growing up, playing or being looked after with their cousins and siblings as the adults of the family worked. There were frequent visits to Gower, where the Ship Inn remained the hub of family life for many years.[2]

The coastline provided a natural playground for Lois and Edgar to explore together with their siblings and cousins, splashing in the waters of Rhossili Beach and climbing over the wreck of the ship *Helvetia* which had run aground in 1887. Its timber frame and ironwork poked out through the sand at low tide, and clambering over it must have been thrilling to children brought up on tales of pirates and smugglers plying the seas around their home. There were caves and gullies to hide in too, and when the sea was out they could run across the causeway to Worm's Head, the rocky island resembling a sleeping dragon, where sheep grazed on the salty grass to produce the best mutton in Gower.[3]

When he was ten, Edgar was permitted to attend school in the morning and go to work in the afternoon. He became a messenger boy at the Post Office in Swansea by the North Dock, where he met sailors from all over the world. Sometimes he and his friends were allowed onto the ships to see what life on board was like. When he left school, he worked at the Castle Hotel where sea captains drank and told stories of their travels. Their tales of exotic adventure joined the stories that his father had told him and filled Edgar with a passion to see the world. His mother tried to dissuade him, but he joined the Royal Navy as soon as he was old enough, seeking excitement and a chance to travel around the globe.[4]

In 1899, Edgar was transferred to HMS *Majestic*. He served on it for two years under the ship's torpedo officer, Lieutenant Robert Falcon Scott.[5] During their time on *Majestic*, Edgar and Scott forged the basis of a relationship of mutual respect and friendship that cut across class barriers and naval hierarchy. Scott valued Edgar's physical strength, practical abilities and good humour. Edgar, meanwhile, found Scott to be a man worthy of following. It was this loyalty to his senior officer that encouraged Edgar to volunteer to join the *Discovery* expedition when Scott was appointed as its commander in 1901.

Twenty-eight-year-old Edgar returned a hero. He was one of only six seamen commended by Scott in his report to the Admiralty and was promoted to petty officer first class. His arrival in Swansea for a period of leave in September 1904 was reported in the local paper.[6] His adventures gave him a new glamour and fascination to his friends and neighbours.[7] He had the world at his feet, and had been rewarded with a naval promotion and a pay rise. The local girls must have thought he was a good catch, square-jawed, tall and muscular, but it was to his very pretty, petite twenty-five-year-old cousin Lois that Edgar gave all his attention.[8]

It's not clear when their relationship turned to something more romantic, but whatever Lois's feelings had been before he left, she very quickly fell under the spell of the brown-haired, blue-eyed Edgar.[9] He had always been a wonderful storyteller with an inexhaustible supply of anecdotes, such as the time at the Ship Inn when he'd ejected a group of raucous visitors from Swansea two at a time in a way that guaranteed they'd never come back.[10] Now he could tell tales of his extraordinary adventures around the world. He'd seen South Africa, where Britain was fighting a war, and had experienced the extremes of the country, visiting prisoner-of-war camps and attending a picnic hosted by the Governor of Cape Town and a garden party hosted by an admiral. Huge crowds had greeted them in New Zealand, and each day the ship was full of excited visitors, including Māori women in traditional costume. He and his crewmates had attended a dinner hosted by the mayor and people of Christchurch.

In between the ports of call, Edgar had endured storms, high winds and 40-foot waves that tossed *Discovery* from side to side and soaked them through. He had spent two years on the icy unexplored continent of Antarctica, the coldest, windiest and remotest place on earth, where in the winter months temperatures could drop to between -40 and -70 degrees centigrade. He'd experienced weather that could switch from dead calm to howling winds in an instant, and long periods where you simply couldn't leave the ship. On other moonlit nights there was an uncanny stillness and a silence so great you could believe you were on the cold, dead surface of the moon. When the sun rose, its light caught the clouds and was broken into all the colours of the rainbow: pale rose, pure lilac, emerald green, lemon yellow and fiery red.[11]

Edgar had man-hauled sledges over a total of 173 days and covered hundreds of miles in often perilous conditions.[12] During a two-month sledging trip with Scott and Chief Stoker William Lashly, he'd fallen into a deep crevasse. Still harnessed to Scott, Lashly had, with great difficulty, pulled them both out. He recounted how Scott and Wilson had endured a devil of time making their 'furthest south' record and how nineteen dogs had died on the journey.[13] He'd survived on limited rations, bemoaned the lack of a hot meal on occasions and not enjoyed eating seal meat, though it was a staple along with stewed or fried penguin, fried penguins' liver and seal kidneys.[14] He'd marvelled at the Antarctic landscape, washed in thawing snow and ice, enjoyed the camaraderie of expedition life, and become one of the most valuable men on Scott's team.

Lois's handsome cousin, with his tattooed forearms that held stories of their own – particularly the left with its stabbed heart, hinting at a loss or a broken heart – may have become one of the most exciting men that she had ever known.[15] How she must have thrilled at these stories of places and people she could hardly imagine. Just fourteen weeks after his return to England, Lois married her Antarctic hero. They were well suited, a musical pair with a shared family heritage.

The wedding took place on Tuesday 13 December 1904 at St Mary's, the tiny medieval church in Rhossili to which the winds brought the briny smells of the sea below. The marriage of the famous local boy was a big occasion, and as the happy couple arrived at the church the rat-tat-tat of rifle fire filled the air as the villagers performed a ceremonial *feu-de-joie.* This may have been a vestige of the centuries-old tradition of bidding weddings in Gower, when guns were fired over the bride's house to frighten away evil spirits.[16] Lois wore a crepeline silk dress trimmed with chiffon and a matching picture hat, and carried in her hand a small ivory-bound prayer book that Edgar had given her. Her bridesmaids were her cousin Gladys and niece Ida, and both wore dress rings that were presents from the bridegroom. Her brother Enoch was waiting inside as Edgar's best man.

As she walked through the church porch, Lois entered a space resonant with family history. Edgar and so many of their relatives over many generations had been baptised in the stone font by the south door, and each Sunday Lois sang with the choir in the carved Gothic choir stalls and listened to the sermons given from the oak pulpit.[17] Walking down the nave towards the altar, she must have thought of her mother and Edgar's mother taking the same path to their weddings. The joyful service was full of song as befitted the musical talents of both, particularly Lois. Her willingness to donate her time and voice to community events over the years had made her as popular in the local area as her famous spouse, and family and friends thronged the church to celebrate their marriage.[18]

Because of Edgar's celebrity after *Discovery*, the wedding was covered by the local newspapers, which named his bride incorrectly as Miss Louie Baynon.[19] This was Lois's first exposure to the press. Edgar had noticed when he was in New Zealand that a lot of lies had been printed about *Discovery* and warned friends not to believe all they read in the papers.[20] For Lois, the wedding marked the start of a relationship with the press that would at times be devastatingly destructive. Later, she would have to struggle with it alone during one of the worst times of her life.

But that was all yet to come. For now, Lois and Edgar were a young couple in love and looking forward to the future. Their wedding breakfast was laid out in the picnic rooms next to the Ship Inn, decorated with festive ivy and evergreens. So popular was the couple that there were two sittings.[21] It's not recorded if theirs was a traditional Gower wedding or not, but if it was, on the evening before, relatives would have brought gifts of currant loaves and slices would be sold to the young men at the wedding breakfast. These they gave to the girl they liked best, and whoever had the most at the end of the celebration was the 'belle of the ball'. Another local wedding tradition was the serving of 'tin-meat', a large, shallow tin containing mutton with a pie crust that was baked in a brick oven. Guests could buy a pie, which would serve four, and portions were given out to anyone who couldn't come to the wedding.[22] At two o'clock, as rifle-fire filled the air once more, the newlyweds were waved off by their guests as they left Wales to begin married life in England.

Edgar was due in Portsmouth at the end of his leave, but first he took his new bride for her first trip to London. He was a man of the world, but Lois had been brought up far away from the bright lights of this metropolis. It must have been an extraordinary time for her, especially as it involved a visit to Buckingham Palace. On 18 December, the crew of *Discovery* was invited to an investiture where King Edward VII presented them with the new Polar Medal in recognition of their service under conditions of extreme hardship. Specially designed for the occasion, the silver octagonal medal had an image of the king on one side and on the other, an image of *Discovery* with a six-man sledge party in the foreground and Mount Erebus in the background. It hung from a pure white ribbon, and a clasp was added with the dates of the expedition and the legend, 'Antarctic 1902–04.'[23]

Each man was allowed to bring one or two guests to the investiture, and so this would have been Lois's first exposure to the other polar wives and also to the hierarchy of the Navy.[24] It must have been daunting for her; within five days of her wedding she was in Buckingham Palace, in the presence of the king and surrounded by Edgar's friends and colleagues, as well as their families. Ory was there, of course, reunited with Hilda Evans only months after their voyage home from New Zealand, and meeting the new Mrs Shackleton. Emily Dorman, six years older than Ernest and from a wealthy family, had faced opposition from her family who regarded him as not good enough for her. She didn't take him seriously at first either, considering him to be an adventurer and dreamer. But Shackleton was smitten, and after a promotion and his acceptance onto the *Discovery* expedition Emily's father finally agreed that they could become engaged. Three years later, on 9 April 1904, they were married at Christ Church in Westminster.

Hilda, Emily and Lois had all married *Discovery* men that same year, and Emily and Lois were both pregnant with their first children. They had so much in common, but it is not certain that they even met. Lois was a petty officer's wife, and her presence wasn't publicly recorded. As the Welsh working-class wife of a non-officer, Lois's place in the hierarchy was clear. She was probably just one of the many people who filled the room, refracting the light of *Discovery*'s stars like Scott, Wilson and Ory.

Scott admired and liked Edgar immensely, but in this very public and ceremonial event he did not seek out his colleague's bride of only a few days to introduce himself.[25] Lois's position was not as stellar as Ory's, but almost certainly this did not matter to her; after all, Edwardian society was hierarchical, and people tended to know their place. Lois was newly married to a man whom she adored, and was overwhelmed with pride as she saw him presented with his medal by the king. She had everything to look forward to. How could she know that this hierarchy would come to matter very much indeed?

A Sailor's Wife

Lois and Edgar arrived in Portsmouth where they were to live for five and a half years. *Discovery* had returned home to a rapturous welcome from the town less than a year before, and Edgar would almost certainly have shown his new bride where the ship had arrived and where he was greeted after his great adventure. Arriving in Portsmouth, Lois might have felt some similarity with Swansea. Both towns were dominated by docks and welcomed ships and their crews from all over the world. But this was Lois's first experience of being a naval wife, indeed of being anybody's wife. There were no married quarters for seamen at this time, and so she did not find herself living among other navy wives; instead they set up home at 12 Walden Road, in the Tipton area of Portsmouth.[1] Their home was a terraced house in an area covered by rows of them, all built in the last few years.[2]

Lois was fortunate that her husband would be land-based for virtually all the years that he was in Portsmouth with her, although he was working hard. In recognition of his role on the *Discovery* expedition, he'd been promoted to petty officer first class and given permission to train as a gunnery instructor at HMS *Excellent*, the Royal Navy gunnery school on Whale Island, off the coast at Portsmouth and only about a twenty-minute walk from their new home.[3] Built around a large open-air drill ground, the school had long gun battery sheds where firing practice took place and various types of gun were kept on-site for training in firing and maintenance. The officers' mess and barrack blocks provided accommodation and a social focus for those resident on the island. Edgar completed his training quickly, finishing in one year instead of two.[4] The instructors at the gunnery school became renowned as the Navy's experts in drill and ceremonial, and HMS *Excellent* became the home of the Portsmouth Field Gun Crew, which competed in the Royal Navy field gun competition at the Royal Tournament every year. Its origins lay in the defence of Ladysmith, a town that had come under attack during the war in South Africa. A naval crew from HMS *Powerful* had become famous for hauling their mighty guns up to defend the town, and the competition was a re-enactment of this incredible feat.

As a gunnery instructor, Edgar was strict and expected hard work. His approach paid off, and he led a crew in a demonstration of how to dismantle and reassemble the huge guns at the first Royal Naval and Military Tournament at Olympia in London in 1906. The next year he led a team in the competition, and the year after that his team won the cup.[5] HMS *Excellent* also took over responsibility for the state gun carriage after 1901. During Queen Victoria's funeral, the army horses pulling the gun carriage that carried her body began rearing up and catastrophe was averted when nearby sailors from HMS *Excellent* stepped in. The men pulled the gun carriage at every state funeral afterwards, up to that of Winston Churchill.[6]

Language was no barrier to establishing her new life in Portsmouth because Lois had been brought up as an English speaker, but she initially had little chance to get to know her new home and neighbours because she was pregnant when she married Edgar.[7] Premarital sex was not at all unusual among working-class Victorians and Edwardians so long as it was followed by marriage. Proposing made it acceptable, binding the man by his word of honour and creating a bond and trust that could, if the couple wished, allow them to begin a sexual relationship.[8] Lois and Edgar had become engaged as soon as he returned from *Discovery* in September 1904, and so her pregnancy would have been no cause for alarm.

Their first child, Norman, was born in August 1905, not long after they arrived in Portsmouth, and Lois had to cope with pregnancy and looking after her baby without the support of the family and friends that she had left behind in Wales. There were visits home during periods of leave, and the Ship Inn remained the family focus, but in Portsmouth Lois had to build a new network of friends and activities.

As a devout woman who had been a churchgoer all her life, joining the local congregation provided an opportunity for her to meet new people. St Saviour's, a little iron mission church, was only a short walk away from their house and would have been a regular part of Lois's social life as she settled into her new home.[9] Edgar's position at the Gunnery School also brought opportunities for his family. Every year the warrant officers of HMS *Excellent* held a children's summer party on Whale Island. About two hundred children with their parents and friends were invited to play on swings and take pony and donkey rides, compete in running races with prizes and take trips around the island on a gunboat. The band played while the children ate their tea in a big marquee and the adults were entertained in the mess room.[10] However, Lois would also discover that being a naval wife in Portsmouth allowed her to call on a unique form of support.

For just over twenty years, Agnes Weston had been running a Sailors' Rest in Portsmouth which looked after naval men and their families in the town. It had begun as a way of mitigating the effects of drunkenness, particularly when crews were paid off and sailors found themselves in a place full of strangers and pubs. Commercial Road, where Agnes Weston built her Sailors' Rest in 1882, was one of the most crowded thoroughfares in southern England, bustling with music halls, theatres and pubs.[11] There she welcomed sailors, even drunk ones, and offered a meal, a hot bath, a bed for the night and breakfast. There were reading rooms and writing rooms, and Agnes also hosted Saturday night entertainments. Along with piano accompaniments for the sailors and musical performances, there were displays of agility and strength involving throwing Indian clubs and battle axes.[12]

At first Agnes and her partner Sophia Wintz, who lived openly as a couple, endured a great deal of criticism for spending time with sailors in what was described as a 'disgraceful innovation'. The women who volunteered to help 'could be no ladies, that was very certain', opined the *Portsmouth Evening News*.[13] Aggie, as she became known among the sailors, shrugged off this disapproval. She was not only a devout Christian but also a prominent member of the Temperance movement, which was one of the largest social campaigns in late Victorian England. Thousands of people, across all social classes, joined its resistance to alcohol. Oriana's father was a member, believing as many did that drunkenness was the scourge of the working classes and the cause of most social ills.[14] It was seen as a particular problem for the Navy, and Aggie wished to develop similar Sailors' Rests all over the country to encourage sailors to understand the evils of drink and pledge to forego their grog rations and become teetotal. She hoped that her popular Saturday night concerts, where non-alcoholic drinks were served and sailors were wonderfully entertained, would encourage them to come back the next day or during the week for the Bible classes that she ran there on Sundays and Thursdays.[15]

The idea of Sailors' Rests and of trying to create a sober, Christian navy did not originate with Aggie Weston, but she was hugely successful because she spoke to the sailors as if she was their mother, imbuing her with great authority in an all-male world. Indeed, she became the 'Mother of the Navy'.[16] Her work came to the attention of Queen Victoria, who agreed that her establishments should now become known as Royal Sailors' Rests. The Prince and Princess of Wales were supporters, sending presents at Christmas, including clothes made by the princess and her ladies.[17] The royal family's enthusiasm was not shared by everyone, however. Local pub landlords saw Aggie as a threat to their profits. In Devonport, where Aggie opened another Sailors' Rest, publicans threatened to break its windows while promising free beer to sailors to attract them into their pubs.

Despite such pressure, Aggie continued to welcome many hundreds of naval men every day and many signed the pledge to stop drinking. She also realised early on that the wives and families of sailors needed support too. In good times pay could be drunk or spent before it arrived home, and in bad times families could starve before pay arrived or be left penniless by a death at sea. Through her Sailors' Rests, Aggie put in place a system of support for wives and their children. By the time that Lois was living in Portsmouth, there were over one thousand naval wives involved regularly. Lois soon became one of them.[18]

The Sailors' Rest and Aggie's philanthropic organisation provided a social life, friendship and much-needed support for Lois, a young mother in a new town. She may have heard about it from other naval wives, or Edgar may have mentioned it as the band from his base, HMS *Excellent*, played often at the weekly entertainments.[19] However she discovered the place, Lois became a regular, attending the Monday afternoon wives' meetings, which revolved around Bible readings and singing and included access to the library and a variety of stalls selling goods. Over one hundred children were often put into the nursery, which had toys, mattresses to tumble on and cradles to sleep in. She could walk around carrying Norman, browsing for fabrics, ready-made clothes, cakes and other things while chatting and catching up with news. She could also go into the restaurant with the other wives and their children for a cup of tea. The restaurant was open to the public on Saturday nights and was always crowded. Lois could sit at a marble-topped table and order sausage and mash or fish and chips, followed by a tart or a cake. Kitchens in the basement operated throughout the day, often starting at four o'clock in the morning to bake fresh bread, tarts, cakes, rolls and turnovers. The basement throbbed like an engine as sausage-making machines and potato-peeling gadgets whirred over the sound of lifts delivering food and non-alcoholic drinks being made in the mineral-water plant. Ginger beer, lemonade and many other varieties of temperance drinks were made on-site.

All donations and money made went into philanthropic work. Aggie and Sophia supervised sick committees and maternity clubs run by sailors' wives. Lois gave birth in Portsmouth at a time when there was no National Health Service and no free maternity care; membership of these sailors' wives' groups gave her access to skilled nurses and, after having her baby, visits from other wives bringing groceries and little comforts. There were other groups too: wives' branches of the Royal Naval Temperance Society, which encouraged wives and husbands to take the pledge together, and of the Royal Naval Christian Union, which did missionary work and sent senior wives to visit less experienced wives and to support sailors who had been invalided out of the Navy.[20]

Lois wasn't a subscriber to the mission – perhaps the family budget wouldn't run to that – but this didn't mean that she was excluded from its benefits. There was also no requirement to take the pledge before joining a wives' meeting.[21] Aggie's approach was a very evangelical one; she encouraged men and women to join in her activities, hoping to win them over to her cause. There is no evidence as to whether Lois took the pledge or not. She came from a pub-running family and had experience of the Temperance movement in Gower, where, after her parents retired from the Ship, local Methodists campaigned successfully to have the pub shut down. The Temperance movement had its roots in non-conformity, and it was the local Methodist Chapel that had organised events promoting a teetotal lifestyle, such as Band of Hope tea parties where the Blue Ribbon of Temperance was presented to the children. There was a long-running tension between chapel and church in Gower, and Lois, a worshipper at St Mary's parish church in Rhossili, was unlikely to be part of any social activities organised by the Methodists.[22] However, Aggie was also a member of the Church of England, and this might have made Lois more susceptible to her Temperance message.[23]

It seems unlikely that Edgar would have joined her if she had decided to take the pledge. He'd been at sea since the age of fifteen and enjoyed a drink in his time off. Edgar would almost certainly have been more comfortable with the Navy's view, which was that drunkenness and not drink was the problem, and consequently it was a disciplinary and not a moral issue. The Admiralty never seriously considered abolishing alcohol. Many sailors criticised Aggie's approach, which was in their view overzealous and offensive. She preached that only a teetotal sailor could be a good husband, father, sailor and Christian, and that those who drank made their families suffer. Many sailors wrote to her saying they objected to her portrayal of them as drunken sailors, dishonourable husbands and irresponsible fathers.

Edgar, who had made a career in the Navy and was immensely proud of his service, may well have objected too. He was skilled, fit, a good leader and a strict disciplinarian and Aggie's comments about his area of expertise may well have chafed. A gunner, she wrote, would have 'downright good brains, well exercised, and kept bright and clear from drink. You don't make a torpedo gunner out of a drunkard. A man must be calm, cool, best of all if he trusts in God, and must do his duty at whatever risk.' When she set up a temperance canteen in the Portsmouth naval barracks in mid-1907, it was very short-lived.[24] Edgar was posted there at that point and, like his colleagues, would almost certainly have decided that he just didn't need to be mothered.

In the spring of 1906, Edgar left Portsmouth for two months away on board HMS *Barfleur*, taking part in the navy's annual manoeuvres.[25] The purpose of the exercise that year was to simulate surprise attacks by another major European power on Britain's commercial shipping. A red fleet led by Sir Arthur Wilson, Commander in Chief of the Channel Fleet, defended the trade routes between England and the Mediterranean. It was bigger and stronger than the blue fleet, led by Vice Admiral Sir William May and Rear Admiral Prince Louis of Battenberg, representing the foreign power, so the blue fleet could only dominate the seas by capturing, destroying, and intercepting as many of the enemy's ships as possible. Between 14 June and 2 July, the two fleets, flying red and blue flags to identify themselves, fought it out around the coast of Britain and Ireland and around the Mediterranean.[26] The red fleet was joined by merchant ships whose owners cooperated with the Navy but were concerned about damage to their property. Responsibility for this fell to Scott, who now had a desk job in London, first with the Admiralty and then with Naval Intelligence. He successfully negotiated insurance cover so that merchant shipping could take part in the manoeuvres without fear of loss.[27]

As professional naval men, it was not surprising that both Edgar and Scott would be involved in such a significant event. They were both building their careers after *Discovery*, but they also both had itchy feet and were finding it hard to settle back in. Scott had been focused since his teens on a glittering career that could support his dependent mother and sisters, but increasingly he was finding other imperatives at work. His naval ambitions and sense of duty were being challenged by his desire to go back to Antarctica.[28] Edgar's craving for adventure had caused him to join the Navy as a boy, and these few weeks of war games at sea were perhaps the most exciting that he'd had since his return from the south.

Betrayal

Marriage, a land-based job and a child may have been a challenge for the gregarious and sociable Edgar. Only a short while before he'd been freewheeling across the world, exploring virgin land and experiencing one of the greatest adventures of the age. If he did still crave excitement, then Portsmouth was a place that offered great temptation. Apart from pubs, there were cabaret shows at the Hippodrome, the Royal and the People's Palace with acts from all over the world. Edgar experienced these delights for the first time in Portsmouth, sometimes going to the stage door to meet the performers.[1] And Edgar had some allure of his own. For many of the women who marvelled at the stories and adventures of polar exploration, men like Edgar were incredibly attractive. The lure of his adventures was matched by his gym-honed physique and merry personality. This was not a new phenomenon; other polar explorers had experienced this attraction too. In 1821, Eleanor Anne Porden had written a star-struck letter to Captain John Franklin about his endeavours in the Arctic. This fan letter was the start of a relationship that culminated in her becoming his first wife.[2] Ernest Shackleton had several admirers throughout his career too, some of them wealthy women who sponsored his expeditions.[3]

We can't know if it was Edgar the polar explorer or Edgar the gregarious, handsome sailor that attracted Beatrice Glazier, but we do know that they had an affair. Beatrice was a local girl, born in Portsmouth, a couple of years older than Edgar and five years older than Lois. Educated and intelligent, she had grown up with her sister Maria in the household of her stepfather, Edward Anderson, a greengrocer.[4] After his death, her mother Martha ran a tobacconist shop in Commercial Road in Portsmouth, helped by Maria while eighteen-year-old Beatrice worked as a teacher. During the next ten years the women must have come into some money or accrued sufficient means because by 1901 neither Martha nor Beatrice was working.[5]

The following year, the twenty-eight-year-old Beatrice married, and her new husband moved into the house that she shared with her mother in Lake Road.[6] Beatrice had fallen in love with a sailor from Devon whose career was flourishing. Thomas Henry Glazier had been decorated for his service in Africa and had recently been promoted to petty officer first class.[7] Just over two years later, in November 1904, their son Manfred Thomas Glazier was born. The future must have seemed bright to Beatrice, raising her first child while her husband's career progressed, but terrible tragedy was stalking her. Just three years after they married, Thomas, aged thirty-four, died. His cause of death was recorded as valvular disease of the heart. Ill for a short while before his death, he had been unable to work and had suffered for two months with anasarca, a horrific swelling of his body related to his failing heart. When he died on 6 April 1905 it was at home, with Beatrice at his bedside.[8]

Just how this young, widowed mother met Edgar is unclear, but there might be a clue in her deceased husband's career. A year before his death Thomas had become a gunner at HMS *Excellent*, where just under ten months later Edgar began his gunnery instructor training. When he arrived at Whale Island in January 1905, Edgar may well have become aware of Thomas, who had health issues in the early part of that year. Perhaps they had become friendly or trained together; perhaps Lois knew Beatrice from the wives' network at Aggie's that visited invalided sailors. However the first contact was made, it seems likely that through her husband's illness, his being invalided at home and then his death, Edgar came to know Beatrice. In this emotionally heightened atmosphere of grief and shock, they were drawn together.

By October, Beatrice was pregnant and Edgar, married less than a year and with a two-month-old son, found himself in a dreadful predicament. This escalated further when Lois fell pregnant four months later.[9] On 31 July, just over three weeks after Edgar's return from manoeuvres, Beatrice gave birth to twin girls and registered their names as Kathleen Lilian and Lilian Kathleen Evans. Not only did she give them their father's name but did so on their birth certificate, also giving her own name as Beatrice Evans, formerly Anderson – all indications that to her this was a serious relationship.[10]

It's not clear when Edgar's relationship with Beatrice ended, but she obviously knew where he was a year and a half after the twins were born. Lilian became very ill and died, aged only seventeen months, on 23 January 1908. Her death certificate lists her cause of death as dentition, or teething, and bronchopneumonia. Teething was considered at the time to be a process fraught with risk and was a common diagnosis in the death of very young children. Medical professionals attributed all sorts of ailments to it, including convulsions, diarrhoea, bronchitis, fever and vomiting. This tendency meant that more serious illnesses could be missed. When Lilian was feverish and suffering from the breathing difficulties caused by pneumonia, Beatrice might quite reasonably have assumed that she was teething. The situation was made much worse by the toxicity of teething powders at the time, many of which included dangerous levels of potassium chlorate or morphine.[11] When Beatrice registered Lilian's death, her father's details were given as Edgar Evans, 1st Class Petty Officer Royal Navy, HMS *Victory*. Beatrice knew that he had moved from *Excellent* to *Victory* since the girls' birth, which suggests they may have kept in touch or had mutual friends who could tell her. Lilian died at Beatrice's home in Sultan Road, which was only a few streets from the Evans home in Walden Road, so how could Edgar not know? Of course, that depends on whether Edgar was still there.

Lois's daughter Muriel was born just five months after the twins, in November, and was baptised on 19 March 1907, almost certainly at St Saviours.[12] After that date there is a period when it's not clear where she and Edgar were living. They were not at Walden Road for the rest of that year or most of the next. It's not until December 1908 that Lois, Edgar, Norman and Muriel are definitely resident in a new home, 52 Chapel Street.[13] It's possible that this represents a period of separation, a time when Lois was coming to terms with Edgar's infidelity. Perhaps she returned to Wales for a time and Edgar moved into the barracks at HMS *Victory*, as reflected by Beatrice listing that as his address on the death certificate. Whether this was the case or not may never be known, but it is certain that Lois was pregnant again by spring 1908. If she had known about Beatrice and the twins, then she had decided to put the betrayal behind her. She loved Edgar, and they were more than spouses – they were cousins, with lives that interconnected back over generations. They had children, and it appears that Edgar chose to focus on them.

Although she continued to live a few streets away in Portsmouth with her mother, there is no evidence that Edgar had any sort of long-term relationship with his daughter Kathleen. Beatrice was in a better position than many to bring up an illegitimate child. She wasn't a young girl, financially dependent on her family or the man concerned, which was just as well as there was no compulsion for the father to provide any financial support. Women could not legally enforce a man to provide if they weren't married.[14] Having a child out of wedlock didn't necessarily carry the stigma that is often imagined, however. In the vast majority of cases, working-class families presented with an illegitimate child took them in. If it was an issue, it was usually because of religion, the age of the parents, the circumstances of the seduction or a concern about respectability.[15] Beatrice clearly wanted to protect her reputation as a respectable widow because Kathleen Evans was presented to friends and neighbours as her niece. When she gave the household's details for the 1911 census, she also declared that she had only one living child and no dead ones, acknowledging Manfred but denying both Kathleen and Lilian. When she married Lieutenant Commander Charles Amsden in 1914, she rectified this by describing Kathleen as her daughter with her new stepfather's name.[16]

Lois and Edgar's new home represented a fresh start in more ways than one. It was just a thirty-minute walk from the Royal Naval Barracks in Queen Street where Edgar had been posted after he completed his training at Whale Island. Known then as HMS *Victory*, the barracks was where field gun crews trained for the Royal Tournament. Edgar threw himself into the hard work and excitement of competition, keeping himself at the peak of fitness as a gym instructor. It was *Victory*'s team, trained by Edgar, that won the tournament in 1908.[17] St Saviours was still within walking distance for Lois, so she could continue to worship there, but when their third child, Ralph, was born in December 1908, he wasn't baptised in Portsmouth. When it came to baptising their sons, Lois and Edgar chose the parish church of St Mary's in Rhossili, where their boys were welcomed into the church in the same stone font as their father and grandparents had been. The man who had married them, the Reverend Lewis Hughes, performed the ceremony, demonstrating that although their children had been born in Portsmouth, their links to Rhossili and their family bond remained strong.[18]

With three children, a roof over her head and a husband who not only loved the Navy but was thriving in it, Lois could count her blessings. Millions in Edwardian England were very, very poor. Fifty per cent of the national income was in the hands of just fourteen per cent of the population, and there was an enormous gulf between rich and poor.[19] Lois, married to a Royal Navy petty officer, must have felt very fortunate indeed to have a steady income that would keep them above the poverty line. She had high hopes for her life with Edgar and her young family in Portsmouth. She could not know that another Antarctic expedition was in the offing, and that a new polar wife would be instrumental in its planning.

Kathleen

In all, ten different countries sent seventeen expeditions to Antarctica during what has become known as the Heroic Age of polar exploration.[1] This period, from the end of the nineteenth century until just after the First World War, saw the boundaries of scientific and geographical knowledge thrown wide by new discoveries. It was dominated by heroic figures; explorers who became celebrities. These men were taking on the unknown world, subduing its wild terrain and redrawing the map. They had tales to tell of derring-do and unimaginable bravery.

Still the most inhospitable place on earth, Antarctica is covered in a blanket of snow and ice which reflects the heat of the sun away, producing some of the lowest temperatures ever recorded. Thermometers there have dropped to -89.6 degrees centigrade while winds rage up to nearly 200 miles per hour.[2] Each year Antarctica is in total darkness for many months. The achievements of the explorers of the 'Heroic Age' were acquired through endurance; they faced dreadful deprivation, exceptionally harsh conditions and no contact at all with the outside world for months, often years. Some did not survive the challenge. Those who did won fame across the world.

The newly promoted Captain Robert Falcon Scott was the undisputed superstar of the British 'Heroic Age' after his return from the *Discovery* expedition. He had embarked on a lecture tour and became only the third explorer to address the fellows of the Royal Geographical Society at the Royal Albert Hall, following in the footsteps of Stanley and Nansen. His account of the expedition, *The Voyage of the Discovery*, was a huge success. Everyone wanted to know him, and he was invited into the salons and dining rooms of London Society, where members of the aristocracy and the governing classes dined, drank, danced and dressed up at parties and balls. Anyone who was invited was 'in' and those that weren't were definitively 'out'.

During Edward VII's reign, the structure of London Society changed. When his mother Victoria was queen, its members had been gentlemen or ladies by birth, intelligence or ability and no amount of wealth could change that. The making of money was seen as vulgar and best left to others. In contrast, Edwardian England saw the rise of a new breed of hugely successful men, millionaires who'd made fortunes as newspaper magnates, tea merchants, bankers and owners of gold and diamond mines. English aristocrats were also marrying for money, as evidenced by the regular creation of American duchesses.[3] It's estimated that by the end of the Edwardian period these American heiresses had enriched their husbands to the tune of approximately £40 million.[4] Admitting this 'new money' shook up London Society and changed the nature of its gatherings. Actresses, artists, leaders of fashion and other celebrities were invited, and finding a heroic explorer at an event wasn't at all unusual – as Kathleen Bruce was to discover.

She barely noticed her first encounter with Scott. It took place early in 1907 at a lunch given by her great friend, the actress Mabel Beardsley. She spotted him at the far end of the table: 'He was not very young, perhaps forty, nor very good-looking, but he looked very healthy and alert, and I glowed rather foolishly and suddenly when I clearly saw him ask his neighbour who I was.'[5] They chatted very briefly after lunch and Scott asked her where she had got her wonderful sunburn. She told him she'd been vagabonding in Greece, travelling and sleeping outside, which he thought was marvellous. Almost at once Kathleen had to hurry away to catch a train. It would be ten months before they met again, and this meeting would be the culmination of the destiny that Kathleen had chosen for herself.

Many years before she had decided that the goal of her life would be to bear a heroic child, and for that she needed to marry a heroic man. It was a romantic and idealistic dream, not a literal one; he could have been a heroic artist or a heroic writer. Kathleen was high-minded and believed in love, and she knew that she needed to admire the man she loved.[6] This was quite an unusual aim for a girl of her upbringing, but Kathleen proved to be quite an unusual girl. She was born into a typical middle-class Victorian family: large, religious, stiff-upper-lipped and with its fair share of eccentrics, but also artistic, cosmopolitan and royal in origin.[7] Kathleen's grandparents had met in Athens when her sixteen-year-old Greek grandmother had jumped onto a table after being terrified by a small dog. Its owner, a twenty-one-year-old Scottish soldier from Edinburgh called James Henry Skene, lifted her down and promptly fell in love with her. James was the son of Sir Walter Scott's best friend, the brilliant Scottish watercolourist James Skene. The young girl he saved was Rhalou Rizo-Rangabe, daughter of the last Grand Postlenik of Wallachia and Princess Zoe Lapidi, of a Greek family from Constantinople that had held important positions in the Ottoman Empire; one member was briefly Emperor of Constantinople, and another married an illegitimate child of Charlemagne.

James and Rhalou married and stayed in Athens where their seven children were born, including Kathleen's mother Janie. They travelled all over the world until Janie was seven and then she and her sister Zoe went to Britain with their grandparents. Both girls married men of the Church. Zoe's husband, Reverend William Thomson, became Archbishop of York, and they had four sons and five daughters. Twenty-seven-year-old Janie chose a seemingly less impressive man, thirty-four-year-old Reverend Lloyd Bruce. Janie was a beauty whom Rossetti once asked to pose for him, and Zoe thought her sister's husband 'dull, shabbily dressed and too old'. But Janie was in love: 'Oh, dear Zoe,' she wrote, 'I wish you could see him a little more with my eyes!'[8] Lloyd came from a distinguished family. The Bruces were descended from the Scottish king Robert the Bruce, and related to Lord Elgin. Lloyd's father, James Robertson Bruce, a former Tory MP who had fought at Waterloo, was now the 2nd Baronet Bruce and Lloyd had been born at Downhill, his father's house in Northern Ireland. He and his brothers would take the traditional aristocratic routes: the eldest, Henry Hervey, succeeded his father as 3rd Baronet; Robert became a soldier; and Lloyd, the youngest, entered the Church.

Lloyd and Janie were married in Oxford by her brother-in-law on 6 October 1863, and he eventually became the rector of Carlton-in-Lindrick, near Worksop in Nottinghamshire.[9] His congregation comprised coal miners and agricultural workers as well as the households of the local gentry. The rectory was a lovely house with stables and a mill pond, and they were helped by a housemaid and a cook, and then a nurse once Janie began to have children.[10] Lloyd had the archbishop to thank for his good position. Zoe also supported her sister's growing family with gifts of clothes and other necessities. And a large family it was, with Janie giving birth to six children in three and a half years. Douglas came first, then Irene, followed by two sets of twins: Zoe and Elma, and Gwen and Lloyd.

Janie had a complete collapse five years after her marriage. Rather than consider that she might be exhausted by having produced so many children in such a short space of time and having to look after such a brood, a London doctor diagnosed her with 'hysteria'.[11] At a time when the domestic sphere was seen as entirely separate to the public sphere, a woman's place was very firmly in the home. She was its keeper and guardian, and because the home was regarded as a moral sanctuary safe from the corruption of the outside world, women needed to be protected from sin. They were viewed as gentle, both physically and emotionally weaker than men and more susceptible to illness. Middle-class and upper-class Victorian women were therefore dependent on their husbands or fathers, and for many this total dependency and lack of control over their own lives led to depression and anxiety. When these women behaved erratically their behaviour was deemed inappropriate and diagnosed as 'hysteria'. A spell in an asylum was often recommended to protect family reputations.

Hysteria was regarded as an exclusively female illness because it had been linked by the Ancient Greeks Hippocrates, Aristotle and Plato to the female reproductive organs. Hippocrates was the first to use the word 'hysteria', deriving it from the Greek for uterus, *hysteron*, and to identify its cause as a wandering uterus. He asserted that when a woman was not sexually satisfied or pregnant, the uterus became restless and melancholy and began to move around the body, producing toxic fumes as it did so. Women in this state could suffer from anxiety, feelings of suffocation and tremors. The cure for this madness caused by an unfulfilled sexual desire or lack of conception was to have sex or give birth to release the fumes and cleanse the body. This understanding of hysteria was commonly held well into the nineteenth century. Most Victorian women carried smelling salts with them in case they swooned when their emotions were aroused, probably unaware that they were still following Hippocrates' advice that the wandering womb dislikes a pungent smell and will be forced back into its place.[12]

Janie's doctor clearly followed current thinking when he recommended that she have more babies as a cure. In the next seven years she gave birth to another five children: Rosslyn, Wilfred, Hilda (known as 'Presh'), Jane (known as 'Podge'), and finally Edith Agnes Kathleen, their eleventh child, born on 27 March 1878.[13] Rather than the hoped-for cure, the pregnancies contributed to Janie's increasingly poor health. Kathleen later wrote,

> This long-suffering lady went blind when I was born, and for the brief time that she lived afterwards she lay gently feeling her last, lusty baby's face, tracing the small features ... How would it have been had she been able to hear, twenty, thirty, forty years later, this same me stretching out my arms to love, or the sun, with a 'Thank God, my mother had eleven children; just suppose she'd stopped short at ten!'[14]

Janie Bruce died on 1 October 1880 of pneumonia aggravated by chronic nephritis; she was forty-two. Her baby Kathleen was only one year old. Lloyd was now a single parent of eleven children and remarried six months later, more for the sake of his children than anything else. He chose a wealthy woman in her late fifties called Ann Parker who had been widowed five years before.[15] Her husband of twenty-six years, Samuel Parker, had been a surgeon, and at the end of his life was a surgeon at the General Infirmary in Sheffield.[16] They had lived comfortably with a domestic staff including a cook, housemaid and groom, and Ann had been left an annuity after Samuel's death.[17] She had been a friend of Janie's, and was known to the children, but did not prove to be the loving stepmother that Lloyd had desired. She virtually ignored the Bruce children, except baby Kathleen, to whom she read picture books. The marriage was not a great success either. After an argument over fish for dinner, during which she slapped Lloyd's face, Ann absented herself from the family for long periods.

Unbeknown to the family, another tragedy was stalking them. Lloyd became unwell, and with their stepmother not around to help, Elma took over the care of her younger siblings. To lighten the load several of the children were sent north to Edinburgh to stay with a great-uncle on their mother's side, William Skene. Kathleen stayed with her father and the oldest of her siblings. Her stepmother made a brief reappearance to offer to take her as her own child, but Lloyd turned her down. After a year of separation, Kathleen was sent to Scotland to join her other siblings, much to the delight of Podge, who had missed her terribly. Shortly afterwards, their great-uncle called them together to tell them that their father had died. Kathleen was seven and an orphan.

William continued to give the Bruce children a home in Edinburgh. He was an elderly Episcopalian academic who had not had children of his own but was fairly used to nieces, nephews and great-nieces and great-nephews roaming in and out. Preoccupied with his studies in Gaelic and Celtic history, he didn't keep much of an eye on how the children occupied themselves; he left that to their governess. He might have expected that the Bruce children, well brought up and from a very religious family, might have been better behaved, but the younger siblings were constantly in trouble. They ran rings around their governesses. Rosslyn got expelled on numerous occasions, Wilfred had a fight with a nursery maid over washing his neck, and Kathleen and Podge played truant in the city's Botanical Gardens and fiddled the account for their schoolbook budget so that they could get more sweets.

Their great-uncle was very short-sighted, and this may have been a blessing in the end as it meant that he didn't notice something that might have upset him a great deal as Historiographer Royal of Scotland. Kathleen and Podge found an old family chest that had been owned by Bonnie Prince Charlie and wrote the names of their dolls on each of its drawers. They then took out a kilt that was hidden inside, which the prince had apparently worn when he escaped to the Isles, and cut it up to make an outfit for their doll Gerald. The younger Bruce children were not intentionally naughty; they were simply independent and used to occupying themselves. Nobody really kept a very close eye, although Elma tried, and they were used to being left to their own devices. As the youngest, orphaned at seven and living with a great-uncle who was affable but distant, Kathleen in particular sought attention and affection.

In 1893, great-uncle William died. The household was broken up and the house sold off. Douglas, who was now twenty-five, became the head of the family and the fifteen-year-old Kathleen was sent to live with Elma and her husband Canon Keating in Scarborough. After a year she went to a convent boarding school and then reunited with Podge at a school in Bognor. During the holidays Douglas made arrangements and Kathleen stayed at the house of whichever relative volunteered to take her. She was expected to become a teacher, like Irene and Presh. Religious faith and duty ran strongly through the family, with three of her brothers becoming vicars – Wilfred was the exception, joining the Navy – and two of her sisters marrying churchmen. Gwen lived her whole life as her twin brother Lloyd's housekeeper, and Podge ran a children's home.

Such were the standard routes for impoverished, unmarried middle-class women, but Kathleen began to rebel against this destiny at sixteen. Having arranged for her to stay the holiday with relatives, Douglas was surprised to receive a letter from his younger sister telling him she could no longer 'endure being a charity child'. She would go to stay with a school friend's family because they wanted her to and because 'I want to dance and I can't dance with Aunt Sophie or Uncle Edward'.[18] When her uncle, the 3rd Baronet Bruce, suggested that she live permanently at Downhill, where her father had been born, she was tempted. She loved the wild, windswept location of the house on a barren cliff with a spectacular view of the Isle of Jura, and she knew how happy it would make her siblings, aunts and uncles. But Kathleen knew that she wanted more. She wanted to get into mischief. Always more rebellious and independent than her older siblings, she decided to be an artist. She also decided that, whatever happened, she wanted to be happy.

Con

Kathleen moved to London and enrolled at the Slade School of Art. She had a small allowance from her great-uncle's estate; not a great deal, but sufficient to gain her some freedom. Regardless of her independence and enthusiasm for life, an unmarried woman from a respectable family could not live on her own in 1900 and so Kathleen moved in with relatives. But her life soon became anything but conventional. She was introduced to a theatrical crowd by her brother Rosslyn, who had become vicar of St Ann's in Soho. She soaked up the opportunities for self-improvement that London offered, visiting museums and art galleries, lectures and exhibitions. Her interests ranged beyond art to music, theatre and philosophy. She drove everyone to the Arts Ball in a motor bus while wearing a crinoline.[1] She loved her studies at the Slade and discovered that she had a real talent for clay modelling, receiving consistent praise from her tutor. Two years later she moved to Paris.

Paris at the turn of the century was a Bohemian paradise. The teaching was better too, with more opportunity to work with live models and greater study of anatomy. For an aspiring artist who also relished freedom, it was an attractive prospect. Kathleen later wrote that the young woman who went prancing off to Paris to study art at that time 'had gone irretrievably to Hell'.[2] She pranced off very respectably, however. Two friends from the Slade went with her; one was Eileen Grey, who would become one of the leading designers of the modernist movement. They lived together at first, enrolling in the Académie Colarossi and then moving to the Académie Julian where they drew, painted and sculpted from life.

Despite her *joie de vivre* and her independence, Kathleen was still young and, at heart, a convent-educated Victorian vicar's daughter. Her first encounter with a nude male model was a shock: 'I turned and fled, shut myself into the lavatory, and was sick.'[3] She learned quickly in the face of all her experiences in London and Paris to cover up her innocence and inexperience with a show of nonchalance. After joining the sculpture class Kathleen very quickly excelled, and within three months she had her statue of a mother and child accepted for the Salon. She met the great sculptor Rodin, who allowed her to visit his studio every Saturday. She learnt by watching him.

Despite the bright lights of London and Paris, Kathleen was not seduced either physically or emotionally by the creative and unusual people that she met. She was intelligent and independent, but she was also chaste and maternal, and it was these qualities that steered her life. Her view of the world was that marriage curbed a woman's freedom, that adventure and travel were the real riches of life, and that art and babies were its greatest achievement. Her love of adventure and travel began with her move to Paris and continued throughout her life. When she found herself in difficult situations, she had a habit of bolting and travelling to some corner of the globe. In December 1903 she journeyed to Macedonia, where an uprising against the Ottoman Empire had resulted in bloody massacres and newborn babies being abandoned. The tragic fate of these war orphans was all the incentive Kathleen needed. She helped in a hospital and was confronted by the horrific realities of death, rape, starvation and disease. She shivered with terrible cold at night and struggled through mud during the day to help the communities that were being destroyed. When she sat with a fourteen-year-old boy desperately hoping that he would live only to watch him die, any remaining spark of a belief in God was put out: '... very suddenly, with his eyes still open, he stopped breathing ... My religion, which had been waning and waning, went out with a spirt.'[4]

Travelling home via Italy, she recuperated in Florence's spring sunshine, revelling in the art of the great masters that she loved. She wrote later, 'There were queer and ugly things in Paris. There were ugly and terrifying things in Macedonia. Here, to me at any rate, all seemed as spontaneous as a Botticelli picture.'[5] In Paris she had slept on the roof of her studio in all weathers, and in Florence she found an apartment with a terrace so that she could further indulge her love of sleeping outdoors. The balcony hung out over the River Arno with a wonderful view of the Ponte Vecchio. Once she felt stronger, she left with her artist friend Hubert to travel around the countryside for three weeks, walking many miles a day, sleeping outdoors, swimming in rivers and lakes and finding food in mountain villages. Kathleen adored vagabonding and did it whenever she could. She spent a blissful few weeks in Greece, sleeping outside and exploring the land where her grandmother and mother were born.

She later explained why vagabonding and sleeping outside gave her so much pleasure:

> A sleeper who wakes but for a moment in the open, be the night starlit, moonlit or black, gains, be he never such a clod, some feeling of grandeur, of variety. Activities of the day dwindle and dim in the vastness of the night. A lightness envelops and lifts him, making him one with infinity. He wakes the richer. He has adventured.[6]

Religion did not play a big part in Kathleen's life. For her the miraculous was found not in God but in new life; she was passionate about babies. At her convent school as a teenager she didn't have visions of Christ coming down from the cross as many girls did, but of the baby Jesus cuddling into her yearning arms. From an early age Kathleen decided that the most important goal of her life was to be a mother, and this meant compromising on her view of marriage. She was in this respect very conventional. She had been around women, including her friend Isadora Duncan, who had become unmarried mothers and considered theirs to be a terrible plight. In 1902, during a picnic in the French countryside to celebrate his birthday, Rodin had introduced Kathleen to the controversial American interpretive dancer. Both women were twenty-four and they shared an innate love of personal freedom but, in the end, very different ways of exploring it. When Isadora became pregnant by her married lover four years later, the ever-loyal Kathleen was there to help at the birth, but she was deeply shocked. That degree of freedom was not for her.

Kathleen's great friend J. M. Barrie described her as half man, half woman, with the woman's half more woman than anyone he'd ever met.[7] She drew men to her like moths to a flame and nearly every man she met fell under her spell, many begging her to marry them. There was a German pacifist who liked to thread her needle when she sewed, a rich Greek who swore that all he wanted was to bite her finger, a Frenchman who furnished a flat in the hopes that she would live there, a teenage fisherman in Greece who wanted to marry her, and a young Italian who sat silently in her studio watching her work. In Florence she awoke with a start on her balcony to find a young artist kneeling there watching her sleep. The closest she came to reciprocating these passions was an encounter with the American photographer Edward Steichen in Paris in 1902. After months of seeing each other every day at the same café, they finally met and he kissed her. This, her first kiss, was a brief and exhilarating moment but it went no further. Kathleen left a trail of shattered hearts in her wake because none of them measured up.

> ... a large and exceedingly varied assortment. They were an enchanting crowd, but I kept my goal, my star, firmly fixed. None of these was the right, the perfect father for my son. None I feared, could even be trained for the role.[8]

After all her travels, and despite all of her suitors, it was in London, at Mabel Beardsley's tea party, that Kathleen found her hero. In October 1907 Mabel had sent a note inviting her for tea and telling her that Captain Scott would also be there. Kathleen, who was not known for her interest in clothes, spent the day before thinking about what to wear. She created a new hat by cutting apart and moulding together her two existing ones.

It was a small gathering of people Kathleen knew, mostly artists, actors and writers. When she went into the back room, however, she found Scott sitting on a sofa next to an elderly lady. Kathleen was a striking, athletic-looking woman with bright blue eyes and a mane of thick brown hair and a classical profile with a strong jaw. She was like nobody Scott had ever met, and the attraction was instant. She didn't know until much later that after their very brief conversation at lunch ten months earlier he had followed her into the street. He'd lost his nerve when he saw her striding along with a suitcase; he had a gentleman's aversion to carrying luggage in the street. He was not going to let her slip away again. Kathleen was drawn to him too:

> With my invariable instinct to avoid what was attracting me, I moved to the furthermost corner of the party ... Then all of a sudden, and I did not know how, I was sitting in a stiff uncomfortable chair with an ill-balanced cup of tea being trivially chaffed by this very well-dressed, rather ugly and celebrated explorer. He was standing over me; he was of medium height, with broad shoulders, a very small waist, and dull hair beginning to thin, but with a rare smile and with eyes of a quite unusual dark blue, almost purple, I had noticed these eyes ten months before, I noticed them again now, though by electric light. I had never seen their like. He suggested taking me home.[9]

Their walk home was joyous: '... we walked, laughing, talking, jostling each other, as we lunged along the river-side in hilarious high spirits.'[10] They were passionately attracted to each other and were inseparable for the next ten days, parting only when he had to leave London for work. Kathleen made up her mind almost straight away to marry Scott. Her choice was confirmed when she told him that she was planning a walking tour to Italy. Not knowing him well, and concerned that he might try to curb her freedom, she was delighted by his response: write often and don't stay away too long. Scott had passed her test. Kathleen wrote later, 'Oh this, is a grand man; no self-pity, no suspicions, no querulousness, no recriminations. Perfect man!'[11]

Kathleen married her 'perfect man' in the Chapel Royal at Hampton Court Palace on 2 September 1908. They had been granted permission to marry there by the king after her aunt Zoe made a formal request. As the widow of the Archbishop of York, she had been granted a grace-and-favour apartment at the palace. These apartments were allocated to people who had performed great service to their country, although usually to their widows or other female dependents. They were a diverse group, overwhelmingly made up of women but from families of minor royals, aristocrats, military heroes, clergymen, diplomats, gardeners and politicians.[12] Kathleen was living with her aunt at the time and so the location was perfect.[13]

Zoe's apartment was close to the Chapel Royal and Kathleen walked there down a flower-decked corridor on the arm of her favourite brother, Wilfred, who was to give her away, accompanied by two bridesmaids, one of them Scott's little niece Phoebe Macartney. Never one to bother much about what she wore, Kathleen made a supreme effort to look the part for her new husband who was very sensitive to appearances, knowing as he did how important it was to be well dressed if you wanted to get on in the Navy. She wore a white satin dress trimmed with Limerick lace and a chiffon bodice with a wreath of natural myrtle. Her tulle veil was fastened with sprigs of real orange blossom. The chapel was lit by candles and decorated with lilies, and it was there, with the permission of the king, that Kathleen married her hero.[14] Her brother Rosslyn assisted with the service.

Crowds cheered outside the entrance to the palace as the one hundred and fifty guests arrived, including Rodin and his wife, and Sir Clements Markham and Dr John Scott Keltie representing the Royal Geographical Society. Many of the officers and men from *Discovery* were there too and gave the newlyweds a lovely silver rose bowl as a gift. It was set on a wooden plinth made from timbers taken from the ship.[15] Ory accompanied Ted to the wedding, setting eyes for the first time on the woman with whom she would share the greatest tragedy of her life. Kathleen and her new husband left the Chapel Royal to the strains of Mendelssohn's 'Wedding March', walking up to the Oak Room where Kathleen's aunt held a wedding reception for them and over one hundred guests. Afterwards, Captain and Mrs Scott set off for a short honeymoon in the south of France.[16]

The newspapers printed the particulars of the day in great detail. This was Kathleen's first taste of public scrutiny. She didn't relish it but must have been gratified that her achievements were recorded in the newspaper reports as well as her husband's. She was described as a pupil of Rodin, having exhibited at the Royal Academy and Salon and 'one of our few notable women sculptors'.[17] Rather than simply the wife of an explorer, she was described as having 'a career almost as adventurous as that of her husband' after her visit to Macedonia and because she had 'a Byzantine Emperor, who married one of Charlemagne's daughters' in her ancestry.[18]

Kathleen was thirty, by which age most Edwardian girls were long married and with a home full of children. Her romance with Scott was a whirlwind. They had known each other for just under a year, and it hadn't been easy. They had decided to marry within a month of meeting but didn't announce it until just before the wedding because they very nearly didn't make it to the altar. Two issues emerged early on as potential flaws in their relationship; the 'healthy, fresh, decent, honest, rock-like naval officer' she had chosen to be the father of her son was a complicated human being like any other, and he came with a family that depended on him.

Robert Falcon Scott was born on 6 June 1868 into a naval family from Devonport near Plymouth. At thirteen he joined up for naval training and at fifteen he was sent off to sea. He progressed well in the Royal Navy, coming to specialise in torpedoes. This life of service taught him from an early age to be obedient and disciplined and to make the best of any situation. As he moved up the ranks and his living expenses grew, it also became more difficult for him to keep up with his naval colleagues, many of whom had private incomes. But he could not fail; his family depended on him. Ten years before his marriage, Scott had become financially responsible for his mother, Hannah, and his sisters. Their father, John, had run a small brewery and when he later sold it, the family believed that their life was being funded by the interest accruing from the sale. When Scott was twenty-five, his mother announced that this was not the case. They had been living on the capital, which was now nearly depleted. They were virtually bankrupt.

Scott and his younger brother Archie did all they could to help their family in its time of need. Archie left the Royal Artillery and joined a Nigerian regiment for better pay and fewer expenses. Scott requested a transfer to HMS *Defiance* in Devonport to be close to home. Both boys sent money and their four sisters took jobs; Ettie went on the stage, Rose became a nurse, and Grace and Katherine became dressmakers. Their father took a job at a local brewery, but only three years later he died. Scott and Archie moved their mother and their sisters Grace and Katherine to London to run a small dressmaking business in Beauchamp Place.[19] Ettie had married just two months before their father had died and Rose was a nursing sister in the Gold Coast (present-day Ghana), so did not need providing for, but the boys agreed to find more money between them to support their mother and two unmarried sisters.[20] However, eleven months later, Archie died of typhoid. From November 1898 onwards, the entire financial security of Scott's female relatives fell onto his shoulders.

Hannah Scott and her daughters were understandably nervous when a new woman entered his life ten years later. They were wary of Kathleen and whether she would discourage his financial support of his family, and a little jealous of losing the affection of their beloved Con (short for Falcon, Scott's middle name). Perhaps hoping that the family's financial problems might be solved by Con marrying a wealthy woman, instead Hannah was confronted by a penniless artist, nearly thirty years old, who had lived alone in Paris. She invited her prospective daughter-in-law to meet and received in return a letter in Kathleen's exuberant handwriting, the large letters careering across the page, not necessarily in a straight line. Kathleen apologised for not having been able to meet sooner: 'I do hope you aren't hating me very much, I'm afraid I should if I were you.'

The strait-laced, deeply religious Hannah may have been surprised by the emotional freedom with which Kathleen always expressed herself, and she certainly would have been shocked when Kathleen proposed cancelling with Mabel Beardsley in order to meet.[21] Mabel was rumoured to have had an incestuous affair with her illustrator brother Aubrey and was friends with other scandalous society figures. But Hannah loved her children deeply, and her beloved Con had fallen in love. After meeting Kathleen, she wrote to her son on New Year's Eve 1907 giving him her blessing: 'You have carried the burden of the family ... It is time now for you to think of yourself and your future.'[22] It didn't prove to be as simple as that.

Kathleen and her solid naval officer could not have been more different. She struggled with the thought of losing her freedom and he struggled with insecurities about their relationship. He worried that he would be too dull for his artistic vagabond, that he would come between her and her work and that they wouldn't have enough money to live on. His letters were full of his concerns about the 'waves of difficulty washing all round our feet'.[23] Theirs was a difficult mix of personalities; she loved him but loved her friends and freedom too, while he loved her for her free spirit but was insecure and afraid of it meaning that he'd lose her. She was the only woman he could talk to, and he came to rely on her strength. He had to be the support for his family and his crew, and he needed Kathleen to support him, particularly when he was suffering from what she called his 'dread thundercloud'.[24]

Kathleen had enjoyed the freedom to do as she wished, and perhaps she now realised that her dream of a heroic son had one quite important flaw: it required her to live with a man. She would have to accommodate his feelings, dreams and needs, and she had fallen in love with a man of light and shade, a man who was shy and moody and prone to self-doubt but also an attractive, intelligent man, full of action, sensitive and with the soul of a poet. Kathleen had been untouched by all the men who had fallen in love with her in the past but now she was experiencing for the first time the responsibilities of loving and being loved, and it frightened her. She wrote to Con on 4 January 1908:

> Don't let's get married. I've been thinking a lot about it and though much of it would be beautiful, there is much also that would be very very difficult. I have always really wanted to marry for the one reason, and now that very thing seems as tough it would only be an encumbrance we could scarcely cope with ... We're horribly different, you and I, the fact is I've been hideously spoilt.[25]

They were reconciled after Con wrote back urging her to 'be patient and we'll pull things straight – have faith in me. But you must work with me, dearest, not against me.'[26]

Kathleen still struggled. She broke off the engagement again briefly in March and in the spring was pursued by a handsome young novelist and playwright, Gilbert Cannan, who tried to convince her to marry him and not Scott. When Kathleen set off on a tour of Italy, Con thought she was bolting from him. He wrote to her that beneath the rigorous exterior of a professional naval officer was a vagabond like her:

> I love the open air, the trees, the fields and seas – the open places of life and thought. Darling you are the spirit of all these to me though we have loved each other in crowded places. I want you to be with me when the sun shines free of fog...[27]

Con won through. He was the polar opposite of most of the men that Kathleen had known but he had proved himself, despite his insecurities. He didn't want to curb her freedom or her career, and he was going to provide something she had never had: a home. They found a lovely Georgian terraced house in London with a studio for Kathleen at 174 Buckingham Palace Road. Kathleen's excitement shines through her letters: 'Oh my dear, how lovely we are going to make everything! You and me. You and me. You and me. I've always been just me before. Now it's you and me and its good.'[28]

Just four months after the wedding, Kathleen discovered that she was pregnant with her long-desired child. Confident that her baby would be a strong and healthy boy, she carried on swimming, dancing and camping outside. He was born on 14 September 1909 and named Peter Markham Scott after Peter Pan, the creation of their great friend J. M. Barrie, and Sir Clements Markham. The two men became his godfathers. For Kathleen, the birth of her son brought an unexpected wave of emotion and a recalibration of her life's goal:

> ... and then a very strange thing happened to me. I fell for the first time gloriously, passionately, wildly in love with my husband. I did not know I had not been so before but I knew it now. He became my god; the father of my son and my god. Until now he had been a probationer, a means to an end. Now my aim, my desire, had been abundantly accomplished. I worshipped the two of them as one, father and son, and gave myself up in happy abandonment to that worship. Now my determined, my masterful, virginity, sustained through such strong vicissitudes, seemed not, as I had sometimes feared, mere selfish prudery, but the purposeful and inevitable highway to this culminating joy and peace.[29]

Kathleen was now ready to help her beloved husband achieve his greatest goal. The account of their wedding in *The Times* had stated that marriage would make no difference to Captain Scott's future plans regarding Antarctic exploration, and that was correct. To the women they married, the great explorers offered more than their glamorous celebrity; they promised an exciting life, vicariously lived. The social restrictions of the early twentieth century meant that adventurous women who dreamed of similar exploits were denied them. The American Jo Peary, whose husband Robert claimed to have reached the North Pole in 1908, had travelled with her husband in the early years of their marriage and gave birth to their daughter Marie in the freezing expanse of the Arctic in 1893,[30] but she was the exception. That same year, Eva Nansen, who had skied with her husband across the sort of rugged Norwegian terrain that no other woman had dared to cross, begged to go with him to the North Pole, but she was pregnant when he sailed away in *Fram*, and she never did go with him on his adventures.

The majority of Edwardian women, tied to their homes and families by convention, could only imagine such travels, but those who were drawn to polar explorers hoped that they might at least experience the world through their husbands' expeditions. Independent, intelligent, and used to her own adventures, Kathleen was this sort of polar wife. She believed that adventure was one of life's greatest treasures. She and Con had talked about a return to the Antarctic before they were married and her enthusiasm was clear: 'You shall go to the Pole. Oh dear me what's the use of having energy and enterprise if a little thing like that can't be done. It's got to be done so hurry up and don't leave a stone unturned.'[31] Kathleen understood that Con was only truly happy when he was challenged, when there was something to be achieved. He was a man of action, only truly fulfilled by a goal and a purpose. That goal was already clear when they met.

A Hero's Wife

In February 1907, Ernest Shackleton had announced publicly that he was going to lead his own expedition to the Antarctic. Within days he wrote to Ted Wilson asking him to join him as his second in command. The pair had forged a close friendship during the gruelling 'furthest south' journey that they had endured together with Scott. Ted had written to Ory from *Discovery*,

> Shackleton's conversation is sparkling and witty to a high degree. He has a wonderful memory, and an amazing treasure of most interesting anecdote. That and his quick wit and keen humour are his strong points at table ... He is still my best friend...[1]

Shackleton had been loyal to Ted on his early return, showing some of his friend's paintings to the editor of the *Illustrated London News* and delightedly writing to Ted on *Discovery* to let him know that the paper had agreed to take some of his work.[2] As they settled back into ordinary life, the Wilsons and the Shackletons spent time together in Edinburgh. In 1906, Ted had taken on fieldwork for the Grouse Disease Commission which meant that he had to examine dead birds and look for disease. His time was split between work in the laboratory and fieldwork on the moors in Scotland. During the winter months he came home and made Westal his base as much as possible, and his parents arranged for their disused conservatory to be used to store his dead grouse. The work soon became too much for one person and Ory's help was vital. She went with him to Scotland where they took a house in Colinton, a suburb of Edinburgh and there she became even busier, running the house, working as Ted's unofficial lab assistant and entertaining guests.

The Shackletons lived in the centre of Edinburgh, and there Emily Shackleton's social connections gave the Wilsons access to the best social circles. By the summer, however, Ted and Ory had tired of the city. They found it vulgar and excessively drunken, and relocated to Lord Lovat's shooting lodge at the head of Loch Ness.[3] But the great friendship remained, and Ted was tempted by Shackleton's offer. However, he was committed to his grouse work. In the face of an avalanche of persuasion, verging on begging, from Shackleton and a flurry of letters from him to those involved in the grouse project asking them to release Ted, he held firm. Even an offer to pay Ted and Ory's passage to New Zealand couldn't persuade him. It's clear from the series of letters from Shackleton in February that Ted felt honour bound to finish the grouse work, though his heart lay elsewhere. He must have written that Ory would have supported him if he'd chosen to go because Shackleton responded, 'Your wife is splendid to be glad for you to do this work if you could have done it.'[4]

Scott only heard about Shackleton's planned expedition when it was announced in the press and was upset that he had not shared his plans with him directly. He immediately got in touch with Ted to tell him about his own plans to return to the South Pole and in March Ted replied, 'Can you really mean that you would like me to go South again with you. If you do I may tell you that nothing in the world would please me more, and my wife is entirely with me.'[5] Ted had written to Ory while he was away on a grouse trip, 'I should not feel it was right now to desert Scott if he goes.'[6] Scott's distress at Shackleton's news was compounded when it became clear that he assumed that he could use the old *Discovery* base of McMurdo Sound. Scott was incensed:

> I don't want to be selfish at anyone's expense and least of all at the that of one of my own people but still I think anyone that has had to do with exploration will regard this region primarily as mine ... It must be clear to you now that you have placed yourself directly in the way of my life's work – a thing for which I have sacrificed much and worked with steady purpose...[7]

Ted and Shackleton were good friends, but Ted was also intensely loyal to Scott. Both Scott and Shackleton trusted him as a voice of reason and honour. When he intervened, he told Shackleton,

> Now Shackles, I think that if you go to McMurdo Sound & even reach the Pole – the gilt will be off the gingerbread because of the insinuation which will almost certainly appear in the minds of a good many, that you forestalled Scott who had a prior claim to the use of that base.[8]

After visiting Ted at Westal on 4 March, Shackleton convinced his old friend that he had known nothing about Scott's plans to return south when he had allowed his to be published. Dr John Scott Keltie, Secretary of the Royal Geographical Society, certainly knew about both potential expeditions but had informed neither Scott nor Shackleton of what the other was planning. Ted was able to explain this to Scott when he wrote to him afterwards; most importantly he was able to tell him that Shackleton had agreed not to use McMurdo Sound.[9] Unfortunately it transpired that when faced with conditions in the Antarctic which made it impossible to do anything else, Shackleton put his duty and the lives of his men before his pledge. He set up base at McMurdo Sound, reluctantly breaking his word to Scott, who felt betrayed by his former subordinate.

Scott's feelings of resentment are revealed in a recently discovered letter that he wrote in 1907 to the map seller Edward Stanford. It was a response to Stanford's map of the Antarctic which marked the point of 'furthest south' reached in the *Discovery* expedition. Although Shackleton had set out with Scott and Wilson, he had been too unwell to join them for the final effort and yet Stanford had labelled the point on his map 'Scott and Shackleton'. Scott's restrained but clearly angry letter demanded to know why Stanford chose to use this inscription, which went against all of the facts by implying dual leadership. He insisted that Stanford can't have intended to record the names of all of the expedition members because Wilson's was omitted.[10]

In March 1909, the news came that Shackleton had not reached the South Pole. He had got within one hundred miles of it but turned back, saying later that his wife would rather be married to a live donkey than to a dead lion. However, he had succeeded in travelling further south than Scott and Wilson had and the record was now his, and his alone.

On Shackleton's return in June 1909, thousands turned out on the streets of London to welcome him. He was driven in an open-top carriage with Emily and his children, and according to accounts at the time the horses were uncoupled and men from the crowd stepped forward to pull their hero's carriage through the crowded streets.[11] Then, in honour of his bravery and leadership in the face of terrible danger, Shackleton was knighted. Scott offered his congratulations publicly but privately resented the way that Shackleton had behaved. The souring of the relationship between these two great explorers was to become central to future British efforts to reach the South Pole. His rival's elevation to celebrated hero Sir Ernest Shackleton galvanised Scott. He started planning a new expedition in earnest.

Scott's new expedition would attempt to reach the South Pole but would also seek to complete and build on the scientific work begun by *Discovery*.

When he announced it, he declared that 'the effort to reach a spot on the surface of the globe which has hitherto been untrodden by human feet, unseen by human eyes, is in itself laudable' but that his objectives were more than this; he wished 'to achieve the greatest scientific harvest which the circumstances permit'.[12] Kathleen supported him wholeheartedly. She was an intrepid and independent woman and loved that Con had plans and ambitions of his own. She wasn't scared of separation, thriving on time to herself, but while the expedition was being readied she intended to be at Con's side, involved in his plans for as long as she possibly could be. Over the next few months she supported him despite her pregnancy.

The expedition was announced on 13 September 1909; Kathleen gave birth the following day. Her entire married life so far, and her pregnancy, had coincided with expedition planning, taking Con's attention away from their personal life. But this was just as Kathleen wanted it. She never intended that marriage or motherhood would curtail her freedom or that of her heroic husband. Kathleen was as committed to the new expedition as Con was.

Discovery had been bought by the Hudson's Bay Company and so Scott had purchased a new vessel, the three-masted whaling boat *Terra Nova*. It had been to the Antarctic before when it sailed south with the *Morning* to relieve *Discovery* after it became stuck in the ice. In March 1910, Kathleen accompanied her husband to Norway to test the caterpillar-tracked motor sledges that he planned to use in the Antarctic. They tried to meet Amundsen, who had made public his plan to reach the North Pole and with whom Con was keen to discuss scientific collaboration if they were to tackle the North and South Poles at the same time. Amundsen was evasive, and the meeting did not take place.[13] They did, however, meet Amundsen's mentor, the great Norwegian explorer Fridtjof Nansen, who advised Scott to use skis and dogs in his attempt on the Pole. Nansen, Peary and others had shown that dogs and skis were the most effective way of travelling over snow and ice. Scott rejected Nansen's advice. He put his faith in the new motorised sledges and horses to move supplies and then dogs and man-hauling to get his men to the Pole.

It has been suggested that Scott's reluctance to use dogs was influenced by the attitude of his mentor and close friend Sir Clements Markham, who had dominated British efforts to reach the Pole since *Discovery*. He believed that the polar regions were a place where British seamen could display their most heroic qualities and was impressed by the Navy's man-hauling of sledges, which he had witnessed in the Arctic.[14] This had been the start of Markham's long-term prejudice against using dogs. But the nobility of harnessing an explorer to a heavy sledge and asking him to pull it in extreme conditions over hazardous terrain for months on end was Markham's notion alone. Scott may have been squeamish about killing dogs for food, but he certainly didn't think man-hauling was more heroic. He just thought it was the only way.[15]

Scott was planning to put his faith in new technology combined with experience. After all, Shackleton had got within a hundred miles of the Pole using the same methods. Despite rejecting Nansen's advice, he did appreciate the value of the young Norwegian skier that Nansen introduced to him and Kathleen. Tryggve Gran was planning his own expedition, but Scott persuaded him to join the *Terra Nova* expedition instead.[16] News of the expedition spread, and over 8,000 men applied to join, including Kathleen's favourite brother Wilfred Bruce. Priority was given to naval men like Wilfred and those with Antarctic experience. The majority of the chosen team had been recommended to Scott or were former colleagues. Naturally, these included his great friends and Antarctic stalwarts Ted Wilson and Edgar Evans.

Oriana and Lois may have felt much less enthusiastic about their men returning to the Antarctic than Kathleen did. However much a polar wife shared her husband's ambition, her support was matched by the burden of knowing how much she would have to sacrifice to facilitate it. Often these men were driven by goals that seemed more important than the women they loved and more attractive than their family lives. Some were only truly happy when they were away. Many wives hoped that each expedition would be the last, that this time the goal would be reached. Jo Peary described this relationship between polar husband and polar wife very clearly:

> When a man goes out off the beaten track he possesses qualities which separate him from the mediocre, and when he blazes a new path and writes his name in big letters on his times, then every-one must concede he is neither commonplace nor conventional. But his wife, if he has one, is generally patterned after woman-kind in all times and ages. She loves her home and her husband ... my supreme thought [when] my husband had reached the pole was not that of jubilation, although I did rejoice over that, but of deep thankfulness that, having attained the goal of his ambition, such perilous trips would no longer be necessary.[17]

This was seldom the case: the perilous trips usually continued, and more separation had to be endured. Emily Shackleton described her powerlessness in the face of her husband's unquenchable wanderlust in these terms: 'How could you keep an eagle tied in a backyard?'[18] She knew that her husband struggled to settle and find his place in the family home and that while he loved his wife and children, he loved adventure more.

There would always be just one more expedition. When Lois and Oriana welcomed Edgar and Ted home from *Discovery* in 1904, they may have been looking forward to a settled family life, but this was not to be.

On 16 September 1909, when the formal request came, Ted was invited not only to lead the scientific staff for the new expedition but to choose the staff himself. It was a foregone conclusion that he would agree. He wrote to his father the same day:

> Scott is a man worth working for as a man ... No one can say that it will only have been a Pole-hunt, thought that of course is a *sine qua non*. We *must* get to the Pole; but we shall get more too ... We want the scientific work to make the bagging of the Pole merely an item in the results.[19]

Oriana knew that Ted and Scott's great friendship, the opportunity to finish the scientific work that they had begun on *Discovery* and Ted's faith in God's plan for him were too much to resist. Not even the great happiness that Ted had found in their marriage could compete with that. Any concerns that Ory might have expressed about being left behind again, or about Ted's safety, were firmly brushed aside. He had no fears about her ability to cope, and because he would not be able to do his duty if he had to worry about her it was implicit that Ory should not object. There was no written contract required of her this time, because she was his wife now and she had promised to obey. He knew what he was asking of her, but as he wrote to her later, they now had a shared destiny: 'It all seems cruel and cold but it is God's will to make good stuff of us both. Anyhow you will do your duty, my brave kind lady, and your "kind sir" will do his.'[20]

Oriana was thirty-five years old and had been married for eight years. She had no children and may still have hoped for them but Ted's plan to sail south again must have almost snuffed out any hope of motherhood. By the time he returned she would be close to forty. But throughout their relationship, Ory made few demands on Ted. He went his own way, even after they were married, and she did not seem to resent it.[21] They were great friends, and she shared his passions, and so Ory stiffened her lip and her resolve, rolled up her sleeves and helped her beloved husband to get ready to leave her again. She packed all his clothes, separating them by appropriateness for each port of call as well as the Antarctic, and stayed up late with him while he toiled into the night to finish his outstanding work. They were exhausting but happy days.

If Ory had hoped to find any solidarity with Kathleen at this time she was to be disappointed. They had tried to forge a friendship during a rather awkward lunch at Buckingham Palace Road the year before but had failed. Scott and Ted were very close and expected as a consequence that their wives would become friends too, as had been the case with the Smiths. Reginald Smith, the head of the publishing firm Smith, Elder & Co., had produced Scott's *Voyage of Discovery* and would publish Ted's book on grouse. These projects had forged a deep friendship between the three men, and so it was that Reginald had invited Scott and Ted to spend time at his shooting lodge in Cortachy near Kirriemuir in the Scottish Highlands. He and his wife had transformed Burnside from a shepherd's cottage into a holiday home with a rose-covered veranda and a garden that sloped down to a row of birch trees.[22] It was during this holiday, in the summer of 1907, that Ory met Isabel Smith, the woman who would become her best friend and one of her closest confidantes for the rest of her life.

Her meeting with Kathleen a year later couldn't have been more different. Scott was away at sea when Ted and Ory came to lunch and that probably did not help to ease the atmosphere or to disguise the fact that the two women had very little in common. Despite very similar upbringings as vicars' daughters who'd both lost their mothers at a young age, their lives had diverged quite dramatically. Kathleen was the youngest of a large family, used to being independent and making her own decisions. She moved in a world where she had access to leaders of thought, politics and culture, and where she was used to stimulation and change. Ory was the oldest child and had stepped into the void left by her mother, helping to raise her younger siblings. Family duty guided her, and supporting Ted's work was the focus of her being. Then there was the matter of faith. For Ory and Ted this was the guiding light of their life together, but Kathleen's belief in God had been snuffed out by the suffering that she'd seen. She found herself unable to overcome the weight of scientific evidence ranged against it either: 'It is sad to me to see people striving after what they desire against the opposed weight of all that they know.'[23]

At the end of the evening, both realised that they had little in common beyond their husbands. Kathleen wrote to Con that she thought Ory was pretty but drab and that Ted was a good-looking fellow; she clearly found them dull and priggish, writing that they'd disregarded each other's sense of humour almost at once.[24] She wrote rather damningly of Ory in her diary, when she said about Ted, 'I gather he thinks women aren't much use, and expect he is judging from long experience, so I bear him no malice.'[25] To the free-spirited Kathleen, Ory seemed serious and boring. Ory had always admired independence and what she called 'the reckless, gay, adventurous plungers', and Kathleen might have fitted this bill. But for Ory these weren't qualities to admire if they conflicted with right and duty. Perhaps Kathleen just seemed too hedonistic to her. When she and Ted got home, she may not have managed to curb her strong critical tendencies. She would later describe Kathleen as 'that horrid Mrs Scott'.[26] Ted wrote very diplomatically to Scott after their meeting to say that Kathleen 'made us feel at once that we were old friends; we were simply delighted by her kindness and abundant hospitality and welcome'. His letter went on to say that his dearest wish had been for his friend to find a wife who suited him as much as Ory did and he could now imagine their next holiday with the Smiths in Scotland as three very happy couples.[27] Clearly that was unlikely to ever happen.

Lois heard the news of her impending separation from Edgar when Scott wrote on 23 March 1910 to explain that he'd requested to the Navy that Edgar join the expedition in a matter of weeks.[28] Edgar knew the dangers, but there was no question that he wanted to go. The Pole was still theirs to take and so was the fame that Edgar knew so well following *Discovery*. He still yearned to get further south than he had before and to be in the first party to reach the Pole.[29] Lois supported him; it was part of their marriage bargain. Edgar had not hidden his desire to go south again if Scott returned, and they had made an engagement pact that if he was selected she would let him go.[30] It was a prospect that had hung over their marriage from the start.

If Lois had harboured any hopes that marriage and fatherhood might change Edgar's mind, they had been shattered. As she said later, 'I knew he would go if Captain Scott wanted him at any time and I had to make up my mind to it.' But Edgar assured her that this would be his last absence and so reluctantly she had agreed.[31] Her reluctance lay not only in being separated from her husband for the first time and being left with three children under the age of five, the youngest of whom was only fifteen months old, but also in the financial risk that she was being asked to take. To join Scott, Edgar had to be granted leave by the Admiralty and come off the naval payroll, throwing his lot in with an expedition whose finances were by no means secure. Edgar argued that it was a risk worth taking. If Scott succeeded, and they were first to the Pole, then fame and money would follow, and this would mean a secure financial future for their family.[32]

Lois may have known for years that an expedition was in the offing, but when the call came the separation was rapid. She had very little time to get used to the idea. Just over three weeks after the letter, Edgar was released from his post at HMS *Victory* and joined the expedition team in London.[33] To be fit for the journey, *Terra Nova* needed a full refit and a thorough clean to remove all traces of whale blubber from its hull. Scott asked Edgar to join him at the expedition headquarters at 36 & 38 Victoria Street as soon as possible to help with the refit and to supervise the sledging gear. It was important work, but on 20 May, as millions filled the streets of London for the funeral of King Edward VII, Edgar may have paused to watch. The procession, which included the largest ever gathering of European royalty, made its way from Buckingham Palace via Westminster Abbey to Paddington Station. Edgar may have wished that he was waiting at Windsor Station with his former colleagues from HMS *Excellent* to pull the funeral carriage up to the castle where the king would be laid to rest in St George's Chapel. But his duty lay elsewhere now. Scott needed him, and that was enough for Edgar; he would follow his leader anywhere. In Portsmouth, Lois remained with their three children, not knowing when she would see him again.

The Departure of *Terra Nova*

Scott's most pressing task now was to raise money. The *Discovery* expedition had enjoyed the financial backing of the Royal Geographical Society and the Royal Society, but the *Terra Nova* did not. He estimated that the cost would be approximately £50,000 (the equivalent of approximately £6 million today). He and Kathleen were not wealthy and so he appealed to the public for funds, aiming to raise £40,000 by public subscription in Britain. The remaining £10,000 he hoped would arrive as donations from South Africa and Australia, where the ship would call, and particularly New Zealand, where the expedition would be based until it sailed on to Antarctica. A national fundraising campaign was launched at the Mansion House in London on 12 October 1909, after which Scott set off to fuel interest in the expedition. He travelled the country holding meetings, giving talks and trying to inspire businessmen in major British cities. This sort of thing didn't come naturally to him, and Kathleen couldn't always be there to encourage him. There was huge excitement among the public and a swell of patriotic fervour around a new British attempt to take the South Pole, but they didn't seem so keen to pay for it. The exception was in Wales.

Cardiff and its leading citizens were to provide the *Terra Nova* expedition with more money and resources than any other group of backers. It has been argued that without Cardiff the expedition might never have set sail.[1] Support was largely whipped up by the editor of the *Western Mail*, W. E. Davies, a highly influential journalist and member of Cardiff's Chamber of Commerce, who used his newspaper and business connections to encourage a fervour for the expedition. When the national fundraising campaign was launched in London, Davies stood with representatives of the Royal Geographical Society and other dignitaries alongside Scott. This invaluable support had been won initially by Teddy Evans, former second officer of the *Discovery* expedition's relief ship, *Morning*, who had abandoned his own plans for an Antarctic expedition to throw his support behind Scott. In return he was made Scott's second-in-command on *Terra Nova*. Teddy, who had ancestors from Cardiff, not only forged the relationship with Davies but also gave lectures and interviews on the advantages to the city of supporting the expedition. He played down the scientific objectives and played up patriotism and civic pride, arguing that this high-profile venture would give the city unparalleled opportunities to advertise its commercial prowess and civic achievements across the world.

During the first decade of the twentieth century, Cardiff had become one of the great industrial cities of the British Empire. Plentiful coal supplies in the Rhondda Valley formed the basis of an export trade which saw Welsh coal power industry across the globe. The vast coal dock in Cardiff, with its network of rail connections, was the hub of this lucrative business. In recognition of its contribution to the Empire, King Edward VII made Cardiff a city in 1905; it was the only city to be created in his reign. Cardiff's businessmen saw their support of the *Terra Nova* expedition as an opportunity to publicise their entrepreneurial city and to rebrand it globally as more than just a coal producer. Teddy Evans forged a close relationship with the leading members of the Cardiff Docks community, which brought with it supplies, equipment and expertise to help with the refit and timely departure of the ship. Cardiff was to donate £2,500 to the expedition in total, which was more than any other city. Its businessmen and dockside community also promised coal, dry docking, painting and towing free of charge. The city's generosity led Scott to announce in January 1910 that Cardiff would be *Terra Nova*'s point of departure.[2]

As it stood, however, the coffers were still too empty for this to happen. Early in 1910, Chancellor David Lloyd George had given Scott £20,000 on behalf of the Liberal Government. A proud Welshman, he knew the *Western Mail*'s W. E. Davies and it has been suggested that the editor twisted his old friend's arm to give money to the expedition.[3] Scott still needed to raise more, and around this time he offered a guarantee of inclusion in the expedition in return for a donation. Two men were appointed through this means, both of whom gave £1,000 to the fund.

The first was Captain Lawrence Edward Grace Oates, the only Army man on the expedition. He was a very wealthy member of the landed gentry and his family had made its money through wool and landownership. His father and his uncle Frank were big game hunters and gentlemen travellers who had journeyed into Africa. Frank had died there of malaria aged only thirty-five, but William Oates survived to pass this adventurous gene on to his son. After Eton he had joined an elite cavalry regiment and was posted to Egypt and India. He fought in the South

African War and returned a hero at twenty-one, albeit wounded. His bravery made him a hero to his regiment, the 6th Inniskilling Dragoons, who nicknamed him 'No Surrender Oates'.[4] Now aged twenty-nine, he was disillusioned with the army and didn't think he was doing enough for his county in India. He was a man motivated by duty and was seeking a new challenge.

Perhaps it was the furore surrounding Shackleton's return from Antarctica or perhaps it was a desire to emulate his father and uncle by tackling the last great terrestrial challenge of exploration, but Oates decided that he wanted to be part of the journey to the Pole. It is easy to see why Scott spotted his among the 8,000 applications. He was an Eton man, a cavalry officer, a war hero and an expert with horses, not just as a cavalry officer but as a hunter and polo player. Horses were to play a crucial part in Scott's attempt to reach the Pole, and after a lifetime at sea he had little experience with animals; the sailors and scientists that made up the rest of the crew weren't much better. Furthermore, he liked the idea of an Army man taking a spot in the expedition. Oates offered to work in any capacity, asked for neither title nor responsibility, and refused payment. He was also happy to pay £1,000, the equivalent of roughly £125,000 today, into the expedition coffers – or rather his mother was, since Caroline Oates controlled the family fortune.[5] Lawrence Oates became known to his *Terra Nova* shipmates as 'Titus' or' 'Soldier'.[6]

The second man recruited this way was Apsley Cherry-Garrard, the young cousin of Scott's publisher and friend Reginald Smith. Cherry, as he became known, had met Ted and Ory in the autumn of 1908 when he'd travelled up to Reginald and Isabel's shooting lodge in Scotland and found them holidaying there. His father had been dead less than a year and the twenty-two-year-old was floundering. With a vast fortune at his disposal and the responsibility for running Lamer, the family estate near Wheathampstead in Hertfordshire, Cherry had all the resources in the world but no idea what to do with them. Raised as a member of the landed classes and educated at Winchester, Cherry had been brought up on tales of imperial glory and was a sturdy conservative and supporter of Britain and Empire. He had been too young to fight in the South African War like Oates, but heroic stories from the conflict had thrilled him and his schoolmates and he longed for adventure and a chance to prove himself.

Meeting Ted changed the course of Cherry's life; he looked up to him ever afterwards as a mentor and a model of how life should be lived. Here was a man whose life had purpose and adventure. Knowing that his cousin Reggie was a close friend of both Scott and Ted, Cherry asked him to approach Ted about joining the expedition. Ted was very supportive from the start, but thousands had volunteered, and all the scientific roles had been filled; the idea was then mooted that Cherry could subscribe to the expedition and go along as an unskilled volunteer. Despite no promises being made, Cherry decided to donate £1,000 anyway. Perhaps it was this gesture, and seeing that his friends Ted and Reggie were so enthusiastic about the young man, that prompted Scott to ask to meet him. He was impressed, and on 27 April 1910 Cherry was given a place on the scientific staff despite failing the medical due to his very poor eyesight.[7]

The expedition was still short of the total funds needed, but Scott now had enough money to depart and enough faith to hope that the rest could be raised in time. He announced that he would stay in England for six weeks after the ship sailed to make sure that the expedition was properly financed. *Terra Nova* left the East India Docks in London on 1 June 1910 and sailed via Portsmouth to Cardiff, where a welcome party of dignitaries on board the tugboat *Falcon* greeted the ship and escorted it into harbour nine days later. Scott and Kathleen, together with Teddy Evans and his wife Hilda, were invited to stay with the city's lord mayor at the Mansion House for the five days of the ship's stay in Cardiff.

Thus began a period of many months that Kathleen and Hilda would spend together, which would prove to be far from easy. Con left that night for London for further fundraising and Kathleen stayed in Cardiff, spending her time socialising with the *Terra Nova* officers. After the ship was filled with coal on Saturday morning, most of the officers and crew were given the rest of the weekend off, to report back on Monday morning for the final preparations. There was a trip to the Music Hall with the lord mayor and his wife, and Kathleen went with those expedition members who were free on the Saturday night to see a variety show at the Palace Theatre Hippodrome. On Sunday vast crowds of sightseers travelled to Cardiff Docks to see *Terra Nova*, although only one hundred or so paid to go on board and explore it.

Scott returned to Cardiff on Sunday night, and the last two days before departure were very busy for everybody as *Terra Nova* was loaded with supplies, equipment and scientific instruments. Nonetheless, time was made for the people of Cardiff to celebrate the presence of the expedition's members in their city and its choice as their departure point. On Monday 13 June, the officers were treated to dinner by Cardiff's Chamber of Commerce at the Royal Hotel. One hundred guests dined on fillet of beef Terra Nova, soufflé Captain Scott and South Pole ice pudding.[8] Edgar went to the dinner provided for twenty-eight members of the crew at the nearby Barry's Hotel, but afterwards he and his shipmates joined the officers at the Royal for a smoking concert. These were popular events at the time, where men met to smoke and talk while listening to live music. That night there were comic singers and a harpist. Edgar, who was lionised in Cardiff, was seated between his captain and the lord mayor. It was Scott's idea to recognise the local hero in this way, and when the lord mayor presented the expedition with a flag bearing the arms of the City of Cardiff it was entrusted to Edgar for safe keeping.

Scott encouraged Edgar to say a few words, and he gave what *The Cambrian* described later as a 'breezy speech'. It was brief, but it was funny and showed Edgar's enormous loyalty to Scott. There was a laugh from the audience when he declared, 'I know him well and he knows me very well...' Every one of them he said would do their very best to succeed this time, and were committed heart and soul: 'No one else would have induced me to go again, but if there is one man in the world who will bring this to a successful issue, Captain Scott is the man.' Referring to the prospect of bringing back 'the Pole', Edgar joked, 'We cannot put it in the Museum, but if we do bring it back I hope you will let it go to Swansea.'[9] It was a very big night for Edgar. His speech was a huge success, prompting cheers and laughter from officers and city dignitaries. He was treated like a celebrity and thoroughly enjoyed the dinner, the concert and the flowing alcohol. Six men had to carry him back on to *Terra Nova* that night.[10] But why not? Already excited to go south, he was enjoying his local fame and wasn't going to see home for quite some time. Edgar had been in the Navy since he was fifteen and was from a family of pub owners, so to celebrate in this way was hardly out of the ordinary. He was a big man, too, and the fact that six men had to carry him might reflect his size just as much as how drunk he was. Edgar certainly wasn't aggressive in any way, nor was he the only one to get drunk that night.

The next evening – the expedition's last night before departure – wives were included in the celebrations. The lord mayor and the lady mayoress held a reception at Civic Hall in honour of the *Terra Nova* officers. Eight hundred invitations were issued, and as guests entered they found the hall decorated with palms, plants and flowers, with firemen in burnished helmets lining the entrance route. The Royal Welsh Ladies' Choir, in full national costume, entertained the assembled crowd and sang 'The Sailors' Chorus' as the crew of *Terra Nova* entered. It was a proud moment for Edgar as a proud Welshman. Kathleen and Hilda Evans stood alongside their husbands as they were showered with good wishes. Autograph hunters besieged Con too, asking him to sign their pocketbooks.[11]

Lois did not see any of these events, nor was she there to share Edgar's celebrity. Despite having family in Wales, he had asked to say goodbye in Portsmouth and would not let her go to Cardiff to see him off. As the mother of three children under the age of five, she might have struggled with the journey, and there was a great deal of work for Edgar to do to get the ship ready, so he would have little time to spare. Saying their farewells privately would also keep her and their children safe from the glare of publicity, and so Lois said goodbye to her husband at their home, waving him off on his great adventure and praying for his safe return. Ironically, a photograph was later published purporting to show Lois standing on the deck of *Terra Nova* in Cardiff at Edgar's side, holding their eighteen-month-old son Ralph.[12] This was one of the many occasions when the press got things wrong. Lois never went on board the ship; in fact, she had never even seen it. *Terra Nova* had sailed out of Portsmouth en route to Cardiff and Edgar, back home from London, had taken her down to Southsea to catch a glimpse, but it was too foggy. Obscured in the gloom, Lois was not able to see the ship that would take her husband away from her.[13]

Edgar used the last remaining days before the ship sailed to return to Gower and say goodbye to relatives and friends, particularly those who would not be coming to Cardiff to wave him off.[14] Lois's parents had given up the licence of the Ship Inn by this point and had retired, so there were no get-togethers in the family pub, but Edgar went to see his widowed mother Sarah, who had gone to live with her sister Anne in the village of Pitton.[15] He said his final goodbye to her there.

Edgar's three surviving siblings also lived nearby: Charles, a farmer at Cwm Farm in Sketty; John, who was a furnaceman at Gowerton Steelworks; and Eliza Jane, who ran a lodge on the Mumbles Road.[16] Edgar and Lois were both used to walking long distances after living in Gower, through which roads didn't fully penetrate and where there was no public transport.[17] Edgar walked 16 miles from his mother's house to his brother Charles's farm to say his goodbyes. He swung his young niece up in his arms and promised to visit her again when he came back.[18] He spent his last night at home in the Rose and Crown pub in Morriston, a suburb in the north of Swansea where Lois's sister Beatrice lived. The pub's sitting room was a popular haven for the area's businessmen, who welcomed Edgar because his brother-in-law, the iron merchant John Faull, was one of them.[19]

These precious few days gave Edgar a chance to say farewell to Gower, his friends and family and all the other familiar sites of home. Beatrice and John Faull had opened their home, Falmouth House in Clydach Road, as a place to stay for those family members who wanted to see the ship and wave Edgar off. His twenty-two-year-old niece Sarah Evans went on board with her two sisters, Annie and Sally, and Scott gave her a taste of what her uncle would be eating by letting her try a ship's biscuit.[20] On 15 June 1910, Sarah sailed with other family members on one of the pleasure steamers that accompanied *Terra Nova* as she sailed along the Bristol Channel. Edgar raised to the foremast the flag that he'd been given by Cardiff's lord mayor; when it fluttered proudly in the breeze, the crowds on the shore broke into a mighty cheer.[21] As the ship sailed out to sea, other members of Lois and Edgar's family stood on top of the cliffs at Rhossili and waved frantically as the sea thumped against the rocks below and the guillemots and gulls flew above their heads.[22] This glimpse of *Terra Nova* was the last they would ever see of Edgar.

The Influence of the Petticoat

For Kathleen and Ory, the final goodbyes were yet to come. As officers' wives, they had the option to go to New Zealand with the expedition and both were determined to travel as far as they possibly could. Ory packed up and prepared to accompany Ted, but Kathleen's position was a little different. She was the mother of a very young child. Sailing with Con would mean leaving nine-month-old Peter for four months. But she felt that she should; she needed to go with Con.

> ... looking back over my life I can think of nothing that hurt more hideously than unlocking the sturdy fingers that clung round mine as I left the laughing, tawny-haired baby Hercules... (but) I had chosen, and joy never left me for long. In agonies and ecstasies of reciprocated love I followed my husband.[1]

Peter was left in the care of his grandmother Hannah Scott at her home in Henley, where three of Con's sisters lived too. Rose, whose husband had died in 1906, leaving her almost penniless, had moved into her mother's home with her ten-year-old daughter Erica. Katherine had married Harry Lurgar Brownlow, a surgeon, in 1901 and lived in St Andrew's Road. Grace, the only one of Con's sisters not to marry, had also set up home in Henley.[2] Peter would have the love and attention of his grandmother, aunts, and cousins while his mother was away – but he would never see his father again.

As Ted sailed away from Cardiff's harbour on board *Terra Nova*, Ory travelled to Southampton to board the ship that would reunite her with her husband on the other side of the world. She was to travel in greater comfort than he because RSS *Saxon* was a passenger liner, part of a fleet run by the Union Castle Line, which operated between Europe and South

Africa. Ory was not the only *Terra Nova* wife aboard. Hilda Evans's husband Teddy was commanding *Terra Nova* as it sailed to South Africa so she, like Ory, would see her husband again there. Kathleen was on board too, but she was not alone. Con had stayed behind to try to raise more of the funds that the expedition needed, and so she now shared a cabin with him, enjoying the last few precious weeks together.

Six weeks later when they reached the bay at Simon's Town, near Cape Town, Kathleen went straight off with Scott on a fundraising mission, which included giving lectures in Pretoria and Johannesburg.[3] There was time to relax together too as she wrote to Con's sister Ettie, 'We've just arrived in this most glorious of countries the place is ablaze with flowers although it is mid-winter. The sun shines, the sea is blue and house we're staying in is right on the sea.'[4] They received letters from Con's family with updates on Peter which they pored over together: 'You must think how we look forward to your letters and how gratifying they are. We went over every word you tell us of our Doodles and I read your letters aloud over and over – and bless you for them.'[5] Meanwhile, Ory and Hilda spent nearly two weeks in Simon's Town waiting for *Terra Nova* to arrive. They weren't concerned that the ship was late; they understood the vagaries of the sea and the winds. When it did sail in on 15 August, they were able to tell the crew that the papers at home had suffered a mild panic but that they hadn't been anxious at all.[6]

Scott greeted his crew with a change of plan. On the next leg of the journey from Cape Town to Australia, he would command *Terra Nova* and Ted would accompany the wives on *Corinthic*.[7] The journey was a trial for Ted, who much preferred the busy atmosphere on the expedition ship. Ory tried to entertain him as best she could when she wasn't reading or sewing kit for him, and Hilda was an eager helper, joining in with games of deck coits, deck golf and table tennis, and charming Ted with her company.[8] But Kathleen, missing Con, whom she would not see until they arrived in Australia, and suffering badly from seasickness, retreated to her cabin for most of the voyage and kept to herself. Her main preoccupation was the diary that she began writing for Con in which she planned to record all that happened while they were apart and which she would give to him later when he returned from Antarctica.

When on 12 October *Terra Nova* sailed into Melbourne harbour, Kathleen insisted that she be taken out to the ship to meet Con. It was dark and raining heavily and the sea was rough, and Ted, who was still in charge of all three wives, tried to dissuade her by saying that the others were cold and hungry, but she was insistent. Ory and Hilda were soaked and shivering, holding on for dear life as their small boat crossed the choppy water in the dark to find *Terra Nova*. For Kathleen there had been no question that it was the right thing to do:

> ... I knew my man would expect me ... I heard my good man's voice and was sure there was no danger, so insisted, getting more and more unpopular ... we at last got close to the beautiful *Terra Nova* with our beautiful husbands on board.[9]

Ory and Hilda stayed in the launch, but Kathleen went on board and into the wardroom, which was cosy and warm with smiling faces and pipe smoke. In Con's cabin she changed out of her drenched stockings and into a pair of his socks to accompany her husband ashore.[10] But the joyful reunion was marred by the arrival of some devastating news. A telegram was delivered to Scott which read, 'Beg leave to inform you *Fram* proceeding Antarctica. Amundsen.'[11] Amundsen was an experienced and professional explorer whose aim so far had been to reach the North Pole, but on hearing that both Robert Peary and fellow American Frederick Cook had claimed to have reached it he changed his plan. Without telling Nansen, who'd lent him *Fram*, his financial backers, which included the Royal Geographical Society, or even his crew until they were en route, Amundsen had changed course and set sail for the South Pole instead. Scientific discovery took a backseat to his ambition as he decided he'd rather be first to the south than second (or third) to the north. His actions went against the convention of the time to be public with plans as Scott had been. Many, including Ory and Kathleen, thought this forestalling was underhand, but Scott at least publicly played it down, reiterating to the newspapers that his was primarily a scientific expedition. The press, however, had a terrific story in their grasp. For them this was now a race to the pole.

Preparations continued apace as the *Terra Nova* team arrived in New Zealand on 28 October. The ship dropped anchor in the port of Lyttelton, near Christchurch, where they spent a month loading the ship and readying it for departure. Equipment and supplies were put on board including three motor sledges, nineteen ponies and thirty-three dogs. The Siberian dogs and Manchurian ponies had been shipped from Vladivostok via Japan, Hong Kong and Sydney on a journey that took seven weeks. The ponies had been forced to stand for fifty-two days and were now exhausted and fractious.[12] When *Terra Nova* eventually departed, hardly any deck was visible on the overcrowded ship. Henry Bowers, nicknamed 'Birdie' by the crew because of his hooked nose, became indispensable during this period. He was an experienced seaman who had served in the Navy and then in the Royal Indian Marine Service but had no Antarctic experience. Appointed at first as a junior officer in charge of expedition stores, the small but strong, sturdy and extremely hard-working Birdie soon excelled himself.[13] He would play a key role in the shore party, in charge of landing, stores, navigation and sledging rations.

Kathleen was at Con's side throughout, rolling her sleeves up to take part in the preparations, even sorting and marking clothes for other expedition members including Oates and Birdie Bowers.[14] They stayed at the Kinseys' home on top of a cliff near Christchurch with its spectacular panoramic views of the ocean and snow-capped mountains. Kathleen and Con slept in the garden under the stars, and he wrote in his diary, 'The scene is wholly enchanting, and such a view from some sheltered sunny corner in a garden which blazes with masses of red and golden flowers tends to feelings of inexpressible satisfaction with all things.'[15]

Ory's precious last few weeks with Ted were hectic too. They spent a month in a whirl of social activity and expedition business. The Bowens, who had become such friends to Ory while she waited for Ted to return on *Discovery*, had them to stay at their house, letting them treat it exactly as if it was their own home. But they spent a great deal of time with the Kinseys too, their house becoming the centre of the expedition's social life.[16] The Scotts, the Wilsons and the Evanses were reunited at a farewell garden party there. Nearly two hundred people gathered in the garden for tea and the opportunity to catch a glimpse of the ship's crew. Ory, Kathleen and Hilda, with their husbands, were the guests of honour, as champagne was drunk, canapes were nibbled and photos taken from the roof by the press.[17] Privately however, things were not quite so harmonious.

Kathleen, Hilda, and Oriana had had a terrible argument. Perhaps it was not surprising that emotions were running high as all three were preparing themselves for a long separation from their husbands. Oates described what happened in a letter that he wrote to his mother on 23 November. Intended to entertain her, his account exaggerated and replayed the event for maximum drama:

> Mrs. Scott and Mrs. Evans have had a magnificent battle, they tell me it was a draw after 15 rounds. Mrs. Wilson flung herself into the fight after the 10th. round and there was more blood and hair flying about the hotel than you would see in a Chicago slaughter house in a month...[18]

Because of this account and because the argument was between women it has sometimes been dismissed as a 'catfight', but this rather misogynistic description misses the point that it represents so much more. Although it's not clear what sparked the row, it became the conduit for the tensions, resentments and irritations that had grown during the three months that the women had spent together on the expedition, and which now bubbled to the surface. The argument says something about what it was like to be a polar wife and also what was expected of one.

Kathleen and Ory, together with Hilda Evans, were the first women to travel on a British polar expedition and as such they were breaking new ground. Before travelling to New Zealand they had been involved in the preparations and in doing so had already become something more than was expected of wives of the period. They had found themselves taking on the roles of counsellor, muse, nurse, fundraiser, assistant and confidante. They were invested in the expedition, in its success and in the safety of their husbands, and each reacted in their own way to the pressures. Oates's account suggests that the disagreement started between Kathleen and Hilda. The two women had contrasting ways of dealing with their anxiety. Kathleen was determined to be positive and may have felt that Hilda wasn't helping anyone by being too open about her fears and clinging desperately to her man.

But behind this clash of temperaments there was also a clash of loyalties to two husbands whose relationship had soured very early in the expedition. Teddy felt his role as second-in-command was being undermined as Scott increasingly put his trust elsewhere, and resented it all the more because he'd given up his own plans to lead an expedition and thrown his support behind Scott. Hilda may have smarted at what she saw as her husband being side-lined, while Kathleen wouldn't have appreciated Con being challenged. Ory, at thirty-six, was the oldest of the three women and her husband wasn't in the Navy, so she wasn't subject to its hierarchy. She could perhaps bring some much-needed perspective and help to calm the situation, but her loyalties would probably always have been with the much younger Hilda. They had been friends since they'd sailed home together from *Discovery* and she may have felt that she needed to support the twenty-six-year-old in her confrontation with the polar wife who was not only six years older but more confident and the wife of the captain. It was an unavoidable truth, too, that Oriana and Kathleen simply did not get on.

Birdie Bowers thought that the friction was caused by Kathleen's jealousy of Hilda's popularity. He believed she used her influence over Scott to hurt Hilda by having her husband side-lined, as he wrote home:

> I did not understand then as I do now the lengths one woman jealous of another can go to ... Mrs Evans is a person apart – in my esteem – She is not my style in most ways but for a womanly woman of remarkable beauty & general charm she stands out of the crowd as almost everything a wife should be. Unfortunately, her excellent qualities have

> laid her open to much jealousy & that's where the trouble has been between Scott & his second-in-command ... In minor ways the influence of the petticoat has raised that uneasy feeling among a party of men whose loyalty was otherwise irrefutable. The hand behind Capt. S. could be seen in many minor ways not against anybody but at Mrs E through Teddy.[19]

However, jealousy was not a trait that Kathleen possessed. Nor did she desire to be popular. Birdie's interpretation of events is based on his assumption that if Hilda was 'almost everything a wife should be' then Kathleen must surely be jealous. But he did not know Kathleen. She didn't want to be that sort of wife at all. The ideal Edwardian woman was Queen Alexandra: beautiful, glamorous, good, virtuous, and dutiful to her husband.[20] Hilda clearly found it easy to inhabit this nurturing, supporting role. She was cheerful and beautiful and 'she was a wonderful woman ... regarded with respectful admiration and affection by every member of the Expedition ... she gave up much time and worked very hard to provide comforts for the men of the Expedition, and her numerous useful gifts to them were treasured as sacred things'.[21]

Kathleen found this ideal irritating. She had no time for women who put up with it and chose to be passive, impractical and decorative in order to fit the womanly ideal, as she wrote later: 'Nothing is expected of a woman in my class, neither brains, energy, nor initiative.'[22] That is not to say that Kathleen wasn't feminine; indeed, she was romantic too, but she was used to interacting with men on equal terms and believed that women should just be able to get on and do what they wanted. She had limits, of course, and although she may have stepped close to the line drawn by society, she never transgressed it in ways such as having sex or children outside marriage. Kathleen simply preferred the company of men because she found most women dull, and in her mind Oriana and Hilda certainly fell into that category. She found it wearisome to have to spend so much time with them, and confided in her diary, 'If ever Con has another expedition the wives must be chosen more carefully than the men – better still, have none.'[23]

For some of the men of the expedition, the issue with Kathleen seems to have been that she did not behave in the way that they thought a woman should. When Birdie wrote home in September 1910, he said,

> Mrs. S is very ambitious & has too much say with the expedition for my liking ... In fact she may not do so but certainly she appears to influence her husband & to make this apparent is a crime.[24]

There is one particularly telling phrase in the letter: 'I don't like to see women out of their provinces.' Birdie asks his mother not to mention this to his sister May, who obviously wouldn't agree with his commitment to the idea of separate spheres for men and women. It's an indication that the real problem was that Kathleen was interfering in what most regarded as a totally male domain; it was her determination to be involved and to be alongside Con in all his planning that really made her unpopular, as Birdie wrote to May:

> I don't know who to blame but somehow don't like Mrs Scott. I don't trust her – though I have always been prepared to give her her due. Nobody likes her on the expedition & the painful silence when she arrives is the only jarring note of the whole thing. There is no secret that she runs us all just now & what she says is done – through the owner. Now nobody likes a schemer & yet she is one undoubtedly ... We all feel that the sooner we are away the better. She will go home to her small son & will so no more discord.[25]

But Birdie was conflicted in his feelings about Kathleen, as perhaps others were too. In the same letter he continues,

> I am sorry for her as she has tried hard to be one of us & always does anything she can for any of us. She actually bought our initials & came down & sewed them on our winter clothes for us. Very nice of her, was it not – I wish I could like her but I am suspicious.

And then in later correspondence,

> ... I like Mrs Scott & admit her many excellent qualities – for myself I can honestly say she has been kindness always ... invited herself to tea with me over & over again ... For all this I feel she has done me proud...[26]

He seems happy to praise her when she's doing the traditional wifely things, such as tending to the crew and helping with their clothes and comforts, but is simply too uncomfortable with her influence. He is much more at ease with the womanly Hilda and with Ory, who was a huge support to Ted when he was preparing for the expedition and when they arrived in New Zealand. However, her focus was always on him and his needs. She did not assert herself publicly in the planning of the expedition nor lord it over the others as Kathleen was accused of doing. It seems likely from his comments that many of his colleagues agreed with

Birdie. Phrases like 'very ambitious' and 'too much say' were used against Kathleen, phrases used then as now against strong, independently minded women.

After the argument, the discord was not quite over. *Terra Nova* sailed from Lyttelton on 26 November, and two days later Kathleen and Con boarded the express train from Christchurch to Port Chalmers to meet up with it. They enjoyed some time together on a private carriage, but their peace was fractured on arrival. On the wharf were Teddy and Hilda Evans, both in what Kathleen described as a tearful condition. Clearly upset, the couple had been brooding on several issues and Teddy was on the point of leaving the expedition. Both Kathleen and Con felt that Hilda was behind it and couldn't really understand the grievances, as Kathleen wrote later: 'Apparently she had been working him up to insurrection, & a volley of childish complaints was let fly. Such as that Con had cut his wife's dance! & many others too puerile to recount.'[27] That night, at a dance thrown to celebrate their last evening in New Zealand, Scott and Teddy managed, with Ted Wilson's help, to smooth things over. Oriana was able to reassure some of the crew members that all was well, much to everyone's relief. Kathleen left the ball early, bored with it all, and was still annoyed with Teddy and his tantrums the next morning.[28] The upset of the night before spoiled some of the last hours that she would spend with Con.

On 29 November 1910, *Terra Nova* sailed from Port Chalmers and set out on its way to Antarctica. Kathleen, Ory and Hilda put their disagreements aside and stood on deck, watching the cheering crowds and the small boats that surrounded the ship. Then a tugboat – appropriately called *Plucky* – came alongside to take them back to shore.[29] It was required of them now as polar wives to be brave, to show unflinching courage as they were separated from the men they loved. Kathleen didn't say a public goodbye to Con because she didn't want anyone to see him sad, and Oriana succeeded in sending Ted away happy as she waved cheerily until *Terra Nova* disappeared from view. This earned her Kathleen's respect and the only positive comment that she ever made about her: 'Mrs Wilson was plucky and good.' But afterwards, as the women drank tea on the tugboat as it sailed towards the shore, Oriana sat in silence, staring sphinx-like at the horizon.[30] Neither Kathleen nor Ory would ever see their husband again.

PART 2

Waiting

I am always thinking of you here on this great ice platform ten thousand feet above sea level.

Edgar to Lois

1910: The Penelopes

When they waved goodbye, Kathleen, Oriana and Lois knew that it might be months before they heard from their husbands and years before they saw them again – if they returned at all. The wives of polar explorers have often been likened to Penelope, the wife of Odysseus who, according to Homer, waited faithfully and with great patience for many years until her husband returned from the Trojan Wars. Enduring years of loneliness and separation was the norm for a polar wife. Jo Peary, interviewed by the *New York Herald* after her husband Robert reached the North Pole, described what this waiting was like:

> Twenty-three years he has been working for this, and during all this time I have just existed, that's all. Hardly a year of real happiness during all that time have I had because of the worry and anxiety and fear. But it is all over now.[1]

However, while it is true that patience and resilience were crucial qualities for a polar wife, these women were rarely waiting passively. Kari Herbert, whose father was a polar explorer, has written from her own family experience that an explorer's wife must match him in spirit if their relationship is to survive; she must be understanding, adaptable, intelligent and confident.[2] Consequently, polar wives were not, on the whole, typical of women of their time. They were called on at different times to support the expedition, defend its aims and outcomes, help to publicise it and sometimes to finance it. Jo Peary, despite her assertion that she 'just existed', was extremely active in support of her husband. She gave lectures to raise funds, liaised with publishers, encouraged newspapers to write positive stories, secured storage for expedition artefacts, and, in perhaps the ultimate rejection of the passive Penelope, sailed out to the Arctic to bring him back.[3] All this while running a home and raising her two children.

It was Jane, the second wife of Captain John Franklin, however, who set the gold standard of loyalty and activism on behalf of her husband. He had set out to find the North West Passage, a sea link between the Pacific and Atlantic oceans, and in 1845 he and his entire crew of 129 men, together with his ships *Terror* and *Erebus*, disappeared. Jane Franklin made sure that the search for him became a national issue. She used the press to whip up public support and she became so well known that Staffordshire potteries made figurines of the Franklins. 'Lady Franklin's Lament' became a popular ballad and is almost certainly the origin for the idea of polar wives waiting patiently like Penelope. But Jane was much more active than that.[4]

After several rescue missions failed to find any trace of her husband and his men, Jane paid for her own, making her the only nineteenth-century woman to raise the money to fund three polar expeditions.[5] She spent the rest of her life and her fortune as well as much of her stepdaughter's inheritance funding the search for him. Some forty expeditions were sent out after Franklin and his men, and at one point fifteen were occupied with the task simultaneously.[6] Jane's decade of searches cost her the equivalent of £41 million in today's money, and although her husband was never found, during the search for him more than 40,000 square miles of new territory was covered, and 8,000 miles of coastline mapped. In 1860, fifteen years after her husband disappeared, Jane Franklin was awarded the Founder's Gold Medal by the Royal Geographical Society for her noble and self-sacrificing endurance.[7]

Emily Shackleton has often been portrayed as the personification of the passive polar wife: unselfish, long-suffering, loyal, willing to endure publicity and surrender her life to her husband's ambitions while raising their children alone. However, this does not do her justice. Intelligent, well educated and well connected, Emily was good at being self-sufficient. She played golf well, she raised her children, and she became actively involved in the Girl Guide movement, becoming Eastbourne divisional commissioner after the family moved there. When required, she went on tour with her husband, attended talks and helped to raise money. It was a struggle at times, however, being an intelligent woman whose class meant that she could not pursue a career of her own. She gave an unusually frank interview in the United States when Ernest was on lecture tour there in which she admitted that she never read her children stories that ended 'And they got married and lived happily ever after' because that would encourage girls to think that was their only option, which she felt was wrong.[8]

Just as the men they married were complex, so were these women. They accepted their role as Penelopes for their own reasons but didn't always find it easy. There were times when it was hard to be alone, and many times when they doubted that their husbands loved them. During these dark periods, it was difficult not to conclude that a man who chose to be away for years at a time could not be a man in love. Jo Peary's letters to her husband reveal occasions when she felt that there was no point continuing their marriage, and Eva Nansen felt such despair that she contemplated suicide.[9] Sometimes, when the explorers did come home, they could not settle, and the lives of their wives and their children were thrown into periods of disruption and unhappiness. This private turmoil was hidden by an outward façade.

Polar wives had to accept that their husbands belonged to the public and were conscious of their own appearance and comments, sharing the homecomings and unable to speak freely, particularly if there was a press exclusive. In this regard they were like the American women who chose to marry pilots but found themselves becoming the wives of the first astronauts. The space missions attracted huge media interest, and while the men were in space the press descended on their wives. They were young and unprepared for the attention, but they learned to smile and keep their emotions concealed, giving the NASA mantra in response to questions: they were 'proud, thrilled, happy'. But what else could they say? I'm terrified, exhausted, and screaming into my pillow? It was a life of fear but also of enormous perks. Astronauts and their wives were glamorous and exciting, and everyone wanted one at their party.[10] The *Terra Nova* wives hadn't all chosen to marry explorers, and now, in their thirties, they found themselves having to adapt unexpectedly to a life of risk and sacrifice that was at times lived very much in the public eye.

Unbeknown to Lois, the risk that she had accepted for her family nearly brought financial disaster very early on in the expedition. On 26 November 1910, *Terra Nova* was due to depart from Lyttelton but a drunken Edgar had fallen into the water as he tried to board. Many of the crew had enjoyed the entertainment in Christchurch, and a celebration prior to departure was a lapse that could surely be forgiven, but this was a very public lapse. The Bishop of Christchurch had just blessed the ship in front of cheering crowds when Edgar fell drunk into the water. He'd embarrassed the expedition and was sacked on the spot. The ship had sailed without him to Port Chalmers. Scott had stayed behind but would travel by train in a couple of days to join the ship there and would leave for the Antarctic on the 29th.

Left behind in Lyttelton, Edgar must have soon realised that he was in a desperate position. His family's sole income was his expedition pay, which he had now lost. He was 11,000 miles from home and would have to find the money to return to Lois and his children. In Portsmouth he might well face naval disciplinary action and a possible demotion. His actions would reduce the income of his family and bring public shame to them in Portsmouth.[11] Edgar would also lose his chance to reach the South Pole and would have let down his leader. Fortunately, he had two days before Scott left for Port Chalmers and one more after that before he was permanently left behind. Edgar asked Scott to give him another chance, and he was eventually reinstated. The two men had history, of course. Scott knew how useful Edgar was on the ice, and he was popular and unquestionably loyal. Teddy Evans thought letting him back on was a mistake and undermined discipline, but Scott did not want to lose a tried and trusted Antarctic veteran and a man he liked very much. Had Scott not been persuaded, Edgar would have lived to see his family again. As it was, their financial crisis was not to be avoided.

After Edgar left, Lois returned briefly to Gower where, on 28 August, her youngest child, Ralph, was finally baptised in St Mary's Church in Rhossili, the place where she had married her Antarctic hero. It's likely that it was a trip home that had been planned before the invitation came from Scott to join him. After that Edgar must just have been too busy or unable to get time off for a trip to Wales and so Lois went alone after he'd gone. Without him there this happy family event was tinged with some sadness, but there was much excitement too as Lois could tell of his departure on *Terra Nova* and his hopes for the expedition's success. Ralph was baptised in the same stone font as Edgar, reinforcing the family's strong connections with Gower, the place where they met and married, and where both their sons had now been baptised.

Leaving her family and friends must have been a wrench for Lois, and returning to their home in Portsmouth alone must have made her feel Edgar's absence even more keenly. During their married life he had only been at sea for a few weeks, and now for the first time she had to manage alone. Life in Portsmouth soon became very difficult. Lois faced the normal everyday struggles of a mother with young children. They had to be supported at school and shoes, clothes and food had to be funded. Norman had very poor sight in his left eye and Edgar had realised that this would mean that he couldn't join the Navy and serve king and country as he would have wished. As a result, it was vital to open up avenues to him through education.[12] Lois also had to find money to pay their rent at Chapel Street.[13]

With Edgar away for years, Lois had to deal with all these challenges alone. Their family, nearly two hundred miles away in Wales, could do little to help and in fact were something of a responsibility. Her parents relied on the financial help of their children, and so did Edgar's mother. Lois sent money regularly, and so did her siblings Beatrice and Stanley.

This group of elderly relatives was part of the first generation to benefit from the state pension in Britain, which had been introduced only four years before. It was a real boon to the poor as no contribution had to be made, but it wasn't an automatic right. An application had to be made and considered and a pension was only granted if the recipient had been resident for twenty years and had means not exceeding thirty-one pounds and ten shillings. A deliberately low weekly payment of five shillings a week (approximately £30 in today's terms) was set so that people would continue to make their own provision for retirement and not just rely on the state. Those who had been convicted for drunkenness, avoided work without justification or made themselves poor to qualify would be banned.[14] But a recipient also had to be seventy years old, and whereas Edgar's mother Sarah was seventy-three, Lois's parents Jane and William were only sixty-five.[15] With no money coming from the state to support them in their old age, William was working as a gardener, and they were relying on the support of Lois and her siblings.[16]

Daily subsistence and family commitments became a more and more difficult juggle for Lois the longer Edgar was away. Following Scott once more to the ends of the Earth was dangerous for him but the risks extended to Lois too. She had known when he signed up that to join the *Terra Nova* expedition Edgar had to be taken off the Navy payroll and that without an income from the Navy she would have to make ends meet on the expedition salary. However, funds became seriously depleted, and after a year volunteers in the crew were asked to follow Scott's example and give up their pay. When she read Con's letter on the subject, Kathleen proudly wrote to his mother Hannah, 'He is to cease to have an Antarctic Salary – This I think is splendid, he once said he believed one did one's best work when there was no question of financial gain, I believe he was right, and it gives me great pleasure to think he won't make anything at all out of it.'[17]

Edgar was one of the volunteers, and his decision was to have very serious consequences for his wife and children. Lois couldn't take pride in the gesture as Kathleen had; she simply didn't have the resources. Things became so bad that she was reduced to selling her husband's precious Polar Medal from the *Discovery* expedition.[18] Her concerns for the future must have escalated when she received a letter from Scott, written in October 1911. While she would have been relieved to know that Edgar was strong and in very good health, she must have grown distressed when she read on. Scott wrote that they might have to stay for another season to finish their work but that if so she must not worry: ' ... you must try and remember that he is certain to be in the best of health and that it will be all the better when he does come home. When that time comes, I hope he will get some good billet and not have to leave you again.'[19]

The promise of financial security for her family and a comfortable retirement was one of the reasons that Lois had agreed to this time apart. If this one last trip would bring them closer to their dream of a comfortable retirement, almost certainly back in Wales, then she could have girded herself for another year without her husband for such a great reward; but it would take more than her determination to see out his prolonged absence. In the short term, Lois and her children needed money.

Although he didn't really like to write letters, Edgar did try to keep in touch with friends and family.[20] When it came to his wife and mother, he was a dutiful correspondent, writing regularly and at least once a week to Lois.[21] He was very aware of the difficulties that she was facing in his absence. This was the lot of the Navy wife, and Edgar had experienced it first hand as his own mother raised him and his siblings largely alone. He reflected in one letter to his mother that Lois must have had quite a job getting the children to school, so he evidently thought about the family life that his wife was maintaining by herself.[22] However, none of the letters that he wrote to Lois and none of those that she wrote back survive, and so it's impossible to know how much of her financial difficulties she shared with him. In the end it does not matter, because Lois did not have a real correspondence with her husband. She could not ask his advice or seek comfort from him, for although they wrote often, hardly any of their letters reached each other. Approximately a year after he left Cardiff, Edgar's letters stopped arriving. Lois would hear nothing from him for a year.

1911: The First Year Apart

Kathleen described her parting from her husband and the period that followed as 'the long, enforced separation from Con. I did not mind; my worship continued unabated. Christians do not see their God, but they worship and love Him with unabated ardour.'[1] This was written years later in her autobiography, but the rawness of her feelings is much more apparent in a letter that she wrote at the time to Hannah Scott: 'I haven't begun to realise that he's really gone yet and I don't want to.' Although she had taken photos of her 'adorable man and his ship', she wrote, 'I don't allow myself any photographs of him yet, just surround myself with the Boodles who must be my only love for a while.'[2] She stayed at Admiralty House in Sydney until her ship arrived on 17 December to take her home to Peter. Each night she wrapped herself in a blanket and slept out on her bedroom's balcony, overlooking Sydney Harbour. Trying to be the nice and dutiful wife of a naval officer and leader of a high-profile expedition didn't suit Kathleen, who longed to break away. Con didn't mind what she did as long as she didn't get talked about, so while she waited she slipped away to trek through the Blue Mountains with a discreet South African she'd met on the ship on the way out.

On the voyage home, they docked in Port Said, and Kathleen, who had always longed to see the treasures of Ancient Egypt, asked herself, 'Pyramids or Peter?'[3] She made a quick dash to Cairo, Luxor and Karnak, and an archaeologist took her down into a newly found tomb where they opened an intact sarcophagus to reveal three mummies inside. One further stop on the way home allowed her to disembark at Marseilles and travel to Paris to see Isadora Duncan, who, disappointingly, was away in New York. Her children were there, however, including Deirdre, whom Kathleen had helped to deliver. Edward Steichen, the American whom Kathleen might so easily have fallen for, visited the apartment. Finding herself again with her artistic and exciting Parisian friends after so many years must have felt odd to Kathleen. Her life had changed so much; she was a wife and a mother, and she loved Con and Peter. She wrote in her diary of Edward, 'It was interesting to see him again but no more.'[4]

On 7 February she arrived home and rushed to Henley to retrieve her son from Con's mother and sisters. She had been worried that he would be shy of her after her absence, but she needn't have been.[5] They settled down in Buckingham Palace Road and into a happy routine which was heavily influenced by Kathleen's more unorthodox traits. She believed in fresh air and fruit, and deplored medicine and children being trussed up in suits and bonnets. Peter ran freely about, often in the scantiest of clothing and sometimes naked, and despite having servants his mother put him to bed herself, all of which was unusual for a respectable family of the time.[6] Spending time with the son she adored helped Kathleen to fill the void left by Con, but it wasn't enough, and she threw herself into a frantic round of activity. She played golf, went vagabonding in Kent, and visited Isadora in Paris. She went dancing, attended the theatre, dined out, partied, and flew.

The latter was a new, exciting but dangerous pastime and Kathleen found it exhilarating. It appealed to her sense of adventure and her love of freedom. That August, forty-seven-year-old Hilda B. Hewlett had become the first British woman to pass her flying test; she received the 122nd pilot's certificate issued by the Royal Aero Club.[7] Kathleen flew as a passenger and longed to get her pilot's licence but her family weren't so enthusiastic: 'Everybody is shocked at my flying even as a passenger.' They felt that she had a duty to her husband and her child not to take risks, and so Con's family sent an envoy, her brother-in-law William Ellison-Macartney, to ask her to stop.[8] Kathleen knew that, unbeknown to his wife Ettie, William was a flyer too and so found the situation ridiculous. Nonetheless, she saw their point. She didn't take flying lessons but wrote to Con in her diary, 'Worse – I believe you'd like it if I did fly. Damn!'[9] Her first commission for a public statue was a reminder of the hazardous nature of early flying. Charles Rolls, the founder of Rolls-Royce, had been killed in an aeroplane accident the summer before and his mother and father wanted a memorial. It was a challenge with no live sitter for a model, but nonetheless his parents were moved and delighted by her preparatory statuette.

When this round of activity took Kathleen away from her son, she missed him and felt guilty. She wrote in her diary, 'The angel boy was so pleased to see me and called me so often and made me fetch your photo, saying, "Dada too!" and then he kissed us both in turns and made me too.'[10]

When it was all too much, Kathleen took Peter down to a rented cottage in Sandwich, Kent, called Shingle End, which was set among the dunes and unreachable by road. Here she installed a hammock on the beach and swam in the sea by moonlight, giving her full attention to her son and enjoying the solitude. Despite trying to stay positive, she was at times lonely and sad. She worried about Con in private and in September wrote in her diary that she'd woken from a terrible dream about him, 'and then Peter came very close to me and said emphatically, "Daddy won't come back" as though in answer to my silly thoughts.'[11] Desperate to share the sunsets and swims with someone but knowing that the only person she really wanted to share it all with was Con, Kathleen was experiencing for the first time the bittersweet nature of being in love. She adored Peter and she adored Con, but missing them both so much meant that her intangible ties to them were curbing her independence:

> It's curious to me to think how unwittingly in a way I've got my heart's desire, at least what I used to think my heart's desire. I used to say I wanted a baby but not a husband, and I've got it, but with a difference, one hasn't got one's husband in the body, but one has got him so very firm in the spirit that it spoils everything!![12]

Men continued to be attracted to Kathleen, as they had always been, but she only made an exception for Fridtjof Nansen. She had met him with Con in Norway and so went to the lecture that he gave in London on 6 November, and afterwards they lunched together and became great friends. Her letters to him don't survive but it is clear from his that he fell head over heels in love, writing of Kathleen, 'It is nice to know there is a woman so like what one has dreamt of but never met.' He felt that they could be soulmates, that he had met his equal, and he wished they had met earlier. His letters to her were so romantic and had such a frisson of sexual chemistry that it was speculated years later that they had had an affair, but this was not the case. When he wrote of her lips it was to say that he had not kissed them, and he knew that her great love for her husband and baby meant that his feelings could only ever be a romantic dream.[13] Kathleen's relationship with Nansen was in the pattern of her lifelong relationships with men; they fell under her spell, and she was drawn to the heroic and the romantic.

Nansen was intelligent and knowledgeable and one of the world's great explorers; more importantly to Kathleen, he admired Scott. He told her that he would not have lent his ship to Amundsen if he'd known that he planned to take it south. His hope was that the two expeditions would meet and go on together or that Amundsen would let Scott get there first, but Kathleen thought that was a ridiculous idea.[14] At a time when she was missing Con, Nansen appeared in her life, a man who supported her husband and knew at first hand what he was experiencing, and he was a magnificent man who admired her as much as she admired him. She wrote for Con, 'He really is an adorable person, and I will tell you all the lovely times we had together when you get back. He thinks you are marvellous, and me still more!'[15] Kathleen and Con shared a marriage where each could be independent while loving and being completely loyal to the other. She explained what this meant in terms of Nansen many years later: 'I was going to remain a completely faithful wife, only I was not going readily to throw aside such a divine friendship.'[16]

While Con was away, Kathleen had obligations as wife of the expedition leader and as the most senior *Terra Nova* wife. She tried to keep a polite distance from polar politics, but her status meant that she could not keep as much distance as she might like. Money was an immediate issue. In September she received a distressing letter from Sir Lewis Beaumont telling her that there was only enough money to cover the expedition's expenses until October. The extra year in the Antarctic and the need to repair the ship in New Zealand had cut a great hole in the finances. She suggested asking the Royal Geographical Society and said she would look for funds elsewhere too.

Kathleen's personal position wasn't much better. In the summer her bank account had become overdrawn for the first time in her life, and when the new king, George V, was crowned, Kathleen took advantage of the clamour for accommodation by very reluctantly taking in a paying guest.[17] These financial worries were constantly present, and so to help raise much-needed funds for the expedition Kathleen had to grit her teeth and overcome her fear of public speaking in order to give a fundraising talk. She wrote letters to potential donors, including the Chancellor of the Exchequer and the Treasury.

Despite her own financial position, Kathleen was happy to support Con when he wrote to say that he'd decided not only to forego his salary but also to put 'all moneys from whatever source (book, cinematograph, articles, photographs, lectures, stamps newspaper news etc) all with no qualification into the Antarctic fund'. Shackleton had made a similar gesture when he had returned from his *Nimrod* expedition in 1909 and donated his appearance fees to charity. Emily was lucky enough to have a small allowance of her own from her father, but her husband's actions meant that he did nothing to pay off his debts or provide for his family. Kathleen might have felt resentful when Con gave away his income, but this was just the sort of heroism that had drawn her to him, and she was bursting with pride when she wrote to Hannah:

> ... you must be very proud and happy to possess him, and all I pray is that I make Peter into as fine a fellow as you have made Con – I can't desire more. His letter to me is the most amazing document of sacrifice and unpretentiousness I ever read, and makes one feel more and more (if that be possible) our extraordinary good fortune in being associated with a man of such calibre ... I have as you know known many men of many nations, but I think I have never met a man one can so wholly admire as your son; he astounds me.[18]

As Kathleen's granddaughter later pointed out, her enthusiasm outweighed her tact in this instance. With her worries about money, Hannah surely would not be impressed by her son giving it up; moreover, the reminder that her daughter-in-law had 'known many men of many nations' wouldn't have been a welcome one.[19]

Kathleen's ability to smooth ruffled feathers within the polar establishment became invaluable as tensions over money and competing expeditions came to a head. Shackleton was still persona non grata with many, and there were sensitivities to navigate. Kathleen had been asked at an event if she minded meeting him, but she didn't. Her attitude was to shake his hand, be courteous and change the subject if necessary.[20] Then, when the news came that Amundsen had been spotted in Antarctica, the press descended on Kathleen's doorstep.

Amundsen had taken the daring step of making camp directly on the Great Ice Barrier, and consequently was 60 miles closer to the South Pole than Scott. She had heard the news the day before, on 27 March, her thirty-third birthday, when she had packed fifty-two guests into her daffodil-bedecked studio for a party. A telephone message from a news agency had interrupted the festivities and then further messages the next day came from New Zealand to clarify the situation. Eventually, when it was understood that a race to the Pole was really on, Kathleen told the reporters, yes, but our expedition still needs money![21]

On 8 May, the *Daily Mail* printed a long appeal from Shackleton on behalf of an Australasian Antarctic Expedition to be led by his former colleague Douglas Mawson. It had important scientific aims, and according to Shackleton should be supported, but it also had a sentimental side as 'we are as anxious to-day as we have ever been that Britons shall keep their place in the vanguard of Polar exploration'. Shackleton appealed to the public to send donations in to help raise the £12,000 needed if Mawson was to set sail in June.[22] Mawson had written a very nice letter to Kathleen before he arrived in London and she was very friendly towards him.[23] She had offered him a place to stay in her home if it would help at all, and so in return he had given her a month's grace so that she could appeal through the press for funds before he did.[24]

Sir Clements Markham was incandescent with rage. Scott was desperate for funds and now had to compete with a rival expedition. He wrote a letter to the paper, co-signed by Sir Edgar Speyer, *Terra Nova*'s treasurer, saying that Scott was actually in the field and surely should be supported before any other expedition as he still needed between £8,000 and £10,000. This counter-appeal fell on deaf ears; within three days, £12,000 in donations had been sent in to the *Daily Mail* in response to Shackleton's plea.[25] Sir Clements had written a further letter to send to the paper, but he asked Kathleen to look at it first and she managed to persuade him against it. He loathed Shackleton, believing that he'd only been accepted on the *Discovery* expedition out of kindness and because he was short of money and then had broken down on the Southern Journey and endangered the lives of others. He was, in Sir Clements' view, a cad, a self-promoter and a 'contemptible self-seeker'.[26] These strong views were clearly expressed in his draft letter, as Kathleen wrote in her diary, 'Such a letter! With all the tact I could muster I wrote back and prevented him publishing it. It was an attack on Shackleton and an eulogy of you which, though I could gloat over it in private, would not have helped us, I fear.'[27]

At the Royal Geographical Society in June, Shackleton sat with Kathleen and said, 'You know, I know your husband very well, perhaps better than any man. I have never seen him hesitate; he is the most daring man I ever met, extraordinarily brave.' She replied, perhaps rather pointedly, 'Yes he is brave morally as well as physically.'[28]

While Kathleen was happy for the press to help raise money for Con's expedition, she did not enjoy the fact that she had become a celebrity. She did not want press attention and she certainly didn't want it for Peter. The *Daily Mirror* offered her £4,000 at a time when the expedition was desperate for money, but she turned it down. They had wanted to photograph Peter writing a begging letter for his father. Worse yet, a cinematographer who was making a private film of Peter for Con took photos of him without permission and used them in newspaper adverts to publicise the project. Kathleen hated her child being used in this way and was bitterly upset.

Ory had arrived home in February too, and had been staying at Westal with her parents-in-law. Ted had urged her to visit the other women left behind by the expedition, and so over the course of the next few months, amid the hottest summer on record, Ory visited Caroline Oates, Emily Bowers and Evelyn Edith Cherry-Garrard.[29] She met Kathleen as well, although she wasn't invited to her birthday party in March. This group of wives and mothers sent copies of the letters they received from their sons and husbands to each other, knowing how important it was to share any information or news when contact with their loved ones was so limited. As the only one of the women who had lived through the experience before, Ory was able to give advice and offer support. Ted had written of her just after he left how much better prepared for the trial she was this time than nine years ago.[30] Nonetheless, by the end of 1911 she was missing Ted so much that she decided that she would go to New Zealand in the new year. She would visit friends and be there in case Ted came back after the second year of the expedition. Kathleen, who was distracting herself with plenty of activity, thought that waiting around in New Zealand sounded dreadful.

In November 1911, cinemas around the country showcased the first of Herbert Ponting's films of the expedition. As the expedition's official photographer and cinematographer, he recorded approximately 25,000 feet of film during his two-year stay in Antarctica. Gaumont, the first and oldest film company in the world, held the exclusive cinematograph rights for the expedition and the profits were to be shared between the company, the expedition and Ponting. The film, *With Captain Scott, RN, to the South Pole*, played in more than eighty towns and cities and was a huge success, bringing in much-needed money for the expedition.[31] Kathleen, Ernest Shackleton and her great friends George Bernard Shaw and J. M. Barrie were among a crowd of 1,500 people who went to a midday screening at the London Coliseum.[32] Peter went too, and when Scott appeared on the screen he shouted out, 'That's my Daddy!'[33] Ory travelled to London from Cheltenham with Ted's mother and father to see it, and with the film on such a wide release Lois must surely have watched it too.

As the film burst into life on the big screen, showing twenty scenes of *Terra Nova* sailing away from New Zealand, its voyage to Antarctica and the crew setting up base camp, the wives must have watched intently, trying to catch a glimpse of their husbands for the first time in a year. For Lois it had been even longer. These flickering, silent images were a confirmation that their men had arrived safely and had begun their work. Kathleen watched with pride as her husband's expedition arrived in the land that she hoped would bring him such glory. She had already seen the film on 19 October at a private viewing for some of the key people involved in the expedition, but seeing it again cheered her up after a gloomy period of missing Con.[34] Lois could reassure herself that her husband's final expedition, the one that would bring their family financial security, had completed its first stage. Ory knew that the real scientific work could begin now. This scientific exploration was Ted's mission and his whole purpose for going away. It was only the importance of this work that made her separation from him bearable.

Just four months after the wives watched this film, which was so full of hope and excitement, the news came that the Pole had been reached.

1912: Losing the Pole

On 7 March 1912, *Fram* sailed into Hobart, Tasmania. On board was Roald Amundsen. His Norwegian expedition had been a model of planning and efficiency, resulting in a journey from his base camp to the Pole and back in just ninety-nine days. Scott had taken sixty-five men on *Terra Nova*, landing thirty-one – a group which included officers, naval seamen, scientists and two Russian animal handlers – to help him achieve his joint objectives of scientific discovery and exploration. In addition, there were seventeen ponies, thirty dogs and two tracked motor sledges (the third had fallen through the ice and sunk). It was a tremendous logistical challenge. Amundsen, however, focused only on the Pole. *Fram* carried nineteen men and only nine of them made up the landing party. He set out with five men, four sledges and fifty-two dogs, travelling a route with pre-prepared depots and using dogs as a source of fresh food as they went. Seventeen dogs made it to the Pole and twelve all the way back to base camp. Amundsen's Polar Party was hand-picked for their experience and professionalism and the four men, who were hardened ice travellers, included two expert dog drivers, a whaler in Icelandic waters and a Nordic ski champion.[1] On 15 December 1911, Roald Amundsen, Olav Bjaaland, Helmer Hanssen, Sverre Hassel and Oscar Wisting became the first men to reach the South Pole.

At first, there was confusion in Britain about what had actually happened. *Fram* had arrived back earlier than expected and Amundsen made no public statement. He did not contact the King of Norway saying that he had reached the Pole, nor did he inform the Royal Geographical Society about the outcome of the expedition which it had part funded. The press, with its interest in whipping up an exciting race for the Pole, quickly filled this void of information with their own interpretation of events. If Amundsen had not immediately claimed the Pole, then

'This much seems clear – The plucky Norwegian has not succeeded in his quest'.[2] English papers reported *Fram*'s return in their editions on 7 March under headings such as 'Captain Scott's triumph for Britain' and 'Scott reaches the Pole: triumph for the English expedition'. Their confidence in the story was bolstered by news that the *Daily Express* in London had received a telegram from Wellington, New Zealand, which read, 'Amundsen states Scott has reached the Pole.' Newspaper columns fully expected *Terra Nova* to arrive very swiftly on Amundsen's heels to announce Scott's victory.[3] Any excitement that Kathleen, Ory and Lois may have felt at this news, however, was quickly dashed.

The exclusive rights to Amundsen's messages had been obtained by the *Daily Chronicle* and they announced the next day that a cablegram had been received from Amundsen saying that the Pole had been 'attained'. Reuters issued a telegram from Christiania (now Oslo) which backed up this report. It stated that a message had been sent to two Norwegian newspapers on 7 March from Hobart saying, 'Amundsen reached South Pole 14-17 December 1911. All well.' The British press reported that there was now a great mystery surrounding the attainment of the Pole. Amundsen had reached it and his telegram of the previous day said that Scott had too, but who had got there first?

With no news from Scott, the papers speculated that he may have accelerated his expedition plan once he knew of Amundsen's. Before he left, Scott had stated that 22 December 1911 would be his ideal date for reaching the Pole and so it was quite possible that if he had started out earlier than planned he could easily have beaten Amundsen. Scott's expedition was more heavily manned and more heavily equipped and would take longer to return even if he had reached the pole first. Media excitement about what it saw as a race to the Pole was palpable in the newspaper coverage. The *Pall Mall Gazette* even speculated that Scott and Amundsen might have met at the foot of the Beardmore Glacier, giving their contest an even more visceral quality as they raced in plain sight: 'Nothing more exciting can well be imagined than such a meeting and its inevitable results.'[4]

Kathleen was sceptical. 7 March was an awful day for her as she was besieged by telephone calls, telegrams and reporters. When representatives of newspapers showed her the cables they'd received, she was wary: 'I told them at once and with all the insistence I could that those cables were worthless and unsigned, and that they would only make themselves and everybody else ridiculous by publishing them.'[5] The press ran with the story and the next day Kathleen put a notice in *The Times* saying that there was no news from Captain Scott nor any reliable information from Amundsen. She would not be meeting any reporters or giving any interviews.[6] She was proved right. When Reuters telegraphed from Hobart that Amundsen denied sending the telegram about Scott reaching the Pole, it started to seem more certain that the Norwegians had got there first. The *Daily Chronicle* began publishing Amundsen's account on 9 March, publicising itself in advance as 'the first newspaper in the world to announce the discovery of the South Pole'.[7]

Kathleen was worried about Con and how disappointed he might be when he heard. She also worried about him being out so late in the Antarctic season, but she trusted that he knew his job and wouldn't take too great a risk. She tried to keep herself busy and not dwell on it. Certainly, she harboured Amundsen no ill will. Nansen had sent her a cable to say he was thinking of her, to which she replied, 'Hurrah for Norway in spite of all.' When the Royal Geographical Society told her, rather nervously, that they had cabled Amundsen to congratulate him, she wrote back, 'But of course, Let us at any rate if we don't win be good losers.' She knew that Con would do the same. When Peter asked her, 'Is Amundsen a good man?' she told him, 'Yes, I think he is.' Then he said, 'Amundsen and Daddy both got to the Pole, Daddy has stopped working now.'[8]

Such good will wasn't universal, however. Fiercely loyal to Scott, Sir Clements Markham was still smarting at what he saw as Amundsen's dirty trick in starting a race to the Pole without warning Scott. Kathleen worked hard to restrain his criticisms of Amundsen and used all her power to stop him publishing awful things about him. Lord Curzon, the former Viceroy of India, who had become president of the Royal Geographical Society in 1911, praised Amundsen's achievement at the annual meeting in May 1912 but was critical of his failure to notify Scott.[9] When Nansen wrote to Kathleen in June offering to write to *The Times* to defend Amundsen against Curzon, Kathleen asked him not to: 'It would only be the signal for the overflowing of pent-up feelings.'[10]

Resentment about his behaviour was still simmering among some at the Royal Geographical Society when Amundsen arrived in London during the winter as part of his lecture tour. After speaking with him, its secretary, Dr John Scott Keltie, wrote to Kathleen saying that they had a very frank discussion and that Amundsen had admitted that he'd told only his brother of his plans because he knew that his funders would have stopped him if they knew he wanted to divert south. Amundsen said he'd really wanted to tell Scott but just couldn't for fear that the secret would leak out. In Keltie's view he had as a result done something 'which no Englishman with a spark of chivalry in him would have dreamt of doing – trying to get in front of a man who had practically devoted 12 years of his life to the attainment of his object'.[11] After reflection, he crossed this out and replaced it in another version with '... doing a thing which to say the least shows a lack of chivalrous feeling'. Curzon clearly felt the same, and when invited to dine with Amundsen at the Norwegian Embassy he sought Kathleen's opinion about whether he should go. Her view was that he should of course be civil, but Clements Markham was upset at the thought that those who had shaken Amundsen's hand should have the impertinence to speak to Scott when he returned home. He was even angrier when Kathleen told him she was going to hear Amundsen speak, but she wanted to hear what he had to say.

Not wanting to be drawn into any press speculation, Kathleen crept quietly into the lecture that Amundsen had been invited to give for the Royal Geographical Society at the Queen's Hall on 15 November.[12] She thought his talk was modest but dull, and, as Keltie forewarned her, contained 'very little, as you will see, of any scientific value'.[13] He only mentioned Scott briefly but Lord Curzon, who was presiding, made a point of saying that he was sure they were all thinking of Scott who was still in the field and had no doubt reached the Pole only a few weeks after Amundsen. He was busy gathering scientific information which 'would be found to render his expedition the most notable of modern times'.[14] Afterwards at dinner Curzon upset Amundsen by calling for three cheers for the dogs.[15]

Ory had travelled out to meet Ted at the start of the year and was in New Zealand when *Fram* sailed in. Her friends there may have been wary of mentioning Amundsen to her, but they needn't have worried. Science and not the Pole had always been Ory and Ted's main concern, and much was still to be done even if he couldn't be among the first men to reach the Pole. Ted's work was exciting, and Ory defended the expedition and its objectives at every opportunity. She wrote later to Cherry's mother,

> ... I get tired of talking to people who know little or nothing about it and 'can't see the good' in going to the South Pole – I tell them they are being commercial – for they would see the good directly if they found a gold mine down there – but they don't see the use of scientific and geographical knowledge.[16]

It was nearly another month before *Terra Nova* finally returned to New Zealand.[17] Ory and Connie were staying at the Kinseys' summer house in Sumner when a phone call came from the Central News Agency's special correspondent to say that the ship had been spotted and all was well. A second call followed later in the morning, and because Mrs Kinsey couldn't hear the speaker very well she passed the phone to Ory. It was quite a shock. The voice on the other end told her that not all the members of the expedition had come back. Teddy Evans was aboard, but Ted was not. Was he dead? Had there been an accident? Gathering herself, Ory asked bravely for clarification and the voice on the other end of the telephone, realising what had been implied, reassured her that Ted was quite well but had remained in Antarctica. A relieved Ory raced down to Kinsey's office, where more information had arrived. She was told that Ted was safe but was staying on for another year.[18]

Scott had prearranged a message to be sent from New Zealand when *Terra Nova* docked, and on 1 April 1912 it had been transmitted to the world: 'I am remaining in the Antarctic for another winter in order to continue and complete my work.' Scott had written to Ory the previous October to tell her that he was staying south for another year and that he was keeping Ted with him, but she had already left England for New Zealand by the time it arrived, and she had missed it. All these months she had been anticipating a wonderful reunion like the one they'd shared after *Discovery*. If only Scott's letter had arrived earlier, then her hopes would not have been so dashed. But Ory had of course been in this position before. She'd had to wait another year for Ted in New Zealand nine years ago, and so she could do it again. It was a country she loved, and she had lots of friends; besides, she was thrilled for him. Although it meant a longer separation, his scientific work was going to continue.

On 3 April, when *Terra Nova* sailed into Lyttelton harbour, Ory, Connie and Hilda Evans were there to meet it. They had travelled down the night before and stayed in a hotel, setting their alarms for three o'clock in the morning. As they walked to the tugboat an hour later, they saw the ship sailing in, silhouetted against a gorgeous red sunrise. The hugely popular and capable Lieutenant Henry Pennell, navigator and acting captain, had brought the ship home because Teddy Evans, the most senior officer, had been too ill. He had not been selected by Scott to be part of the final Polar Party and on his way back to base camp had been so ill with scurvy that he'd only made it back through the efforts of his sledge mates Petty Officer Tom Crean and Leading Stoker William Lashly. Recovering now, he hobbled up to meet his wife, Kathleen and Ory as they came aboard, and the three women stood on the bridge as the ship slipped quietly into harbour with not a soul on the quay to witness their arrival.[19]

Safely home, the ship's crew learned for the first time that Amundsen had reached the Pole. They were in turn able to give the world some news about Scott and the Polar Party. Although Pennell and the crew had not been able to wait for them to return because the pressure of ice building up around *Terra Nova* had forced the ship to leave in early March, they were in good spirits when last seen. Oriana was told that Ted was one of the four men whom Scott had chosen to accompany him to the Pole.[20]

Teddy Evans had last seen her husband with the others on 4 January, just 148 miles from the Pole, and he was probably the fittest of the five-man Polar Party. The news that Ted was fit and well and would reach the Pole was enough to make Ory forget any disappointment that she may have felt at a longer separation. She sent an excited telegram to the family at Westal from Christchurch: 'Last news from South Pole/Plateau Ted absolutely fit exceedingly/happy Ory.'[21]

Pennell did not forget Lois, waiting for news at home. She had heard nothing from Edgar for nearly a year, but like everyone else in the world had heard that Amundsen had reached the South Pole. Edgar had longed to reach it first, for the glory of the achievement but also because it would bring the sort of fame and money that would secure a comfortable, financially independent future for his family.[22] Lois knew that the news would have been a bitter blow, but with no possible means of contacting her husband she couldn't tell him that his family cared only that he came home safely. It was a huge relief, then, when she received Pennell's letter written on board *Terra Nova* as it sailed into harbour in Lyttelton.

At long last, there was news of Edgar: he was safe and well. Best of all, Lois learned that Scott had chosen him to go to the Pole: 'I heartily congratulate you on his being in the Polar Party, for there can be little doubt that they will reach the pole, though of course the news cannot come through for a year.'[23] Pennell explained that the Polar Party had started out late and was therefore late returning to base camp, and because the season had ended earlier than expected the ship had been forced to leave. This explained why Edgar hadn't been in touch for so long. He and his comrades had left for the Pole before the mail ship arrived to bring his letters home. The news of their achievement would come through when *Terra Nova* went back to Antarctica in January to collect them. In the meantime, Lois could be happy that Edgar would finally get to the Pole. He wouldn't be the first, but he would get there.

1912: Messages from Antarctica

On board *Terra Nova* were letters for the wives, precious details and confirmations that their men were safe and well. Reading Ted's letters to her, Ory understood how agonised he had been by the decision to stay in Antarctica for another year. He had known that he could not get back to the ship in time to return to New Zealand even if she'd left him messages saying that she needed him. Ory was 'overjoyed to think that I sent him happy letters and a cable through Mr Kinsey at the last to say that all was well at home and that I was happy and quite prepared to wait another year for him either in N. Zealand or at home'. The messages from Ted included notes, neatly written in pencil, from the key points on the route to the Pole, two from the Great Ice Barrier and two from the Plateau and Beardmore Glacier.[1] She was very proud of them and the achievement that they represented.

The final letter, written in December 1911 at a point less than 300 miles from the Pole, was full of his excitement at the prospect that he would be picked for the final push: 'I am as fit and strong as a horse and have great hopes of being one of the final party ... Everyone on this journey is as fit as can be ... We are over the worst of it all now though, and we come home with light loads from depot to depot.'[2] Teddy Evans also handed Ory Ted's journal from a sledging trip that he had made the year before, and this is how she heard about what is now known as the Winter Journey.

The Winter Journey was organised by Ted to try to prove the link between dinosaurs and birds. It was a general scientific belief at the time that as an organism grew, it passed through each stage of its species' evolution. Emperor penguins, as flightless birds, were held to be a primitive form of bird and so Ted hoped to find in its early embryos vestiges of teeth and links between feathers and scales that would show that birds came from dinosaurs.[3] He had discovered the emperor penguin rookery at Cape Crozier during *Discovery* and had been determined to go back to collect eggs at a stage of incubation where there were early embryos. Because emperor penguins incubate their eggs on the sea ice in winter it meant a journey across the ice shelf in polar darkness, in the Antarctic winter. Nobody had done that before.

Ted chose Birdie Bowers and Apsley Cherry-Garrard to go with him. The latter, writing later about the expedition, described it as 'the Worst Journey in the World'. The three men survived for five weeks pulling heavy sledges in a darkness so total that they could only sense the presence of crevasses, and temperatures so cold that their breath froze immediately, coating their faces with ice. Even in these brutal conditions, Ted was thinking of Ory. In the entry written on their wedding anniversary, he recorded that they had built a rocky hut on a stony ridge near the rookery and that he had named them Oriana Hut and Oriana Ridge. On Ted's thirty-ninth birthday, 23 July, after a night where the snow had crept through every gap in the walls, the roof of the hut blew away. The three men lay huddled in their sleeping bags, exposed to savage winds. Bowers and Cherry had wanted to change the name after that, but as Ted wrote in a letter to Ory, 'I wont ever cancel the name, for I learned so much good there in a very short time, and therefore I love the place as I love you.'[4]

They returned with three intact penguin eggs, frostbite and scurvy. They were lucky to be alive.[5] Ponting, the expedition photographer who'd come back on *Terra Nova* too, told Ory how painful it had been to see the look on their faces when they returned, all three strained by lack of sleep and so much anxiety. Reassured that Ted was now fine, Ory felt incredible pride in his having been through something so awful and yet so wonderful. He had done something that nobody else had: survived an Antarctic winter.[6]

Ory could see from Ted's other letters how wonderful the time away had been for him and his health. He'd realised that he had been 'overdoing things badly, and I should have come a cropper but for this Expedition'.[7] He wrote of a fitter, less stressful future, of trips together to Japan and of exploring New Zealand. He painted a picture of a future that Ory could be excited about; a blissful reunion and then shared work. She would happily wait another year if such a wonderful future would be the reward. Writing to Isabel Smith and her husband Reginald just a few days later, Ory was bursting with pride. Able to write to her best friend in a way that she couldn't publicly, in her letter Ory offers an unrestrained expression of her admiration of Ted and brims with excitement. Her support of his decision to stay south is clear:

> I was quite annoyed with people who rang me up on the telephone to sympathise with me because Ted had not come back! – I asked them if they had read the paper – & they hadn't – so I told them that when they had done so they would see why I was glad he had stayed South that I was so very proud of his work and to think that he had been chosen to go on the final journey to the Pole and that no one else in the world had ever done such a winter journey as those three men did...[8]

Her pride in Ted's achievements were bolstered when she met Amundsen at a talk that he gave in Christchurch and they chatted afterwards at the Kinseys' home. She felt that no real scientific breakthroughs had come from his dash to the Pole, and certainly nothing to compare with Ted's work. She was reassured too by the great explorer's conviction that if Ted could survive the Winter Journey then he could probably survive anything.[9]

Ory decided to stay in New Zealand and wait for Ted. She couldn't really justify the cost of an additional voyage home and back when she knew so many people who would accommodate her. She received invitations to all parts of both islands, so many in fact that she really couldn't afford to honour them all.[10] Writing to Isabel, she reassured her friend that this time she understood much better how to keep herself well over the long winter when the wait would start to seem very long. She wouldn't exhaust herself with endless short trips and would try to stay in the country, which she so much preferred to the towns. There was needlework and singing practice to distract herself with too. She was certain she could be resilient, feeling as she did so certain that Ted was doing the right thing.

Staying on at first with the Kinseys in Christchurch meant that Ory was surrounded with Ted's *Terra Nova* colleagues who had come back with the ship and who were going to overwinter in New Zealand before returning to collect those who had remained in Antarctica. Pennell was a particular favourite, and Ory thought him the nicest man on the ship party: 'A delightful character and an extraordinarily hard worker, very clever and he is always saying kind things about people and finding excuses for them if he can't do anything else – it's so nice to have him in the house every evening. We play great games of cribbage!'[11]

The Kinseys had always opened their home to her but now, with a year-long wait ahead, they created a perfect base for Ory, a private place where she could sit out the days until Ted's return. *Terra Nova* had brought back one of the flat-packed meteorological huts purchased for the expedition, completely unused and still in its packaging. Kinsey bought it and had it transported by train and bullock wagon to his summer home in Sumner, where it was erected in the garden. It was tiny, only three metres by four, but the wooden tongue and groove walls and teak floor provided a cosy home for Oriana. The Kinseys added a fireplace to make sure. An external stairway by the door led to a rooftop observation platform, meant originally for meteorological observation but now used by Ory to watch birds and to gaze out across the sea.[12] While it was her home, and while Ory dreamed of Ted coming to live with her there before they sailed home, the hut became known as 'Uncle Bill's Cabin'.[13] Uncle Bill or just Bill was the name by which Ted was known affectionately by everybody on *Terra Nova*.

Kathleen had been very depressed and restless and had taken herself off to Paris to cheer herself up. When she returned, she at last received her letters from Con on 10 May. Summaries of his diaries were cabled home too, and when Kathleen read them two days later she recorded in her diary, 'The more one reads and weighs it, the more apparent the splendid achievements against awful odds appears, and the smaller the value of Amundsen's dash to beat you. I'm so glad, so very glad, you are staying another year. It would have been a thousand pities to return with such opportunities before you.'[14]

In May 1912, a bundle of letters was delivered to Lois in Portsmouth; there were at least fifty of them, representing a year's worth of correspondence from Edgar.[15] Teddy Evans had brought the precious bundle of letters that had missed the mail ship home on *Terra Nova*. Reading them now, Lois realised with great sadness that Edgar had not had a line from her since he left.[16] He had had no contact with home and the comfort that came from that in those long months at the bottom of the world. Boosting morale and sending love from the family was a key role of the polar wife, and through no fault of her own Lois had failed in this respect. Edgar was made of strong stuff, however. He had been in the Navy, away from his family since he was fifteen, and had thrived on *Discovery* without much contact with home. Scott described him as a man of Herculean strength, inexhaustible energy, a ready sense of humour and eager for the wildest risks. He could not imagine a man more suited by temperament or physical prowess to polar exploration.[17]

Edgar's letters show if anything that he was happy instead to chivvy his wife's spirits, saying how their time apart would quickly pass and he would soon be back with her and the children once again. His cheerful, picturesque letters were full of hope and bore her up.[18] The last letter in the bundle, written in December 1911 or possibly January 1912, reassured Lois that she was in his thoughts: 'I am always thinking of you here on this great ice platform ten thousand feet above sea level.'[19] It was written in pencil from a position about 150 miles from the Pole, and said that all of them were well and that they had every chance of reaching the Pole. For Lois, there was nothing to do but wait another year.

Ory and Ted's engagement photograph, 19 October 1899. (© Cheltenham Borough Council and The Cheltenham Trust)

Ory and Ted on their wedding day. His sister Polly is on the left and her sister Connie is on the right. (© Cheltenham Borough Council and The Cheltenham Trust)

A picnic at Cortachy, Scotland, 1907. Left to right – Reginald Smith, Isabel Smith, Ory and Robert Falcon Scott. (© Cheltenham Borough Council and The Cheltenham Trust)

Lois with her children Norman, Muriel and Ralph. (John Evans)

Edgar in 1904 when Lois married him.
(Photograph by H. A. Chapman)

Rhossili in the early twentieth century when it was Lois's home.

The remains of the shipwreck on Rhossili Bay beach with Worms Head in the background where Lois and Edgar may have played as children. (© Anne Fletcher)

Rhossili Bay. (© Anne Fletcher)

View of Middleton, early 1900s. The building in the background is the Ship Inn, run by Lois's family for generations. (From Robert Lucas's *Rhossili: A Village Background*)

St. Mary's Church, Rhossili, where Lois married Edgar and where their sons were baptised. (© Anne Fletcher)

Kathleen. (© Illustrated London News Ltd/Mary Evans Picture Library)

Kathleen and Con on board *Terra Nova*, 1910. (Mary Evans Picture Library/Interfoto Agentur)

Above: With the Mayor of Cardiff before *Terra Nova* departed, 1910. Kathleen and Con are on the left and Teddy and Hilda Evans are on the right. (© Dundee Heritage Trust)

THE ANTARCTIC TRAGEDY: THE LEADER'S WIFE AND TWO OF THE DEAD.
ABOARD THE "TERRA NOVA" BEFORE THE JOURNEY OF TRAGIC ENDING: LIEUT. H. R. BOWERS, WHO DIED WITH CAPTAIN SCOTT AND DR. WILSON; MRS. SCOTT; AND CAPTAIN L. E. G. OATES, WHO "WENT OUT INTO THE BLIZZARD."—(LEFT TO RIGHT.)

Right: Kathleen was unpopular on board *Terra Nova*. In this rather uncomfortable-looking photograph, she is captured on deck with two of the men who would later perish with her husband. 'Birdie' Bowers is on the left and 'Titus' Oates is on the right. (© Illustrated London News Ltd/Mary Evans Picture Library)

The TATLER

Vol. XLIII. No. 559.
London, March 13, 1912

[REGISTERED AT THE GENERAL POST OFFICE AS A NEWSPAPER]

Sixpence

MRS. SCOTT AND HER LITTLE SON

THE WIFE OF CAPTAIN SCOTT, THE FAMOUS ARCTIC EXPLORER

Captain Scott, who is well in the public eye at present, is the leader of the English South Pole expedition. Mrs. Scott is a gifted sculptress and is here seen at work with her little son, Peter, a sturdy young man of two and a half years, who is watching his mother with critical eye

Above: Terra Nova, with Con inset. (Library of Congress)

Left: While Con was away on the expedition, Kathleen and Peter attracted a great deal of press attention at home. This photograph of them in her London studio was on the front cover of *The Tatler* on 13 March 1912. (© Illustrated London News Ltd/Mary Evans Picture Library)

At the South Pole. From left to right: Lawrence 'Titus' Oates, Henry 'Birdie' Bowers, Robert Falcon Scott, Edward 'Ted' Wilson and Edgar Evans. (Library of Congress)

The snow cairn and cross that mark the final resting place of Scott, Wilson and Bowers in Antarctica. (Library of Congress)

The press went to find Lois as soon as the news of the Antarctic tragedy broke. This photo of her, her father and her youngest child Ralph was taken on the same day that she was told that Edgar was dead. It was published in the *Daily Telegraph* and many regional newspapers. (© Local and Family History Library, Leeds Libraries)

Lois's two eldest children, Norman and Muriel, were photographed by the press on their way home from school. They did not know that their father was dead. (© Local and Family History Library, Leeds Libraries)

Kathleen at her London studio in 1928 at work on her 10-foot statue of Edwin Montagu (former Secretary for India) destined for Calcutta. (© Illustrated London News Ltd/Mary Evans Picture Library)

Kathleen with her sons, Peter Scott (right) and Wayland Young (centre), 1932. (© Yevonde Portrait Archive/ ILN/Mary Evans Picture Library)

Ory in later life. (Image reproduced with the kind permission of Archives and Special Collections, St George's, University of London)

Lois at the premier of *Scott of the Antarctic* with her son Norman, 1948. (John Evans)

1912: Another Year of Waiting

While Oriana waited for Ted in New Zealand, Kathleen remained at home, caring for Peter and working. Sculpting continued to be both a passion and a much-needed source of income for her. She was the only sculptor invited to exhibit at the Grafton Gallery as part of a show of women's work and had been commissioned to carve statues of bishops for the chapel of Winchester College. She also worked on busts of the writer Compton Mackenzie, her great friend Fridtjof Nansen and the Prime Minister, Herbert Asquith.[1] She had first met him in February 1912, and he sat for her several times throughout the year, becoming a close friend. Through this friendship Kathleen gained access to some of the most influential people in the country.

Asquith's Liberal government put the highest emphasis on social and economic reform, and legislation was passed that laid the foundations of the welfare state, including National Insurance, old age pensions and free school meals. But there was one area where Asquith did not support change, and that was women's suffrage. When he repeatedly blocked attempts in Parliament to give women the vote, he found himself in direct conflict with the WSPU, the Women's Social and Political Union, founded by the Pankhursts in 1903. Given the title 'Suffragettes' by the *Daily Mail* to belittle them, the WSPU embraced the name, created their own identity and branded it with their colours of green, purple and white. Their slogan 'Deeds, not words' matched their policy of militant action.[2]

The conflict between the government and the Suffragettes had escalated two years earlier when three hundred women had marched on Parliament. When the Home Secretary, Winston Churchill, had sent in mounted police a great many people were injured in the ensuing violence. Black Friday, as it became known, was a turning point for the Suffragettes, many of whom decided to abandon the rule of law for the rule of rebellion and to get the vote at any cost.[3] Now, in 1912, under the leadership of Christabel Pankhurst, a much more dangerous group emerged. Nicknamed 'The Young Hot Bloods', these young unmarried women formed the most aggressive, violent and radical branch of the Suffragettes and volunteered for 'danger duty', which was code for extreme militant action.[4] The newspapers began to run regular reports on Suffragette 'outrages', and when some of the arrested women went on hunger strike they were force-fed. Asquith was attacked in July when four English Suffragettes travelled to Ireland, where he was on an official visit, and threw an axe at him, narrowly missing him but cutting the hand of an Irish MP in his party.[5]

Kathleen might have been expected to support votes for women, but she didn't. She shared Asquith's vehemently anti-women's suffrage views. She disapproved of their tactics, writing in her diary on 12 March that 'the brutes have been breaking all the shop windows', and the attack on her friend Asquith four months later might well have entrenched these views even further. Her antipathy was rooted in more than just her dislike of their violence, however. Many women disapproved of the Suffragette attacks but were still in favour of giving women the vote; after all, there was a vast suffrage movement that did not support militant action and was still campaigning through legal means. But Kathleen did not support the extension of the vote to women through any means. She was one of many thousands who felt that it was unnecessary and, in some cases, damaging to let women vote, and she became an active supporter of the anti-suffrage movement. The fight for the vote was a long one not just because of the opposition of men like Asquith, but because a significant number of women felt like Kathleen and were against it too.

On 28 February 1912, the National League for Opposing Woman Suffrage organised a meeting at the Royal Albert Hall in London. Nine thousand people filled the hall to capacity, but twenty thousand had applied to attend.[6] The great and the good of all political parties were in the audience, including the dukes of Devonshire, Norfolk and Northumberland.[7] Kathleen was there too and clearly among friends.[8] Although Asquith couldn't attend, he sent a message of support and his son Raymond and daughter Elizabeth represented the family.[9] On the stage was Lord Curzon, who was on the executive committee and known to Kathleen as president of the Royal Geographical Society.

The social reformer Violet Markham, the only woman on the platform, gave a barnstorming speech encapsulating the key argument made by women anti-suffragists:

> We believe that men and women are different – not similar – beings, with talents that are complementary, not identical, and that they therefore ought to have different shares in the management of the State,

> that they severally compose. We do not depreciate by one jot or title women's work and mission. We are concerned to find proper channels of expression for that work.[10]

Many educated and intelligent women shared this view. They did not believe that women were inferior to men, but that they had different strengths. It was a commonly held view that women were more emotional and moral than men, and anti-suffragists argued that these maternal and caring qualities made women valuable not only in the home but in education, philanthropic work and the expanding field of local government. By fighting for a vote and a say in politics, they claimed, the Suffragettes were showing not only their lack of interest in doing good by serving society but also their desire for power.[11] This view tapped straight into the main male objection to giving women the vote: the fear that families could be destroyed, children damaged, and the natural order of things completely overturned if women ruled the country. Women needed to be running their homes and raising their children.[12]

Lewis Harcourt MP, Secretary of State for the Colonies, in his speech that day stated that they would be taking women from spheres where they shone and duties they adored into matters for which as a sex they were less suited. The men of *Discovery* might have agreed. On board they'd had a 'most amusing' discussion about women's rights and concluded that it would be an impossibility while women 'suffered from disabilities, in comparison with man'.[13] Lord Curzon, who had written a pamphlet entitled *Fifteen Good Reasons Against the Grant of Female Suffrage*, shared the commonly held view that women lacked the 'calmness of temperament or the balance of mind' necessary to take decisions and make laws, especially 'in emergencies or on occasions of emotional excitement'.[14] But as a former Viceroy of India and a stalwart supporter of Britain's imperial ambitions, Curzon also expressed the view of many men that day that female suffrage could damage the empire: '... there would be introduced an element of instability and uncertainty into our politics which would have a demoralising effect – I even think a corrupting effect – upon politics in this country and might seriously weaken our work as an Empire abroad'.[15] Many believed, like Curzon, that Britain would become a laughing stock in the colonies, particularly India, if women were given a greater role in government.[16]

These points of view certainly resonated with Kathleen and not only because she felt, in line with social etiquette of the time, that being involved in violence or being arrested, and force-fed was not respectable, particularly for a married woman.[17] Her strong maternal impulses had guided her life and she might well have agreed with Violet Markham's comments about social causes, especially those involving children, being of more interest to women than matters of national politics. She may also have had sympathy with Curzon's view that that 'Political activity will tend to take away woman from her proper sphere and highest duty, which is maternity.'[18] But her real strength of feeling lay in her belief that most women were either not interested or just too silly to be given a vote and if they had a point of view, then they could make it known perfectly well through men. It may seem strange that such an independent woman would not support her fellow women in something that would provide them all with more of a voice and more freedom, but Kathleen simply didn't see herself as part of that group.[19] She was used to operating alone and she was used to exercising soft power with some of the most influential men in the country, including the Prime Minister. Kathleen could exert her influence without needing to take part in politics but her lack of empathy with other women perhaps led to her not appreciating how unusual her position was.

There is no doubt that Kathleen thoroughly enjoyed the event at the Albert Hall. She'd had an exhausting day, but it really energised her, and she wrote with relish in her diary that night that 'several people were carried out kicking'. She had witnessed the Suffragettes in the audience taking exception to some of the comments, particularly those of Lewis Harcourt MP. When he declared that now was the time for people who were against giving women the vote to make their view known, a voice shouted, 'The majority of women have no representation!' After that a 'rowdy man or two and three or four misguided young women' were ejected.[20]

Kathleen had started work on Con's journals, typing them up and getting them ready for publication. He had trusted her with his words and his legacy, and she felt the weight of the responsibility: 'I find it difficult being your wife. I hope none of my blunders will make indelible marks. I am quite a good mother, and a moderate sculptor; but beyond that I seem rather a failure.'[21] As she worked on Con's journals, she read about Edgar and was keen to write to Lois to tell her that he was not only thriving but had more than proved his worth to Scott:

> ... Captain Scott has sent his diary back from the Antarctic and I think you will be glad to hear how well he speaks throughout it of your husband & his work. Apparently he has made himself more than useful, he has worked so hard and so willingly through every sort of difficulty – and finally has been chosen to go on to the Pole. I am sure you will like to hear how indispensable he has made himself to Captain Scott and how fit and hardworking and thorough he has been – My husband asked me to tell you how splendid he has been ...[22]

Edgar was wildly loyal to Scott and would have been thrilled to be so indispensable and valued, but any pride that Lois felt was tempered by her immediate financial circumstances. By the end of the year, she was struggling to make ends meet and made the decision to leave Portsmouth and take her children back to Wales.[23] Although Edgar was temporarily off the naval payroll, Lois was still a Navy wife and her involvement with the Sailors' Rest in Portsmouth may have brought some financial help. Aggie had been instrumental in the establishment of new ways of distributing money to widows and dependents following naval disasters. She had campaigned successfully for public donations to be shared out more fairly and in greater proportion to those dependents left behind. Through her own philanthropic channels at the Sailors' Rests, she was also able to act quickly to help families in trouble. The local press was full of stories of Aggie and her team distributing temporary relief after ships had sunk and on occasions maintaining dependents on full pay for a period. She made a donation to the Portsmouth Titanic Fund.[24]

Even if Aggie did help Lois at this desperate time, it would not have been a long-term solution and Lois did not know how long it would be before Edgar returned. Leaving Portsmouth must have been made even harder for her because her younger brother Stanley had just been bereaved. Like Edgar, he had joined the Navy as a teenager and was just seventeen when he served as a boy 2nd class on HMS *Impregnable* at the start of a twenty-four-year naval career.[25] He was at sea a great deal of the time but when he was on shore his base was at Devonport. It was there that he met his wife, Amelia Ann Andrews, whom he married in July 1911. Just over a year later she was dead, and Stanley found himself the widowed father of a little girl, Amelia Beatrice Beynon, named after her late mother and his sister.[26] It must have hurt Lois to leave Stanley, but without enough money to look after her own children she had no choice but to move back to Wales.

The family in Gower had been worrying about Lois and felt deeply sorry for her. Blame did not fall on Edgar for the situation, however; it was understood that the opportunity to go south again with Scott was too great to miss. But when it was clear that Lois needed help, it was her Welsh family that acted. Her relative William Tucker travelled down to Portsmouth to bring her and the children back to his home at Pitton Cross Farm.[27] For the time being, her furniture was left behind.[28] Lois's parents had retired from the Ship Inn and moved a little way out of Middleton to West Pilton Cottage, and that is where they welcomed their daughter and three grandchildren into their home.[29] Edgar's widowed mother Sarah was living nearby in Pitton, in the cottage of her older sister Anne, and so Lois had a great deal of daily support at a time when she must have needed it very much.[30] She was a resourceful woman, used to making ends meet, and living back at home where she knew everyone and everyone knew her, she could subsist better than in Portsmouth. She could help her parents in their retirement, and they could share the rent. She could barter and trade her time and resources, looking after a friend's children for an afternoon in return for a spare piece of meat or trading some extra eggs for some milk.

Gower was also self-sufficient in food production; a peninsula cut off by poor roads and 18 miles from Swansea, it had no choice. Farmers across the region produced lamb, beef, pork, chicken, milk and eggs, and the climate suited the growing of root vegetables, particularly potatoes and swedes. Rabbits were plentiful too. Lois's ability to feed her family would have been further helped by a system of agriculture in Gower which had survived since Norman times. For hundreds of years, an open-field system of cultivation was retained there even as it disappeared virtually everywhere else in Britain. In an area called the Vile – a name which comes from the Gower pronunciation of 'field' – land was divided into strips that were separated by low green banks. Each was cultivated by a different member of the community, and each family had more than one strip to ensure that the best land was shared out fairly. Every family had land where they could grow corn, swedes and potatoes, and virtually everyone baked their own bread and had a couple of pigs and some ducks or geese. There was common land too for those who had sheep or horses that needed to graze.[31]

The sea was an abundant source of free food too. Sorrel and samphire could be foraged around the coast while purplish-black edible seaweed was plentiful on the beaches and could be boiled down into a thick puree known as laverbread. Fishermen worked the waters while crabbers and cocklers scoured Gower's rocky beaches looking for seafood which could sustain their families and bring in some income. Limestone layers perforated with holes and ledges were revealed at low tide, and this is where crabs and lobsters were found, mainly between April and September. One of the best hunting grounds in Rhossili was an area called Crabart, which was revealed as the sea retreated from the Worm's Head causeway. Crabbers pulled the crabs out of their holes by hand, working their own area of rocks over many years and handing down knowledge of the best locations to younger members of the family.[32] Cockling was mainly done by women, who worked the cockle beds which were exposed when the tide went out. While the beach was still covered by a very shallow layer of water, they picked the cockles out of the sand using hand rakes and sieved the sand away using a riddle, collecting them in bags and baskets and transporting them by donkey and, later, pony and flat cart to Swansea. It was hard work, done in all weathers and often very early in the morning.[33] Lois could therefore subsist at home in Gower and wait for her husband's safe return with their extended family around her. Their children could play on the beaches and cliffs and explore the rockpools and caves as she and Edgar had done, and they could attend the same school that their father had.

In the autumn of 1912, the last instalments of Herbert Ponting's films were screened by Gaumont in cinemas around the country.[34] Audiences knew that the British expedition had not reached the Pole first, but this did not diminish their interest. The films were still a commercial success. The first, released on 30 September 1912, concentrated on the Antarctic landscape and its natural history as well as the expedition's scientific work. The second film, released on 14 October 1912, featured the planned assault on the Pole and showed the ponies, dogs and sledges that were a key part of the expedition. Kathleen saw her husband in his element as leader and explorer as she watched him and his men discovering their new environment, going about their daily life in camp and preparing for the next stage of their journey. Lois must have strained to catch glimpses of Edgar and would have laughed with everyone else as images of crewmen playfully running after Adélie penguins filled the screen. Ory's Ted appeared smiling and happy in his scientific work, which must have filled her heart with joy. And then a parting shot of Scott, Ted and Cherry filled the screen as they walked out into the vast white expanse of the plateau at the start of the journey, waving a last farewell. 'What fun it will be when we're home again and see this at the cinema,' Scott had said to Ponting. Kathleen and Ory must have felt that they were waving to them, an intensely private moment in a very public place.

It had been months since *Terra Nova* had returned to spend the winter in New Zealand, and after the joy of reading the letters and other documents that the ship brought home there had been no more news of the Polar Party. Where were they? Neither Kathleen nor the Royal Geographical Society knew. But watching these films must have fuelled their growing anticipation of a homecoming. Writing to Cherry's mother Evelyn in September, Ory was buzzing with excitement:

> I think March will be the worst month of all. Why every telephone ring will make one jump to the conclusion there is news of the *Terra Nova* – It makes one feel quite sick with excitement and anticipation to think of it even. & what it will be when the month is really here, I can't imagine.[35]

Of course, Ory did know what it was like. She was the only one of the wives or mothers to have been through all of this before, and although she longed to see Ted she didn't relish the fuss or sharing him with others.

She wrote to Evelyn Cherry-Garrard that if 'it is at all like old *Discovery* times out here, life will be one continual rush and fêting – and there is not much satisfaction in that'.[36]

As the year ended, the wives spent their third Christmas without their husbands. Lois was with her children, perhaps some of her family too, and Kathleen was with Peter at Lewis Beaumont's home where they ate their Christmas dinner alone and drank a toast to Con's joyful return.[37] Ory was in New Zealand with her sister Connie at the home of her friends the Dennistouns in Peel Forest, and as 1913 dawned she wrote excitedly of Ted's return: 'Isn't it lovely to be able to say "this year" – now...'[38] None of them knew that they had already been widows for nine months.

1912: Finding the Bodies

Scott had chosen a site for his base camp in McMurdo Sound on Ross Island, near to the base of Mount Erebus. He called it Cape Evans. Here, expedition scientists used the makeshift lab while other team members were deposited in areas further afield to explore and collect geological and botanical samples. Meanwhile, in readiness for the attempt to reach the South Pole, a vital depot-laying journey had taken place, creating deposits of food and fuel for the final stages of the return journey, beginning at One Ton Depot. Scott had wanted to go further towards the Pole before laying this first depot, but the weather had counted against him and so the first store of supplies available to the men coming back from the Pole would be 150 miles from base camp.

On 1 November 1911, Scott had led his men out of Cape Evans, towards the Pole. It would be a round trip of over 1,700 miles with three distinct stages: the Great Ice Barrier, the Beardmore Glacier, and finally the Plateau. The Barrier (now called the Ross Ice Shelf) is a vast sheet of floating ice that joins Ross Island to the Antarctic mainland. Once they had walked 425 miles across it, they would pass through a gap in the Transantarctic Mountains via the 125-mile-long Beardmore Glacier. This would lead them to the Polar Plateau, on which the South Pole was located, approximately 350 miles away. Scott planned to cross the Barrier using motorised sledges with ponies and dogs carrying supplies; on reaching the foot of the glacier they would kill the ponies and send the dogs back if they'd made it that far. The men would then pull their own supplies on sledges, 'manhauling' all the way to the Pole in leather harnesses. Cherry believed that Scott's hope was to abolish the cruel practice of using horses and dogs, a very British view of polar exploration which the sentimental Scott had embraced wholeheartedly.[1] However, Scott was also convinced that he couldn't rely on animals. Since he had seen an entire dog team fall into a crevasse in 1911, he believed that animals simply could not survive the extreme weather conditions of the Beardmore Glacier and its treacherous, fissured surface. It was a setback, then, when the motorised party, which had left on 24 October, came to a spluttering stop and the motorised sledges had to be abandoned. Scott had made provision for this eventuality, but it was still a huge disappointment.

On 10 December, about a week later than Scott had planned, the group arrived at the bottom of the glacier. The last five ponies were shot for meat and the dogs were taken back to Cape Evans together with letters home from the men who would carry on to the next stage. This left twelve men to man-haul three 500-pound sledges over 100 miles of glacier. Another four were sent home ten days later when the party reached the top of the Beardmore Glacier.[2] The returning men included Dr Edward Atkinson, a naval doctor known affectionately as Atch who, as the most senior naval man there, would assume command when he got back to Cape Evans. Scott told him to make sure that somebody brought the dogs out to One Ton Depot in February; they should use the dog food stored there to then go on as far as they could to meet Scott and the returning Polar Party.[3]

Eight now remained: Scott, Wilson, Edgar Evans, Lawrence Oates and Birdie Bowers together with Teddy Evans, Tom Crean and William Lashly. They began their walk across the Plateau in two teams of four; Scott, Ted and Edgar pulled together with Oates. Before leaving England Scott had said that his ideal day to reach the Pole would be 22 December, and so he was already later than he had hoped. He decided to improve their speed by changing the sledge runners from 12-foot ones to new 10-foot models to make the sledges lighter. Edgar was responsible for the sledges, harnesses, tents and sleeping bags, and he had designed and made crampons and ski shoes during the winter, so it was he who changed the sledge runners. While doing so, he cut his hand. He didn't mention the injury to the rest of the party. It didn't seem much, and he was determined to get to the Pole. But this cut was to be his Achilles heel.

As the year 1912 dawned, Scott took the decision to take five men with him to the Pole instead of four and the final Polar Party was confirmed; his team of Wilson, Edgar and Oates would be joined by Birdie Bowers. They were only about 168 miles from the Pole, and as Teddy Evans, Lashly and Crean began their long trudge back to base they were sure that a British flag would be flying there soon.[4] This is what had been reported back so confidently to Ory, Kathleen and Lois. On the return journey Teddy became seriously ill with scurvy, this very grave illness allowing him to save face because it obscured the fact that Scott had already ordered him home. He had decided that he did not want Teddy to be left in charge if he was late returning; he doubted the man's ability to do the job.

The relationship between the two men was now in tatters, having deteriorated rapidly once ashore in Antarctica. Teddy's boyish enthusiasm had been popular during the voyage, particularly compared to Scott's rather aloof style of leadership, but once the hard work of the expedition began, especially the sledging, Teddy was sometimes found wanting. Bowers was also upset by Teddy's criticism of Scott.[5] Before they parted at the top of the glacier, Scott gave Teddy new verbal instructions about bringing the dogs out to meet the Polar Party; they should come even further south from One Ton to hurry Scott back to Cape Evans in time to catch the ship and get out the news that they'd reached the Pole. But in the drama of Teddy's ensuing illness this instruction was forgotten.[6]

Trudging across the Plateau, on 16 January Bowers thought he saw something in the white expanse. It looked like a cairn and then a black speck in the snow. As the five men drew closer, the dark, indistinct spot in the landscape took the form of a black flag tied to a sledge and they knew in an instant that they were not the first men to walk there. Looking around them, the signs were unmissable. Sledge and ski tracks had cut through the snow and the remains of a camp were clearly visible. Worst of all, there were

> ... clear trace of dogs' paws – many dogs. This told us the whole story. The Norwegians have forestalled us and are first at the Pole. It is a terrible disappointment, and I am very sorry for my loyal companions ... Tomorrow we must march on to the Pole and then hasten home with all the speed we can compass. All the day dreams must go; it will be a wearisome return.[7]

The next day the party followed the Norwegian tracks onward for a distance and then Scott decided to follow his own calculations to find the Pole. On 17 January 1912 they found a tent and inside was a record of the five Norwegians who had reached the South Pole, dated 16 December 1911, and a note for Scott. Amundsen's expedition had got there nearly one month before them. It was devastating news. The five men built a stone cairn and 'put up our poor slighted Union Jack'.[8] They photographed themselves next to their flag and their disappointment is clearly captured there. Haunted eyes and deflated postures express the enormity of the mental challenge that they now had to face, one that Scott so clearly expressed in his diary:

> Great God! This is an awful place and terrible enough for us to have laboured to it without the reward of priority ... Now for the run home and a desperate struggle. I wonder if we can do it.[9]

The Antarctic winter had begun, and to get back safely required speed and regular food pick-ups. But the men were already in poor shape and the freezing temperature and savage winds pushed against their efforts to walk their way home. Frostbite was ravaging their extremities, particularly in the case of Edgar and Oates, who seemed particularly vulnerable to it. Oates's toe had turned black within days of starting home and Wilson suffered greatly with his eyes. In his diary entry on 25 January, Scott wrote that only he and Bowers were without troubles at that time. But it was Edgar who appeared to be causing Scott the most concern. His cut hand was no longer a secret; the wound was full of pus.[10] By the end of January, Scott was confiding to his diary that he had noticed a worrying decline in Edgar.

On 4 February, Scott and Edgar fell suddenly and unexpectedly down a deep crevasse. This was the second fall for Edgar, and that night Scott wrote that he had become 'rather dull and incapable'. And two days later, 'Evans is the chief anxiety now; his cuts and wounds suppurate, his nose looks very bad, and altogether he shows considerable signs of being played out.'[11] A concussed Edgar became withdrawn and very unlike himself. He couldn't help with duties and gradually this began to hold up the group. Despite this, Wilson and Scott kept an eye on the scientific aims of the expedition. Ted discovered rocks containing plant specimens, beautifully traced leaves, and plant stems.[12] The fossilised remains in these rocks, which Scott had allowed Ted to collect even though the men were struggling, were later identified as *Glossopteris*, a plant from warm, temperate climates. They were further proof of the theory that the climate had changed, that Antarctica had once been warm, but Ted would never know how important his rocks would prove to be.[13]

These few days of exploration proved a brief moment of calm in a rapidly deteriorating situation. Over the coming days, food rations were reduced as progress was slowed by Edgar's condition. On 16 February, Scott recorded his anxiety about his old friend in his diary: 'Evans has nearly broken down in brain, we think. He is absolutely changed from his normal self-reliant self.' These words, written by an exhausted, hungry man working under the burden of enormous stress and responsibility, would prove to have enormous consequences for Lois. But Scott was right to be concerned because the following day, 17 February, was, in his own words, 'a very terrible day'. Edgar stopped to adjust his shoe as his foot had worked out of it. The rest carried on, and when they saw that he'd fallen back a bit they stopped to cook a meal. They weren't alarmed at first, but after they'd eaten Edgar had still not caught up; in fact he still appeared to be far away. All four men skied back and were shocked to find him crawling in the snow with his clothes in disarray and his frostbitten hands exposed. He had a wild look in his eyes and his speech was slurred. Edgar had no idea how he came to be like this and assumed that he must have fainted, but he couldn't remember. Getting the huge man to his feet was a struggle, and when he collapsed again after only two or three steps, Oates stayed with him while the others went to get the sledge. They got Edgar back to the relative warmth of the tent, but he was already unconscious. He died quietly at 12.30 a.m. His friends covered his body and left it to be engulfed by the snow and ice. Edgar was just a few weeks short of his thirty-sixth birthday.

The four remaining men struggled on for another month against unexpectedly harsh conditions and some of the coldest weather ever recorded in Antarctica.[14] On some nights temperatures fell below -40° centigrade, the winds picked up and the surface over which they had to pull the sledge became increasingly more difficult. Food ran low as their progress slowed and they also worried about the amount of fuel left at the depots as some had evaporated from the tins. There was little respite from the biting cold, and shoes, gloves and sleeping bags were difficult to dry out. Scott recorded in his diary on 'Friday 16 or Saturday 17 March Lost track of dates' that Oates had said that he could not go on. Gangrene was causing unbearable pain in his leg, and his hands were so frostbitten that Ted Wilson was having to feed him. Oates had said earlier that a sick man's duty was to eliminate himself rather than hold back his comrades, and so he reached the decision that the time had come. He crawled out of the tent, saying as he went, 'I am just going outside and may be some time.' Scott wrote,

> We knew that poor Oates was walking to his death, but though we tried to dissuade him, we knew it was the act of a brave man and an English gentleman. We all hope to meet the end with a similar spirit, and assuredly the end is not far.[15]

Scott's final diary entry was written on 29 March 1912 from the tent in which they had been trapped for several days by a storm. Wilson and Bowers had hoped to make a dash for One Ton Depot, which was only 11 miles away, but the weather was too ferocious. As food and fuel ran out, the three men died from exhaustion, starvation and extreme cold. Scott's last words were,

> I do not think we can hope for any better things now. We shall stick it out to the end, but we are getting weaker, of course, and the end cannot be far. It seems a pity, but I do not think I can write more … For God's sake look after our people.[16]

As the Antarctic winter took hold, *Terra Nova* left for New Zealand and only thirteen men remained at the expedition base at Cape Evans. The quiet, popular and hard-working naval doctor Atch was in command, and he tried to keep their minds occupied and their spirits high, but it became increasingly hard as the months passed and there was no sign of Scott and the others. During that dark, cold winter, they came to the inevitable conclusion that all five men were dead. Atch asked the men to vote. Would they try to relieve their colleague Victor Campbell and his scientific party, who had been out in the field exploring the north since February 1911, or would they go south? The majority voted to go south and try to find out what had happened to Scott, Wilson, Oates, Evans and Birdie. Campbell's team had supplies and could survive, and moreover the men at the base felt that they had a responsibility to report back to the world what had happened to the Polar Party – if they could find out.

Against all expectations, the search party found the bodies on 12 November 1912. They had assumed that their friends lay at the bottom of a crevasse, or had perished under the driving snow, never to be found. They had not expected to find them and so tragically close to home. They spotted a mound of snow with 3 feet of bamboo sticking out from the top, and when the snow was brushed away the green flap of the tent's ventilator became visible. Still inside their tent and buried beneath the snow, Ted Wilson and Birdie looked at first as if they were asleep, their sleeping bags closed over their heads as they would be each night. Scott, lying between them, had flung his sleeping bag and coat open and his arm rested across Wilson, his greatest friend. Tryggve Gran, the young Norwegian skiier whom Nansen had introduced to Scott in Norway, was part of the group and described the scene in his diary:

> All ghastly. I will never forget it so long as I live – a horrible nightmare could not have shown more horror than this ... The frost had made the skin yellow & transparent & I've never seen anything worse in my life. The Owner seems to have struggled hard in the moment of death, whilst the two others seem to have gone off in a kind of sleep.

They found Scott's diary in a bag tucked under his arm, and as it was picked up, a sharp retort like a gunshot rang around in the Antarctic silence. It was the sound of Scott's frozen limb breaking.[17] The horror of the scene would not be disclosed until many decades later, and the widows would never hear of it. Instead, they and the world would be presented with a sanitised and less distressing picture.

With nobody left alive, the story of what had happened to the Polar Party was held in the diaries and letters that were retrieved from the tent.

Atch was the first to read Scott's account. His instructions, written on the cover, were that the finder was to read it and then bring it home. Atch took in enough to understand what had happened and read some of it, including the account of Oates's death, to the others. This was how they discovered that Amundsen had beaten them to the Pole, but they didn't care now. Having expected to find little or no trace, they had been profoundly shocked upon discovering the bodies of their friends and their accounts of what had happened to them. Carefully they gathered up diaries, notes and letters, along with the geological samples gathered by Wilson and the films the party had shot, and started on their way back to Cape Evans.[18]

Two months later, on 18 January 1913, *Terra Nova* arrived in Antarctica to bring all the remaining expedition members home. Teddy Evans, recovered from scurvy and recently promoted, was in command of the ship. On board, a tremendous feast had been prepared and champagne, chocolates, cigarettes and cigars had been brought up from the stores. Little flags and silk ribbons decorated the wardroom table and letters from home had been done up in neat packets for each expedition member. They had been placed on the bunks that had been made up with clean white sheets for Scott and the others.[19] As the senior officer on land, Victor Campbell had taken over command of Cape Evans from Atch. He and his men had sledged back into base after an extraordinary terrible final winter with little food or fuel, confined to an ice cave in which they couldn't stand up.[20] Delighted to see that he had returned safely, Teddy Evans called down to him from the ship, 'Campbell, is everyone well?' After a moment's hesitation the reply came: 'The Southern Party reached the South Pole on the 17th of January, last year, but were all lost on the return journey – we have their records.'

A moment of silence and overwhelming sorrow swept over the ship's crew. Teddy wrote later that the same feeling came over him each Armistice Day. The ship, which had been prepared for a celebration and a homecoming, was stripped of its decorations and festive table settings and the flags were dropped to half-mast as the ship was plunged into mourning. Within thirty-six hours, the entire expedition was packed up and all its men boarded. Before they left, they erected a 9-foot cross, made by the ship's carpenter from Australian Jarrah wood, on Observation Hill with the names of their dead colleagues and a quote from Tennyson's *Ulysses* carved on it: 'To strive, to seek, to find and not to yield.'[21] On board *Terra Nova*, the letters that it had carried from New Zealand from Kathleen and Ory and other loved ones were packed away, never to be read by the men for whom they were intended. They were joined by the journals that the Polar Party had left behind and the farewell letters that they had penned in their final hours. Contained within were their last goodbyes to the women they loved.

PART 3

Widows

... you know I have loved you ... and oh dear me you must know that quite the worst aspect of this situation is the thought that I shall not see you again ...

Con to Kathleen

If His Death Can Help People ... I Can Be Happy in Giving Him Up

Anyone watching *Terra Nova* closely as it sailed into Lyttelton Harbour at dawn on 12 February 1913 would have realised that it was the bearer of terrible news. Its flag was flying at half-mast. The ship had arrived two days earlier at Oamaru, but because of the £2,500 deal that Scott had struck with the Central News Agency (worth approximately £300,000 in today's terms) it was not permitted to sail into shore immediately. The loss of the Polar Party was Central News's story to break, and so the crew had to wait at sea until the news had been cabled to the United Kingdom. Only once the press exclusive was guaranteed could they disembark and share the tales that they had to tell. Pennell and Atch had slipped ashore very quietly, early on 10 February, to send a telegram to London from Oamaru post office. It said that Scott had reached the Pole but all had perished on the way back due to a blizzard. Sworn to secrecy, they said nothing, even when Tom Crean was chased as he rowed the little boat back to the ship and a New Zealand vessel approached *Terra Nova*, shouting, 'Where's Captain Scott? Is all well? Did you reach the Pole?'[1]

Atch and Pennell took the train to Christchurch to see Kinsey and give him the official report of the expedition, which they had written on the voyage home with Teddy Evans, Victor Campbell, ship meteorologist Francis Drake and Kathleen's brother Wilfred.[2] Kinsey immediately wired a short despatch so that the bereaved could be notified. Both telegrams arrived at the Central News Agency in London at lunchtime on 10 February, but, not wanting to wait for the full report in case they lost the exclusive to their New Zealand rivals, the agency released the news. The Royal Geographical Society was telephoned, and at 7.55 p.m.

King George V sent a telegram to Lord Curzon which expressed the shock felt by the nation:

> I am deeply grieved to hear the very sad news which you give me of the loss of Captain Scott and five [*sic*] of his party just when we were hoping shortly to welcome them home on return from their great and arduous undertaking.[3]

By that evening the death of Scott of the Antarctic and his brave companions had begun to ripple out on to front pages across the globe.[4] Despite Kinsey's attempt to get the news to the bereaved as quickly as possible, the three women widowed by these terrible events were not the first to know.

The expedition's control of the dissemination of news was so good that even though *Terra Nova* and the survivors were there, the story did not reach the New Zealand papers until London wired the story back to them the next day.[5] There had been rumours circulating, but nobody could believe them to be true; surely if such a calamity had happened it would have been reported when the ship called in at Oamaru?[6]

Ory had been staying with Kinsey's daughter May in Dunedin when he heard that *Terra Nova* was coming in and told his daughter to get Ory on a train to Christchurch. She set off excitedly on the journey that would deliver her into the city in the late afternoon of 11 February for a romantic reunion with Ted. At around lunchtime, as the train stopped en route, her carriage door was flung open and she was surprised by her great friends the Dennistouns, who had galloped from Peel Forest to intercept Ory and share her joy. When the train eventually pulled into Christchurch, amid the usual clatter and racket of the busy city was a new and unusual sound. The voice of a newspaper vendor cut in and out of the noise, gradually forming into the chilling phrase 'Antarctic Tragedy'.[7] The news had broken that morning in New Zealand. The cathedral bell had been tolling, flags were at half-mast, people stopped in the street to share their shock and sorrow and the fate of the Polar Party was printed on all the front pages. That is how Ory discovered that Ted was dead.

This, of course, was not how Ted's colleagues had planned it. Teddy Evans had been particularly concerned about Ory: 'I feel somehow that the blow to her will be far worse than to the others. Mrs Scott has her son, but Uncle Bill was all the world to his wife.'[8] Atch and Pennell had been waiting at Kinsey's house to break the news to her and were distraught at how she'd heard it. Ironically, the family back at Westal found out in a similar way. A telegram had arrived on the 10 February from a colleague from *Discovery* days saying that *Terra Nova* had come home early due to disaster, followed by another that evening giving sympathy and hoping the rumours weren't true. It was the evening papers that dealt the shattering blow to the family, whose thoughts turned to 'our dear, good Ory, vainly awaiting his return in New Zealand'.[9] Atch and Pennell had Ted's diary and the final letters that he had written, and they now answered Ory's questions about what had happened. Atch told her about finding Ted, how he had died peacefully and that he had read the burial service before they erected a simple cross over the cairn of snow that buried the tent and the bodies within. In private, Ory read Ted's last words to her, magnificent words that in the crucible of her grief brought her some relief, demonstrating as they did that he had died at peace with his fate and that his final thoughts were of her.

> To my beloved wife,
> Life has been a struggle for some weeks now on this return journey from the Pole, so much so that I have not been able to keep my diary going. Today may be the last effort. Birdie and I are going to try and reach the depot 11 miles north of us and return to this tent where Capt. Scott is lying with a frozen foot. We have been short oil and short food for so long and such low temperatures and bad weather that we are all done up. Evans and Oates are dead. Our effort today is rather a forlorn hope but I hope this will reach you ... I look forward to meeting you after this life is over. I shall simply fall and go to sleep in the snow and I have your little books with me in my breast pocket ... God will bring us together again ... Don't be unhappy darling all is for the best. We are playing a good part in a great scheme arranged by God Himself and all is well. I find absolutely no terror in the thought that this is my last day of life. Yet it almost certainly is. It is, I think, dear. I am only sorry I could not have seen your loving letters and Mother's and Dad's and the Smiths' and all the happy news I had hoped to see, but all these things are easily seen later, I expect, when we are with Christ which is far better. God be with you – my love for you is as living as ever ... We will all meet after death and death has no terrors. God keep you in this disappointment – We have done what we thought was best ... my own dear wife – goodbye, for the present... I do not cease to pray for you – to the very last.

Then a few days later he wrote again:

> ... I leave this life in absolute faith and happy belief that we shall merely know nothing till we are together again and if God wishes you to wait long without me it will be to some good purpose ... Bless you my own dear wife – take heart and live your life out ...

> ... God knows I am sorry to be the cause of sorrow to anyone in the world, but everyone must die – and at every death there must be some sorrow ... All the things I had hoped to do with you after this Expedition are as nothing now, but there are greater things for us to do in the world to come ... My only regret is leaving you to struggle through your life alone ... All is well dear.[10]

Ted had died peacefully; Ory could take solace in that. After he had slipped away in his sleep, Scott, now the only man alive in the tent, had written to her:

> My dear Mrs Wilson,
> If this letter reaches you Bill and I will have gone out together. We are very near it now and I should like you to know how splendid he was at the end – everlastingly cheerful and ready to sacrifice himself for the others, never a word of blame for me for leading him into this mess. He is not suffering, luckily, at least only minor discomforts.
>
> His eyes have a comfortable blue look of hope and his mind is peaceful with the satisfaction of his faith in regarding himself as part of the great scheme of the Almighty. I can do no more to comfort you than to tell you that he died as he lived, a brave, true man – the best of comrades and staunchest of friends. My whole heart goes out to you in pity.[11]

Ory's gratitude at being able to read Ted's final words was the greater for knowing that Ted had intended to write farewell letters to other members of the family, but they received only empty envelopes.[12] He had died before he could fill them. The importance of the letters to her is expressed in a note she wrote to Tom Crean from Christchurch on 23 February 1913:

> I shall always be grateful to you all, that you persevered in looking for the tent – for as a result of your search I have had the comfort and help of receiving the last words Dr. Wilson wrote to me and I am more thankful to you all than I can say ... His friends shall be my friends and I shall always take an interest in your fortune – and if it is ever within my power to do anything for your and yours at any time, I hope you will tell me.[13]

On 13 February, Ory asked Cherry to visit her. He had been with Ted on the Winter Journey and was the cousin of her greatest friend and she was very fond of him, as Ted had been. Cherry went to a memorial service for his friends that day at Christchurch Cathedral; maybe Ory attended too, but more likely she remained in privacy at the Kinseys' house. It was there that she met with him.[14] He was recovering from a complete mental collapse, brought on by the grief and shock of losing Ted and Birdie, the two men he had come to consider his best friends. He was also crucifying himself with guilt, tortured by the belief that he might have saved them.

Atch had put into effect Scott's orders and sent Cherry with a dog team and the dog handler Dimitri Gerof to meet the Polar Party at One Ton Depot. Atch told them to look after the dogs as they would be needed the following season to continue the scientific work. Scott had left orders for human and dog food to be left at One Ton for this relief party, but in the delayed returns of parties and the confusion of Teddy Evans' illness, food had been laid for humans but not for the dogs. Unable to travel further south without killing dogs to feed the rest of the pack, Cherry waited, and he had no reason to think that this was a problem. He could not possibly have known that the circumstances had changed, that this had now become a life-or-death rescue mission. He waited as long as he could and then left supplies and a note for Scott and began the eight-day return journey. Perhaps if he'd known that they were dying and in desperate need of food and fuel he might have risked the terrible conditions and killed the dogs, and maybe even found his friends in time. But he didn't know, and just five days after he left One Ton, his friends pitched their final tent just 11 miles away and died there. Atch had reassured Cherry that given the circumstances and their orders nobody could have done more, but this would never be enough for Cherry. He tortured himself for the rest of his life and never recovered fully from the profound trauma caused by the loss of his friends.[15] He wrote later how his grief even entered his dreams:

> I am asleep in my bunk at Cape Evans; the hut door opens, letting in its mist of cold air, and the Polar Party walk in, shaking the snow from their clothes and ice from their faces. Scott is there, and Bill with his usual cheery grin, and Birdie Bowers, just utterly done. Titus Oates and Taff Evans are not there. The disappointment of finding that it is only a dream will last for days. There is another of us survivors who has much the same dream, I find.[16]

Ory had read Ted's letters and was keen for Cherry to know just how highly regarded he'd been and so she read extracts to the fragile young man. She also tried to give back to him the copy of Tennyson that he had loaned Ted, and which had been found in the tent. He refused to take it and pressed it into her hands together with a piece of lava that he'd brought home for her from Observation Hill when they erected the cross.[17]

Cables and letters of sympathy from friends and strangers flooded in, all united in their desire to help, and it was a tremendous support to Ory, as she explained in her reply to the sender of one:

> God is indeed helping me though my friend and I am sure my beloved one is very near & God knows how he has helped me all my life & is helping me now. His life was so perfectly unselfish & Christ like, and I can only be thankful that he was not the one to be left behind. It only means that I have to wait a little longer and then I do believe God will let us work together again. He never got any of our letters but I am sure he knew that all was well – at any rate he does now – and if his death can help people, more than his life, I can be happy in giving him up.[18]

My Husband Died Bravely

Despite the news breaking first in Britain, Lois didn't hear that her husband was dead until after Ory, nearly 12,000 miles away in New Zealand. The telegram that had been sent to inform her was delivered to the wrong place, arriving in Portsmouth because neither Edgar nor his shipmates had known that she had been forced to move home to Wales. And although the story of the tragedy had been in the evening papers in Swansea on 10 February, Lois had not seen any of the coverage because she was out in Gower, staying with the children on the farm belonging to her relative William Tucker.

Early on the morning of 11 February, she had decided to make the best of a beautiful sunny day and had taken four-year-old Ralph and her fourteen-year-old cousin Lilly Tucker to look for cockles on Oxwich beach. William had driven them the short distance from Pitton in his pony and cart and was going to come back at 5 p.m. to collect them. Cockles were scarce that day, but they had plenty of time to hunt. They were very surprised when William returned much earlier than expected. Lily knew it was her father crossing the beach because of his limp. In his hand he held a telegram. As William handed her the piece of paper, Lois must have known what it meant. She'd had no news of Edgar for nine months. Still she hesitated, unable to gird herself to read the words printed on it. She asked William to read the telegram but he shook his head sadly; she must read it for herself. The words, chosen carefully by Teddy Evans in Christchurch on behalf of the *Terra Nova* crew, read, 'Members wish to express deepest sympathy in your sad loss.' Lois read them without shedding a tear, saying afterwards that it was the news she had been expecting.[1] Edgar had been dead for a year, and she had not known.

All the real detail about the tragedy was still held by those in New Zealand. In Britain, nobody really knew what was going on. This had been a private expedition, but the press still descended on Lowther Lodge, the headquarters of the Royal Geographical Society in London, expecting it to have information and to take the lead in responding to the tragedy. Although the society had been telephoned at 3 p.m. with the news as soon as it came in, its members had no more detail than anyone else, including the government. Like many others, they were dependent on the Central News Agency for information. Keltie, the society's secretary, told Lord Curzon nearly a week after the story broke that if there was no fresh news in the papers that evening then perhaps they could cable Teddy Evans directly because the Central News Agency had 'the monopoly of the news'.[2]

Keltie and his colleagues were in shock, desperately scrabbling for information with everyone else and now dealing with press enquiries too.[3] They were simply too distracted to think of Lois. In contrast to Ory, who had been whisked immediately to Kinsey's house to meet Atch and Pennell and to read Ted's diaries and ask questions, Lois was isolated out in Gower with no support or information. From the telegram it was clear that Edgar was dead, but how and where? What had happened to his body? All sorts of thoughts and horrors were set running, but there was no more information than the stark and brutal news that she was a widow. William took her back to her parents' cottage, and there she broke the news to them and to her aunt Sarah, Edgar's mother. Many of the other family members heard via the newspapers. Lois's brother Stanley in Devonport sent a telegram which arrived not long after Teddy's and read, 'Just read terrible news. Bear up. Will write – Stan.'[4] Shocked and heartbroken, they consoled each other, but their privacy was soon to be shattered.

One of the journalists in London who had, in their desperation for news, surrounded the Royal Geographical Society the previous day set out in his motor car to the chilly, fog-bound Gower Peninsula to try to find Lois, the only one of the three widows in the country. The *Daily Telegraph* must have found out very quickly that she had left Portsmouth and returned to her family. He was fortunate that the road from Swansea went as far as Pitton Cross because Lois was living not far from there, but even if he had her address it would be difficult to find. West Pilton only comprised a farm and a couple of cottages, but it was out in the expanse of fields that lay between the road and the sea. He would have to pick his way across the land, the fog obscuring his view and the uneven ground under his feet alternating between boggy dips and hummocks prickly with gorse. Perhaps he had to knock on what doors he could find there to ask for her. Perhaps somebody took him in a cart. But eventually he arrived at the little cottage in the vast landscape, nestling under the bare trees near a farm. It was easier for the local press and journalists from *South*

Wales Daily Post and *Western Mail* who very quickly descended on the area too. Lois still did not fully understand the tragedy that had engulfed her and her family until these reporters turned up at her parents' home to interview her. This was how she found out for certain that she was a widow, doorstepped by strangers.

While Ory was secluded in her grief, nothing was done to protect Lois from the attentions of the press, and it was to become even more intrusive. During the course of that terrible day, while trying to come to terms with the shock of Edgar's loss, Lois tried to absorb the few details of the tragedy that the journalists had to tell her. They had gleaned their information from the official report that had been wired from New Zealand early that morning.[5] Lois had to hear the detail of her husband's death from the journalists and be interviewed by them about it at the same time. During these extraordinarily stressful hours, there was no support from London but there was contact. When the *Western Mail* reporter asked to see Edgar's last letter to her, Lois told him, 'I cannot show you his letter, we are debarred from in any way publishing them.'[6] Lois must have been given this instruction almost immediately on hearing of her husband's death. Whoever instructed her need not have worried, however; she would not have shared her treasured letters in any case. Edgar's final words were precious and personal and meant only for her. Lois would never have agreed to have their contents printed for all the world to see.[7]

To make matters worse, throughout this ordeal Lois was worrying about what was happening to her two oldest children. Seven-year-old Norman and five-and-a-half-year-old Muriel had left for school that morning without hearing the news of their father's death.[8] Had they been told in the playground without her there to comfort them? She must have been frantic with worry; did they know? If not, how would she tell them? There was no shield from public gaze for Lois or her family in their grief, no appeal for privacy while they came to terms with their loss. The press did not treat the children with great delicacy either. A photograph of a smiling Norman and Muriel walking home from school that day was printed in the newspapers. Oblivious to the tragedy, the children must have wondered why a photographer had appeared in their path to capture their carefree faces. The caption under their picture in the *Daily Telegraph* reads, 'Norman and Muriel Evans being fetched from school by a relative when the news reached Mrs Evans.'[9] When they got home their mother explained. Newspaper accounts of their reaction were written by journalists after they had again interviewed Lois and her father. Norman was reported as saying 'I shall see him in heaven' and 'I must work hard for you now mamma'. Muriel, according to the newspaper report, had always said the same prayer: 'Please God take care of my daddy and send him safely home.' When she asked her mother what she should say now, Lois could say nothing as tears rolled down her face.[10]

Press scrutiny continued for several days, with journalists visiting the cottage for updates. The *Daily Telegraph* appeared again at the door on 13 February to see how Lois was and to present her with five pounds from a fund set up by the newspaper. Another correspondent came the next day with a further fifteen pounds and left with more details of the family's grief for his readers.[11] Lois had to deal with public interest from the moment that she heard of Edgar's death, and despite these appalling circumstances she held herself admirably. One reporter wrote that he found her to be 'quite a superior and refined little woman'.[12] This patronising comment says much about his preconceptions of a working-class family in rural Wales, but it also demonstrates just how remarkable this young woman from Gower was when thrust into the spotlight in the most brutal of personal circumstances. Lois spoke proudly and with great loyalty about her Edgar: 'My husband was such a brave, strong man ... and he was kind and such a devoted father!'[13] It was a sentiment supported by her father when he was interviewed: 'He was a fine boy ... A good husband and a good son to his old mother.'[14]

The official notification of Edgar's death and an account of what had happened arrived in a letter to Lois from Atch dated 31 January:

> I have a very sad duty to perform in writing to you the news of your Husband's death on his return from the South Pole in February 1912. He had a very severe fall coming down the Beardmore Glacier and hurt his head. Captain Scott and his companions stuck by him but he got much worse and died on the 7th [*sic*] February and was buried there, at the foot of the Glacier by them. Your husband on many occasions has shewn me very great kindness, and in any way I can repay it, it would give me very great pleasure ... his diary from the South Pole will be sent to you ...[15]

Atch's letter gave Lois the information that she craved about how her husband had died. She knew now too that he did not die alone and that his great friend Scott had been with him. There was no last letter for Lois as there would be for Kathleen and Oriana, as Edgar had not expected to die. But there would be his diary, and this would be of some comfort. Atch had written that Edgar died 'in a very great undertaking, and one that was a very honourable one'. Lois could take solace in her husband's bravery and that he had died doing his duty, because duty was important to Edgar, so much so that he had hoped Norman would follow him into the Navy to serve king and country.[16]

The importance of Edgar's sacrifice was a sentiment that ran through the numerous condolence letters and telegrams that arrived from the great and the good; the sort of people that Lois would never have dreamed of meeting, let alone corresponding with. Lord Charles Beresford, retired admiral and serving Member of Parliament for Portsmouth, wrote that Edgar's name would be 'honoured for all time by the Navy, by his country, and by the whole of the civilized world'. Scott's sister Ettie, Lady Macartney, wrote that Edgar died doing his duty: 'For you, his dear wife, and his three children, his loss is hard to bear but I trust that your future will be smoothed for you by the country he served so well ... I hope your three children will grow up to comfort and support you.'[17] Agnes Weston wrote from Portsmouth too, remembering the woman who had been a part of her Sailors' Rest family.[18] She wrote often to women who had lost their husbands at sea, and it was quite fitting that she should write to Lois now in her loss. There were so many letters that Lois was not able to write to everyone personally. She was quoted in the newspapers as thanking everyone for their messages of sympathy at this very sad time, it being impossible to reply to each individual letter.[19]

Teddy Evans wrote too:

> I am writing to sympathise with you on your terrible bereavement. Your husband died a gallant death on the return march from the Pole after faithfully serving his leader, Capt. Scott, through a most trying time. He lost his life for the honour of his country, and the British Navy will be proud of having possessed such a brave man. His 'grit' will for ever be an example to the lower deck, his ability was remarkable and I wish to convey to you from the whole expedition our sorrow. I also write to tell you of the admiration we felt for your dead husband. I shall soon be in England, and I will see that you and yours will never want... I cannot tell you how sorry I am for you.[20]

This letter is important because of the poor relationship that had always existed between Teddy and Edgar. Their bad blood had begun in Cardiff when Edgar had criticised the skis and Scott, listening to his opinion, put him in charge of equipment instead of Teddy.[21] Relations had worsened in New Zealand when Edgar had got drunk and been fired from the expedition, a misdemeanour that Teddy was never quite able to forgive.[22] But it seems that all was forgotten in the wake of the South Pole tragedy. Teddy had only arrived home on 22 April, but, true to his word, on 4 May he travelled to Swansea from Cardiff to see Lois, meeting with her at her sister Beatrice's house.[23] While they talked about Edgar, he can't have failed to notice how very much four-and-a-half-year-old Ralph looked like his father. Teddy had brought with him Edgar's personal effects and his diary, closed with a government seal so that only Lois could read it. He thought it appropriate that he, as one of the last surviving men to see Edgar alive, should deliver it. Teddy's parents had written to Lois in February, 'We trust that you, your children and your husband's mother will in time recover from the effects of the terrible misfortune which has fallen upon you.'[24] They acknowledged that it could so easily have been their Evans that had been lost instead of hers. Perhaps this was a reason that Teddy let go of his negative feelings about Edgar. It could so easily have been him buried alone at the foot of the glacier.

Teddy was also a man coming to terms with his own shattering loss. After leaving New Zealand to sail home to England, his wife Hilda had been taken ill as the ship taking them home via the Mediterranean sailed along the Italian coast. The ship's doctor and a passenger who was a medical specialist diagnosed peritonitis and a surgical operation was performed on board. Hilda seemed well at first but only four days later, at about midnight on 18 April, as the ship was sailing away from Naples, she died. She was only twenty-nine years old. After burying his wife in Toulon, Teddy had to continue the journey alone.[25] In a poignant tribute, he added her maiden name of Russell to his surname, thereafter calling himself Edward Ratcliffe Garth Russell Evans. Having lost the wife he adored suddenly just two weeks before, Teddy now found himself sitting with Lois and sharing her terrible, unexpected grief. Before he left, he assured her that he would make sure that she didn't want for anything. Afterwards he described her as 'the brave widow of a brave man'.[26]

I Regret Nothing But His Suffering

Kathleen had set out from England to meet Con in January 1913 and travelled via the United States. She had dined and partied in New York and then headed by train via New Orleans to El Paso where she climbed mountains, rode with cowboys, slept under the stars and cooked at a campfire.[1] After an exhilarating adventure she boarded the *Aorangi* at San Francisco on 5 February for the voyage to Wellington, New Zealand, and a glorious reunion with Con. She was now somewhere on the ocean, and although attempts had been made to contact her, the wireless signals were just not strong enough to reach the ship and wouldn't be until she was closer to land. Kathleen's family in England knew of Con's death, of course, and had been overwhelmed with nearly 400 letters of condolence.[2] Her brother Rosslyn told the newspapers that the terrible duty of telling their sister now fell to their brother Wilfred, who was waiting for her in New Zealand: 'I cannot picture any more pathetic figure than that poor little lady going out there, expecting all the triumph and delight of getting her husband back, and knowing as she does, how keenly interested is the whole world in the expedition.'[3] As it turned out, Wilfred was spared.

On 19 February, Captain Stevens approached Kathleen after breakfast, asking her to come to his cabin. She had no idea why, but she saw that his hands were trembling. He said that he had some news, and he didn't know how to tell her. She knew then that it must be about the expedition. He showed her the message that had been cabled. She recorded in her diary that in her shock she had responded, 'Oh well, never mind I expected that. Thanks very much. I will go and think about it.' Kathleen needed time to come to terms with the devastating news and so asked that the other passengers not be told so that everything could appear normal. She went to her usual Spanish lesson and then to lunch and then read a book about the *Titanic*, determined to be able to control herself before the news came out and she had to face people. For the rest of the day, she lay on the deck and thought about Con.

The remaining eight days of the voyage were agony. It was hard to keep the tragedy a secret and privacy became hard to find as passengers gradually found out. Kind condolence messages from home came through all night, but they blocked the line and stopped any further news reaching the ship. Kathleen sat in the wireless room each night receiving the messages into the early hours, but no more detail came about what had happened to Con. Afterwards she slept or lay awake on the deck for the rest of the night, her mind wracked by the agony of not knowing. She worried that he might have been tortured by thoughts of leaving the job undone, about the deaths of his friends and of leaving her and Peter. She agonised about his pain and hoped he'd died quickly in the cold but couldn't get the awful, haunting picture out of her head. It was a few days before she learned the terrible truth that Con had starved to death.[4]

Each night, as she lay on the deck, a young third officer stood nearby, discreetly watching and bringing her messages. Later Kathleen realised that he'd been posted there to watch over her in case she jumped overboard in her grief. Little did the crew know that she would never have done that. Kathleen didn't believe in life after death. She would never see Con again, and she knew that she had to go on without him. Determined not to be self-pitying, she believed that in time her pride in Con and her joy in their son would overcome this terrible crushing grief: 'Had he died before I had known his gloriousness, or before he had been the father of my son, I might have felt a loss. Now I have felt none for myself.'[5] Kathleen wanted to be brave and stoic in public and express her grief the way that she believed Con would want her to:

> I think he has made me twice the man I was. Certainly, I couldn't have faced this with complete self-control but for his teaching. Ever since I knew him I have worked, striven and strained that he might applaud ever so little ... He has been my motive-power all this while. I feel as though even now it will not give out. I wonder. He's raised my standard anyhow, shown me what men can be, and what he expects me to be. Can I keep to it without the hope of his applause?[6]

When Con's final message to the world was wired to the ship, Kathleen's broken heart was eased a little and her pride swelled. 'That was a glorious, courageous note, and a great inspiration to me,' she wrote. 'If he in his weakness could face it with such sublime fortitude, how dare I possibly whine. I will *not*. I regret nothing but his suffering.'[7] The letter that she wrote later to Hannah Scott is the perfect expression of her determination to be happy, proud and grateful. Addressed to 'Dearest Mother of Con', in it she told her mother-in-law that although the light has gone out of their world,

> ... and tho the price is heavy I feel it was worth it. For myself I regret nothing save only the racking anxiety he suffered in his thoughts of unfulfilled obligations. He didn't see that he had far overpaid all obligation in giving us something that we can look to with pride and enthusiasm for ever. The last month of his diary is one of the most inspiring things I ever read and I wonder if anything he could have done in life would give my Peter a greater start in life than that heroic story ... There is no whimper no complaint through it all. A fine standard he sets us. I never dreamt there could be so noble a spirit.[8]

For the rest of the voyage, with all eyes on her and little privacy to be found, Kathleen retained her composure. With great self-control she endured the journey, and this bravery became the model for the public face of her grief. In private, of course, there were tears. She wrote later that the sight of Con's handkerchief had made her weep for the first time.[9] As she disembarked at Wellington on 27 February, she knew that her brother Wilfred would be waiting for her. He'd cabled her on board, and she must have been thankful for his comfort and support. Atch was there too with Con's diary and last letters, and Kathleen spent that night reading her husband's words. His final letter to her was addressed 'To my widow':

> Dearest Darling – we are in a very tight corner and I have doubts of pulling through – In our short lunch hours I take advantage of a very small measure of warmth to write letters preparatory to a possible end – The first is naturally to you on whom my thoughts mostly dwell waking or sleeping – if anything happens to me I shall like you to know how much you have meant to me and that pleasant recollections are with me as I depart ... I shall not have suffered any pain ... Therefore you must not imagine a great tragedy ...
>
> We have gone down hill a good deal since I wrote the above ... Well dear heart I want you to take the whole thing very sensibly as I am sure you will – the boy will be your comfort I had looked forward to helping you to bring him up but it is a satisfaction to feel that he is safe with you. I think both he and you ought to be specially looked after by the country for which after all we have given our lives with something of spirit which

makes for example ... I must write a little letter for the boy if time can be found to be read when he grows up ...

Dearest you know [I] cherish no sentimental rubbish about remarriage – when the right man comes to help you in life you ought to be your happy self again – I wasn't a very good husband but I hope I shall be a good memory certainly the end is nothing for you to be ashamed of and I like to think that the boy will have a good start in parentage of which he may be proud.

Dear it is not easy to write because of the cold ... you know I have loved you, you know my thoughts must have constantly dwelt on you and oh dear me you must know that quite the worst aspect of this situation is the thought that I shall not see you again ...

Since writing the above we have got to within 11 miles of our depot ... there is a painless end so don't worry ... make the boy interested in natural history if you can, it is better than games – they encourage it at some schools – I know you will keep him out in the open air ... Oh my dear my dear what dreams I have had of his future and yet oh my girl I know you will face it stoically.

... what tales you would have for the boy but oh what a price to pay – to forfeit the sight of your dear face – Dear you will be good to the old mother. I write her a little line in this book. Also keep in with Ettie and the others – oh but you'll put on a strong face for the world – only don't be too proud to accept help for the boy's sake – he ought to have a fine career and do something in the world. I haven't time to write to Sir Clements – tell him I thought much of him and never regretted him putting me in command of the *Discovery*. – Give messages of farewell to Lady Baxter and Lady [Sandhurst] keep friends with them for both are dear women & to also both the Reginald Smiths.[10]

The next day Kathleen was able to hear from Atch the details of finding Con. She was pleased it had been him as he was quiet, tactful and respectful, but she still agonised over the details and wanted to know so much more. She spent the rest of that day with Ory. They had messaged each other while Kathleen was still at sea and Ory had been there to meet her off the boat. These two women, who had never liked each other, put aside their feelings to support each other at this time of profound emotional crisis. They had both seen their husbands' diaries and letters and could talk together about what had happened. Perhaps they shared the contents or perhaps they didn't, feeling possibly that these last messages were too personal and their bond too temporary and fragile. But they were valued hours, spent together at a time when nobody else, save Lois, could understand how they felt. Kathleen wrote later in her diary, 'She was sweet and gentle. I am glad we could be nice to each other; it is comforting for us both I think. She of course has had more than a fortnight to get used to it, I only a few hours, but we were both very sensible, I think.'[11]

Later, just a day after arriving in New Zealand, Kathleen left for Sydney where she would board *Medina* on 5 March for the long voyage back to England. Her brother Wilfred was by her side.[12] She and Ory were now public figures and so they had issued a joint statement before she left:

> Before leaving this country we would like to express our very real gratitude to the Government and people of New Zealand for their sympathy and thoughtful help to us. The forethought for our welfare has touched us very deeply, and will not be readily forgotten.
>
> Kathleen Scott,
> Oriana Wilson.[13]

On the final leg of her journey, Kathleen crossed the channel from Calais, lying on the deck, covered by a blanket, watching a monoplane fly out from the French port and another flying over Dover harbour. Her dear friend Lewis Beaumont was there to meet her when the ship arrived, and she slipped home quietly by train for a reunion in London with Peter.[14] Kathleen was now Lady Scott, having been granted the honour by the king in recognition that her husband would have been knighted if he'd lived.[15] She would rather have remained plain Mrs Scott and sailed home with Con.

By April, the three widows were all back home. Ory and her sister Connie had boarded SS *Remuera* at Wellington on 7 March 1913.[16] She had been very brave and joined in with ship life, being as jolly as she could. Connie recorded how beautiful she looked but how poignant it was to see her dressed in black instead of her usual blue. Atch had been on board too, tasked with escorting the two women safely home. Always kind and solicitous, he found a little diving petrel that had been blown on board and took the bird to Ory to hold.[17] When she arrived in England, she returned to Westal to mourn privately with Ted's family. Kathleen, Lois and Ory were experiencing something unique; they were grieving for a private life lost, but in the public eye. They were mourning men they loved but who had been appropriated by the nation and the world as heroes. It might be expected that they would cling to each other, to console and support one another, but these were women of very different characters and backgrounds. All that they really had in common was the Antarctic tragedy.

Very few letters to Lois survive in any public archives, and none that were written by her, so it's uncertain what contact Kathleen and Ory had with her after they heard of their husbands' deaths. However, Kathleen and Ory did meet in New Zealand and Oriana did write to many of the crew after the tragedy. Kathleen had also been in contact with Lois during the expedition at Con's request. It seems impossible, then, that there was no contact between the three women at this point, although frustratingly no evidence of it survives. Any meeting or correspondence may have been complicated by their feelings about each other's husbands because, beneath the public façade, each of the widows must have battled privately with the conflicting emotions of their grief. What if their men could have found another challenge, a different way of proving themselves? What if they were the cause? Had it all been to prove themselves to their wives? Kathleen had told Con not to let her and Peter stand in his way. Ory had acquiesced twice to Ted's desire to go, and he was happy to assume that it was what she wanted too. Lois had made a marriage bargain with Edgar, promising that he could go back if the chance came again, but after the birth of three children did she wish she'd protested more? Did any of them in hindsight regret that they'd been so supportive?

They had known that there were risks, but they also knew that they had married men with restless ambition and a determination to return to the Pole. But did they feel anger that the love and home they offered could never be enough? Did they resent the pull that Antarctica had over their men, an attraction so great that they would risk their lives for it? They had each spoken to survivors and had received numerous letters which allowed them to start to piece together what had happened, and they must have dwelt on the fear and suffering of that final journey. They had seen that awful photo of them taken at the pole with their haunted eyes and Scott's look of agony.[18] Now, alone with the precious diaries that had been returned to them, each could read about events in their husbands' own words. Edgar had not been able to write to Lois at the end, but she was secure in his love for his family, so clearly expressed in his loving and optimistic letter written just miles from the Pole. Kathleen and Ory had received the heartbreaking last words of Con and Ted and knew that they were in their thoughts in their dying moments.

This must have brought both solace and desperate regret. Did they begin to cast blame? Did Ory and Kathleen feel that Edgar's illness had slowed the party down? Was Kathleen resentful that Scott had continued to slog along with the burden of Ted's precious geological finds when he could have moved faster without? Did Ory think that Ted and Bowers might have made it if they had left Scott and made a dash for safety through the storm? In those first few weeks and months the widows must surely have tortured themselves with what-ifs, struggling to understand how the five men who had set out with such high hopes of making history could now be lying dead, frozen into the landscape that they'd failed to conquer.

Whatever their private struggles may have been, the widows eventually focussed their thoughts on a vision of their lost husbands which gave them the strength to carry on alone. These coalesced from the flotsam of their lost lives onto which the three women had clung to keep themselves afloat in their grief. For Ory, it was all God's plan and Ted had died for scientific discovery. For Kathleen, Con was a hero. For Lois, Edgar had died bravely serving his country. All three would find these consoling views tested over the coming years.

Our King upon His Knees

The popular press had arrived in Britain with the launch of the *Pall Mall Gazette* in the 1880s, followed by the *London Evening News* and the *Daily Mail* in the 1890s, heralding an era of cheap newspapers, bringing interest and excitement to a wide readership. When the news of the Antarctic tragedy broke, the public reaction was extraordinary and the press's demand for coverage seemed insatiable. Column inches were filled day after day with the story of the heroic sacrifice made by Scott and his men and details about their bereaved families. Fuelling and feeding it was an enormous and engulfing wave of public grief but also national pride. The media whipped these shared feelings of shock, loss and admiration into a reporting frenzy that ensured the story of 'Scott of the Antarctic' became known very quickly to everyone in the country and many across the world. The *Evening News* had reported on 12 February that 'people think of nothing else, talk of nothing else, read nothing else'. A special edition of the *Daily Mirror* on 21 May was the first to publish the photos that the explorers had taken at the Pole, and it was the bestselling edition that year – indeed, the bestselling edition of any daily newspaper published before the First World War.[1]

The newspaper coverage and the outpouring of public grief exceeded even that of the *Titanic* disaster the year before.[2] That tragedy had gripped the nation with its tales of men giving up their lifeboat spaces for women and children, of a captain who went down with his ship and of mankind's terrifying struggle with nature. Newspapers talked of self-sacrifice and of the heroism that Britons exhibited in the face of unsurmountable odds. Glorifying the deaths of innocent passengers, however, was problematic in a way that the story of 'Scott of the Antarctic' wasn't. The polar story had all the elements that the *Titanic* story had and more because explorers were meant to suffer.[3]

Almost immediately, Scott and the Polar Party were held up as the absolute embodiment of the Edwardian hero. This ideal was inextricably linked with the British Empire and the uncomfortable truth that it was created through conquest at the hands of superior military might. Much more preferable was the idea that it was founded on the principles of liberty and commerce, benefitting the colonised as much as the colonisers. So as British men began to fight and conquer in far-flung parts of the world, their exploits were described in terms of discovery – scientific, geographical and cultural – and not as a land grab. This rhetoric was extended to the explorations of Antarctica. Expeditions were not about conquering, gaining land and being first, they were about gaining knowledge. Thus the definition of a hero evolved into something peculiarly Edwardian. Men were revered when they died in pursuit of the higher imperial ideal of knowledge and the improvement of the world for everyone. Failure was a key part of this. It was much easier to demonstrate that the heroes of empire were benevolent rather than tyrannical if they failed. Heroic failure became the new heroism, and it was determined not by acts but by character. Its key components were fair play, sportsmanship and magnanimity. Heroes had to strive willingly for a noble goal and then, after failing to reach it due to unsurmountable obstacles, demonstrate physical and mental courage in the face of defeat by sacrificing themselves. Scott, Wilson, Evans, Oates and Bowers displayed these qualities in abundance during their final journey.[4]

When the official expedition report was wired to London, giving an account of the fate of the Polar Party drawn from their own records, it was accompanied by two extracts from Scott's diary: a description of the death of Oates, which included his last words, 'I am just going outside and may be some time', and Scott's 'Message to the Public'. Chosen by his colleagues and typed up by Cherry while they were still at Cape Evans, they formed the basis of what was printed by the press.[5]

Scott's conclusion to his 'Message to the Public' in particular was the perfect expression of the Edwardian notion of heroism, and it was to form the bedrock of his legend:[6]

> We are weak, writing is difficult, but for my own sake I do not regret this journey, which has shown that Englishmen can endure hardships, help one another, and meet death with as great a fortitude as ever in the past. We took risks, we knew we took them; things have come out against us, and therefore we have no cause for complaint, but bow to the will of Providence, determined still to do our best to the last ... Had we lived, I should have had a tale to tell of the hardihood, endurance and courage of my companions which would have stirred the heart of every Englishman. These rough notes and our dead bodies must tell the tale...[7]

These words represented everything that made people proud to be British and described perfectly the nation's character; playing the game was more important than winning it.[8] Rudyard Kipling's poem 'If–' encapsulates this British heroic ideal, and the chaplain who led the memorial service for Scott at the Royal Navy College at Dartmouth quoted it, saying that victory stems from the point when somebody says you have failed. The hundreds of condolence letters sent after the news broke focused on these virtues; praising Scott and his men for their endurance, fortitude, suffering and self-sacrifice.[9]

The insatiable public interest in Scott and his men was generated not simply by the fact that they were seen as heroes of empire, but also perhaps because it was a time when heroes were needed more than ever. The flag-waving imperialism of the time hid the country's less confident face because these years before the First World War were not a golden age of long hot summers, garden parties and tranquillity. Edwardian England had its fair share of anxiety. There was an enormous gulf between rich and poor, and while those with money could be seen to flaunt it in ostentatious displays of extravagant dinners, elaborate clothing, fast cars and aeroplanes, those who were struggling could do nothing but watch. The rise of the Labour Party and the belligerence of the trade unions showed that a large part of the population wanted real change, and this frightened the more conservative members of the governing classes who thought too much change would encourage an uprising of the working class.[10]

New technology was bringing bewildering developments, the urbanisation of the country was generating social problems and there was a very real possibility of civil war in Ireland. Meanwhile, Suffragettes were causing widespread terror and destruction and 1913 became one of the most violent years in their history. Mills, railway stations, postboxes, post offices, golf courses, MPs' homes, racecourses and churches were targeted by arson attacks and bombs. In May there were fifty-two attacks including twenty-nine bombs and fifteen arson attempts.[11] On the day that Suffragettes blew a hole through the second floor of the Royal Observatory in Edinburgh, a bomb was found on a London bus packed into a cocoa tin with a 6-inch string fuse.[12] Two weeks earlier, a bomb had been planted in St Paul's Cathedral; a ticking parcel wrapped in brown paper was found on the dais of the Bishop's Throne. Underneath the paper was half a pound of gunpowder inside a one-pound mustard tin wrapped in a sheet from the Suffragette newspaper. No warning of attacks was given, and many public places were forced to close for fear of attack, including some rooms at Hampton Court, Kensington Palace, Windsor Castle, the Victoria &

Albert Museum, the National and Tate Galleries and the Jewel House at the Tower of London.[13]

This shake-up of the traditional structures of society was matched by a fear that Britain's role on the international stage was diminishing. Germany's navy was getting stronger just as Britain's military might appeared to be dwindling.[14] In the South African Wars the British Army had encountered fierce opposition from farmers who fought unexpectedly well to protect their land. Their tactics were much better than anticipated and their knowledge of the landscape and excellent horsemanship meant that they would not surrender. British policy changed to one of scorched earth, and they burned farms, killed livestock and imprisoned the farmers and their families. In 1900, there were approximately one hundred concentration camps where at least 100,000 men, women and children were kept in appalling conditions behind barbed wire. When the stories of famine, disease and polluted water reached home, it damaged the empire's reputation and undermined the view of the British Army. It may have succeeded in South Africa, but it had done so by callous and brutal tactics, not military skill. The empire had made people in Britain feel safe; if it could no longer be relied upon, then what could be? The tragedy of Scott, Wilson, Evans, Bowers and Oates was seized upon by the public as proof that there were still heroes of empire, meaning Britain could still rule the waves.

Without bodies to bury, there would be no funerals to focus the nation's grief; instead there would be memorial services. The widows and mothers had been in complete agreement about what should happen to their loved ones. There were suggestions that the bodies might be brought home, and men from the *Discovery* expedition among others had volunteered for the task.[15] But Oriana was categorical in her view: 'I need hardly say that on no account would I wish my Husband's body to be touched. I feel that it could not have a more fitting resting place – and I know Lady Scott feels the same about Captain Scott's and also Mrs Bowers about her son's body.'[16] Hannah Scott supported this view about leaving her son's body where it lay, opining that 'any other thought seems desecration'.[17] 'Desecration' may seem a strong word to use, but almost at once the dead became not only heroes but also took on a saintly quality because they had sacrificed themselves for their country.

On 14 February 1913, a service was held in London at St Paul's Cathedral to commemorate Robert Falcon Scott, Lawrence Edward Grace Oates, Edward Adrian Wilson, Henry Robertson Bowers and Edgar Evans. Only a year before, a service had been held in the same place to remember the victims of the *Titanic* disaster. As the nation mourned it was important that everyone had a chance to grieve, and so only two hundred seats in the cathedral were reserved, the rest being offered on a first-come-first-served basis. By nine o'clock in the morning a huge throng of people had gathered in St Paul's churchyard. They surged up the steps, making for the varioius entrances to the cathedral. By ten o'clock there was no more room inside and a 'church full' sign was erected. Thousands were turned away from the cathedral, which just could not accommodate all of those who wanted to pay their respects.[18] They crowded into the churchyard and surrounding streets, which were closed off and their traffic diverted. Souvenir sellers plied their wares which included hastily manufactured 'in memoriam' items.[19] At the same time, schoolchildren all over the country were sitting spellbound. A version of Captain Scott's story written specially for children by a London journalist, Arthur Machen, was read aloud in every school.

It was extremely unusal for a king to attend a memorial to anyone who was not royal, but King George V came to the service, signifying that this was a nation's loss. This extraordinary precedent did not go unnoticed:

> Can you see the Dome of the Golden Cross
> And our King upon his knees?[20]

There was no state entry; the king simply walked down the nave to his seat under the cathedral's great dome while the Coldstream Guards played. Their scarlet coats were one of the few splashes of colour among the largely black-clad mourners. The ministers of state took their seats on either side of the king, among them the Prime Minister and the Leader of the Opposition.[21] Winston Churchill, the First Lord of the Admiralty, was represented by his wife Clementine. Envoys from grieving nations across the world sat in the choir, including members of colonial governments and ambassadors from Russia, Germany, Italy, Austria and Japan.[22] Kathleen and Oriana were out of the country and so they were represented by close family members and friends. This group of stricken relatives took their place in the choir with the president and members of the Royal Geographical Society.[23] Scott's mother, Hannah, and his sister and aunts were there as well as Ted's sister Polly. Caroline Oates came to mourn her son and was joined by his sister and cousins. Birdie Bowers was represented by his sister.[24]

There is no mention in press reports of Lois or of any of Edgar's family being part of this group. It is possible that some of them were there but simply not noticed by the press, but surely this would not have been the case for Lois. Had she attended, the only one of the three widows to have done so, the attention would have been overwhelming. Perhaps she was too grief-stricken to put herself in public view so soon after hearing the news of Edgar's death. She'd certainly had more than her fair share of press attention. Perhaps the journey was too much for her with three young children, or maybe it was just too expensive. Instead, Lois grieved at home surrounded by her family and friends. A memorial service was held in the small parish church of St Mary's in Rhossili on the evening of 16 February, the first Sunday after news of the tragedy broke. It was here, where she had married Edgar eight years before and where their sons had been baptised, that Lois prayed for her lost husband. There were services at churches elsewhere in Gower too and in Swansea.[25] In Cardiff, huge crowds gathered to watch a procession from Cardiff City Hall to a service at St John's Church. Numbers were so large that many couldn't get into the church.

Similar memorial services were held in churches all over the world that day. The most poignant were in those locations where the dead men had been known and loved. The Sailors' Rest in Portsmouth held theirs in the vast hall where Lois had attended wives' meetings and events, and it was crowded to excess. The memorial address, delivered by John Harris, was entitled 'Greater love hath no man than this that a man lay down his life for his friends'.[26] The Dockyard at Devonport remembered Scott, who had been born in the town. Ted's former college at Cambridge, Gonville & Caius, commemorated him, as did St Matthew's Church in his home town of Cheltenham. Cheltenham College deferred their memorial service to the first anniversary of his death at the request of his parents, who had not attended the church service. Many of the servants from Westal had done so but Dr and Mrs Wilson declined, 'owing to the strain endured by them during the past few days'.[27]

The Polar Party were now more famous than they might have been if they'd lived, and their deaths made celebrities of their wives. The press had put the dependent widows, mothers and children at the heart of their narrative, but Kathleen and her son Peter were firmly set on centre stage. The young, golden-haired only child of Scott became 'the orphan of the nation' and Kathleen, the only one of the widows to truly become famous in her own right, became an icon for both feminists and non-feminists. She may have smarted at Christabel Pankhurst's assertion that all militant women could recognise in the courage of the Polar Party the courage of the Suffragettes who were prepared to sacrifice themselves for an ideal too. But Kathleen may have grudgingly appreciated Pankhurst's sympathy with the lot of the polar wife, sharing as she did all the hopes and anxieties of the expedition and requiring the greater strength to stay behind. More conservative women, and those who were anti-suffragist, praised the manliness of Scott and his colleagues while lauding Kathleen as a devoted wife and mother and a model of courage. Both points of view cast her publicly in the role of the patient wife and brave widow. Other aspects of Kathleen's life, such as her sculpting career, were quickly obscured.[28]

For God's Sake Look after Our People

Kathleen had been thrust into the limelight with almost no time to process her grief. When she arrived back in London on 11 April 1913, she continued to be a focus of attention. Her approach to unwanted pressure and scrutiny had always been to work hard and play hard, to then struggle from the effort of self-control and finally to escape on a vagabonding journey somewhere. Little surprise, then, that she resumed her life of socialising and keeping busy with work to distract herself from thoughts of Con. He had written to J. M. Barrie as he lay dying asking him to look after Kathleen and Peter, and now his old friend proved to be especially good with his little boy, taking him to see *Peter Pan* and playing with him.[1]

Barrie was, unusually for Kathleen, a man who was a friend for her son and not an admirer for her. They liked each other and comforted each other in their grief, but such was her celebrity that their relationship eventually attracted rumours. She was a romantic figure, the widow of a hero, and as such the press and the public became fascinated by the thought that she might marry again. A letter from the news editor of the *Daily Chronicle* in May the following year enquired whether she had married Barrie and if she'd like to make a comment. Another rumour spread that she'd married Teddy Evans, and as the stories of Kathleen's potential bridegrooms were picked up by the newspapers in the United States, Australia and New Zealand, Teddy would be forced to issue a firm denial.[2]

Perhaps the widow best equipped to carry on alone, Kathleen had enjoyed an independent life before Con and had work and friends to fall back on now. Her return had been heralded by a great deal of publicity and succeeded by a great deal of expedition business and stress. Con's will was granted probate on 13 May, leaving everything to Kathleen, who was also his estate's executor.[3] She now owned all that he had relating to the *Terra Nova* expedition and was empowered to make decisions about it. But she also inherited Con's responsibility for his mother, taking on the management of his estate to support Hannah as he had requested in his will.

In contrast, Oriana found herself with considerably less independence. Since her marriage she had not worked, and they had never owned their own home. In his will Ted had arranged for a trust fund to be created which would support Ory, but it was to be administered on her behalf by his brother Bernard and her brother Noel. He gave Bernard and Noel complete control over the investment of the trust in public stocks, funds or government securities in Britain, India or the colonies.[4] Ory would come to resent being dependent on Ted's brother for money.[5] However, her in-laws did give her refuge at Westal when she returned home and they began making plans for the creation of a separate flat for her there.[6] They were kind and supportive, and reluctant to take any financial help from her, but she knew that Edward and Agnes Wilson were rather impoverished by the standards of their class and had relied on the money that Ted used to give them when he and Ory lived there. A very real possibility existed that Ted's beloved Westal might have to be sold.

Although the detail of the widows' financial circumstances was private, their husbandless plight was championed by the press, which led the campaign to fulfil Scott's dying wish to 'For God's sake look after our people'. It had called for action almost immediately, but the official response had been chaotic. Asquith had addressed Parliament the day after news of the tragedy broke, saying that Scott's last words to the nation were 'one of the most moving and pathetic utterances in the annals of discovery' and that his appeal 'will not fall on deaf ears'.[7] But nobody took the lead in responding to Scott's request at first, and journalists were turning up at the headquarters of the Royal Geographical Society enquiring what they were going to do to help the families. Keltie, the society's secretary, wrote to its president, Lord Curzon, saying, 'Of course Mrs Scott ought to be provided for and her boy and Scott's own mother I believe was dependent on him to a considerable extent.' But his recommendation was indecisive: 'If we or the Mayor make an appeal now or the two combined then the Press will support and we'll raise a good sum.'[8]

By 13 February the chaotic situation had resulted in a plethora of funds having been set up for the bereaved. The British Antarctic Expedition committee, the Lord Mayor of London at London's Mansion House, the *Daily Chronicle* and the *Daily Telegraph* were all raising money in addition to numerous local councils, churches and newspapers. These funds were asking for money not solely for the bereaved but also to pay off the expedition's debts, to publish its scientific findings and to erect statues to the dead. Despite the outpouring of national grief, the public response was muted. It wasn't until the *Daily Express* intervened to detail how the situation had been mishandled, and Scott and Kathleen's friend J. M. Barrie wrote an open letter to the *Daily News and Leader* asking 'How Much Are You Sorry?', that the official response to the tragedy came.[9] The funds were pulled together into a single Mansion House Scott memorial fund, administered by the Lord Mayor's private secretary. The Lord Mayor had written to Lord Curzon proposing this solution on 17 February: 'It is to my mind quite obvious that there should be eventually one committee to deal with all the Funds, and I will make a fitting opportunity of communicating with the editors of the *Daily Telegraph* and the *Daily Chronicle*...' This reorganisation inspired confidence, as did a donation from the king, and money poured in from all over the world. *The Times* reported on 19 February that the widows and orphans of Scott's expedition were the wards not only of England but of the empire.

When the fund was closed in June, it had raised £75,000, a vast sum equivalent to £9.2 million today.[10] Before the money was distributed, Kathleen wrote to Lord Curzon from her home in Buckingham Palace Road to say that she had been hearing all sorts of rumours about the money being spent elsewhere and thought she ought to let him know. She urged him to make sure that the share given to the families was not too small: 'I think there would be a great outcry from the public if only £12,000 (one-fifth of the sum subscribed in response to my husband's message) be devoted to the object he wrote about.'[11] Asquith, Kathleen's great friend, must have had her very much in mind when he had promised that the bereaved should be left in the same financial situation as if the disaster had not happened and so to the sum from the fund were added, where applicable, government and Admiralty pensions, salary from the British Antarctic Expedition and projected income from publishing articles and journals. These were generous sums, but they were not means tested or distributed according to need. They were distributed in line with the very strict naval and social hierarchies of the Edwardian world.

Kathleen and her mother-in-law had been the main focus of the correspondence about who should benefit from the fund, perhaps not surprisingly as Scott was the expedition's leader, had incurred debt by funding it and because he and Kathleen were known to so many of the committee and had influential friends. On her return to England, Kathleen had delivered Con's final letters to Lewis Beaumont and Vice Admirals Bridgeman and Egerton, in which each man was implored by his late friend to petition the Admiralty on his family's behalf. Oriana was mentioned in correspondence too, principally because of the high regard in which Ted was held, as the Lord Mayor of London wrote to Lord Curzon, 'Had Wilson himself survived he would certainly have deserved some special recognition. Next to Scott he was regarded as the most important member of the expedition.'[12] Sir Clements Markham shared these sentiments:

> The most important matter is the provision for Scott's mother. She has no means at all, and was supported by her son, and daughter. He was certainly thinking of her when he wrote his last words. Next comes Mrs Wilson. I think that she ought to have the pension of a Fleet Surgeon RN who fell in action ... the battle ought to be fought for Mrs Wilson to the last...[13]

In the end, £34,000 was shared between the dependent female relatives who comprised widows, mothers and sisters.[14] The rest of the funds raised would be used to pay the expedition's debts, to raise memorials and to publish the scientific findings. Of the widows, Kathleen received the most, and her son Peter was the only child to be given their own fund. Together they were awarded a lump sum of £2,676, pensions worth £325 per annum and income from a combined trust fund of £12,000. Kathleen's mother-in-law Hannah Scott also received £6,000 from the Mansion House fund for herself, her unmarried daughter Grace, and her widowed and penniless daughter Rose. There was also a government pension. Kathleen's worries about supporting Con's family would be greatly mitigated two years later when Hannah moved into a grace-and-favour apartment at Hampton Court Palace, granted to her by the king. She lived there, in apartment 44, until her death.[15] Kathleen was delighted with the small but well-appointed ground-floor rooms, which suited Hannah very well, and wrote to Keltie, 'You were right, her son would be very pleased at the luxurious comfort he has made for all of us that was always the thing that worried him most...'[16]

Ory was granted an annuity of £300, which was to be shared with her sister Connie, who was unmarried and whom she and Ted had supported.[17] She gratefully received all that was offered and was touched when later in the year Scott's diaries were published and Kathleen sent her a cheque for £125 in recognition of Ted's artistic contribution. Ory wrote to thank her, saying about the publication of the diaries, 'I feel quite ill with nervous excitement. I don't know what you can feel except a rejoicing that the world can now see a little more what a wonderful man your husband was – one can only feel full of gratitude for having known such men – and what a heritage for the beloved Peter.'[18] Ory would not, however, accept Kathleen's offer of a share of her income for the sculpting of polar memorials. Perhaps that kind gesture felt a little too much like charity. Ory suggested saving it for Peter's future and his education instead.[19]

There was no mention of Lois in the correspondence that had flown around Curzon in those first few months, even though Scott had mentioned her specifically in his letter to Barrie, saying that Edgar had left 'a widow in humble circumstances' who needed to be looked after.[20] He had been right that she might be the most desperately in need of financial support, and when a reporter from the *Western Mail* interviewed her the day after the newspapers published news of the tragedy, he found her to be very poor and worried about whether she would get a naval pension: 'Oh she cried... his loss means the loss of my all.' The reporter wrote that Lois was quite without means and that worries about their financial plight were shared by Edgar's mother:

> ... although he was much absent from us he was always a good son. He left his half-pay right up to the time he married. He would, shortly have been entitled to his pension. Not being an officer, his widow would, I suppose, be entitled to nothing now, but we must live in hope.[21]

Sarah's concern about her son's pension may have been heightened because to qualify he would have had to serve twenty-one years and Edgar had died on the cusp of that, but she needn't have worried. The Admiralty announced that the two naval men, Scott and Edgar, had died 'in action' and would receive naval pensions. Despite the press reporting incorrectly that this entitled them to improved pensions, Lois must have been relieved at this confirmation that she would have an income after all.[22] Money from the appeal to the public would not be available immediately, and so on 12 February Teddy Evans' brother G. E. Evans, who was acting secretary of the British Antarctic Expedition, had gone to Rhossili to give his condolences to Lois and to Edgar's mother. He gave them sufficient funds to cover their mourning expenses and to meet their immediate needs until money could be sent from the fund.[23] He reassured Lois that although Edgar had not been an officer she would be looked after. Evans was accompanied by a journalist from the *Western Mail* who reported Lois as saying, 'It has removed a great load from my mind ... as of course I have these three children to bring up, and our sole support has gone.'[24]

Despite these very public promises, life continued to be extremely difficult for Lois for several months. On 30 April, Lord Charles Beresford raised her situation in the House of Commons, telling the Prime Minister that Lois was only receiving 13*s* 6*d* a week from the Admiralty to support herself and her three children. He urged that steps be taken to distribute the money raised by the public as soon as possible. Asquith was rather dismissive of Lois's plight; his understanding was that the fund would be closed in a few days and the money speedily distributed, but in any case he felt Beresford's concern was based on 'very imperfect information'. Lois, he stated, had received £52 in accrued pay from the Navy and £55 from the Expedition Committee along with other funds, and that there was 'no reason to think that her case has not been and is not being adequately treated'.[25]

Asquith's confidence was misplaced. Only six days before, Lois had told a *Western Mail* reporter that she was subsisting on the Admiralty pension but that it wasn't enough to survive on independently. She still had to rely on her relatives for a home. No representative of any fund had contacted her and although Mr Asquith had promised her a grant, she had not received anything yet.[26] These were desperately worrying times for her, unsure if she'd receive any further money and unable to support herself or her children. She said that she had been told, presumably by G. E. Evans, that if she needed emergency funds she must contact the expedition committee.[27] Evans had given her money to tide her over, but when Norman needed help for his 'acute affliction of the eyes' Lois had no option but to call on the offer of help. Before the establishment of the National Health Service, medical treatment was expensive and beyond the means of many. The emergency grant from the committee made sure that Norman could receive expert help and treatment without delay.[28] But this was a hand-to-mouth existence, dependent on others for the security of her family.

When the funds were eventually paid out, it must have been a relief that Edgar's mother Sarah Evans was awarded a grant of her own. However, out of the three widows, Lois received the least. She was a working-class widow of a petty officer and so despite having three children to support, her status put her lower on the list for funds than both Kathleen and Ory. She was awarded a lump sum of £1,250 from the Memorial Fund as well as an Admiralty pension worth about £48 per year. These pensions included 2 shillings a week for each child from the Navy, ending when Ralph and Norman were fourteen and Muriel sixteen, and 3 shillings each from the government until they reached the age of eighteen. Lois turned down an offer from the London Orphanage Asylum to board and raise one of her children until they were fifteen. Despite her financial difficulties she wanted to keep her family together and wouldn't countenance giving up one of her children.[29]

The government pension that was awarded to Lois did come with a condition, however. To claim this money for her children, Lois had to prove every year that they were still alive.[30] She received considerably less than Kathleen and Ory and had her integrity challenged by having to prove that she wasn't claiming money fraudulently for children that were no longer living. Kathleen was never asked to do the same for Peter. Lois had been very brave to publicly criticise the government for the delay in helping her, and the funds and pensions that she received did take her off the poverty line, but she struggled financially for the rest of her life.[31] The divide between the treatment of the widows revealed itself in other ways too during this time. The press and the public began to think more deeply about what had happened in Antarctica, and as the events surrounding their husbands' deaths were discussed, not all the widows were consulted.

Heroic Failures

It didn't take long before the wave of national grief turned into a torrent of questions. Why had they died? How was it possible for such brave men to perish? Where should the blame lie? In his 'Message to the Public', Scott had outlined what he saw as the causes of the tragedy: extreme and unprecedented weather conditions, the health problems of Oates and Evans, and a seemingly unrelenting string of bad luck. Sir Clements Markham, who had been Scott's close friend and loyal supporter for over twenty-five years, and regarded him almost as a son, passionately supported this view in letters sent from Lisbon where he was spending the winter: 'All Scott's arrangements were, as they were sure to be, quite perfect. The risks and perils were known to be possible, and they were faced. They overwhelmed him.'[1]

Douglas Freshfield, the vice president of the Royal Geographical Society, also praised the noble qualities of Scott and his team and how they had gallantly taken on the harshness of the environment but been beaten by the weather. The society saw no reason to disagree with the account of the expedition leader, at least in public. Privately, though, some concerns were expressed. A flurry of letters between president Lord Curzon and secretary John Scott Keltie reveal their shock and grief at the tragedy and genuine concern for the bereaved but also a scramble to find more information and to protect the reputation of the society. Keltie wrote to Curzon on 11 February 1913 stating that there were one or two things in Scott's last message that perhaps they should look at, in particular the unexpected shortage of fuel in the depots on the way home, the relief party not being able to wait long enough to save them and the fact that nothing was done to find them until the following October.[2] The press had already picked up on these and other issues and debate had begun almost immediately in the newspapers, not only about what had gone wrong but also about the superiority of Amundsen's method.[3] Curzon proposed a private meeting of the society where returning members of the expedition could be questioned about what had happened, but not everyone agreed this was a good idea.

In death, male explorers empowered their female relatives. Widows, mothers and sisters could take control of the narrative and protect the legacy of their heroes. Kathleen now became a hugely influential voice in how the story of her husband's life would be told. She was well connected and strong enough not to be ignored. She owned everything that had come back from Antarctica, and she had Scott's diaries. The men in London and New Zealand may have been trying to agree a party line, but here was a woman who could, if she chose, blow their version apart. She had written to Keltie in March from Sydney asking him to 'see to it that none of the ridiculous reports of dissension, lack of support, tampering with depots or other harmful fabrications of detrimentalists be allowed to have a light. There is no blame anywhere.'[4] She had read Con's diary and was inspired, moved, and filled with admiration for him as she wrote to a friend: 'Con's journal ... is I think the most beautiful thing I have ever read and his writing to me not excelled even by the Death of Socrates.'[5] Her son had a heritage to be proud of and she would protect it.

When Kathleen met with Curzon in London on 16 April, her view was very clear. He made notes of their conversation in a list of bulleted points written in his scrawling handwriting which record that he and Kathleen discussed 'Scott's words in his diary on exhaustion of food and fuel in depots on his return'. They talked of the deaths of Edgar and of Oates and the impact on the others but acknowledged that Scott had been so badly frostbitten that his feet 'would have to be amputated if ever he returned'. The note concluded, 'They were killed by the weather and ill luck.'[6] Clearly this was an interpretation that Kathleen endorsed, because her very good friend Lewis Beaumont, who was also a fellow of the society, wrote to Curzon the next day: 'Lady Scott, I was glad to find, takes a broad and generous view of the sad end and would rather that nothing happened to mar the splendid record of her husband's work which she has to give to the world out of his diaries and in his own words.'

Kathleen's obvious desire not to challenge Con's words was shared by Beaumont. He wrote to Curzon saying that he was glad that he had 'taken up the consideration of the delicate and yet important points which lie hidden in the narrative of the Antarctic Expedition' and that the necessity now was to decide 'what attitude the Society should take with regard to your questions (a) and (b) that is:- the exhaustion of the supplies of food and fuel-and the conduct of the relief parties'. But Beaumont stressed that he would not want an informal meeting of the society to take on the appearance of a formal enquiry because this would require them 'to poke very deep and would have probably to disapprove of what was done in many particulars – it would be different if good could come of the enquiry, but I fear that nothing but controversy would come of it'.[7] He reiterated his point in a letter two days later in which he expressed his view that if they called the survivors to a meeting then it would appear to all the world that it was an enquiry. The rumours would circulate in the press, and they would be condemned for holding a 'secret enquiry'. He was also very keen that Kathleen should be spared the ordeal of attending such a meeting if at all possible.[8]

When the matter was discussed later with Oriana, she shared Kathleen's view.[9] Under Curzon's flamboyant 'C', which signs off his notes of his meeting with Kathleen, there is a postscript written in his hand which records what Oriana said:

> Mrs Wilson told me later there was a passage in her husband's diary which spoke of the inexplicable shortage of fuels and provisions on the return journey, relating to depots which had not been touched by Meares and which could only refer to an unauthorised subtraction by one or other of the returning parties. This passage however she proposes to show to no one and to keep secret.

It seems that Ory was true to her word as this phrase does not appear in the published version of Ted's diary. It has been suggested that she may have gone as far as to rub out his pencil entries in the original version, but it's uncertain what she would have gained if she had.[10] Ory was happy to share Ted's diary with her father-in-law, and after letting Cherry read it wrote to him: 'There is nothing that I would mind you reading in the least, you see he wrote it for relations – to go all round the family – so that it was a very general account of everything & he dismissed people but little.'[11] Whatever the truth about the diary, perhaps the most important point is that Curzon's note suggests that, despite what Ted had written, Ory was happy to support the party line.

It appears that *Terra Nova*'s surviving officers felt the same way. Beaumont wrote again to Curzon on 21 April to tell him, 'I am under the strong impression that the officers of the expedition want to be loyal to the memory of their leader and will think an enquiry an act showing want of confidence in them.'[12] The Royal Geographical Society decided in favour of the narrative that Scott and his men had been beaten by bad luck and the weather. This protected it from any criticism and preserved the reputations of the dead. Nobody was to blame. They were heroic failures.

Lois was not consulted as Kathleen and Ory were. She certainly wasn't ignored; she had received condolence letters from the sort of people that she would never have had contact with under normal circumstances, and Teddy Evans had driven down specifically to see her and her family. But there was not the same discussion with her about what had happened in Antarctica as there was with the other widows. She was told the details of what had happened, of course, but the expectation seems to have been that she would accept what she was told. And why wouldn't she? She was a naval wife and as a working-class woman was accustomed to deferring to her 'betters'. If the Admiralty and the committee in London told her what had happened, then why should she disagree?

There was another of the bereaved, however, who didn't believe the official version of the story and who was desperate to be heard. Caroline Oates was struggling to accept what had happened. After reading her son's diary and letters she had become convinced that the official version of events was flawed. A wealthy widow and mother of four, she was a devout Christian, a stern moralist and above all obsessively devoted to her eldest son, whom she called Laurie or Baby Boy. In his alternative view of events, which he shared only with his mother, Oates painted a picture of poor leadership, poor decisions and poor preparation. He felt that the entire expedition had been undermined by Scott's decisions. In particular Oates, who had in part been taken on for his horse expertise, had not been sent to purchase the horses for the expedition and when they arrived and he told Scott that they were unfit for the job in his opinion, he had been waved off. He regarded Scott's ignorance about marching with animals to be colossal, and his aversion to killing them for food a weakness. It was the start of Oates's questioning of Scott's abilities as a leader, and therefore the rapid deterioration of their relationship.[13] Caroline spoke to everyone she could after *Terra Nova* returned, including Atch, Ponting, Lashly and Crean. She came to trust Teddy Evans in particular, and he visited her on several occasions, supplying information about the expedition. During this very private and personal enquiry, Caroline spoke to all three of the widows, and, quite extraordinarily, she kept notes. She met Kathleen at least three times between her return to London in April and the end of May.[14]

The record that Caroline made of their meeting on 18 April at Kathleen's house in Buckingham Palace Road suggests that these two grieving women were rather uncomfortable with each other:

> She was not at her ease and evidently embarrassed throughout the visit, perhaps quite natural. She was kind and told me a great deal which was fresh to me. Seemed anxious to give me information. At first she was very nervous ... but soon she settled down and talked more naturally.[15]

Very different in character and outlook, the devout and stern Victorian matriarch had little in common with the thirty-five-year-old Kathleen, who was an independent, creative, modern woman who loved to dance. Caroline was quite shocked when Peter was brought down, scantily clad in blue sateen, but she nevertheless thought him a fine-looking child. What the two women did share was the pain of their bereavement, but in her crushing grief Caroline had come to see Scott as a bungler who had caused her son's death. Faced now by his young widow and child, she employed tact. She asked Kathleen if she'd known how dangerous the expedition was and she replied that yes, she had known that the risks were considerable. Caroline said that she had not, but then Oates had played down the dangers in his letters to his mother.

Then she asked why Kathleen thought the expedition had failed. It was only two days since her meeting with Curzon and their discussion about what had happened, and so Kathleen's response reflected that. She said that they had simply been unlucky; everything had gone against them from first to last and they had faced weather conditions that it had been impossible to battle. But she told Caroline, just as she had Con's mother, that even if they'd lived the men could have done nothing finer in their lives. This was the way that Kathleen was coming to terms with Con's death; she was determined to be proud and happy. The difficulty was that Caroline did not feel the same way about her son's death. She wasn't satisfied with what she heard but felt she couldn't press further.

Caroline may well have interpreted Kathleen's nervousness as being a sign of guilt about Scott's role in her son's death that she was attempting to cover up, but it was quite the opposite. Kathleen's discomfort came from her gradual realisation that this distraught mother was indirectly blaming Con. She had a beloved son too and must have felt compassion, but her loyalty lay with her husband who was not there to defend himself. Kathleen had been determined from the very start that, as she had written to Keltie, the 'harmful fabrications of detrimentalists' not be allowed to see the light of day. She may well have seen Caroline as one of these detrimentalists, and so despite empathising with her loss felt it necessary to be very clear with her that as far as she was concerned there was no blame to be allotted. Her tension might also have come from the feeling, however fleeting, that Caroline's son had slowed the expedition. Perhaps she thought that if Oates had taken the opium tablets that he'd been given sooner, then Con might still be alive.[16]

When she talked with Caroline, Oriana was friendlier but gave very much the same response as Kathleen. She said that Ted had always written to her as if he would not return.[17] There are no notes of any meeting between Caroline and Lois, but they may have had some contact because a crocheted altar cloth at St Mary's, the church near to the Oates home at Gestingthorpe, is said to have been made by Lois.[18] As the bereaved of the two men who had been accused of holding up their comrades, perhaps they shared something unique in their grief. Teddy Evans had told Caroline that several of the officers had been surprised when Scott chose Edgar over Lashly or Crean for the final party, but neither Edgar nor his widow could be held accountable for that. Caroline never accepted the official version of events; she grieved for her son for the rest of her life. Such a formidable woman might have been able to force an enquiry had she wanted to, but she kept her views private, choosing instead to boycott any public commemoration of her son's death.[19]

Both Kathleen and Oriana had seen in their husbands' own words that things had gone wrong, and they'd heard the criticisms of Caroline Oates, so why did they choose to support the official narrative? Surely because they wanted to believe that their lost husbands had died for something worthwhile. The alternative would be resentment and pain at the wasting of their lives. Oriana had no child to focus on or to console her. But she did have faith, a strong Christian faith that she shared with her beloved Ted, and her saving grace was the belief that his artistic and scientific work were what God had intended for him. She was determined that this would be his legacy, and only through this could she accept and make sense of his death. She wrote to Lord Curzon soon after her return home in April with a request that 'some of Ted's work could be given to the Society so that they can be enjoyed and not stored away where it will not be seen ... I feel that it would be fitting if some at any rate could be a permanent gift to the nation ... My pride in his work and the worldwide sympathy is a great help and I have much work that I can still do for him.'[20]

Whatever had happened on the route home, there is no doubt that Scott and his men had shown incredible courage. They were heroic, and what could possibly be wrong with focussing on that in their grief rather than dwelling on what might have been? There was plenty of cause for pride. When Kathleen read her husband's diary she wrote,

> Any more magnificent invigorating document I never read, and one would be a poor creature if indeed one could not face one's world with such words to inspire one ... wonderful record of valiant, clear-headed courage. Indeed, indeed he has left a goodly heritage. We must be proud and happy and make our gratitude drown our pain at the thought of his terrible mental suffering in thinking of responsibilities unfulfilled.[21]

Kathleen made a decision to be proud and happy. In his letters Con had urged her to be brave, declared his love and said that he had no regrets, and so she decided to regret nothing but his suffering. She shared with her husband an intense sense of honour and duty and a desire to support and not stifle each other's actions. Con had left for the Antarctic with a note from her which he kept in his pocket and which implored him,

> ... when you are away South I want you to be sure that if there be a risk to take or leave, you will take it, or if there is a danger for you or another man to face, it will be you who face it, just as much as before you met Doodles [Peter] and me. Because dear *we can do without you* please know for sure we can. God knows I love you more than I thought could be possible, but I want you to realise that it won't [crossed out] wouldn't be your physical life that would profit me and Doodles most. If there's anything you think worth doing at the cost of your life – Do it. We shall only be glad. Do you understand me? How awful if you don't.[22]

This letter is about duty and honour. It is imploring Scott to do what he is destined to do and not to let any worries about his family get in his way. Whatever he needs to do, Kathleen and Peter will love him and be proud of him. Peter later wrote that his mother, who 'was one of the gayest people I have ever known, could never have tolerated any kind of continuing tragedy'.[23] Kathleen decided to be as brave as her husband and to bring their son up in love and happiness and with hope. She sublimated her eviscerating grief beneath an outward life so positive that her very dear friend, the author George Bernard Shaw, later wrote in a letter that she didn't seem to feel any loss at all.[24] Only those who looked very closely could see that the crippling headaches she regularly suffered were a sign of her inward battle.

Gloriously Widowed

Lois may not have been consulted as the other wives had been, but she was very much made a part of the commemorations that followed her husband's death. She was invited to attend Teddy Evans' talk at the Royal Albert Hall on 21 May 1913 and the evening before she was a guest at the reception thrown by Lord Curzon at the Hyde Park Hotel where she quite possibly stayed the night.[1] At a time when she was living hand to mouth in Wales, uncertain when she would receive anything from the fund or the government, her expenses must have been covered, perhaps by the expedition or by the Royal Geographical Society. It was at Teddy's talk that Kathleen, Oriana and Lois met together for the first time.

Lord Curzon hosted 10,000 invited guests who came to welcome home the *Terra Nova* survivors and to remember its dead. The talk was to be the first public airing of the official expedition story. Curzon's introduction declared that it had been one of the most – perhaps *the* most – efficient, complete and successful expeditions ever sent to either of the poles. The men sitting on the platform should, Curzon stated, be offered the thanks not only of the nation but of the world for their daring, their suffering and their achievement. As the official leader of the expedition, Teddy Evans was then invited to speak, becoming only the sixth explorer to lecture at the Royal Albert Hall.[2] As the audience listened to the full story of the expedition for the first time, seated behind Teddy on the platform in a show of unity were Campbell, Atch, Drake, Meares, Ponting, Cherry, Griffith Taylor, Priestley, Gran and Mather. However, Kathleen and Ory's attendance hid from public view what was becoming an increasingly fractured relationship with Teddy Evans.

On Kathleen's return in April, Curzon and his colleagues had been made aware that Scott had lost confidence in Teddy fairly early on and that their relationship had deteriorated badly. On 1 May, Keltie had written to Lord Curzon about arrangements for the talk and expressed his view that Teddy's 'ideas with reference to his position in relation to the expedition seem developing: he is evidently disappointed that no honour has been conferred on him'.[3] Keltie seems to have been a little wary of Teddy back in February when he asked Kathleen, 'What do you think of all the honours that have been conferred upon Evans on the continent and here and about his lecture tournaments?'[4] When Teddy had asked for one hundred tickets to send to those that had donated to the expedition, Keltie felt this was unnecessary and offered fifty.

Ory certainly shared this opinion that Teddy was getting above himself. She was smarting at the attention that he was getting in the press when others, whom she felt did more, were being side-lined. She felt so strongly that she wrote to Curzon two days before the event at the Royal Albert Hall asking him to make sure that Teddy gave praise to those who had continued to work hard in the Antarctic while he was recovering from scurvy. She singled out Atch, who had to wait for the whole of that last winter at Cape Evans; Pennell, who quietly brought the ship home; and Cherry and the other men who had found the tent and brought the records safely back.[5] All of them did a full two years, unlike Teddy. She was also irked that he had recently been made a Companion of the Order of the Bath and went on to say, 'Somehow I feel that they are being left out in the cold when I see that once more Commander Evans has been honoured by the King, though he had already received promotion for his one year's service in the Antarctic.'[6]

Ory's sense of fair play was reacting against Teddy's elevation in the story of the expedition which she and others felt went far beyond the reality of the situation. He was, in her view, promoting himself, and certainly didn't demur when referred to as Scott's second in command. But if you asked anyone who'd been on *Terra Nova* whom Scott had relied on most, the answer would be Ted. She certainly wasn't going to let that be forgotten.

Ory's indignation was shared by Cherry who had, in his attempts not to blame Scott for Ted and Birdie's deaths, transferred all his hostility and rage on to Teddy Evans. He had become obsessed with his taking over the expedition, as he saw it, and for taking credit where it just wasn't due. He regarded Teddy as a traitor and a liar and saw conspiracy everywhere.[7] Ory spent a great deal of time with Cherry, who visited often and happily slept in the garden at Westal when space was tight.[8] Alongside Isabel, he was to become her greatest confidant and friend.[9] Twelve years her junior, this sensitive, intelligent man suffered greatly with anxiety and he and Ory were drawn to each other in the aftermath of Ted's death. Her beloved husband had admired this young man, now the only person alive to have experienced that gruelling journey with him when they had collected emperor penguin eggs earlier in the expedition. For Cherry, Ory was a way of keeping Ted near; perhaps she was the only person who could assuage his guilt that he might have saved his friends. He was upset when the press criticised the conduct of the relief party and felt that Teddy Evans and the committee could have done more to scotch the rumours and put the record straight. Instead, he felt that he'd been thrown to the wolves.[10]

That night at the Royal Albert Hall, however, Ory needn't have worried. Teddy did thank the men seated on the stage, and all of his comrades, and had also asked the Royal Geographical Society if a circular with the names of all of the expedition members printed on it could be distributed to the guests.[11] Nevertheless, the role of Teddy Evans continued to be an ongoing issue for Ory. Her close friendship with Cherry may well have fanned their mutual distrust and dislike of him into something that was to become lifelong and deeply felt. She would write to Kathleen in June, asking her to use her influence to prevent Teddy bringing *Terra Nova* into Cardiff and taking all the credit from Pennell as he had in Lyttelton. She added 'You may think I am foolish about this or small minded.'[12]

Later that year when she was asked to send Ted's notes to him, she was affronted: 'Why is Teddy Evans writing to ask me to send any records of my husband to the office as "the official records or charts" are being now written ... As Teddy Evans is no longer in command I don't see why I should send anything to him.'[13] Then, when Teddy's lecture tour came to Cheltenham in November, Ory didn't attend; when he came to Westal afterwards, she made sure she wasn't there.[14] Her father-in-law said he had been very nice about Ted during the lecture and afterwards at their home, but this did not change Ory's opinion of him.[15]

Kathleen didn't seem as concerned, presumably because she was happy with the narrative of the expedition that Teddy delivered. She had met him privately at Charing Cross station when he'd returned to London in April, offering her condolences on Hilda's loss and welcoming him home.[16] Her priority was her beloved Con's legacy, and nothing that was said in the lecture that day endangered it. To put his talk together Teddy had to rely on Kathleen's permission to use Scott's diary and she clearly had not withheld it.[17] She was possessive of Con's legacy and highly sensitive to any criticism of it and was certainly up to challenging Teddy if he overstepped the mark. During the Royal Albert Hall talk, Kathleen was seemingly more concerned by Shackleton's presence. Years later, Shackleton's wife Emily wrote that he had been very hurt when he was told that he was not allowed to speak at the request of Lady Scott. It seems that as far as his widow was concerned, the enmity between

Scott and Shackleton was far greater than that between Scott and Teddy Evans. Kathleen was not prepared to let the man who had forestalled her husband overshadow him at his own commemoration.[18]

Five days later, Kathleen and Ory were presented with their husbands' awards from the Royal Geographical Society. They sat together on the front row of the meeting at Burlington Gardens, both dressed all in black except for Kathleen's white collarette. Ory received the Patron's Medal awarded to Ted in recognition of his special contribution to the expedition.[19] Now, in death, the society claimed him as a fellow; much as he had longed to be one in life, he never had been able to afford the fees. Ory made sure to tell Keltie this, rather pointedly writing, 'I always felt he ought to have been made one in recognition of his work on the *Discovery* expedition. However that does not matter now.'[20] Because Scott had already received a Patron's Medal and a medal for *Discovery*, the Society presented Kathleen with an inscribed antique silver casket in which to keep them.[21] In his address, Lord Curzon reiterated the view of the expedition that he and his colleagues had settled on:

> ... Captain Scott was beaten not by some isolated catastrophe, still less by want of forethought or provision on his own part, but by a combination of misfortunes, raining down one upon the other with a relentlessness that reminded one of a Greek play in sombre fury.[22]

The *Daily Mirror* described the women the next day as 'gloriously widowed in the Polar calamity', but they could not have felt less glorious.[23] They had learnt of the deaths of their husbands only three months before, and while still grieving had been thrust into the spotlight. They were overwhelmed by attention and were not comfortable attending the many events to which others invited them. These two women, who had never warmed to each other, now relied on each other heavily to face up to their responsibilities as widows of national heroes and to get through these very public first few months of their widowhood. Ory wrote from Westal on 10 May that it was the greatest help to her 'to know that I can come and talk over things with you if I want to at any time'.[24]

Just a few days before the presentation of the casket, Kathleen had clearly considered not attending. Perhaps she felt that she'd done her bit and wanted to be left to her grief, and that the casket and the medals just didn't matter. Or perhaps she'd found the Albert Hall event too much. Ted's father had certainly assumed that Oriana would feel this way and had written to Keltie before she arrived back in England saying, 'I should scarcely think that she would feel able to be present at the meeting of the R.Geog. Soc on May 26th.'[25] Oriana, however, wrote very quickly on her return saying that she would like to attend and would be very grateful if her mother and father-in-law could have tickets too. Although she would not be alone, Oriana must have known that she'd be more of a focus of attention without Kathleen, who was much braver in the glare of publicity. Not relishing that prospect, she wrote two letters urging Kathleen to reconsider, telling her, 'I should be really miserable to be there without you – please, please come', and then 'I want to be with you at these times – and I would have given much to have you, as it won't be at all easy to go alone ... If you could screw yourself up at the last moment you know it would give me great joy. It only means standing for 3 seconds.'[26] Whether it was due to Oriana's urging or not, Kathleen did attend.

As Kathleen and Oriana worked closely together during this period, Lois was not part of their circle of support. Sympathetic to her plight as they must have been in their own grief, she was not their social equal, nor somebody in whom they could confide. Nevertheless, she was a *Terra Nova* widow and as the spring of 1913 turned into summer Lois found herself at the centre of some of the most public commemorations. Scott had promised that *Terra Nova* would return to Cardiff and so it did, under Pennell's command, on 14 June. The surviving expedition members were on board. Ory had written to Cherry saying, 'I don't know a bit whether I am going to Cardiff but suspect not – unless Lady Scott goes. I have written to ask her.'

In the end, both women travelled to see their husbands' ship return.[27] They met at Cardiff Docks where, with a small group including Cherry and Emily Bowers, they boarded the tugboat *Nelson* and sailed out to *Terra Nova*.[28] There they shared a private reunion with their husbands' friends and colleagues away from the glare of the public and the hordes of press waiting on the quayside. Rockets were fired and a huge crowd, including hundreds of schoolchildren, cheered from the shore as the ship sailed nearer and they could see, among the ranks of silent crew members on the deck, the two black-clad figures of Kathleen and Ory.[29] A blond, curly-haired little figure did respond to the excitement, however. Three-year-old Peter Scott waved enthusiastically from *Terra Nova*'s deck at the crowd below.[30] Lois was not there that day. She may have thought it was something that she could not endure publicly, or she may have been prevented from attending because she had small children to care for, but three days later she did attend the formal ceremonies that welcomed the survivors home.[31]

The Cardiff Coal Exchange was the hub of the city's most important industry, where coal mine owners, shipowners and their agents traded and made deals. At one point the price of coal across the world was set there. Thousands of people passed in and out of the building each day, and during the peak trading hour between noon and one the trading floor would be filled with the noise and bustle of at least two hundred men doing business at a rapid speed. However, at noon on Monday 17 June business was suspended. The oak balcony filled with women in brightly coloured summer outfits, contrasting with the soberly dressed men on the trading floor below, surrounded by rich wooden panelling and ornate decoration. A seating area had been reserved there for the most important guests, and when Lois entered, dressed in the deep black of mourning, Ory immediately went to her and they spoke together, quietly, for some time before taking their seats in the front row.[32] There, in that public place, where the officers and crew were officially welcomed home by Cardiff and condolences offered to Lois and Ory, the two widows sat together, each silently supporting the other.[33]

The next month saw a return trip to London for Lois. On 26 July, the officers and crew of *Terra Nova* marched through the gates of Buckingham Palace to the music of the Scots and the Grenadier Guards, to be presented with their Polar Medals and clasps by King George V.[34] Six of the medals were to be awarded posthumously and so, as the king recorded in his diary that night, Lady Scott and the widows were in attendance.[35] With them were Emily Bowers to collect her son's medal and Mrs Brissenden whose husband had drowned in New Zealand.[36] Caroline Oates, blaming her son's death on Scott and the expedition, refused to collect his medal and instead it was collected by Teddy Evans.[37] All clad in black, the group of women waited for their turn. There were no speeches, but the king spoke quietly to each of them.[38]

Kathleen went first to receive Con's award and Lois came next. The king was especially sympathetic to her and as he spoke, she had to wipe away her tears. It must have been overwhelming to hear such words from the king and to contain her emotions in such a public setting. Perhaps she was embarrassed too that she had been forced to sell the Polar Medal that Edgar had been awarded after *Discovery*. Oriana, who was presented to the king next, still had Ted's and could add his *Terra Nova* clasp to it. The following year the situation was rectified, and Lois was given a replica medal to replace the one that she had been forced to sell, but its absence on that day at Buckingham Palace must still have been keenly felt.[39] It highlighted very publicly how very desperate for money Lois had been. Afterwards everyone went to a reception at Caxton Hall, and it was the last time that the three women would ever meet.

Much as Ory and Kathleen struggled with the expectations of others at this difficult time, it must have been so much harder for Lois to be present at these public events. She had not been raised to mix with high-profile, educated people of the middle and upper classes and she inhabited a world that was very different, where finding enough money to house and clothe her children was the main priority. It was her pride in Edgar and his achievements that gave her the strength to be present and also her own strong character. No letters or diaries written by Lois survive, but she can be glimpsed through the words of the newspaper journalists who interviewed her in the immediate aftermath of Edgar's death. These men arrived at her door with a preconceived idea of her character, and their reportage is sympathetic but depicts her as a vulnerable figure, touchingly grateful for any support she was offered. Reading between the lines, however, it's possible to catch a sense of the real Lois: a brave and loyal woman who surprised the journalist by being 'quite a superior and refined little woman'. This is the Lois that her grandson John remembers, a tiny but formidable woman.

In the most tragic circumstances and in the glare of publicity, Lois tried hard to find positives in the desperate situation. She had told the newspapers in February that she was grateful that Edgar's end was 'a more merciful process' than the death of the others. He succumbed to an accident and wasn't starved and frozen to death.[40] 'I have this consolation,' she stated firmly, 'my husband died bravely.'[41] Her courage in attending these high-profile events in the summer is even more extraordinary because very soon after making these comments in February she had been forced to stand by them amid an onslaught of doubt. Lois found herself having to contend with something that the other widows did not. Unlike Kathleen and Ory, whose husbands were being mourned as heroes, some people had already begun to point a finger of blame at Edgar. He was singled out as a key factor in the tragedy, and Lois and her children had to face the sort of public reaction that Kathleen and Ory never had to endure as her husband was cast as the villain of the drama.

The Strongest Man of the Party

Scott's words in his 'Message to the Public' had drawn attention to Edgar's role in the tragedy. His deterioration was cited as a significant factor in the failure of the Polar Party to return, and it was inferred that Edgar had therefore contributed to the death of his four teammates:

> The advance party would have returned to the glacier in fine form and with surplus of food, but for the astonishing failure of the man whom we had least expected to fail. Edgar Evans was thought the strongest man of the party.[1]

Almost straight away several newspapers ran stories about Edgar's mental state, asking questions about whether he'd broken down physically or mentally. Because so little information had been made public initially, rumours began to circulate that something was being covered up. Official communications had always stated that Edgar had died of concussion, but as the demand for information grew and the atmosphere became more febrile, there was speculation that 'concussion' was a cover-up for the fact that Edgar had gone mad.[2] The *Observer*, *Western Mail*, *South Wales Echo*, *Daily Graphic* and *Times Weekly Edition* all ran a very similar story suggesting that Edgar had lost his mind:

> It would seem from what has escaped some of the survivors that Evans lost his reason for the time being under the great stress of fatigue and privation and was incapable of obeying orders, or assisting his hardpushed companions in the weary work of pulling the sledge. Indeed it became necessary in the end to lay him on it.

The *Daily Mail* stated on 12 February that 'the sudden breakdown of Seaman Evans, who appeared to be the strongest of the party, was a disastrous blow and was probably fatal'. Teddy Evans had given his first official interview on 13 April in Port Said where the ship bringing him home had docked. He denied vigorously that anything was being kept from the press regarding Edgar's death. He said that it was simply untrue that he had been dragged hundreds of miles on a sledge by the others, and that he'd in fact been man-hauling the day he died. Teddy also stated categorically that Edgar had not gone mad and that such stories were cruel and baseless. Despite Teddy's comments, newspapers continued to print stories about Edgar's collapse. When Scott's diaries were published in November 1913, some troublesome comments about him added fuel to the fire.

The day before Edgar died, Scott wrote that he was 'nearly broken down in brain, we think. He is absolutely changed from his normal self-reliant self'.[3] He also insinuated that, at times, delays were Edgar's fault: 'If he had been here in a fit state we might have got along faster.'[4] But Scott was writing against a background of extreme hardship, stress and suffering and in a whirl of emotions including loneliness, worry, fear, depression and irritation. Sir Ranulph Fiennes admitted that in 1993, during his unsupported Antarctic journey, he experienced irrational feelings of resentment and anger toward his colleague, believing him to be working less hard and eating more than him.[5] If Fiennes was affected in this way despite having superior equipment and nutritional knowledge, then it's not surprising that Scott and his colleagues made negative comments at times about each other.

It is not surprising either that the rest of the party should grow impatient with Edgar. He was an invaluable member of the team, skilled, good humoured and a great man-hauler. They had not expected him to deteriorate first, and showed some irritation that he couldn't help around the camp once his cut hand and frostbite began to incapacitate him. They needed his pulling power to get home. Scott was disappointed that the 'strong man of the party' had become so demoralised and had become 'very much annoyed with himself'.[6]

A number of factors contributed to Edgar's deterioration and some of those can only be understood with the benefit of modern medical and nutritional research. All of the men were overworked and undernourished. Each had a daily ration comprising 12 ounces of pemmican (dried meat ground into a powder, mixed with lard and set into blocks), biscuits, butter, sugar, cocoa and tea. This provided them with approximately 4,500 calories, but to haul the 500-pound sledges they needed nearer 6,000 calories a day.[7] Not only were Scott and his men starving to death, but they were also dehydrating. Despite the severe cold, the men sweated heavily as they pulled the heavy sledges for hours at a time and drinking water was not easily accessible. Snow had to be melted with a primus stove, which was also needed to make tea or hot chocolate, and it wasn't practical to stop and set up the equipment or to use precious fuel every time somebody needed a drink. The men simply went thirsty. As they became increasingly dehydrated, they would have experienced headaches and short-temperedness.[8]

Weighing over 200 pounds and with little body fat, the strong and fit Edgar would have felt the effects first. He needed more calories than his companions and lost weight more quickly as a result. Scott noted this in his diary: 'We are pretty thin, especially Evans...' As his body fat reduced, he had less insulation from the biting cold and wind. His dehydration, malnutrition and exhaustion would have made it difficult for him to maintain his body heat. Even at night it could take a great deal of time to get warm, if one warmed up at all, in an icy sleeping bag with wet clothes. Edgar would have felt the effects of hypothermia sooner than his colleagues, and Wilson noted in his diary that Edgar was feeling the cold a lot and getting frostbitten easily. Generating body heat required calories and so the vicious cycle continued.[9] But the insubstantial diet may have had even more insidious consequences.

Shackleton, Amundsen, and Nansen all suggested to the press after the death of the Polar Party that scurvy was the most probable cause. They were all fully aware of its dangers, but why polar explorers often suffered from scurvy was not fully understood. Fresh food prevented it, they knew that, but vitamins were not recognised and named until after the expedition left and the vital role of vitamin C in preventing scurvy was not fully understood until the 1930s. Fit men tend to be hit by scurvy after three months without vitamin C. It had affected Scott, Wilson and Shackleton on the three-month 'furthest south' expedition in 1902–3, Shackleton and his companions nearly succumbed on their four-and-a-half-month journey to try to reach the Pole in 1908–9, and Teddy Evans had nearly died of scurvy on the return march to *Terra Nova*, which took almost four months.[10] Edgar had died after 109 days on a diet that completely lacked vitamin C.

Scurvy symptoms develop gradually, beginning with feelings of extreme fatigue and abnormal laziness and muscle ache, particularly in the legs. Gums begin to swell and bleed, and patients feel pain in their joints and muscles. Flesh can become gangrenous and the skin, particularly in the legs and feet, may ulcerate and bleed, and wounds fail to heal. In the final stages sudden fainting can occur, and death is usually brought about by a brain or heart haemorrhage caused by exertion.[11] Edgar's cut hand refused to heal, suggesting that he may have been suffering from a vitamin

C deficiency.[12] As his frostbite worsened too, he became increasingly incapacitated. The skin on his hands was raw, and as infection and frostbite set in he lost his fingernails, and his hands became an agony of pus-filled sores. Wilson tried to dress them as best he could, but there was no prospect of the malnourished, exhausted man recovering.

A man as fit and full of life as Edgar would feel this incapacity keenly. He was not depressed or more upset than the others about losing the Pole, but he was frustrated by being unable to help his comrades. Frank Debenham and Thomas Griffith Taylor, two of the three young scientists whom Edgar had accompanied on the Western Journey west of McMurdo Sound between January and March 1911, were certain that this is what affected Edgar's morale. They knew him better than most. He was a hugely experienced Antarctic explorer and a man of great skill and ingenuity. He had shown the novices how to put up a tent, how to cook for four and how to mend boots. When Debenham's toes had become frostbitten, Edgar made him lie on his back and place his bare feet on his tummy under his clothing, and gradually the feeling came back to them.[13]

'Merry Taff' as they called him, was a confident and gregarious man. He was witty and jovial and at home with officers and scientists just as much as he was with the men below decks.[14] Some of this character comes through in the journal that Edgar kept during the journey, where he recorded, 'I've used up all my selection of swear words today' and 'I finished Cook tonight Deb[enham] take on tomorrow I'm going to have a tug at his leg next week. He has had a go at me.'[15] Of their journey Debenham wrote, 'We really are a very jolly sledging party and it is practically all due to Evans', elsewhere described as a 'ripping chap'.[16] Edgar maintained morale with his stories and antics, as Debenham recorded: 'Evans has the most frequent falls and after one he peers out of his hole at me to see if I'm laughing and that always breaks me up.'[17]

Debenham identified the injury to Edgar's hand as the thing that brought him down. In his view his loss of morale came firstly 'because he thought he had let his Captain down by having the accident and secondly, later, because he knew he was delaying the party'. He added that Edgar was 'a first-rate sledging companion and under ordinary circumstances I would have expected him to be the last rather that the first to die'.[18]

On 23 January, Scott had written in his diary, 'There is no doubt that Evans is a good deal run down, his fingers are badly blistered and his nose is rather seriously congested with frequent frostbites. He is very much annoyed with himself which is not a good sign.'[19] Scott knew Edgar very well. He realised that the ever-jovial strongman of the party was frustrated with himself because he couldn't perform as well as usual. His frostbitten fingers were raw and oozing and his nails were falling off. Pulling the sledge was agonising, as was pulling his sodden gloves on and off. Yet two days later Scott seemed surprised that Edgar was 'losing heart over it' and commented that he was no longer cheerful.

On 4 February, Edgar fell down a crevasse – his second fall. Wilson believed that he hit his head, causing an injury to his brain. Scott recorded later that day that Edgar was 'becoming rather dull and incapable [the result of concussion in the morning's fall]'.[20] The symptoms of concussion are well known now and include confusion, dizziness, slurred speech, delayed responses to questions, fatigue and a dazed appearance. Edgar's behaviour following his accident fits this list neatly, and, put together with malnutrition, possible scurvy, suppurating hands and exhaustion, it is easy to see why Edgar appeared to his companions two days later as 'being played out'.[21] On the day that Edgar died, Scott summarised the lethal combination of circumstances that he thought killed him:

> On discussing the symptoms we think he began to get weaker just before we reached the Pole, and that his downward path was accelerated first by the shock of his frostbitten fingers, and later by falls during rough travelling on the glacier, further by his loss of all confidence in himself. Wilson thinks it certain he must have injured his brain by a fall.[22]

Of course, the entire Polar Party was suffering. They were all malnourished and dehydrated, suffering hypothermia and possibly scurvy. Both Oates and Scott were badly frostbitten and facing some prospect of amputation should they survive. Oates's feet in particular were in an appalling state, black with frostbite and swollen to double their normal size. A war wound on his leg had opened and was festering, and his difficulties in walking were exacerbated by his shortened leg, which put extra strain on his back when man-hauling. Before Scott announced his final selection for the Polar Party both Wilson and Atch, also a doctor, believed that Oates was not fit to go, and Oates himself did not wish to be in the final party.[23] Scott noted in his diary that Oates was struggling early on; by the time he decided to walk out of the tent to his death, he had already slowed the party down to a significant degree. It was a very brave act, but it was too late.

Both Edgar and Oates had slowed down their comrades, but both also soldiered on bravely, well beyond the limits of most men. Oates had saved his comrades from an appalling choice. They did not have to decide whether to abandon him or not because he took his fate into his own hands. Edgar had woken on the day that he died, saying as usual that he was quite well. In his feverish last few hours, despite everything, he had struggled to obey and support Scott and his colleagues, dragging a sledge with his frostbitten hands almost to his final breath. Cherry wrote later that if Edgar had been at home he would have been nursed in bed, but instead he had to march, and he did so, suffering terribly without complaint.[24] But there was nobody left alive to say what had happened, only the accounts left by the men that died. It was their *Terra Nova* colleagues, inspired by the diaries that they found there in the tent, who decided to wire Scott's account of Oates's death with the official report. It was the only verbatim section of his diary to be shared at this time (except his 'Message to the Public') and it was chosen because when they read what had happened, Oates's teammates were awestruck by his heroism:[25]

> I take this opportunity of saying that we have stuck to our sick companions to the last. In case of Edgar Evans, when absolutely out of food and he lay insensible, the safety of the remainder seemed to demand his abandonment, but Providence mercifully removed him at this critical moment. He died a natural death, and we did not leave him till two hours after his death. We knew that poor Oates was walking to his death, but though we tried to dissuade him, we knew it was the act of a brave man and an English gentleman. We all hope to meet the end with a similar spirit, and assuredly the end is not far.[26]

Any delays caused by Oates seem to have been forgotten in the wake of his sacrifice, while Edgar was left to bear the blame or simply be side-lined. Charles Wright, who'd been on the Western Journey with Edgar and was a member of the group that found the bodies, wrote,

> Found the Owner [Scott], Bill [Wilson] and Birdie [Bowers] in the tent. Evans went mentally first then physically at foot of Glacier ... Titus [Oates] got a bad frostbitten foot but struggled on till March 17. Knowing he had no hope & realising that he was a drag on the party, he walked out into a blizzard ... A damn fine finish.[27]

Debenham, the man who had written so favourably of Edgar when part of the same expedition, declared,

> Taff Evans – already a little weak – had a bad fall and got concussion. He delayed the party and they were late for each depot. At the bottom of the glacier he failed and died before they reached the depot ... Soldier [Oates] failed next. He knew he was delaying them and in one blizzard walked out and away and he was never seen again. He did it intentionally to save his comrades – a fitting death for a real hero.[28]

The admiration that the surviving *Terra Nova* crew felt for Scott, Wilson, Bowers and particularly Oates is demonstrated too in the words chosen by them for the memorials they erected in Antarctica. They also show that Edgar's colleagues did not see his death in the same heroic light:

> This cross and cairn erected over the remains of: Captain R. F. Scott Dr. E. A. Wilson, Lieutenant H. R. Bowers As a slight token to perpetuate their gallant and successful attempt to reach the goal ... Also to commemorate their two gallant comrades, Captain L. E. G. Oates, of the Inniskilling Dragoons, who walked to his death in a blizzard willingly, about twenty miles south of this place, to try and save his comrades beset by hardship; also of Petty-Officer Edgar Evans, who died at the foot of Beardmore Glacier.

At the point where they estimated Oates may have walked to his death they raised a cairn with the words, 'Hereabouts died a very Gallant Gentleman.' No monument was dedicated specifically to Edgar.

This characterisation of the two men was published in newspapers across the globe. While Oates would be cast as the self-sacrificing hero who walked out to his death with the iconic phrase 'I am just going outside and may be some time', Edgar would forever be the strongman who broke under pressure. Oates became not only the embodiment of all that was great about the British Empire, but he provided the standard against which Edgar would be measured and always found wanting. As Scott's words established Oates as a hero, by necessity they cast doubt on Edgar. Teddy Evans, while trying to defend Edgar from the charge of insanity, unwittingly did further damage to his reputation. What Scott had called Edgar's 'astonishing failure' was due, Teddy said, to the continuous hardships that he'd had to endure. Edgar, he added, was a man of tremendous strength but 'it would seem that his staying power was not equal to that of his tent-mates'.[29] By using the phrases 'tremendous strength' and 'staying power', Teddy lit the touch paper on some very specific Edwardian anxieties.

During the early 1900s, many felt that Britain was in decline. Riddled with social problems caused by rapid industrialisation and urbanisation, and faced with competition from abroad, there were fears about the health of the nation. The decadence of a very wealthy elite and the deterioration of the working classes threatened the future of the country. When a significant proportion of men signing up to fight in South Africa were rejected on health grounds, fears grew for the health of the working class. An inter-departmental committee was established in 1904 to investigate and it found that just over a third of volunteers had been rejected and approximately half of those had been turned down because they were too short, underweight, had poor eyesight or bad teeth. Rather than see the poor health of these working men as a consequence of their poverty and malnutrition, the prevailing view was that a progressive deterioration of the working classes generation by generation was now revealing itself.[30] Edgar had been a Navy fitness instructor, an experienced Antarctic explorer hand-picked by Scott for the final Polar Party and one of the fittest in the group, and yet the idea that as a working-class man he must have had a congenital weakness of mind and body was accepted by many. He was from the very first more likely to be blamed than Oates, the Eton-educated cavalry officer and hero of the South African Wars. Doubt fell on Edgar more easily because he wasn't a gentleman like the others.

Strength had particularly negative connotations in Edwardian society, being equated to low intellect and a weak character. The upper- and middle-class ideal lay in 'staying power', a mix of self-control, discipline and willpower. This was the character of a real man and of a British hero. Scott's own efforts to overcome his youthful faults were later described in these terms: 'It was self-control more than anything else that made the man of him of whom we have all become so proud ... He had become master of his fate and captain of his soul.'[31]

As some of the press coverage began to focus on what was described as his mental breakdown, Edgar's lack of manliness was inferred. At this time, when education was focused on producing brave boys to defend the empire and boys' adventure stories thrilled the children of the country, there was a real fear of effeminacy. Hysteria, nerves and other forms of mental collapse were female conditions and not the sort of thing that should be observed in men like Edgar. This view that he may have deteriorated first because he wasn't a gentleman was articulated clearly in the *Daily Express*, which employed an 'expert' to explain why an uneducated man like Edgar would have been unable to cope with the mental strain of the return journey.[32] It focussed on the monotony of the routine, the landscape and the food, which denied the men any mental stimulus:

> To an educated man this strain would be bad enough, but he would be able to stimulate his brain with his store of learning ... The absence of such a stimulus in an uneducated man such as presumably Seaman Evans would have been, might have been succeeded by a kind of self-mesmerism followed by mania and then delusion that he was being kept from food and home, both close at hand.[33]

It was a commonly held view for years afterwards that a working-class man like Edgar simply could not appreciate the scientific value of the expedition and that for him the loss of the race was the loss of everything. He'd broken down because he thought all their efforts were in vain. As late as 1929, Cherry commented that it was the men 'with a background of education – "good blood" – who went furthest, pulled hardest, stayed longest'.[34]

While Edgar was often blamed or simply forgotten, his four colleagues were hailed as heroes. Scott, Wilson and Bowers were all regarded as having died heroically, but they were all eclipsed by Oates. The manner of his death, especially his choice to sacrifice himself together with his background and class, made 'No Surrender Oates' the embodiment of a national hero. When he walked out of the tent into the blizzard to die, Oates walked into the history books. The *Daily Mail* declared on 12 February 1913, 'If there was a contest in heroism between Captain Oates and his comrades, Captain Scott, Dr Wilson, and Lieutenant Bowers, the final honour lies with Captain Oates.'

Of course, not every newspaper, memorial or commemoration ignored or blamed Edgar, but it happened enough to perpetuate the belief that he had gone insane, failed through a lack of education or congenital weakness and simply hadn't died as heroically as his teammates. Little sensitivity in the matter was shown to his family. Perhaps the most distressing example was when the local paper, *The Cambrian*, wanted to get to the bottom of these stories about Edgar's physical and mental health and so sent a reporter to talk to his mother. Sarah Evans, who had only heard the news of her son's death just over a week before, was subject to intrusive questioning about her family history. Under the heading 'FAMILY'S RECORD: THREE CONSUMPTIVES', the article reveals,

> It may come as a surprise to all who have heard so much of his great physical strength to learn that out of twelve children, Mrs Evans has buried nine, and of these nine **three have died of consumption.** Although Mrs Evans holds firmly to the conviction that Edgar was an exceptionally strong man, it will be seen, therefore, that his family by no means shared that characteristic.[35]

Sarah's painful history of childbearing was published for all to see, and this must have been hard for her to bear in such a close-knit community. The reporter succeeded not only in brushing aside her defence of her son but in making her feel responsible for the inherent weakness that she must surely have given him.[36] Heartbreakingly, it was being bombarded with this narrative that made Sarah, in a moment of desperate grief and weakness, say something that she must surely have regretted. Under the headline 'her pathetic grief', the reporter wrote that Edgar's ageing mother, in her 'little cottage', was fretting as old people tend to do and magnifying an issue out of all proportion. The reporter tried to reassure her but she, close to tears, stated,

> I am worried because I feel that if he hadn't broken down they – Captain Scott and the rest of them – would have all been alive today ... I can't help thinking about it all the time ever since I read about them being **forced to wait for him** and carry him along with them, when it was all they could do to get along themselves. Perhaps it would have been better if they had left him behind.[37]

It is tragic that while struggling to come to terms with the loss of her strong, jovial son in such dreadful circumstances this almost unbearable responsibility should be added to Sarah's burden. The entire country was grieving, and it was her son's fault. To add insult to injury, many of the newspapers had used the wrong photograph for the first few days. It wasn't until 13 February that a correction was printed in the *Daily Sketch* to say that the portrait, 'sent out by a photographic agency as that of Evans, and published in the *Daily Sketch* and other newspapers, was in reality a picture of Petty Officer Johnson, another member of the expedition, who is alive and well'. Lois had told one of the *Daily Telegraph* reporters who visited her that the man with crossed torpedoes on the right arm in the photographs was Johnson and not her husband. The same mistake had happened after *Discovery*.[38]

Lois, also doorstepped by the press, held firm. Edgar was a good husband and a good man and she more than anyone knew the truth. He wasn't just the 'strongman of the party', and he wasn't a 'mere' seaman; he was a chief petty officer with an exemplary navy record. He was a leader who had taken his gun team to victory. He was witty, an avid reader and full of wonderful stories and ideas. Never shy to give his point of view, he could hold his own with officers as well as the men below deck.[39] Scott had held Edgar in very high regard too. During *Discovery* they'd spent two months together on a sledging journey with William Lashly, sharing a three-man sleeping bag, and were nearly killed when they fell together in harness down a deep crevasse.[40] So much did Scott appreciate Edgar's ingenuity, practical skills and lively personality that he had asked him to join the *Terra Nova* expedition. When *Terra Nova* was docked in Cardiff, Scott had made a point of spending time with the Evans family and had given Edgar's niece a biscuit.

As he lay dying, composing his final letters, Scott did not write to Lois, but he did remember her in his letter to J. M. Barrie. Lois had the proof not only of how much Scott cared for him but also how much he owed her husband in the letter that he had asked Kathleen to write and in the letter that he had written to her from Antarctica: 'He is such an old friend of mine and has done so well on this Expedition that he deserves all I can do for him.'[41] Scott's diary contained much praise for him too, revealing Edgar as an ingenious and extremely skilled craftsman, responsible for innovations that were vital to the success of the expedition including sealskin overshoes and tent linings. He was able to construct, on-site in the Antarctic, the essential sledging gear on which the expedition depended.[42] Scott described Edgar as having a 'really remarkable headpiece [brain]. It is only now I realise how much has been due to him ... what an invaluable assistant he has been'. But by the time this praise came to light, the damage to Edgar's reputation had already been done.

It was against this background that Lois attended the commemorative events and met Kathleen and Oriana for the first and last time. She may have been wary of how the other widows felt about her husband. Did they blame Edgar for their husbands' deaths? Did the others in the room agree? The public criticism and blame cast at Edgar must have hurt her, but with nobody else to defend him she would have to do it herself. She told a journalist, 'He liked Captain Scott and was a great favourite of that commander.'[43] Lois stated clearly and firmly for all the world to hear that Edgar was 'a very fine, healthy man, nothing ever the matter with him, and he had the will to go through anything'.[44] She was loyal and brave in public but privately the press criticism can only have added to her sorrow.

Not only was her beloved husband portrayed as a man who'd lost his sanity and broken down physically when put to the test, but his condition was said by some to have been exacerbated by his drinking. Edgar had famously got very drunk on two occasions: at the dinner in Cardiff before the ship sailed and in New Zealand again just prior to departure. However, he certainly wasn't the only member of the crew to celebrate their departure a little too well. Teddy Evans wrote later, 'Our departure from Cardiff did not do some of us credit.'[45] Although he clearly enjoyed a tipple, Edgar was not the boozy sailor sometimes depicted. Thomas Griffith Taylor, who was on the Western Journey with Edgar in 1911 and knew him well, stated, 'Regarding whether Edgar Evans drinking bouts had any bearing on his stamina, I don't think it had. He was not a regular drinker – went on the spree occasionally.'[46]

Lois's defence of her husband in the face of this criticism was prompted not just by her love and loyalty to him but also to protect her children. It has been argued that the extent of the criticism of Edgar by the press should not be exaggerated, that his courage was widely praised too and sometimes he wasn't singled out any more than Oates.[47] Although this may be the case in terms of column inches, it is not the case in terms of its impact on his family. Norman, Ralph and Muriel had been thrown into the public arena even before they knew that that their father had died. Peter Scott's fatherless plight was movingly described by the press, and despite Kathleen's attempts to keep him out of the papers he had become a poster boy for the tragedy and a focus of compassion and sympathy. Meanwhile in Wales there were three other children who were exposed to a more negative impression of the father they had lost. Published in 1913 to raise money for the Mansion House fund, the children's' book *Like English Gentlemen* was dedicated to Peter Scott and was the most explicit example of the scapegoating of Edgar:[48]

> ... Evans, the man of mighty muscles, seemed to have lost his strength. He was always a little behind the others, found it harder than they to pull themselves out of the snow drifts ... He stopped dead. 'I'm done,' said he ... But they were English gentlemen these four, the hero [Scott] and Dr Wilson and Captain Oates and Lieutenant Bowers and so, such a thing as leaving Evans behind never came into their heads ... It was their lifeblood the heroes gave for this simple seaman ... Poor Evans! If he had not fallen. If his strength had not failed. If only they could have left him where he fell. Poor heroes! But they were four English gentlemen.

In contrast, Oates's death was noble and self-sacrificing because he knew 'how English gentlemen die'.

Norman and Muriel may have read this children's book; they might even have been old enough to understand some of what was being said in the papers about their father. In any case, their schoolmates made sure they knew. They were bullied mercilessly. The taunts about their father and his role in the Antarctic tragedy followed them for their entire childhood,[49] and these cruel playground jibes had their origins in comments made at home by parents whose opinions were formed by magazines, newspaper reports and gossip. Most would not have read Scott's diary and the more positive comments about Edgar that it contained. Although it ran to four editions in only four months, it was very expensive. Costing forty-two shillings, the equivalent of approximately two hundred pounds today, it was almost certainly beyond the means of most of Lois's friends and family.[50]

Some would surely have acknowledged Edgar's courage, particularly those who had known him, but others responded more readily to the negative views. The stories that Edgar had gone mad were very damaging at a time when mental illness carried a huge stigma. Lois had Teddy Evans' assurance that such claims were groundless, but that was little defence against the slew of newspaper reports to the contrary. Some of her neighbours would have felt that his physical collapse had let everyone down regardless of his mental state. Others may have believed that he neglected his family, leaving Lois and the children to struggle financially in his absence. But Edgar didn't knowingly leave them in trouble; he had signed on to the expedition to secure a future for his family. He couldn't have known about the expedition's financial troubles, and he certainly hadn't intended to leave Lois a widow.[51] The vicar of Rhossili, Reverend Lewis Hughes, who had married Lois and Edgar and baptised their sons, preached a sermon in early 1914 praising him as

> ... one with a wonderful head, equal to any emergency, and brave to face any difficulty ... There he lies amid the eternal ice, a monument of courage and resource at the farthest point from living humanity, but never to be forgotten by his country nor to fade from its annals.[52]

Lois and her family and friends would all have heard these words, spoken from the pulpit in their parish church, but they were not enough to restore Edgar. As the rumours about him continued to circulate, the popular attitude was reflected in ways that his children simply could not miss. In the playground and in the streets, collecting cigarette cards was all the rage. Children waited outside tobacconists asking smokers for the cards in their packets and swapped them at school, trying to complete full sets. Cricketers, movie stars, animals and monuments of the world were hugely popular sets, but in 1916 John Player & Sons produced a twenty-five-card set called 'Polar Exploration'. Scott, Oates, Bowers and Wilson were depicted, but the fifth card of the series illustrated Francis Drake, the ship's meteorologist, taking sea temperatures. There is no Edgar Evans. The set contains Teddy Evans, Amundsen and his colleague Oscar Wisting, Oates exercising the ponies, sledging flags, a sledge party, Adélie penguins, Weddell seals, setting up camp and even a football match on the ice.

The omission of Edgar against the inclusion of the other four is extraordinary.[53] Even more pointed for Edgar's family must have been the texts on the reverse. Card three, which depicts Oates, condemns Edgar by both omission and comparison: 'On the return journey disaster overtook the little band; the most frightful hardships were encountered and one by one the men broke down. Oates' hands and feet were badly frost bitten and realising that he was becoming a drag on the party, this gallant English gentleman nobly walked to his death, hoping by this glorious sacrifice to save his three comrades beset with hardships.'[54] Edgar's deliberate omission from the set would have provided schoolmates with another weapon to use against Norman, Ralph and Muriel.

Lois would never accept this view of Edgar. As memorials were planned for his comrades, she was determined that her husband would not be forgotten. It was a challenge. He had not been linked to the sort of institutions that habitually commemorated their alumni like Eton, where Oates had gone to school, or Gonville & Caius College in Cambridge where Wilson had studied. She may have been in the newspapers, but she did not have the friends or connections to influence events and to advocate for her husband. There had been calls by both the weekly Swansea newspaper *The Cambrian* and by the Mayor of Swansea for a permanent memorial to Edgar in the city or in Gower, but nothing came of it.[55] Four memorials to the Polar Party would be erected in Cardiff within four years of the disaster, but none were dedicated to the only Welshman in the group.[56]

If public perception was also against her efforts, Lois could do little to change it on her own, so she decided to commemorate Edgar by herself. In January 1914 she paid for a white marble plaque to be erected in St Mary's Church in Rhossili dedicated 'to the Glory of God and in memory of Edgar Evans'. It is topped by a marble frieze showing the five men of the Polar Party and, in the background, the cairn of snow built over the tent containing the bodies of Scott, Wilson and Bowers with its cross on top. Lois asked for it to bear the same words by Tennyson that had been carved on the memorial cross erected on Observation Hill by his comrades before they left Antarctica, but with nobody to advise or support her the quotation was wrong. Edgar's memorial reads, 'To seek, to strive, to find, and not to yield' instead of, 'To strive, to seek, to find, and not to yield.' Nevertheless, this plaque, paid for out of her limited funds, in the church where their family celebrated so many happy events, represents Lois's incredible strength. As blame and recrimination swirled around her, it is her clear statement that Edgar was a brave man whom she remembered with pride. It would be the only memorial erected to him in her lifetime.

Men of Stone and Bronze

Kathleen and Ory remained vigilant to their husbands' reputations too. While her own grief had still been raw, Ory had thrown her energies into securing Ted's scientific and artistic legacy, the one thing that would give his death meaning. She had asked Cherry to take care of Ted's things, a task he took on assiduously, and nothing had greater importance than the penguin eggs that Ted, Cherry and Birdie Bowers had retrieved with great difficulty during the Winter Journey. In the late summer of 1913, Cherry personally took them to the Natural History Museum, expecting them to be welcomed with great excitement. Having made no appointment, to his great distress he received a frosty reaction from staff and was kept waiting. Later he went back with Grace Scott and the person that they met denied ever receiving the eggs.[1] He wrote later that he'd handed over the embryos, which nearly cost three men their lives and cost one man his health, and they didn't even say thank you.

Labelling specimens, collecting notes and papers, and gathering Ted's work preoccupied Ory for much of this time. She worried about how it would all be written up and she felt the huge responsibility of it: 'Oh the pity of it all – if only Bill were here to do his own work.'[2] There was frustration too at not having her own home, a place to keep everything safely together: 'It's this sort of thing which makes me wish I had a home in one place where I lived! – so that I could get all my things and Bill's – I always am wanting belongings that are at Westal.'[3]

Ory's efforts reached their first fruition in December 1913 when an exhibition of Ted's paintings went up at the Alpine Club in London. It attracted big crowds as well as royalty; Queen Alexandra, her daughter Princess Victoria and Queen Amelie of Portugal visited. Reviewers marvelled at Ted's work, pointing out that his tremendous artistic talent combined with the depth of his scientific knowledge made his paintings an authentic glimpse of Antarctica.[4] Ory must have been thrilled at this boost to Ted's reputation and proud of her own efforts to remind people that *Terra Nova* had not been a mere dash to the Pole. But she had a great deal to cope with beyond the pain of her grief. She had been thrown into the limelight, she had to make decisions about money, and she had to bear the burden of Ted's scientific legacy. In May 1914, after the opening of another exhibition of Ted's work, this time at the New Museum of Archaeology in Cambridge, Ory wrote to Cherry, 'I can retire gracefully into the background for a time, which will be a real treat.'[5] She was happy to be spared the celebrity and responsibility that came with being Ted's widow, none of which she felt very comfortable with and none of which she had expected.

Kathleen had a very particular and a very personal obligation to Con. He had asked her in his last letter to encourage Peter's interest in nature, and it became clear that his passions lay that way already. He enjoyed trips to London Zoo with Kathleen and to the Natural History Museum where on one occasion a member of staff showed him something interesting: 'It's the range-finder used by Captain Scott, you'll have heard of him.' Giving Kathleen's finger a squeeze, Peter very politely replied, 'Yes, I've heard of him, that's very interesting.'[6] In their cottage at Sandwich in Kent, they explored the beach and the dunes and dipped into rockpools. There were insects and lizards, and Peter never forgot seeing his first wild geese there. Con's colleagues visited too. Cherry was a regular and Dennis Lillie, a biologist on *Terra Nova*, spent hours with them explaining to Peter what he had found in the pools and under rocks.

Kathleen had tried and failed to settle back into normal life on her return, writing in her diary on 12 January 1914, 'I am worn out by the Antarctic work of publicity, so I am off to the Sahara alone.' There she was escorted by a local guide, a cook and two camel drivers and rode ponies and camels, dressed in baggy white trousers, a cloak, a checked red sash and turban, travelling a third of the way to Timbuktu and sleeping outside.[7] While she was away, Herbert Ponting premiered the full version of his film, entitled *With Captain Scott in the Antarctic*. It was first shown to a private gathering at the Philharmonic Hall in Great Portland Street in London on 23 January 1914, and from the next day was shown twice a day to the public, accompanied each time by a two-hour lecture by Ponting. Kathleen may not have been sorry to miss this premiere as it was presided over by Shackleton.[8]

For all her bravado in public, she also may have needed a little more time to gird herself for it. Kathleen had been told the details and she had read Con's diaries, but she hadn't seen his final resting place. Nearly a month after the films opened to the public, she went privately and unannounced to the Philharmonic Hall with friends.[9] Word spread quietly around the room, and when the image of the snow cairn over the grave of Scott, Wilson and Bowers appeared on screen, a dramatic hush fell. Kathleen sat motionless, obviously moved by what she saw; at the end, she hurried from the hall.[10]

Con and Ted's personal effects had been returned to their widows. Without bodies to bury, everything that their husbands had left behind became even more precious. But these items were also of huge interest to the public because since the Franklin expedition there had been an appetite for displays of polar objects. This gave Kathleen and Ory some agency over how their husbands' stories were told publicly as they could decide what objects they would lend and how they would be displayed.[11] There were times when they worked together, for example just after they returned home. Teddy Evans and teammate Cecil Meares had very quickly put together an Antarctic element to the Imperial Services Exhibition at Earl's Court, which centred on items belonging to the Polar Party. Kathleen had not been consulted and neither had Oriana, who alerted her to a display which she regarded as being in very bad taste – it included the inner lining of the tent in which their husbands had died. Kathleen complained and had a number of items removed or redisplayed.[12] The flags that had been flown at the South Pole and which were captured in the haunting photo of the Polar Party taken there had particular significance. Kathleen gave Con's personal sledging flag to Exeter Cathedral and Ory gave Ted's to Gloucester Cathedral, the church that he loved most in the world.[13] The Union flag that Queen Alexandra had given to Scott was returned to the dowager queen by Kathleen and Peter on 12 July 1913.[14]

The more personal items were kept or given away as keepsakes to others who had loved the men. Atch had saved Ted's watch for Ory and the gold and bloodstone signet ring that his parents had given to him for his twenty-first birthday was safe too.[15] After it was returned to her from the Antarctic, Kathleen gave to Con's friend Eleanor Mansfield, Lady Sandhurst the gold, pearl and diamond tiepin that he had worn at fundraising dinners. Con had urged Kathleen in his final letter to stay friends with Eleanor, and so in the message that Kathleen sent with the tiepin she said, 'I think also you will like to know that my dear man thought of you at the very end, for as his pencil stops writing he says "give fondest messages of farewell to Lady Baxter and Lady Sandhurst keep friends with them for both are dear women". Six more words and his writing finishes.' She added, 'May I tell you too that I was always glad of his friendship with you.'[16]

Parents and siblings cared very much about keepsakes and legacy too. Ted had been very close to his family, and Ory appreciated that Edward and Agnes's loss was as great as hers. Their beloved son had been the great hope of the family, his father later writing that 'Ted was a Christian Saint & Hero if ever one was'.[17] Not long after hearing the terrible news of his death, they were told that his clergyman brother Jim had suffered the first of several breakdowns. He was encouraged into semi-retirement and complete rest by his bishop, and for the Wilsons this was a blow almost equal to the loss of Ted.[18] Jim never came to terms with his brother's death and could never talk about it at home.[19]

The photos, sketches, and mementos that Ted left behind were precious to all of them, but with emotions running high and a grief-stricken Oriana's patience running thin, she solved an argument about who should have one of Ted's sketchbooks by ripping it in half.[20] The family put on a united front for the unveiling of a statue of Ted on the Promenade in Cheltenham on 9 July 1914. Amid the crowds that gathered for the unveiling, Ory had her closest friends and family with her to remember Ted. Her father came to Cheltenham, and of course Ted's parents and sisters and brother Bernard were there too. Isabel and Reggie Smith were invited, and Cherry of course, as well as Sir Clements Markham and his wife, and Joseph Kinsey travelled from New Zealand. It was Kathleen who made the sculpture, and Ory had visited her many times in the studio to see the statue as it evolved. She must have been delighted with the bronze likeness of her beloved husband, which now smiled benignly on his home town. Kathleen joined them all at Westal for a wake afterwards and some of the guests stayed the night.[21] In a photo taken to commemorate the event, Kathleen is perched rather awkwardly next to Ory, who is elegantly dressed in black and staring unsmiling at the camera.

Con's mother and sisters were equally sensitive to his memory. As early as March 1913 the suggestion had been made to the family that they might commission a new portrait of him for the Royal Geographical Society, and by July they had agreed that it should be painted by the Scottish portraitist Harrington Mann. The finished work was striking. Con looked splendid in his naval uniform, posing confidently with his arms crossed and with his sledging flag behind him, his polar medal pinned to his chest. It is an image that inspires pride, and the family were pleased that it would grace the society's headquarters at Lowther Lodge in Kensington Gore.

When Kathleen and Mann visited to see the portrait in situ, however, they were very unhappy with its position and the amount of light that was falling on it. There followed five months of correspondence between her, Scott's sister Grace, Lord Curzon and a very unhappy artist who, after threatening to take the painting back, agreed to make some modifications. The society's assistant secretary most sincerely hoped 'that you will find that the alterations made in the portrait … have been so successful that everyone will be pleased with the appearance of the picture wherever it may be hung'.[22] Finally, they agreed that as long as the painting was not hung prior to being varnished then the matter of position and light was less critical. Curzon noted in his draft response that the society must be very tactful, acknowledging that they were dealing with a grieving family. He recognised that for the Scott family the hanging of a portrait had taken on a greater significance, one of memorial but also of legacy.[23]

The responsibility for a national memorial to the Polar Party had fallen to the Mansion House Scott memorial fund committee. Although not officially a member, Kathleen was clearly consulted on what she felt would be most appropriate. When she met with Lord Curzon, he had floated some suggestions. His handwritten list of possibilities records her view that the most appropriate would be a memorial at St Paul's Cathedral, depicting the five men asleep or perhaps starting out, and then an external memorial, perhaps in Kensington near the Royal Geographical Society headquarters, of the five men again or perhaps something more allegorical. The remainder of funds should go towards an endowment to fund research. Kathleen didn't much like the idea of funding hospital beds or a church in Plymouth.[24] A memorial tablet in St Paul's was unveiled in 1916 bearing the inscription, 'Inflexible of Purpose, Steadfast in Courage, Resolute in Endurance in the face of Unparalleled Misfortune. Their Bodies are lost in the Antarctic ice but the memory of their Deeds is an Everlasting Monument.' However, the question of where the external national memorial would stand proved deeply vexing.

There were very strong objections to any statues in the royal parks in case important vistas were destroyed. Kathleen's great friend Lewis Beaumont proposed the cloisters at Westminster Abbey,[25] and days later Sir William Soulsby, the fund committee's secretary, wrote to express the concern that 'the Mall especially had been considerably vulgarised by these accretions'.[26] He wrote again to Curzon three months later, clearly campaigning against a public memorial and stating that something simple in St Paul's would surely be enough: 'If you were to take a census of London statues, you would find that nine-tenths of the subjects are quite forgotten and their achievements obsolete … the public have a very short memory and that in a few years Captain Scott and his companions will have drifted into the same obscurity as many more distinguished men.'[27] In January, Sir William tried again, this time proposing a group statue in the grounds of the Royal Hospital facing the river at Greenwich, a site owned by the Admiralty and with strong naval associations.[28]

In the end, the national memorial to the Polar Party would not be unveiled until 1925, and it was erected not in London but in Devonport,

Scott's home town. Sir William's aversion to the vulgarity of statues in central London and his belief that their subjects were soon forgotten was clearly not shared by Scott's fellow naval officers, who commissioned a statue of him from Kathleen. It was unveiled on 5 November 1915 in Waterloo Place in London. The officers, Beaumont and many other colleagues had wanted Scott represented in his most dignified state, in full naval uniform, but Kathleen ignored them.[29] Her magnificent statue depicts her beloved Con in his sledging gear, a true hero of polar exploration.

Kathleen literally as well as metaphorically put Con on a pedestal, and Ted and Edgar too became men of marble, bronze and stained glass. As their husbands became national heroes, and came to embody nobility and sacrifice, what of the people that they had truly been, the complex and very human men their wives had fallen for? If they had lived, what would Kathleen, Oriana and Lois's lives have been like? Just as had been the case after *Discovery*, Con, Ted and Edgar would have been a focus for the press. They would have been instant heroes, the glamorous and exciting figures everyone wanted at their party – especially if they'd made it to the Pole first. There would have been medals and honours and a knighthood for Scott. There would almost certainly have been more children for Kathleen and Lois, and perhaps a precious first baby for Oriana. While their men met heads of state, gave lectures and made trips to meet the public, Kathleen, Oriana and Lois would have run their homes and raised their families and then powdered up for the parties and special events, proudly stepping out alongside their husbands.

As the excitement of their return faded, the men would have returned to work. Scott and Edgar, almost certainly newly promoted, would have resumed their naval careers; Edgar was very close to retirement and a life at home with Lois. Ted and Ory might have returned to New Zealand if the right opportunity had come along, but he certainly wouldn't have joined the Church as some speculated.[30] He may well have been recognised as a leading ornithologist or an independent medical researcher.[31] In either case, Ory would have been at his side, sharing his work as much as she could.

There would have been tensions too, of course, because these were all real people, complicated and flawed. For Con there would have been expedition debts to pay, and all of the men would have had to endure years without a proper challenge. They might have found it difficult to settle down and enjoy the routine of family life, their wives wondering when the next separation might come. Kathleen and Con's relationship was passionate, and both could be volatile. Even Ory, who never made any demands on Ted and let him go his own way, occasionally felt that marriage was a hard path to tread. She once told her nephew, 'Of course but you know it's very different being married to someone.'[32] Lois had experienced Edgar's infidelity, even though he was otherwise a devoted and loving husband and father.

We can't know how these women would have weathered the storms of their marriages going forward, but we do know that they experienced very different widowhoods. The deaths of their husbands and the appropriation of the tragedy by people all over the world was all the *Terra Nova* wives had in common. United briefly by a shared, profoundly traumatic event which would shape the rest of their lives, they would never meet together again. Their lives would diverge in very different ways as the world was plunged into war.

Knitting for Victory

The story that had been read to over one million children at school on 14 February 1913 had begun, 'Children: You are going to hear the true story of five of the bravest and best men who have ever lived on the earth since the world began.' It ended,

> So these brave men died; and now you know what we mean when we say that they were great. They feared no danger, they never complained, they did their very best, each one was willing to give up his life for the others, and when they knew that there was no hope for them they laid down their lives bravely and calmly like true Christian gentlemen.

These words, spoken at a time of hightened national emotion, can't fail to have had enormous impact on these malleable young minds. How strongly the ideas of duty, sacrifice and fighting against all odds must have been stamped into the psyche of a whole generation of young men and women. The message had been compounded by Robert Baden-Powell, founder of the Boy Scouts Association, who had asked, 'Are Britons going downhill? No! ... There is plenty of pluck and spirit left in the British after all. Captain Scott and Captain Oates have shown us that.'[1] The *Boy's Own Paper* agreed, regularly featuring stories of polar exploration and idolising Oates.[2]

Eighteen months after the schoolchildren of Britain were read this inspiring story, the country was at war. Now grown into young men, thousands of them signed up to sacrifice themselves for king and country. Later a commentator would ask, 'How many of the three million who volunteered within a year of war breaking out owed the deciding impulse to that glorious example of Robert Scott and his companions?'[3] At a time when men needed a British hero more than ever, Ponting's film of the

Terra Nova expedition was shown to over one hundred thousand soldiers all across northern France.[4] As the images of the men who died in the Antarctic flickered before them, an example was set; here was what it meant to die for king and country.

Waiting once more as loved ones risked their lives far from home, Lois found that this time there was a great deal that she could do to support their efforts. She had remained in Wales after Edgar's death, and she and her children were living with her parents in Pitton when war broke out. Almost immediately, young men in Swansea and the surrounding area flocked to do their part. The sons of the farming families of Rhossili, including many of Lois's Beynon relatives, signed up and left their homes in Upper Pitton, Worm's Head, Fernhill Top and Pilton Green to fight.[5]

On 15 September, a meeting of businessmen and employers was held in Swansea to gain their support for the formation of a local battalion. It would leave the city and the area with serious labour shortages, but nevertheless the proposal won their support and, the next day, the approval of the public.[6] The battalion became known as the 'Swansea Pals' and consisted of 1,200 men from the city and its surrounds. They were to see action in some of the deadliest battles of the war, and by 1918 more than half of them had given their lives. Norman and Ralph were of course too young to fight, but Lois's sixteen-year-old nephew John, Beatrice's son, signed up as a driver in the Royal Field Artillery of the Territorial Force in 1914.[7] Lois's younger brother Stanley was already a serving seaman, and so for four years she worried about his safety at sea among the German U-boats. As friends and neighbours brought back the broken bodies of husbands, sons and brothers, their loss was keenly felt in the close-knit community of Gower and women looked for ways to help.

Fundraising drives were organised in communities, and many societies, associations and guilds sprung up in villages and in towns to raise money and supply clothing, gifts and other items for those fighting abroad and the sick and wounded in hospitals at home and overseas. Lois, her sister and other female relatives would almost certainly have joined in with these charitable activities, particularly those involving her church. Many made jam and preserved fruit for the Army, and nearly all women knitted and sewed knitwear for the troops. Woollen items were vital for the men stuck in the cold and damp conditions of the trenches or facing the elements at sea, and knitting circles were established all over the country to provide them. Newspapers and yarn manufacturers advertised patterns for knitted helmets, socks and mittens as well as modified versions such as rifle gloves that left the thumb and forefinger free and balaclavas with ear flaps. When wool wasn't available or affordable, women unpicked old jumpers and socks and recycled them for soldiers and sailors.

These woollen comforts not only boosted morale on the battlefield and on the oceans but gave real purpose to the women at home, desperate to do something to help.[8] More formal groups were set up by the Red Cross, whose working parties were formed by women all over the country. They made and collected socks, shirts, bed jackets and pyjamas as well as hospital equipment including bandages, splints and dressings. Lois might have participated in these activities from her home, as many women did. Swansea had four work depots, each coordinated by a local woman, which collected what had been gathered by the work parties in their areas.[9] They sent the items to Red Cross headquarters or directly to the Red Cross Hospital that was opened at Port Eynon to look after the wartime wounded.

As the war progressed and more men were called up there was a severe shortage of workers throughout the country. Women now took over men's roles, particularly in transport where they worked as bus drivers, ticket collectors, carriage cleaners and porters. They also volunteered in hospitals and worked in factories. Swansea's mines and factories were either already producing coal and materials vital to the war effort or were refitted to do so. Artillery had become the main destructive force of the war, and as shells and munitions became scarce the government pushed for the establishment of more factories. Although women had made up a substantial portion of the industrial workforce before the war, this was largely in textile mills. Now munitions became the largest single employer of women, with nearly one million working in the production line. Uniquely, the government provided childcare in day nurseries for them, but despite the work being more lucrative than being a servant they only got paid half of what their male colleagues did. It was highly dangerous work. Women working with TNT, a highly toxic explosive, were nicknamed canary girls because of toxic jaundice, the potentially fatal condition that they often contracted, which turned their skin yellow. Approximately four hundred of them died from it during the war. Shell production was equally hazardous, and in 1918 an explosion in a munitions factory at Pembrey in Carmarthenshire killed three young women from Swansea. *The South Wales Weekly Post* recorded that they had died 'as surely in the service of their country as any on the battlefield'.[10]

Cut off from transport networks, Rhossili remained as remote as ever, and so it's unlikely that Lois would have regularly taken part in war work in Swansea. However, there was something equally vital to be done in Gower. By the beginning of 1915, over 100,000 men who usually worked on the land had gone to war, and farmers could not produce enough food to feed the country. The situation became even more critical when

German submarines interrupted the flow of food imports to the country and vital commodities like flour ran short. The government encouraged everyone to use their gardens and any spare land to grow food. War Agricultural Committees were established in each county to help increase local food production, but they were reluctant to use women, believing that they would not be able to do the physically demanding work. The government organised demonstrations and competitions to show that women could do farm work well, but it wasn't until 1917 that a Women's Land Army was founded.[11]

In Wales, however, women and children had always helped on the family farms. The Rhossili School logbook for Edgar's last year there records that during haymaking the elder children didn't attend, and the following year there were references to frequent disruptions: 'Was obliged to close the school the whole of the day on Monday owing to most of the children being wanted at the sheep washing' and 'Children away planting potatoes'.[12] Lois came from a family of farmers and was used to the work involved. She is very likely to have joined the thousands of women who contributed to the production of food by milking, feeding, ploughing, planting and harvesting. In Gower, with her children at school and her friends and neighbours around her, the war remained distant. She worried about Stanley and about her nephew John, but she was not confronted with its horrors as directly as Kathleen and Ory would be.

Sculpting Beauty from Horror

Kathleen had planned to spend the summer of 1914 with Peter in Sandwich, but she was very aware of the growing tensions in Europe, writing to Keltie, 'I am off tomorrow to Sandwich for a few weeks, but the uncertainty in the air makes one feel very uncomfortable.'[1] She and Peter were there when Britain declared war on Germany three days later.[2]

True to her nature, Kathleen had a very active war. She already had experience of war zones and military hospitals, and by December 1914 she'd rolled her sleeves up and got involved. She transported cars and ambulances to France and worked there in a hospital where she had to search through the muddied and bloodied clothing of the wounded, string their garments together with their boots and number them for fumigation. She couldn't bear to see the casualties just as numbers, and talked to the wounded men about their wives and families.

On her return to England in 1915 she found new work on the production line at the Vickers factory in Erith making electrical coils. Then, at the end of 1916, her friend Sir Matthew Nathan, now Permanent Secretary to the Ministry of Pensions, asked her to be his private secretary. At first uncertain about long hours away from Peter, Kathleen was persuaded by Asquith to take the job, but she was completely unsuited to it and felt completely useless. Her art was subsumed by the pressure of her war work, and during a year of long hours in the pensions office she sculpted very little. The exception was her statue of Con, which was finally erected on 5 November 1915. Kathleen had been too busy working on the Vickers production line to attend.

Evenings and weekends were precious times to spend with Peter. Barrie was a regular visitor, as were scientific friends who encouraged Peter towards the natural world as Con had wished. There were visits to the Natural History Museum and conversations about snails' eggs, crystals, octopi's suckers, eel spawn and sea urchins.[3] Kathleen continued to move within a diverse social circle of lords, politicians, artists and writers. Her friendships with Prime Minister Herbert Asquith and Home Secretary Reginald McKenna and his wife Pamela put her right at the heart of the country's decision-making elite. Asquith dropped in regularly at 174 Buckingham Palace Road, preferring to sit with Kathleen in her studio where there was no phone to constantly disturb them.[4] There he talked about conscription, rebellion in Ireland, cabinet changes and all manner of issues that were worrying him, looking to Kathleen for wisdom and sympathy. She felt uneducated and useless, but, like Con, Asquith was drawn to her as a sounding board, a sympathetic ear and a source of strength. Even when he was forced out of office in December 1916, Asquith continued to confide in her.

Many weekends were spent at Cherry's country estate, Lamer. He had let the Red Cross open a fifty-bed hospital for officers there and was given a temporary commission in the Royal Naval Volunteer Reserve. He was appointed to the Royal Naval Air Service's armoured car division, a brainchild of Churchill's, and although he went to the Western Front he almost certainly saw no action.[5] Kathleen was able to escape the grind of her London work at Lamer. There was wildlife for Peter, and while he caught newts she sculpted. When the weather was good they slept outside, and Kathleen danced on the lawn in her nightdress.[6] Cherry bought Peter a special junior bed so that he could stay over sometimes when Kathleen had to return to the Ministry of Pensions.[7] She opened her home in London to him too, where he confided in her as well as taking Peter to pantomimes and to dine at Claridge's. He sometimes joined them in Sandwich too.

But Kathleen's relationship with Cherry was not as close as Ory's. For her, the main attraction was Lamer and the frequent visits there by George Bernard Shaw, who was at that time the most famous writer in the world. He and his wife Charlotte owned the rectory at Ayot, just a quarter of a mile's walk through lime trees and over footpaths to Lamer. He and Cherry were close, and as Kathleen became a regular visitor he and Charlotte came to adore her, and she them, despite a thirty-year age difference.[8] He once said that Kathleen was so like a man that his feelings for her were 'the nearest I ever came to homosexuality'.[9] These idyllic weekends at Lamer, with wonderful friends, fascinating conversation, dancing on the lawn and sleeping under the stars were a respite for Kathleen from the grinding routine of her war work and from the Zeppelin raids that dropped bombs on London.

There was contact with other Antarctic colleagues in the war years too. In 1916, Teddy Evans married again after a whirlwind romance with Elsa

Andvord, a Norwegian from Christiania, now Oslo. Their wedding took place in London on 22 January and was attended by Kathleen, Caroline Oates and Emily Shackleton, who was there without her husband.[10] Back in 1914, as the press eulogised Scott and his companions for showing that men were still willing to sacrifice themselves for an ideal, Shackleton had faced criticism for setting off on an Antarctic expedition. He'd been given the king's permission to go, but with many men from *Terra Nova* setting off to fight, few defended him. Now his ship *Endurance* was stuck in the ice of Antarctica's Weddell Sea and he and his crew were stranded, nearly a thousand miles away from the nearest land and hundreds of miles from a food depot. Emily had been writing letters and campaigning for a rescue mission but still there were many who felt that the men shouldn't have been there and that sending a ship out to save them when so many were dying in the war was just not appropriate. Kathleen had never liked Shackleton but seeing Emily at the wedding must surely have sparked compassion for her as a wife and mother enduring an uncertainty that she knew so well. It was only three years since she had lost Con.

When the good news came that Shackleton and his men were safe, their story was one of the most extraordinary in the whole of polar history. After sixteen months they had managed to battle the elements and sail the lifeboats to the remote and desolate Elephant Island. With no communication possible, Shackleton had no idea if help was coming; knowing that they could not survive, he and five men, including Tom Crean, had set out in the 22-foot-long *James Caird* for an 800-mile journey across open seas to the whaling station at South Georgia to get help. Seventeen days later, after a journey in which they could neither lie down nor stand comfortably, the six men arrived only to find that they were on the opposite side of the island to the whaling station. Only three men were fit enough to go on, and so for thirty-six hours, Shackleton, Tom Crean and Frank Worsley battled across the mountainous and glacier-filled terrain of the interior, arriving burnt, blistered, emaciated and barely recognisable.

When a cable arrived in London on 31 May 1916, news of the extraordinary journey made the front pages across Europe, even in Germany.[11] Kathleen wrote in her diary on 2 June, 'For myself I think it one of the most wonderful adventures I ever read of. Magnificent, Shackleton or no Shackleton. I sent a telegram to Lady Shackleton.' Later that month she felt rather less magnanimous about it all when the man sitting next to her at dinner enthused, 'You must be tickled to death by the news about your husband.' It was bad enough to be mistaken for Emily, but referring to death while bringing up her own husband was quite a faux pas.[12]

Sir Clements continued to be a regular part of Kathleen's life too. On 18 January 1916, he wrote in his dairy that Kathleen and Peter had walked with him in the garden outside his house. It was to be his penultimate diary entry, as only days later he died in a tragic accident. Despite having electric light in his bedroom, he was reading as he'd done since he was a young seaman in a hammock, balancing a book in one hand and a candle in the other.[13] The candle fell, the bedclothes caught alight, and Sir Clements died of his injuries. He had been the guiding spirit of the *Discovery* and *Terra Nova* expeditions and had loved Con like a son. He was a terrible loss to Kathleen and to his godson Peter.

In the final months of the war, Kathleen found work that uniquely fitted her skills and experience. She was asked to join the team at the new hospital in Regent's Park where the badly damaged faces of officers would be rebuilt. Kathleen's role in this pioneering work was to sculpt the noses, chins and mouths that had been blown away, providing a model for the doctors to work from. It was difficult and upsetting but it was important work and she got through it by seeing past the terrible injuries and appreciating the young men who bore them: 'I worked on a man with a wonderful face and no nose. These men with no noses are very beautiful, like antique marbles.'[14]

Casualties of War

Ory was keen to play her part, and soon after war broke out a role became clear. The New Zealand War Contingent Association, the NZWCA, was set up in London in August 1914 by the New Zealand High Commissioner, Sir Thomas Mackenzie. As a dominion of Britain, New Zealand had joined the war at its start, with thousands of young men signing up in the first week. The association's aim was to support soldiers who found themselves in Britain, providing small comforts, visiting them in hospital, arranging accommodation for the convalescent and helping them stay in touch with their relatives. After the Gallipoli campaign in 1915, the work of the NZWCA escalated. The aim of the campaign had been to drive Turkey out of the war by taking over the Gallipoli Peninsula with land troops while naval gunships bombarded the Dardanelles Strait. Victor Campbell, who'd survived a winter with his men in an ice cave during *Terra Nova*, had retired from the Navy but came back to join the Royal Naval Division and he went to Gallipoli in 1915. William Lashly was there too, and despite his ship being sunk he survived to the end of the war.[1] But the Gallipoli campaign was a disaster, and the carnage led to thousands of wounded New Zealand soldiers arriving in Britain for treatment and recuperation.[2]

In June of that year the NZWCA took over an estate in Walton-on-Thames in Surrey, turning it into a hospital with a large operating theatre specifically for troops from New Zealand. It opened on 31 July 1915 and in early August was visited by the king and queen.[3] It was to be the first of four New Zealand hospitals in the country, built to look after the growing number of casualties of war. Within two days of its opening, the first patients arrived. One of the wounded was the twenty-year-old son of the high commissioner who had established the NZWCA and the hospital which was now treating his son. Clutha Mackenzie, who lost both eyes in an explosion, was typical of the young men who were so seriously wounded at Gallipoli.[4] Ory met him after an operation which would enable him to have glass eyes put in, and she liked him very much.[5] She wasn't a nurse, but she had lots of experience of caring for others and this was invaluable because the NZWCA also had a ladies' committee comprising mostly well-to-do women who visited wounded soldiers, wrote letters home to their families for them and made sure that they had the comforts they needed. Under the leadership of Lady Islington, they also organised clubs and respectable activities to keep the young men occupied and entertained during convalescence, including free tickets to shows and theatres as well as weekend stays in British country houses.[6]

Ory's considerable organisational skills, honed by her cataloguing and archiving work with Ted, together with her strong bond with New Zealand and its people, made her a perfect fit. In September she was trained and then took up a post as assistant honorary secretary at the NZWCA headquarters in Southampton Row in London, walking every day from the small flat that she rented in Hammersmith.[7] It was over a decade since Ory had worked for anyone else, and now, in a smart uniform, she found herself working in an office in London for the first time. It was a lively place, with New Zealanders coming in and out all day with thrilling and awful stories of the war, but eventually Ory moved into her own office and delegated much of the day-to-day work to her bevy of girls, leaving her to supervise and make visits around the country.[8] She was helped by Bertha Raynham, who had worked for the London editor of *Vogue* and in New York for *Vanity Fair*, and who now became Ory's invaluable assistant.[9] She also brought in the retired Captain Greenstreet, the ship's captain who had brought her back from New Zealand, and he ran the Red Cross stores in Southampton.[10]

Kathleen wrote to tell Ory that she was hard at work making munitions, but after the war it would be Ory's work that was recognised as she became a Commander of the British Empire. After the king presented her CBE at Buckingham Palace in March 1919, her best friend Isabel, her brother Adrian, her assistant Bertha and Captain Greenstreet were all waiting outside to congratulate her.[11] Ory was proud of the recognition of her war work, but proud too of this public and permanent link to New Zealand.[12]

In the same month that Ory began her new job, her sister Connie began a new life of her own. At the age of thirty-six she married for the first time. She had fallen in love with Second Lieutenant Owen Charles Bragge, and their wedding had been delayed when he was sent out to the Dardanelles. He was very badly wounded, narrowly avoiding his arm being amputated, and would be out of the fighting for good.[13] Their marriage took place on 16 September 1915 at St Peter's Church in Eaton Square, close to Owen's home in Grosvenor Gardens. It was a small wartime event with the groom's father and the bride's father and stepmother in attendance – and of course Ory.[14] There was a spate of other weddings that year too, including those of Henry Pennell and Edward 'Atch' Atkinson, the two men who had waited to tell Ory of Ted's death.

Not surprisingly, Ory didn't attend Teddy Evans's wedding. Her feelings about him hadn't changed, and when the Kinseys sent her a review of a romance and adventure novel that he had written while on furlough she wrote it out verbatim for Cherry. What 'silly person', she asked, had written, '"His great personal charm has bought him scores of friends, so that he knows & understands mankind; and he writes as unaffectedly as he talks"'.[15] When Teddy took his new bride to Westal in February 1916 to meet Dr and Mrs Wilson, Ory pretended to be absent. Although she was desperate to see what the new Mrs Evans looked like, she hid herself away and her in-laws thought she behaved very badly.[16]

Although most of Oriana's brothers and brothers-in-law were in reserved occupations as clergymen and teachers, Connie's husband Owen had fought in France, and Ted's brother Bernard was a captain in the 6th King's Own Yorkshire Light Infantry there. Ory had seen first-hand the horrors of war at the hospitals that she visited and in the eyes of the young men she comforted, but in 1916 they were visited on her. Her forty-year-old brother Noel had come over from Canada, where he had been farming, signed up and was sent out to the trenches of northern France. In February he'd written that he was thoroughly enjoying everything and that the rats were making more noise than the Germans, but that soon changed.[17] On 1 July 1916, the first day of the Battle of the Somme, Noel was among the 19,000 men killed in one day.[18] He was the third of Ory's brothers to die young and tragically.

She lost dear friends that year too, men who were linked to Ted and her memories of him. Pennell, who had kept her company at Kinsey's house in New Zealand, was killed when the *Queen Mary* was blown up during the Battle of Jutland, and now, nearly at the year's end, Reginald Smith, her husband's great friend, killed himself. Reggie was known to be suicidal and was being watched around the clock, but he managed to slip away and on 26 December threw himself from a fourth-floor window at his home in Green Street.[19] Ory and her dearest friend, his widow Isabel, were now the only two surviving members of the happy band that had holidayed in the Smiths' lodge in Scotland nine years before.

At Reggie's funeral three days later, Ory saw Kathleen again. They had never been friends, and so it's unlikely that Kathleen knew of Noel's death; all that she saw of Ory was the rather frosty exterior that had irritated her before and with which she had no patience now. She was emerging from the most crippling part of her grief and beginning to enjoy life again. Just the month before she'd written in her diary, 'Oh, how ludicrously happy one is in this sad, grim world! To everyone else it is sad and grim, and to me it is an endless ecstasy of delight, when I am out of pain.'[20] Perhaps she expected Ory to be feeling the same, because she wrote about their encounter that night in her diary: 'We saw Mrs Wilson there. She's an absurd prig.'[21]

Kathleen could not have known all the grief that Oriana was hiding behind her frigid façade. It was later written of her that fate had destined her for tragedy, that her character was forged on the anvil of sorrow, and if so then the senseless, ruthless cruelty that she was experiencing all around her now might have been the final hammer blow. Ory questioned how there could be a god ordering the universe when Ted and Noel were dead.[22] Her faith had been shaken to its foundations, and it could not survive the shock. Her belief in God was extinguished.[23] Ory could still believe in the goodness in the world and in people, but her loss of faith was catastrophic in terms of how she'd lived with Ted's death. They had both believed that they would see each other again in the afterlife, and this, together with the thought that Ted was looking down on her from Heaven, had sustained her. Now she felt like she was suffering a second bereavement. The loss of her beloved Ted hit her again, but this time there was no hope of reunion. War had brought about the death of Ory's faith just as it had finally put out the light of Kathleen's wavering belief in God many years before. Kathleen may have been emerging from the very worst of her grief, but Ory had been dragged back to its first painful cut.

The war was not yet over, and neither were the horrors that it would deliver. Ory's widowed sister-in-law Rosalie had moved in with her and Ory was still working hard to support the wounded men of New Zealand when she heard that Atch had been terribly hurt.[24] She had always had a soft spot for the man who had led the search for the bodies of the Polar Party and retrieved the precious diaries and letters which had eased her grief. He had also made sure that he was there in person to tell her all he knew about how Ted had died when she most needed to hear it. Atch had made it safely to within weeks of the war ending. He'd first been in Gallipoli working in his capacity as a doctor investigating the fly-borne diseases that were ravaging the troops, and the following year he was sent to the Western Front where he was a medic at the Somme. Then, on 16 September 1918, the ship on which he was serving was hit. HMS *Glatton* was a new ship, sailing off the coast of Dover when it caught fire. An order was given to torpedo it before the onboard magazine blew up. Casualties were heavy and Atch suffered horrific injuries. He was blinded and badly burnt but still managed to rescue several men as he escaped, feeling his way in the darkness through the burning ship. Awarded the Albert Medal, he only partially recovered his sight.[25]

Ory couldn't help feeling resentment that while Atch and Pennell had suffered, Teddy Evans had become a national hero for a second time. He had been commanding the HMS *Broke* in 1917 when, with one other ship, it took on six German destroyers that were about to attack Dover. Three were sunk and three retreated. He emerged from the conflict as a classic war hero, consolidating his position as a famous public figure. Becoming known as 'Evans of the Broke', the papers loved him.[26] Ory couldn't deny that Teddy Evans was brave, but she also felt he was boastful and took credit where it wasn't due.

If they had come home safely from Antarctica, Ory, Kathleen and Lois's husbands would have joined their *Terra Nova* colleagues and the millions of others who went to fight. Within a year of returning, Con and Edgar would have been serving on ships and facing the German Navy and U-boats like Campbell, Pennell and Teddy Evans had. They may have been sent to the Dardanelles and they may have fought at Jutland, and they may not have survived.[27] Ted's experience might have been more like Atch's. He could not have killed; he had said at the time of the South African Wars that he would sooner shoot himself than shoot someone else.[28] He would have done his bit, but like Atch he might have looked for a role where he could use his medical skills and not pick up a gun. In any case, he would almost certainly have struggled mentally on the front lines.[29] And how would he have coped with Ory's loss of faith? Perhaps Ted's beliefs would have been shaken by the war too, but could he ever have accepted that she no longer believed that God was shaping their lives?

The First World War brought with it enormous social change. Women became responsible for their families for years at a time and many stepped into the roles vacated by men, showing themselves to be capable and hard-working members of society. Those who broke out of the domestic sphere began to feel differently about their status and wanted more. Men found themselves thrown together in the trenches, living and fighting alongside men of all classes from all over the empire. How could anyone see the rigid social hierarchy of Edwardian England in the same way again?

As the old world was flattened underfoot on the battlefields of Flanders, the demand for social change accelerated. The men and women who wanted more rights and more of a voice weren't afraid to demand it. The end of the war brought with it what the Suffragettes had fought so hard for: the right to vote. The Representation of the People Act 1918 gave the vote to all men over twenty-one and for the first time women could vote too, although only those over thirty. Kathleen may have been firmly anti-suffrage when the Suffragettes were setting fire to postboxes and bombing railways, but that did not stop her from using her vote in the election of 1918.

The jingoistic fervour for self-sacrifice and duty that Scott's story had inspired in 1914 dissipated after the appalling carnage of four years of brutal war. Millions of women now found themselves in the same situation as Kathleen, Ory and Lois. When she celebrated the Armistice in Paris with J. M. Barrie, Kathleen noticed among the wild scenes on the Grands Boulevards young girls dressed as widows, dancing with the rest.[30] This vast regiment of bereaved women had slim chances of remarrying as a generation of young men had been decimated by the conflict. The *Terra Nova* widows were now part of a much wider group of surplus women whose husbands and fiancés had sacrificed their lives and who now faced the future alone.

A New Family

At the beginning of 1919, Kathleen wept as nine-year-old Peter went away to school. Had Con lived there would surely have been more children, and after his death she had railed against the fate that meant that she could have no more babies.[1] In Peter's absence she filled her life with dances and ballet and opera, and with good friends such as Nansen, Barrie and Asquith. In his last letter to her Con had urged Kathleen to go on with her life and to be happy, but despite being only forty-one she did not expect to find love again. However, towards the end of the year she wrote in her diary, 'Hilton Young came to lunch. I think I adore him.'[2] Wounded hero, former journalist, barrister, naval officer and now Member of Parliament Edward Hilton Young, who was only a year younger than Kathleen, quietly became part of her social crowd.

Peter was drawn to this witty and gentle man as much as Kathleen was. Hilton was shy and talked about birds and nature with Peter, and Kathleen began to fall in love. But just as she had with Con, Kathleen doubted herself and her feelings, and couldn't decide whether to choose Hilton or another man who was pursuing her, or indeed any man at all. In her unsettled state, she clung to the memory of Con, writing in her diary in the summer of 1920, 'I grow more in love with Con every year.' She wintered in Peru, hoping that absence would help her decide, but on her return wrote, 'If God said, "You may take whom you like and I'll see he loves you utterly" whom could I say? Just "Con again, please."'[3] Later that year as she left the holiday home in Sandwich, which she had originally chosen for her and Con, she was saddened by the thought that he had never seen it. Then, packing away her things, she found on a high shelf the bundles of his letters that had been returned to her from the Antarctic.

If he had pursued her determinedly during this time, Hilton may have lost Kathleen to the memory of Con; but he did not, and his appeal grew. He allowed her to be herself. He embraced wholeheartedly her independence and understood her perhaps better than her closest friends. When Shaw mistook her stoicism in public as a lack of love for Con, Hilton defended her: 'If she did not seem to feel her loss, that is only seeming. Joy was her principle, and she would not let what she felt be seen and make her friends less joyful.'[4] Kathleen wrote later of him, 'I used to think that it was I myself who made and attracted adventures, but with [Hilton] we are always setting forth on new and unknown tracks.'[5]

Kathleen and Hilton were married in the crypt of the House of Commons on 3 March 1922, in a ten-minute ceremony with only Peter and Austen Chamberlain as witnesses. It all happened so quickly that the press outside her home thought she'd been jilted when she came back after only half an hour.[6]

In August 1923, at the age of forty-five, Kathleen gave birth to her much-longed-for second child during a thunderstorm. He was called Wayland, a name that she had given him while he was still in the womb. Fourteen years after Peter's birth, most of which had been spent as a single parent, Kathleen was now a wife and mother of two. Hilton and her boys, all three of whom she loved passionately, would be the focus of the rest of her life.

Kathleen divided her time between their new London house in Leinster Corner and Hilton's country cottage, The Lacket, in Wiltshire. She still loved to dance and listen to music, and she took up ice skating too. Their house was regularly filled with literary and artistic friends and young writers, artists, poets and dancers whose careers Kathleen encouraged. There was constituency business to attend to in Norfolk, and Kathleen did find being the wife of a Member of Parliament very difficult. She hated having to make speeches at women's' meetings, feeling shy and inept while at the same time smarting at having to curb her behaviour. She also hated that everyone knew who she was. But most of all she was in agonies for Hilton when he was criticised, heckled or attacked, and especially when he was up for election.[7]

When he retired from politics in 1935 and they became Lord and Lady Kennet, this anxiety disappeared. Kathleen's life as a peer's wife took her instead into court circles, attending garden parties, meeting the Prince of Wales and the Duke and Duchess of Kent and dining from gold plates with George V.[8] Moving in such exalted circles did not change her; she still resented spending money on her appearance and thought having to buy clothes for the coronation of King George VI in Westminster Abbey a terrible waste. She found the coronet that she had to wear with her robes very uncomfortable, but she only had to wear it for a few moments – because the ceremony was so long, she took chicken sandwiches and carried them in it.[9]

Sculpting, which had sustained Kathleen through many difficult periods of her life, continued to be central to her world, giving her confidence and self-respect when she was juggling being a politician's wife and the mother of a young child and a teenager.[10] She submitted work to the Royal Academy from 1914 until 1947 and in 1937 became the first woman to be elected to the Council of Royal Sculptors. Her renowned subjects included William Butler Yeats, her friends David Lloyd George and George Bernard Shaw and T. E. Lawrence. Kathleen met Lawrence in 1921 and found him entrancing. Years later, when he was still struggling with press attention, he asked her how she coped with it; Kathleen replied that she just let them do what they like and their interest soon died away.[11] This was not strictly true, of course, because although the 1920s may have opened a new chapter in Kathleen's life, she would still always be regarded as Scott's wife. Interest in her never really waned.

In the same year that Kathleen became a wife again, Shackleton died, and Emily became a polar widow. He had suffered a heart attack in South Georgia and was buried there at Emily's request. Kathleen wrote to offer her any help she needed.[12] When his affairs were settled it was clear that Shackleton had made financial provision for his men but left debts for his family. Emily had to accept support from family and friends, including Caroline Oates, to educate her children Ray, Cecily and Eddie. A memorial fund was set up to support his mother and their children, but Emily asked for the majority to go to her mother-in-law, whom Ernest had supported since his father's death.[13] Emily's income from her father did improve later in her life, and her financial situation was greatly helped by the granting of a grace-and-favour apartment at Hampton Court, which she moved into in 1930. This apartment, where Emily lived for the rest of her life, was the same one that Hannah Scott had occupied just a few years before.[14]

Kathleen and Emily were now the country's two most famous polar widows, but theirs was not an easy relationship. When Emily's son Eddie was set the holiday task of reading *Scott's Last Expedition* in the summer of 1924, she had discovered that a passage that had greatly upset her husband was still included. At the time of publication Shackleton had asked Kathleen to remove it, saying that Scott would never have included it if he'd lived. Emily was very upset about what all the children reading it would think of Eddie's father and thought of writing to Kathleen, 'but she is so hard about Ernest'.[15] Later that year Emily wrote again of her concerns about approaching Kathleen. She 'screwed up [her] courage' and wrote to ask if she could come to see her after telephoning to check that she was at home. When no reply came, she wrote, 'I can't think she would ignore my letter.' Even so, she didn't like to write again.[16]

Kathleen remained fiercely loyal to Con, defending him against any criticism and protecting his legacy. Several of the *Terra Nova* men had written their accounts of the expedition, but when Cherry wrote his, *The Worst Journey in the World*, Kathleen was very upset. They had drifted apart in the years since the war ended, and when Kathleen remarried she had a country house of her own and so didn't need the escape that Lamer had once offered. She was also very busy with Hilton and his career and with her sons. There had been a falling out too over the sale of two cars which Kathleen had given to a friend of Cherry's to do up and sell on; when no money was paid back to her she threatened court and Cherry got caught in the middle, bitterly resenting having to be interviewed on the matter.[17] Their friendship never really recovered, and the publication of his book drove an unsurmountable wedge between them.

Cherry had suffered greatly, grieving for his best friends Wilson and Birdie, and blaming himself. In the years since Scott's diary was published, however, he had also struggled not to blame his leader. He believed that the diary did not tell the full story, that it had been edited to make Scott look perfect. He was right that Scott's twelve notebooks had been edited into one continuous narrative for publication, but what had been removed was not hugely significant. Primarily it was repetitions and multiple entries as well as some of the criticisms of teammates that had been recorded privately and under enormous pressure. It was entirely usual for that sort of comment, reviewed later, to be judged to have been unfair and removed. Much of Scott's self-criticism was left in, revealing to all his bouts of moodiness and anxiety. His 'Message to the Public' was exactly as he had written it as he lay dying.[18] But Cherry's fear that there had been a committee cover-up was still acute. The diaries made no mention of the fact that the dogs had been taken on further than planned and that because of jumbled orders there was no dog food laid at One Ton. He felt that his reputation had been sacrificed to place Scott beyond criticism.[19] He still admired him greatly, but in his own cathartic account he wrote about the mistakes that his leader had made, generating a less heroic portrait of Scott than had existed before.

The Worst Journey in the World was published in December 1922 and received rave reviews, but Kathleen was furious. She wrote in her diary that Cherry had criticised Con in the most appalling fashion. What Kathleen detested was that Cherry had highlighted some of the complexities of Con's character. These were aspects that Con had written about himself – weaknesses, as he saw them, that he tried to conquer – but it was simply not Cherry's place to talk about them. The Scott that Cherry described was a subtle character, full of light and shade, flawed but a hero nonetheless. He was temperamentally weak, prone to depression and with little sense of humour, but his strong character ran through him like grain through wood and it was this that pulled him through:

> Scott was the strongest combination of a strong mind in a strong body that I have ever known. And this because he was so weak! Naturally so peevish, highly strung, irritable, depressed and moody ... His triumphs are many – but the Pole was not by any means the greatest of them. Surely the greatest was that by which he conquered his weaker self, and became the strong leader whom we went to follow and came to love.[20]

Kathleen took strong exception to the description of Con as weak and peevish, and later tried unsuccessfully to have the offending words taken out of the book.[21] Barrie sided with her, and George Bernard Shaw, who had encouraged Cherry to be as honest as possible and helped produce the book, defended him jovially, trying to prevent the group of friends from falling out. He failed.[22] Shaw had never met Con, and he'd kept his rather negative opinion of him to himself throughout his friendship with Kathleen, but now it emerged, and it wasn't particularly welcome.

When Kathleen commissioned the first official biography of Con, *Captain Scott*, from her great friend Stephen Gwyn in 1929, it was partly to redress the impression of him created by Cherry, but she found the process painful. 'Scott' was public property, and she knew that she could not hold back anything that illuminated his character and his achievements, but sharing her beloved 'Con' was another matter. Kathleen balked at the prospect of complete strangers reading Con's most intimate words: 'To think all these years nobody has seen those letters or known a thing of that amazing love; and now everybody who cares to can talk about it. It's twenty years ago, and it seems to me as present as to-day, and shocking to talk of, even to my nearest.'[23]

Kathleen's protectiveness of Con was eventually softened by her desire to look forward and to be happy. Now Lady Kennet, a mother of two sons and with a busy and interesting life, she was determined not to dwell on the past. When Ted Wilson's biographer wrote to her in 1939 informing her that he was planning to write a book about Scott, she replied that she'd rather be left out of it: 'It belongs to the past for me. Another world. And I am a different person.'[24] But of course, Con was never forgotten. That same year, on a March day close to the twenty-seventh anniversary of his death, she stayed in bed all day, reading and re-reading his letters.[25] They were 'letters that have made me weep and will make me weep every time I think of them till I die'.[26]

Family Tensions

With the public view of Ted remaining fairly consistent, Ory hadn't had to contend with criticism of her husband as Lois and Kathleen had. However, his scientific legacy was in danger of being overshadowed by the story of his and his teammates' deaths. For Ory and Ted the expedition had always been primarily about the acquisition of knowledge, not reaching the Pole first, and so overseeing the completion and publication of her husband's research and sharing his artworks with the nation would become Ory's mission for the rest of her life.

In 1920, the Scott Polar Research Institute was founded in Cambridge using money set aside from the funds raised by the Scott memorial fund. Frank Debenham had championed it, and Ory and Kathleen supported him. Ory saw it as a place where Ted's watercolours could be displayed and not left gathering dust as they would at the Royal Geographical Society.[1] When the institute was moved to a new building in 1934, Kathleen gave *Youth*, a statue modelled on T. E. Lawrence's younger brother, to stand in front of it and carved a bust of Con for a niche in its façade.

The widows regarded the institute as the best custodian of the precious documents and relics left behind by their husbands, and it would be over these items that Kathleen and Ory found common ground and had very occasional contact. Sporadically they issued joint statements to the press urging that treasured family items should be stored at the institute, the British Museum or some other safe repository where they could be studied. They both had a horror of their husbands' possessions and letters being traded on the open market.

Over the years, as the rawness of her grief eased and as her life drew further away from Antarctica, Ory was able to put a new perspective on things. She came to understand from Atch's research that the nutritional content of the rations given to Ted and his colleagues was only about half of what they needed. This was why they had starved to death. She accepted now too that fuel in the depots had evaporated and had not been taken by the returning men.[2] Nevertheless, Ory was unable to let go of her resentment of Teddy Evans and, as she saw it, his betrayal of Ted and willingness to grab the limelight. When Atch died on his way home from India in February 1929, she wrote to Cherry,

> Do you think anything could be written for the *Times* about him and the fact that it was owing to his decision to search for the Polar Party that we got all their records? People still believe that Evans led that party. I heard it said quite a time ago – also I have seen it in newspapers in connection with Evans' lectures – and it makes me fairly boil inside. No one seems to realise what Atch did.[3]

Then, in 1933, a sound version of Ponting's film, now given the title *90 Degrees South*, was released with an introduction by Teddy Evans. It can only be imagined what Ory thought about that.

Ory's life was not subsumed entirely by Antarctic matters. Ted had kindled in her a love of birding and walking, and she indulged in these hobbies. Many in the family believed that she was as good an ornithologist as Ted had been.[4] Her day began at half-past five when she did her correspondence or enjoyed the sounds of the birds waking up in her garden. If there were house guests, they were not allowed to show themselves before eight o'clock in the morning; this precious time of solitude was sacred. She loved gardening, she cooked and baked bread, and was an excellent housekeeper.[5] In the evenings she would go into town to see friends or to go to the theatre. She never missed a new production and loved talking about new actors; it was a greater part of her life even than concerts.[6]

Ory was an independent woman who had become used to travelling alone, taking plenty of books and needlework to keep herself busy.[7] She returned often to New Zealand, a place where she felt equally at home and where she had as many friends as she did in Britain.[8] Uncle Bill's cabin was always readied for her and the Kinseys were unstinting in their hospitality. In 1921 she made a trip with a friend to Darwin in northern Australia, venturing into the wilds with Aboriginal guides. She noted wildlife and collected specimens, dissecting and investigating using the kit she'd used during Ted's grouse work. In the stalactite- and stalagmite-filled Kintore Caves, she saw Aboriginal wall paintings by lantern light and spotted an unusual-looking bat; it was among the specimens that she shipped back to the Natural History Museum in London, and while she was staying with the Kinseys for Christmas in 1922 the zoologist who had examined it wrote to tell her that he had concluded that it was a new species. He named it after her.[9]

Five years later, Ory attended a reunion of the New Zealand Women's Overseas War Workers' Association in Wellington, celebrating the work that she and her fellow volunteers had done in the war. During her visit in 1931, New Zealand was hit by one of the worst natural disasters in its history. A 7.5 magnitude earthquake shook the city of Napier, killing 161 people and wounding many more. Ory put her wartime skills back into action, helping in the rescue effort and visiting the wounded in hospital.[10]

There was never any question of Ory remarrying. Ted's letters had talked of their being reunited in Heaven, and although she no longer believed in the afterlife it was perhaps implicit that theirs was a bond for life. She had been utterly devoted to him, and there could never be another man for her. She became used to her independence and to her nomadic lifestyle. Besides, she'd seen how others fared; Connie's marriage was not a happy one, and Ted's sisters Polly and Lily had their own difficulties too. They had married brothers Bernard and Godfrey Rendall; both were aggressive men, and their relationships were difficult.[11] It suited Ory to remain as she was.

In New Zealand in particular, Ory had found a certain degree of celebrity by being Ted's widow and quite enjoyed it. Her presence at the Women's Overseas War Workers' Association dinner was recorded in the 'Women in Print' section of the *Evening Post*. She wasn't afraid to use her fame either, telling Isabel in a letter in 1935 how she had been offered a top bunk on a steamer crossing in New Zealand and asked for a private cabin instead: 'He then asked my name and changed his manner!'[12] Ory was proud of her heroic widow status and felt that Kathleen had ruined hers by remarrying.[13] The Wilson family were not keen on the idea of a remarriage either, seeing Ory as an important link to their lost son, her role made clear by their nickname for her: Mrs Ted.[14]

Ory considered moving permanently to New Zealand, where she had so many friends and was so well regarded, but family troubles kept bringing her home. Her sister Connie had never really recovered from the nervous breakdown that she'd had thirty years before. She continued to suffer severe bouts of depression, not helped by a very unhappy marriage, and needed her sister's support, particularly after she became the mother of two daughters.[15] Ory was called back from New Zealand on several occasions by her brother-in-law Owen to help him deal with Connie and she found it difficult to watch his treatment of her sister, which was damaging her already precarious self-esteem. Then, on a sunny day in August 1931, Connie walked out of her cottage into a nearby field and set herself alight. She did this despite knowing the agony of it from an incident years before when her thin Indian shawl and flimsy evening dress caught the fire she was stoking and her arms and neck were burned;[16] and she killed herself knowing that her two daughters, Betty and Eleanor, were in the house and would be left motherless at nearly the same age that she and Ory had been.

Ory had been travelling home to see Connie at the time, and it was Isabel who had to break the news to her that her only sister had taken her own life at the age of only fifty-two. She couldn't imagine the hopelessness and sorrow that must have driven Connie to hurt herself and her children. She blamed Owen, who remarried very soon after the funeral. Ory wrote to a friend that she could have gladly shot him but instead had to do everything she could to help so that she could keep contact with the children, for whom she was joint guardian. It was for the girls' sake that she committed her future to England, renting 78 Bushey Heath in Hertfordshire, a house opposite Ted's sister Polly and her husband Godfrey Rendall.[17] Ory, the eldest of eight children, had now lost four of her siblings and all in tragic circumstances. She would survive all but one.[18]

Relations with the Wilsons had also become very difficult. There were money tensions as Ory was still dependent on Ted's brother Bernard for her finances, but she had also 'fallen out of love with them'. She had begun to feel jealous, wanting the memory of Ted all to herself, resenting all the years that they had spent with their brother when she had enjoyed only a relatively short time. There must have been bitterness on the Wilson side too, with Ted's siblings feeling that their very close relationship with him had been superseded by that of a spouse who could now make all the decisions about what happened to their brother's legacy.[19] The family was very keen for Ted's biography to be written and blamed Ory for the delay. Kathleen had made sure that Scott's diaries were out within the year, and Emily Shackleton had commissioned her husband's biography equally quickly, but Ory had not wanted to rush. Like Kathleen, she had recoiled from the idea of sharing her private thoughts and letters and was reluctant to revisit a painful past and so she had resisted for eighteen years.[20] Ted's brothers had wanted to write it, but Ory had been horrified at the thought of them reading her most intimate letters. Her frosty disapproval and withering stare were notorious in the family and some of the Wilsons were no doubt on the receiving end of it at this time.[21]

In the end, the perfect biographer had presented himself. George Seaver was sixteen years younger than Ory and physically reminiscent of Ted. He was a vicar but, as she told Cherry, 'not of the usual type', which was important to the now atheist Ory. Ted was Seaver's hero, and he was bowled over by his wife, becoming besotted with her. She introduced him to Debenham and Cherry in 1929 and she stayed at his home in Melksham as they worked on the book together. They punctuated their work and discussions of Ted with trips and visits, Ory sometimes riding in the wicker sidecar attached to Seaver's motorbike.[22] She found it terribly painful to revisit her loss and nearly had to stop, but Seaver coaxed her along, providing a warm and sympathetic ear. Her depth of trust in him was demonstrated when she put into his hands a chest filled with letters and private manuscripts.[23] Among them were Ted's final letters to her, which until then only Isabel and Reggie had seen.

The bond between Seaver and Ory grew very intense, and perhaps too close because Ory fled to New Zealand.[24] But after some distance, when Ory settled into number 78 a few years later, she renewed contact and the writing began again. Ted's biography, *Edward Wilson of the Antarctic: Naturalist and Friend*, was finally published in September 1933, with an introduction provided by Cherry. It was popular and sold well, but not all his friends and family liked it. Some thought it made him too saintly and sentimental, and it included none of his humour or his temper, nor any of the other traits that made Ted human. Ory, however, was pleased. She was inclined to keep him in an ivory tower, and this was the Ted she wanted the world to see.[25]

Unlike Lois and Kathleen, Ory had no children of her own. In her later years, however, she filled her home with young people and was eager to support them. Connie's daughters were regular visitors and in 1933 Ory brought her niece Joan, daughter of Ted's brother Jim, to live with her for a while. Jim had become very depressed again, and the following year Ory loaned Jim and his wife Nora her house while she travelled.[26] Jim's son Michael remembers his aunt Ory very fondly; she got him into birds, opening his eyes to the fact that they could be recognised by their song alone.[27] Ory remained interested in Peter Scott too. She had often enquired about him in her letters to Kathleen, and later she attended one of his lectures on pink-footed geese.[28]

Young New Zealanders came and went through the house, Ory using royalties from Ted's biography to help them in their careers. Esmond Atkinson, the son-in-law of one of her friends, came to England with his wife and Ory paid for the treatment for his 'war epilepsy' and afterwards sponsored him to go to art school in London.[29] Esmond's sister Rosalind was an actress and Ory helped her too, thrilling at the opportunity to see her on stage and to go behind the scenes afterwards.[30]

The closeness of Ory's relationship with Rosalind in particular was demonstrated when she added a codicil to her will after her sister's death. Connie had been Ory's executor and trustee for her estate and for the unspent money from the Mansion House fund. The other executor was a public trustee, usually appointed when there was nobody else appropriate or trusted to take on the role. Their instructions had been that when Ory died the fund money should be split, with half given in equal shares to Ted's siblings and the other half in equal shares to Ory's; the remainder of her estate was to go to Connie.[31] When Connie died, instead of replacing her with another family member as executor of her will and trustee for the fund money, Ory appointed Rosalind. The residue of her estate was then to be split equally between her cousin Geraldine de Courcy O'Grady and Rosalind.[32] This unusual arrangement, which gave financial control and an inheritance to a young woman who was neither a Wilson nor a Souper, is perhaps a reflection of Ory's relationship with her family at that time.

A Family Home

It has been suggested that Edgar Evans might have wanted to open a pub when he came home.[1] He had plenty of experience, having grown up in a pub-owning family and worked in a hotel before he joined the Navy. It was also one of the ways that seamen in their retirement could earn a living, and the life of a publican might have suited the jovial and sociable Edgar. His fame and his stories would have attracted punters to his door. Tom Crean would eventually open his own pub in Ireland in Anascaul, in County Kerry, calling it the South Pole Inn. But when Lois was asked what Edgar would have done had he lived she had replied, 'He would have drawn his pension and settled down to land life.'[2] She made no mention of their running a pub. Perhaps she, with her involvement in Aggie's temperance work, did not relish a return to that life; perhaps it just wasn't something they'd discussed in any detail. In any case, it was irrelevant now. Lois had no choice but to create a new future for her and her children.

Deciding not to settle in Gower permanently, Lois eventually chose Morriston, near Swansea, to be her home; she would stay there for the rest of her life. It was an obvious choice because Lois knew the area very well. Her older sister Beatrice had lived there, in Clydach Road, since her marriage in 1896 to John Faull, who ran an ironmongers while Beatrice raised their four children.[3] She was Lois's only surviving sister and the two women were very close.[4] Her sister's eldest daughter, Beatrice Ida Faull, had been one of Lois and Edgar's bridesmaids and Lois had visited their home many times, both before and after Edgar died. The Faull household had provided much-needed continuity for Lois and her children, temporarily homeless and adrift in their grief. It was there that she had met Teddy Evans when he travelled to Swansea to see her. The youngest of the Faull children, Marjory and Margaret, were close in age to

Muriel, Norman and Ralph, and these cousins grew up spending a great deal of time together, just as Lois and Edgar had.[5]

Morriston – in Welsh Treforys – is a name which perfectly describes the town's origins. In 1726, Robert Morris, who had come to Wales from Shropshire, took over a copper works that had been established along the banks of the River Tawe. His son John took over the business next, and as it grew it attracted men from the surrounding agricultural areas. Housing was in short supply, and so they gravitated towards the unsanitary slum dwellings of Swansea. John Morris, who was a devout Christian and ahead of his time as an employer, came up with an innovative solution: between 1790 and 1796, he laid the foundations of a model town for his workers. He chose farmland 4 miles to the north of Swansea and had the streets laid out in a grid pattern which remains today. There were 141 cottages at first, each with its own garden, and his most reliable workers also had land where they could keep a cow. Morris endowed a church at the town's centre and provided it with an organ. Morris Town, eventually shortened to Morriston, was the first planned industrial village in Wales.[6]

As the copper industry waned in the mid-nineteenth century, tinplate rose in its place. Cheaper than copper, pewter and brass, and less fragile than glass and pottery, it proved to be a popular material for pots and pans and vessels of all kinds. By the time Lois arrived, Morriston was an established town of tinplate workers and three large tinworks formed its industrial heart. They dominated the landscape with their tall chimneys, smoke and noise, and they also dominated the lives of the people who lived there. Most inhabitants of the town found work somewhere along the production chain that rolled iron plates, coated them with tin to prevent corrosion and turned out finished vessels.

There is a frustrating gap in the extant record of Lois's life between the years just after Edgar's death and the end of the war and so it's not easy to pinpoint exactly when she moved to Morriston. Tracing the lives of working-class people, particularly women, is challenging when key events fall between censuses and when their lack of a home or a vote mean they leave little trace in local or national records. Consequently, it's not until 1918 that Lois's residence in Morriston is certain. She and the children moved to 5 Slate Street, a terraced house just fifteen minutes' walk from her sister's home.[7] This relocation may have been made easier because Lois's worries about her parents' financial position had eased; they had both reached the age of seventy and become eligible for a state pension. William had been able to stop work and they moved out of their remote cottage shortly after the war, and into a small home in Rhossili, close to St Mary's Church where they, Lois and many of their family had married and been baptised.[8] Edgar's mother had moved too after the death of her sister Anne in 1919 to share a home with her widowed sister Elizabeth.[9] As young wives, these two women had lived close to each other on Fernhill Top and Sarah had given birth to Edgar in Elizabeth's cottage.[10] Now at the end of their lives, they set up home together at the bottom of the hill in Middleton, in the community where they grew up and near to the Ship Inn. Elizabeth's two unmarried daughters shared the home with them, and these four women supported each other until the end of Sarah's life. Lois's father William not only had his two sisters living just a short distance away, but he and Jane also had both their daughters nearby and numerous grandchildren old enough to visit and help out.[11]

Lois's move from a small community in Gower to a town close to Swansea may, however, have had a financial imperative. Edgar had not left Lois an inheritance and the support given to her by the Mansion House fund was not sufficient to live on for the rest of her life. The money paid to her on behalf of her children would reduce when Norman turned fourteen and the Navy stopped paying his pension in 1919; three years later, when Ralph was fourteen and Muriel sixteen, their payments would end too. There would still be money from the government until each child was eighteen but then all support would end, meaning the loss of approximately £1,500 a year in today's terms.[12] Perhaps Morriston offered more opportunities for Lois's children, because by the time that Norman was fifteen he was working as an apprentice electrician. He was employed at the Upper Forest Steel & Tinplate company, which lay just a short walk from their house, on the other side of the River Tawe and the railway tracks, alongside the town's two other tinplate works and its iron foundries and chemical factories.[13] Norman's salary was important but with two other teenage children to support it seems very likely that Lois would have had to work. In 1923 there is a 'Lois Evans' listed as living at 4 Pentrepoeth Road, a butcher's shop with accommodation. Until she was fourteen Lois's parents had run a greengrocers' shop in Swansea and then, as a publican's daughter, she had worked alongside them in the Ship Inn so shop work and dealing with customers would have been very familiar to her. If this record is for Lois, then it's possible that she moved her family to this address, which provided not only a home but also quite possibly a job for her for at least five years.[14]

The end of the First World War brought a change in the national attitude to housing the working classes, and this was to be hugely significant for Lois. Before the war, private companies had built nearly all new housing, but afterwards it became clear that this was just too expensive. Labour and materials were scarce and rising building costs meant that rents for new houses were pushing beyond the means of the average working-class family. Prime Minster David Lloyd George promised that returning soldiers and sailors would have 'homes fit for heroes', and in 1919 the Addison Act addressed the acute shortage of houses in the country. It placed a duty on councils to provide accommodation for working men and women and, for the first time, provided government funding to build council-provided housing on a large scale.

In the 1920s and 1930s, Swansea saw council housing built in swathes. It was this initiative that meant that by 1929 Lois had moved into 62 Heol Fedw.[15] The house, which was only a few years old, was in Cwmrhydyceirw, a suburb adjacent to Morriston, and Lois paid rent to Swansea council.[16] She was now fifty years old, and this house provided a safe haven for Lois and her family for the rest of her life. Despite the fresh start, however, Edgar was never far from her thoughts, and she named her new home Terra Nova. His portrait hung in the hall, his eyes following every visitor as they entered the house.[17]

Lois and her siblings had always been close, and she and her sister had chosen to live near to each other so that they could be part of each other's daily lives. Although she had moved house after she had been widowed, Beatrice was still only a short bus ride away from Lois.[18] When their younger brother eventually chose to come home to Swansea, they shared this loving relationship with him as well. Stanley had retired from the Navy in 1923 and stayed in Devonport with his only child, Amelia, but after she married ten years later and set up her own marital home Stanley came back to Wales. He moved in with Lois at Terra Nova and stayed with her until he died in 1939.

The house was close to the tinworks, and most of the families in the neighbourhood were involved in the industry. Men worked as tinplate rollermen, tinplate cold rollers, furnacemen and tinplate shearers while their wives raised the children and kept the house in order.[19] Not surprisingly, the tinplate industry played an important role in the lives of Lois's children as they began to forge futures of their own. Norman left home first and was lodging with Edward and Lizzie Rogers in Morriston when he fell in love with their daughter Lydia.[20] He married her in 1928 when he was twenty-three, but for a few years in the early 1930s he moved back into Terra Nova with his mother, siblings and uncle Stanley. Whatever the reason for the separation, Norman and Lydia finally settled into a home of their own in Morriston. Norman continued to work as an electrician in one of the local tin works and Lydia raised their son, Edward John, whom she gave birth to in 1939.[21] When war broke out that year, both of Lois's sons were in their thirties. Without their service records it's not clear what they did during those years, but their older cousin John

Wilfred Faull, Beatrice's son, became a major in the Glamorganshire Home Guard and was awarded an OBE in 1944.[22]

After the war Norman and Lydia moved into Terra Nova for a couple of years before moving into 9 Fendrod Walk, a new home on a prefab housing estate.[23] After the Second World War there was an acute housing shortage because thousands of homes had been destroyed by bombs and also because of the rising birth rate. Churchill's government launched a programme of temporary housing to ensure that everybody, and returning servicemen in particular, had homes in which to restart their family lives. These prefabricated bungalows were meant to last ten years, at which point it was hoped that the building of new housing would have caught up with demand. To encourage young couples to move in, prefabs, although quite small, were designed to have all the mod cons: fitted kitchens, indoor plumbing, built-in cupboards, big windows and gardens. Most also had electric fridges and cookers – very modern luxuries at the time – as well as hot water, an indoor toilet and electric light. Many council houses were still being built with outdoor toilets and no indoor plumbing, and electric light had only found its way into homes on a large scale after the National Grid was established in 1926.[24] Norman and Lydia, like many prefab couples, enjoyed the comforts and stayed on much longer than planned. Their house was close to Terra Nova, and Lois was able to spend plenty of time with her grandson, known to the family as John.

Muriel married when she was thirty-one. Her husband, Stuart Hawkins, worked in the tin industry as a mill roll grinder. She had lived with Lois at Terra Nova until her marriage and then moved only a few miles away to Stuart's family home, Bryn Mount in Gorseinon.[25] Every other Tuesday Lois took her grandson John by bus to Gorseinon to see Muriel and her children, Anne and David.[26]

Lois's youngest child, Ralph, never left home. He was employed at one of the local tinworks as a plater and after his marriage to Sheila in 1947 he moved his new wife into Terra Nova, where gradually they would be able to take over the work of running the house and paying its rent. Their two children, Helen and Edgar Evans, were brought up in their grandmother's house and they all lived with Lois for the rest of her life.[27]

With all her children and grandchildren living a walk or a short bus ride away, Lois's life was full. She continued to worship at the Anglican St David's Church in Morriston and may well have been part of its choir.[28] The town was also famous for its Orpheus Choir, and it had a ladies' choir too. Whether or not Lois was a member, the musical tradition of Morriston must have been an enduring joy to her, a woman who loved to sing.

Forgotten Widows

In the last years of her life, Ory was looked after by Eleanor Forbes, the daughter of *Discovery* geologist Hartley Ferrar and his wife Gladys.[1] She had suffered a stroke at the age of sixty-three and needed help at home. Margaret Bowen, her old friend from New Zealand, now running a school in Yorkshire, came during the school holidays to see her and Isabel came often, taking Ory out in her car to go birding. Eventually nurses from St George's Hospital came to look after her too, and finally there was a full-time resident nurse. Depressed by her inactivity and struggling emotionally, Ory suffered a nervous breakdown, as had so many of the people that she had known.[2] She asked Evelyn to burn all of Ted's letters – every scrap. Perhaps she had regretted sharing them with Seaver and allowing him to quote them in his book, but more likely she just did not want anything so private left behind for others to pick through in the future.[3] In burning this record, the most intimate moments of her life with Ted were protected.

As world war broke out again in 1939, Ory's health deteriorated further and she went to live in a nursing home in Finchley in north London. She was not alone; Seaver sat by her bed writing his book on Scott, and Isabel, her dearest friend, remained with her to the end. Oriana died on 25 April 1945 at the age of seventy and was cremated at Golders Green crematorium, an unusual decision at a time when most people still chose to be buried. At the end, she did not forget Cherry. She returned to him his copy of Tennyson which Ted had taken to Antarctica and which he had so kindly allowed her to keep.

Kathleen, happily married to Hilton, continued to live a vibrant life almost until the end. During the Second World War she had signed up to do facial work again as she had before, but she was not called. She moved between their houses in Fritton in Norfolk and London, staying wherever seemed safest from attack, but to no avail – the Blitz damaged their house in London and in Norfolk their car was caught up in a bombing and machine-gun attack by enemy aircraft which killed twelve. Kathleen worried most about her sons, especially after Wayland reached the age of eighteen and joined up, writing in her diary that she feared the horrors of war were 'nearer now, near my sons'.[4] Both Peter and Wayland were in the Navy, dodging U-boats and aeroplanes, and Kathleen dreaded each broadcast as it might bring news of their ships being sunk. The boys' young friends, who had filled the house in Norfolk and swum and boated on the lake, began appearing in the casualty lists. In her diary entry of 2 June 1940, Kathleen wrote, 'The boys are going thick and fast now. It seems as if it were only a matter of days before it were my own boy's turn: and one just sits by, impotent.'

Kathleen was one of the lucky mothers. Both her sons survived, and her first grandchild was born in 1943 following Peter's marriage to Elizabeth Jane Howard.[5]

As her health began to fail, Kathleen was diagnosed with leukaemia. She died in July 1947, aged sixty-nine. Her last request to her husband was to inscribe her simple headstone with the words, 'Kathleen. No happier woman ever lived.'[6]

Lois continued to live close to her children and with her son Ralph until the end of her life. She died on 23 April 1952 at the age of seventy-three at Gorseinon Hospital near the home of her daughter Muriel.[7] The funeral cortege left from her home, Terra Nova, where she had lain in an open coffin as was the tradition. She was laid to rest in an unmarked grave at her own request, alongside her beloved brother Stanley.[8]

Ory, Kathleen and Lois had only a very short time with their polar heroes. Theirs were all marriages defined by years of separation. Ory was married the longest, but they were apart for half of the eleven years that she was Ted's wife. Kathleen married Con while he was already planning the expedition, and two years later he left. Lois lived with Edgar for five years, knowing that if the call came he would leave with Scott again. A great love was theirs to mourn, and there were four children to treasure, but these marriages represented only a fraction of the many years that these women lived. Nevertheless, they were to define the rest of their lives. When the three women died, over thirty years later, their long-dead husbands were still at their side. The notice of Kathleen's death in *The Times* stated, 'Wife of Lord Kennet, widow of Captain R.F. Scott'. Ory's described her as 'the widow of Dr Edward Wilson (who died with Captain Scott in the Antarctic)'. Lois's death did not feature in *The Times* but her local fame as a polar widow ensured that she was remembered in newspapers in Wales as the 'widow of Petty Officer (Taff) Evans'.[9]

Their husbands had been mourned by a nation and inspired the generation that followed. It was a legacy that was passed on to their children, whose lives would be affected by their famous fathers even though they had hardly known them. Peter Scott wrote later that he was only one and a half when his father left and so was spared feeling his loss, but being the son of a national hero had very definite consequences for him. He did feel that the press treated him as fair game, but his mother protected him quite successfully. People who had admired Scott expected Peter to be like him, and the frequency with which he was asked if he would follow in his footsteps made him determined to take another direction. His father had set a standard to which Peter feared he might never aspire, and so following his father's wish that he pursue natural history was a much more exciting prospect. Peter had a natural love of nature and Kathleen very cleverly and subtly encouraged it.[10] He would far exceed the hopes that his father had expressed in his final letters to Kathleen. Ornithologist, conservationist and painter Peter Scott established the Wildfowl & Wetlands Trust in Slimbridge and helped found the Society of Wildlife Artists. He was central to the creation of the World Wildlife Fund and designed its panda logo. He was knighted for his services to the conservation of wild animals. Through her encouragement of her son's artistic talents and love of nature, Kathleen had kept her final promise to Con.

For Edgar's children the legacy was very painful. Whether it was said directly or whispered behind their backs, the charge that their father had let down his teammates and contributed to their deaths still hung in the background. In the plethora of books written by and about his colleagues, Edgar was increasingly marginalised, blamed or forgotten. Norman, Lois's eldest son, was badly bullied at school and was only able to talk about his father much later in his life.[11] Muriel was affected by the same sadness. Interviewed in her late eighties, she said of her life, 'I would have rather had a living father than a dead hero.'[12] Lois's fight to commemorate Edgar in Wales and to restore his reputation was taken on by other members of the family, first by his niece Sarah, who had taken a biscuit from Captain Scott and sailed with her uncle into the Bristol Channel. But it wasn't until 1994 that an official memorial was raised to Edgar in Wales. Commissioned by the Captain Scott Society of Cardiff, the white marble bust was sculpted in Gower and was presented to the City of Swansea. The following year, the first biography of Edgar was published.[13] Eighty-seven-year-old Muriel was the guest of honour at the launch in Swansea and must have had some satisfaction in hearing the lord mayor of the city say about her father that 'perhaps his recognition has been much too long in coming'.[14]

Thrown together in the aftermath of tragedy and thrust into the limelight in an intense period of public scrutiny in 1913, the three widows gradually slipped to the outer edges of the Antarctic narrative. Kathleen is the only one who became famous in her own right, but the role that she, Oriana and Lois played in supporting their polar heroes in life and defending them in death has been almost forgotten now, despite the enduring appeal of their husbands' story.

On 29 November 1948, Charles Frend and Michael Balcon's film *Scott of the Antarctic* was selected for the Royal Command Film Performance with a premier at the Empire, Leicester Square. Survivors had objected to any potential adaptation of the *Terra Nova* expedition in case the story was changed for dramatic effect and because they felt uncomfortable about money being made from the tragedy. The strongest resistance had come from Kathleen, and earlier plans to make a movie had to be cancelled when she refused to give her permission despite appeals from Gainsborough Pictures and from Teddy Evans. Kathleen told them, 'Not while I am alive.'[15] Her attitude may have been shaped by her visit to see a play about the Antarctic tragedy staged in Berlin in 1930; she wasn't upset or offended but considered it to be inaccurate and dull.[16] By 1946, however, Kathleen's view seems to have softened and she responded positively to an approach by Balcan's screenwriter.[17] Kathleen gave her consent and allowed access to family papers.[18]

When the film premiered two years later, Kathleen was dead and so was Ory. Lois still lived, however, and she travelled to London with Ralph and Norman to see it. At the cinema she met with other surviving relatives, including some of Scott, Wilson and Oates's sisters, for the first time in over thirty years.[19] As the lights dimmed, Lois watched her Edgar brought to life again on screen by James Robertson Justice alongside John Mills, who played Scott. Most of the survivors who saw the film agreed that it was a very accurate depiction. They had been won over, and some had worked with the filmmakers to ensure that every detail was as realistic as possible.

The only part that was not authentic was the depiction of the wives. The producers admitted later that they had rewritten their parts to make them more appealing to contemporary cinemagoers, who perhaps expected their heroes to struggle in manly solidarity and their heroines to be beautiful and passive.[20] The roles played by Kathleen and Oriana in the Antarctic story were whitewashed, and they appeared only fleetingly in the film as 1940s housewives, cheerfully waiting and homemaking, wearing aprons, baking and arranging flowers. Lois, watching from the stalls, was probably not surprised to find that she was not featured at all.

Timeline of the *Terra Nova* Expedition

1910

15 June	*Terra Nova* leaves Cardiff
15 August	*Terra Nova* arrives in Simon's Town, near Cape Town, South Africa (Oriana and Kathleen travelled on RSS *Saxon* with Scott)
12 October	*Terra Nova* arrives in Melbourne, Australia (Oriana and Kathleen travelled on *Corinthic* with Ted)
	Scott receives a telegram announcing that Amundsen is going to the South Pole on *Fram*
28 October	*Terra Nova* arrives in Lyttelton, near Christchurch, New Zealand
26 November	*Terra Nova* sails from Lyttelton to Port Chalmers, New Zealand
29 November	*Terra Nova* sails to Antarctica and will be out of contact for a year

1911

January	*Terra Nova* arrives in the Antarctic. The party skirt McMurdo Sound for suitable landing sites and find Cape Evans on 4 January
February	Oriana and Kathleen arrive back in England from New Zealand
	To avoid being stuck in the ice, *Terra Nova* leaves to overwinter in New Zealand, leaving expedition members and scientists in Antarctica
March	Reports reach Britain that Amundsen has been spotted in Antarctica and has set up base 60 miles closer to the Pole than Scott

November	Polar Party sets out, with a planned return of March 1912
November	The first of Ponting's films are shown in the UK
15 December	Roald Amundsen reaches the South Pole

1912

January	*Terra Nova* arrives back in Antarctica, bringing letters from home, but the Polar Party have missed them
January	Oriana travels with her sister Connie back to New Zealand to meet her husband Ted. Scott had written to tell her that he would be keeping Ted for a further year, but Ory had already set off when it arrived
17 January	Scott, Wilson, Oates, Bowers and Evans reach the South Pole
7 March	Roald Amundsen sails into Hobart, Tasmania on board *Fram*. The press begins to report that he was first to the Pole
Feb.–March	All five members of the Polar Party die on their return journey from the Pole
March	The Polar Party has not returned when *Terra Nova* departs to avoid being trapped in the ice
1 April	*Terra Nova* arrives back in New Zealand, carrying the news that Scott and the Polar Party were last seen safe and well on 4 January and that Scott intends to stay a further year to finish the scientific work. Teddy Evans is on board, suffering with scurvy
	Oriana is disappointed at having to face another year of separation but decides to stay on in New Zealand
November	Atkinson leads a search party which finds the bodies of Scott, Wilson and Bowers lying in their tent. They bring back their diaries and final letters

1913

	Lois moves back to Wales to wait, with family support, for Edgar's return
18 January	*Terra Nova* sails back to Antarctica with Teddy Evans in command to pick up the Polar Party and other colleagues. They are told that the Polar Party are dead
10 February	The news is telegraphed around the world
14 February	A service of remembrance is held at St Paul's Cathedral
April	Kathleen and Oriana return home

Acknowledgements

The idea for this book came while I was on holiday in Sicily. Thinking about the history of Britain that I was taught during the 1970s and '80s, I was reflecting that behind every great man and great event there must have been wives, children and families left to pick up the pieces of their famous and heroic exploits. These wives, often widows, had to worry about all the domestic details of life – feeding their children, keeping a home going and earning money while the rest of the world thrilled at the stories of their husbands, men now consigned to the history books. I wondered what the women who shared a life with Admiral Nelson, the men of the Light Brigade and of course Captain Scott really thought of their husbands' sacrifice and whether it was worth it. I am grateful that my publisher, Amberley, was intrigued by the idea too and that the Society of Authors were interested enough to award me a grant from their Authors' Foundation. This has helped me to fund my research and has been invaluable.

Kathleen, Oriana and Lois all have living relatives and I have been helped enormously by their support and their unwavering politeness and patience in answering my questions. I am extremely grateful to Louisa Young, Dafila Scott, David Wilson, John Evans, Tyler and Anthony Ford for sharing information and for giving me permission to quote from family sources and to use family photos.

Writing a book during a pandemic, when archives and libraries were closed for much of my research time, has been an enormous challenge. Without the help of archivists and librarians who ran ahead of the closure grabbing scans and information, and those working from home who still managed to access documents for me, writing this book would have been impossible. I must thank in particular Naomi Boneham and Laura Ibbett at the Scott Polar Research Institute in Cambridge, Emma Williams at

Swansea Museum, Katie Millien and the team at the West Glamorgan Archive Service, and Claire Tranter and her colleagues at Swansea Council Library Service. The London Library supplied me with books throughout lockdown and allowed my work to continue, for which I'm enormously grateful.

I have also discovered a whole world of wonderful people who are both enthusiastic and extremely knowledgeable about all things polar. They too have been incredibly generous to me, giving advice, sharing sources and making recommendations. I would like to thank in particular Michael Smith, Sara Wheeler, Liam Maloney and Claire Warrior but also Isobel Williams, Gary Gregor, Anne Strathie, Susanna Ferrar and many, many more. My thanks also to Alex Bennett, my brilliant editor at Amberley, Robin Quinn for once again creating an excellent index and my brother David Fletcher for his wonderful map research.

My great friends Briony Sutcliffe and Jane Manson have also been superb. Through our regular walks Briony kept me sane and when I needed a push invited me to talk to her book group which forced me to finish my first draft and provided fantastic feedback. Jane has listened to tales of my widows and accompanied me on my research trip to Wales, showing unstinting interest and support throughout. Thank you both.

Finally, without my husband Jon Teckman I wouldn't have been able to write this book. He has been a supporter, a sounding post, and a reviewer and his comments have, as always, been insightful and invaluable. He also provided a vital supply of coffee and snacks when I was at my most hard-pressed. And so, I thank him and my sons Joseph and Matthew for putting up with me and my widows for the last two years. I hope that you'll feel that this book was worth it.

Sources

Kathleen was the only one of the three wives to leave a diary. She began it in 1910 for her husband and kept it up until 1946, just before she died. The published version, *Self-Portrait of an Artist: From the diaries and memoirs of Lady Kennet, Kathleen, Lady Scott*, also includes extracts from the autobiography that she wrote in 1932. In 1995, Kathleen's first and only biography, *A Great Task of Happiness: the life of Kathleen Scott*, was written by her granddaughter Louisa Young. It draws on the extensive family archives and papers that are kept at the University Library in Cambridge, including Kathleen's diary.

In addition to the papers in the Kennet archive in Cambridge, other primary sources relating to Kathleen can be found in the Scott Polar Research Institute in Cambridge (SPRI), the Royal Geographical Society (RGS), the National Maritime Museum and the British Library. Details are given in my endnotes.

Oriana did not want her letters looked through after her death, but the official biography of Ted that she commissioned from George Seaver, *Edward Wilson of the Antarctic: naturalist and friend*, does contain extracts from the letters that Oriana was happy to share. At the end of her life she asked her friend Evelyn Forbes to burn all of her personal letters and so Seaver's book is a valuable record. Oriana's great-nephew David Wilson wrote a biography of Ted in 2000 called *Cheltenham in Antarctica*, and this includes information about Oriana drawn from the Wilson Family Archive. He also recorded interviews with family members who knew her (recording of interviews between David Wilson and Evelyn Forbes, 25 August 1995, and David Wilson and Michael Wilson, 30 March 1995, Cheltenham Borough Council and the Cheltenham Trust/ The Wilson Family Collection).

The first biography of Oriana wasn't written until 2019, and *Woman with the Iceberg Eyes: Oriana F. Wilson* is particularly useful for its information about her time in New Zealand.

Letters to and from Oriana do survive in various archives in this country, primarily at SPRI and Cheltenham Borough Council and the Cheltenham Trust/The Wilson Family Collection. Again, details are given in the endnotes.

Lois has left the least trace. There has never been a biography of her and the first to be written about Edgar didn't arrive until 1995. Gary Gregor's *Swansea's Antarctic Explorer, Edgar Evans, 1876-1912* was built upon by Isobel Williams' *Captain Scott's Invaluable Assistant – Edgar Evans* in 2012. Both contain information about Lois. However, very few primary sources survive.

Her grandson John Evans told me when we spoke in March 2020 that a stack of letters written by Lois and Edgar to each other, his with a penguin on the paper, were once stored in an old bureau in his family home. When his parents separated temporarily, they left the house and the bureau and the letters inside all disappeared. He doesn't know where they went. In 1984 the family sold a number of items at Sotheby's, including Edgar's diary from the Western Journey and various papers and other letters. Some of these documents are now part of archive collections, accessible to the public, and others are probably in private ownership. None of Lois's letters survive in any archive as far as I know.

Archives

(Details of sources used given in endnotes)

Aggie Weston's Charity, Portsmouth
Bradfield School
British Library
Dundee Heritage Trust
Kerry County Museum
LSE Library
National Library of Wales
National Maritime Museum
Portsmouth History Centre and records office
Royal Collection
Royal Archive
Royal Geographical Society
Saint Andrew's Prep School, Eastbourne
Scott Polar Research Institute Archives, University of Cambridge (SPRI)
Swansea Museum

West Glamorgan Archive Service
The Wilson Cheltenham Art Gallery & Museum
Women's Archive Wales.
The Women's Library (London School of Economics)

Books

Barczewski, Stephanie L., *Antarctic destinies: Scott, Shackleton, and the changing face of heroism* (London: Continuum, 2007)

Barczewski, Stephanie L., *Heroic failure and the British* (New Haven: Yale University Press, 2016).

Barret-Ducrocq, Françoise, *Love in the time of Victoria: sexuality, class and gender in nineteenth-century London*. Translated by John Howe (London: Verso, 1991)

Beynon, Leonard, *Rhossili: The Land, Landscape and People* (Swansea: West Glamorgan Archive Service, 2008.

Black, Ros, *Scandal, Salvation and Suffrage: The Amazing Women of the Temperance Movement* (Troubadour, 2014)

Blackie, John, *Bradfield, 1850-1975* (Bradfield [Bradfield, Berks.]: Warden and Council of St Andrew's College, 1976)

Blum, Hester, *The news at the ends of the Earth: The print culture of polar exploration* (Durham and London: Duke University Press, 2019)

Cherry-Garrard, Apsley, *The Worst Journey in the World* (London: Vintage Books, 2010)

Crane, David, *Scott of the Antarctic: A life of Courage and Tragedy in the Extreme South* (London: Harper Collins, 2005)

Crow, Duncan, *The Edwardian Woman* (Routledge Library Editions: Women's History, 2012)

Gosling, Lucinda, *Knitting for Tommy: keeping the Great War soldier warm* (Stroud: The History Press, 2014)

Fiennes, Ranulph, *Captain Scott* (London: Coronet, 2004)

Frost, Ginger S., *Living in sin: cohabiting as husband and wife in nineteenth-century England* (Manchester; New York: Manchester University Press; Palgrave Macmillan, 2008)

Gregor, Gary C., *Swansea's Antarctic Explorer, Edgar Evans, 1876-1912* (Swansea: Swansea City Council, 1995)

Gregor, Gary, *Edgar Evans of Gower (1876-1912): From Rhossili to the South Pole* (Swansea: The Gower Society, 2008)

Hempleman-Adams, David, Sophie Gordon and Emma Stuart, *The Heart of the Great Alone: Scott, Shackleton and Antarctic Photography* (London: Royal Collection, 2011)

Herbert, Kari, *Polar Wives* (Vancouver: Greystone Books, 2012)

Hanbury-Tenison, Robin (ed.), *The Great Explorers* (London: Thames & Hudson, 2010)

Heffer, Simon, *The age of decadence: Britain 1880 to 1914* (London: Cornerstone Digital, 2017)

Hughes, Wendy, *The story of Gower* (Capel Garmon: Gwasg Carreg Gwalch, 1992)

Jones, Max, *The Last Great Quest: Captain Scott's Antarctic Sacrifice* (Oxford: Oxford University Press, 2003)

Koppel, Lily, *The astronaut wives club: a true story* (London: Headline, 2013)

Langford, Paul, *Englishness Identified: manners and character, 1650-1850* (Oxford: Oxford University Press, 2000)

Lane, Heather, Naomi Boneham and Robert D. Smith (eds), *The last letters: the British Antarctic Expedition 1910-13/the South Pole party: Captain Robert Falcon Scott, CVO, RN; Dr. Edward Adrian Wilson; Lt. Henry Robertson Bowers, RIM; Captain Lawrence Edward Grace Oates; Petty Officer Edgar Evans, RN* (Cambridge: Scott Polar Research Institute, 2012)

Lincoln, Margarette, *Naval wives & mistresses* (London: National Maritime Museum, 2007)

Lucas, Robert, *Rhossili: A Village Background* (Cowbridge and Bridgend: D.Brown & Sons Ltd, 1989)

MacInnes, Katherine, *Woman with the Iceberg Eyes: Oriana F. Wilson* (Cheltenham: The History Press, 2019)

Mill, H. R. et al., *Rejoice my Heart: The Making of H.R. Mill's "The Life of Sir Ernest Shackleton" The Private Correspondence of Dr. Hugh Robert Mill and Lady Shackleton, 1922-33* (Santa Monica: Adélie Books, 2007)

Mountevans, Admiral Lord, *South with Scott* (London and Glasgow: Collins, 1921)

Parker, Sarah E., *Grace & favour: a handbook of who lived where in Hampton Court Palace, 1750 to 1950* (Surrey: Historic Royal Palaces, 2005)

Riddell, Fern, *Death in Ten Minutes: The Forgotten Life of Radical Suffragette Kitty Marion* (London: Hodder & Stoughton, 2019)

Savours, Ann (ed.), *Edward Wilson: Diary of the 'Discovery' expedition to the Antarctic regions 1901-1904; edited from the original mss. in the Scott Polar Research Institute, Cambridge* (London: Blandford Press, 1966)

Seaver, George, *Edward Wilson of the Antarctic: naturalist and friend; with an introduction by Apsley Cherry-Garrard* (London: John Murray, 1933)

Seaver, George, *Edward Wilson of the Antarctic: naturalist and friend; together with a memoir of Oriana Wilson; with an introduction by Apsley Cherry-Garrard* (London: John Murray, 1963)

Scott, Robert Falcon, *Scott's Last Expedition, Diaries 26 November 1910-29 March 1912* (Stroud: Amberley Publishing, 2012)
Scott, Peter, *The Eye of the Wind: An Autobiography* (London: Hodder & Stoughton, 1961)
Smith, Michael, *I am just going outside: Captain Oates – Antarctic tragedy* (Cork: The Collins Press, 2002)
Solomon, Susan, *The coldest march: Scott's fatal Antarctic expedition* (New Haven and London: Yale University Press, 2001)
Spillane, Paul, *St Andrew's School 1877-1977* (Eastbourne: St Andrew's School, 1977)
Spufford, Francis, *I may be some time: ice and the English imagination* (London: Faber, 1996)
Strathie, Anne, *From ice floes to battlefields: Scott's 'Antarctics' in the First World War* (Stroud: The History Press, 2015)
Turney, Chris, *1912: the year the world discovered Antarctica* (London: Bodley Head, 2012)
Weston, Agnes, *My Life among the Bluejackets* (London: James Nisbet & Co., 1909)
Wheeler, Sara, *Cherry: a life of Apsley Cherry-Garrard* (London: Jonathan Cape, 2001)
Williams, Isobel, *Captain Scott's invaluable assistant – Edgar Evans* (Stroud: History Press, 2012)
Williams, Isobel, *With Scott in the Antarctic: Edward Wilson – explorer, naturalist, artist* (Stroud: History Press, 2008)
Wilson, D. M. and Elder, D. B., *Cheltenham in Antarctica: the life of Edward Wilson* (Cambridge: Cambridge University Press, 2002)
Young, Edith, Baroness Kennet, *Self-Portrait of an Artist. From the diaries and memoirs of Lady Kennet, Kathleen, Lady Scott* (London: John Murray, 1949)
Young, Louisa, *A great task of happiness: the life of Kathleen Scott* (London: Macmillan, 1995)

Other published and unpublished sources

Alumni Oxoniensis (1715-1886) vol. 1
Bush, Julia, *The anti-suffrage movement*, 5 March 2018 [URL: www.bl.uk/votes-for-women/articles/the-anti-suffrage-movement]
Christie's auction catalogue, *The Polar Sale including The Shackleton Collection*, Tuesday 25 September 2001
Cobb, Steve, 'Testing Commerce Protection "On the scale of twelve inches to the foot": The Royal Navy's 1906 "Grand Manoeuvres"' (2010)

Conley, Mary A., '"You Don't Make a Torpedo Gunner Out of a Drunkard": Agnes Weston, Temperance, and the British Navy', *The Northern Mariner/ Le Marin du nord*, Vol. IX, No. 1 (January 1999), pp. 1–22

Conroy, Bill, 'The final tragedy: Remembering Hilda Evans', *Antarctic: The publication of the New Zealand Antarctic Society*, Vol. 33, No. 3 (2015) issue 233

Gower: The Journal of the Gower Society (National Library of Wales)

Johnson, A. M., 'Scott of the Antarctic and Cardiff', *Morgannwg*, Vols xxvi (1982) and xxvii (1983)

Lymbery, Mark, *Social Work with Older People* (London: SAGE Publications Ltd, 2005)

Mayberry, Jason Allen, 'Scurvy and Vitamin C', *Food and Drug Law* (Winter 2004)

Morgannwg: Transactions of the Glamorgan Local History Society

Sotheby's auction catalogues: *Orders, medals and decorations* (1 November 1984) and *English Literature and English History comprising Printed Books, Autograph Letters and Manuscripts* (6-7 December 1984)

Tasca, Cecilia, et al., 'Women and hysteria in the history of mental health', *Clinical Practice & Epidemiology in Mental Health*, Vol. 8 (2012), pp. 110–19

Warrior, Claire, 'Rekindling Histories Families and British polar exploration' (PhD Thesis, University of Cambridge, 2016)

Online archives and resources

Ancestry (ancestry.co.uk)

The British Newspaper Archive

Cambridge Alumni Database

Christie's

Hansard, UK Parliament

Legacies of British Slave-ownership – UCL Department of History

Papers Past, National Library New Zealand

LibraryLine, Swansea Council Library Service

Welsh Journals online

Welsh Newspapers online

Notes

Prologue

1. Scott, Robert, Falcon, *Scott's Last Expedition, Diaries 26 November 1910- 29 March 1912* (Stroud: Amberley Publishing, 2012) p. 314.

Oriana

1. Under the Slavery Abolition Act of 1833 he received compensation of £64 0s 1D for one enslaved person. 'Trinidad 826', Legacies of British Slave-ownership database, https://www.ucl.ac.uk/lbs/claim/view/29868 [accessed 14th April 2019].
2. *Chester Chronicle*, 19 August 1814.
3. Cambridge Alumni Database www.venn.lib.cam.ac.uk.
4. Ibid.
5. 1861 census.
6. England & Wales National Probate Calendar, 1880 (James Beaumont) and Admission papers for William Coppard Beaumont, 8 April 1881.
7. *Berkshire Chronicle*, 9 August 1873.
8. Blackie, John, *Bradfield, 1850-1975* (Bradfield [Bradfield, Berks.]: Warden and Council of St Andrew's College, 1976) p. 60.
9. Ibid. p. 62.
10. Spillane, Paul, *St Andrew's School 1877-1977* (Eastbourne: St Andrew's School, 1977) p. 5.
11. Ibid. p. 8.
12. *Eastbourne Gazette*, 17 July 1889 and *Eastbourne Gazette*, 13 November 1889.
13. Spillane, Paul, *St Andrew's School 1877-1977* (Eastbourne: St Andrew's School, 1977) p. 9.

14. *John Bull*, 5 May 1888.
15. Spillane, Paul, *St Andrew's School 1877-1977* (Eastbourne: St Andrew's School, 1977) p. 7.
16. Census 1891 and 1901 and Cambridge Alumni Database www.venn.lib.cam.ac.uk.

Ted

1. Cambridge Alumni Database www.venn.lib.cam.ac.uk. And Church of England Marriages and Banns, 1754-1932 for William Bonner Leighton Hopkins, St Mary's, Battersea, 1896.
2. Battersea, Caius College Mission Chapel Ref. BAT02, *Former places of worship in the Diocese of Southwark*. London Metropolitan Archives.
3. Lymbery, Mark, *Social Work with Older People* (London: SAGE Publications Ltd, 2005). Chapter 2 *The History and Development of Social Work*.
4. St George's Hospital is now in Tooting, South London but when Ted was studying there it was at Hyde Park Corner.
5. From one of Ted's letters to Oriana from Norway quoted in Seaver, George, *Edward Wilson of the Antarctic: naturalist and friend; with an introduction by Apsley Cherry-Garrard* (London: John Murray, 1933) p. 61.
6. Seaver, George, *Edward Wilson of the Antarctic: naturalist and friend; with an introduction by Apsley Cherry-Garrard* (London: John Murray, 1933) p. 34-35.
7. Cheltenham Borough Council and the Cheltenham Trust/The Wilson Family Collection object no: 2015.29.3.
8. The 1901 Census enumerator lists her as 'Lady Matron', but this describes her sex and not her social status. The clerk at the census office has added 'Teach' but this does not mean Oriana was a teacher, it refers to the category in which her job should sit, that is a school. She was a school matron.
9. Ted's diary entry for 10 March 1898, written at Westal and quoted in Seaver, George, *Edward Wilson of the Antarctic: naturalist and friend; with an introduction by Apsley Cherry-Garrard* (London: John Murray, 1933) p. 46.
10. Wilson, D.M. and Elder, D.B., *Cheltenham in Antarctica: the life of Edward Wilson* (Cambridge: Cambridge University Press, 2002).
11. 1881 and 1891 Census.

12. Seaver, George, *Edward Wilson of the Antarctic: naturalist and friend; with an introduction by Apsley Cherry-Garrard* (London: John Murray, 1933) p. 60.
13. MacInnes, Katherine, *Woman with the Iceberg Eyes: Oriana F. Wilson* (Cheltenham: The History Press, 2019) p. 31.
14. Wilson, D.M. and Elder, D.B., *Cheltenham in Antarctica: the life of Edward Wilson* (Cambridge: Cambridge University Press, 2002).

A Scientist's Wife

1. Seaver, George, *Edward Wilson of the Antarctic: naturalist and friend; with an introduction by Apsley Cherry-Garrard* (London: John Murray, 1933) p. 20.
2. MacInnes, Katherine, *Woman with the Iceberg Eyes: Oriana F. Wilson* (Cheltenham: The History Press, 2019) p. 34.
3. Seaver, George, *Edward Wilson of the Antarctic: naturalist and friend; together with a memoir of Oriana Wilson; with an introduction by Apsley Cherry-Garrard* (London: John Murray, 1963) p. 222.
4. Ibid. p. 64.
5. It is now called the Ross Ice Shelf.
6. Jones, Max, *The Last Great Quest: Captain Scott's Antarctic Sacrifice* (Oxford: Oxford University Press, 2003) p. 29.
7. Ted went to hear Nansen speak on 9 February 1897. Seaver, George, *Edward Wilson of the Antarctic: naturalist and friend; with an introduction by Apsley Cherry-Garrard* (London: John Murray, 1933) p. 31.
8. *The Geographical Journal*, Vol. 9, No. 3 (Mar., 1897), pp. 249-256 Published by: The Royal Geographical Society (with the Institute of British Geographers).
9. Wilson, D.M. and Elder, D.B., *Cheltenham in Antarctica: the life of Edward Wilson* (Cambridge: Cambridge University Press, 2002) p. 51.
10. MacInnes, Katherine, *Woman with the Iceberg Eyes: Oriana F. Wilson* (Cheltenham: The History Press, 2019) p. 40-41.

The Discovery Expedition

1. Savours, Ann (ed.), *Edward Wilson: Diary of the 'Discovery' expedition to the Antarctic regions 1901-1904; edited from the original mss. in the Scott Polar Research Institute, Cambridge* (London: Blandford Press, 1966) p. 24-25.
2. Wilson, D.M. and Elder, D.B., *Cheltenham in Antarctica: the life of Edward Wilson* (Cambridge: Cambridge University Press, 2002) p. 52.
3. Cambridge Alumni Database www.venn.lib.cam.ac.uk.
4. Wilson, D.M. and Elder, D.B., *Cheltenham in Antarctica: the life of Edward Wilson* (Cambridge: Cambridge University Press, 2002).
5. *Gloucestershire Echo*, Thursday 18 July 1901.
6. Ibid.
7. Ibid.
8. Recording of interviews between David Wilson and Evelyn Forbes (25 August 1995) and David Wilson and Michael Wilson (30 March 1995), Cheltenham Borough Council and the Cheltenham Trust/The Wilson Family Collection.
9. *Gloucestershire Echo*, Thursday 18 July 1901.
10. Ibid.
11. Last Will & Testament of Edward Adrian Wilson, 25 July 1901. Probate granted in Gloucester on 1 May 1913.
12. Savours, Ann (ed.), *Edward Wilson: Diary of the 'Discovery' expedition to the Antarctic regions 1901-1904; edited from the original mss. in the Scott Polar Research Institute, Cambridge* (London: Blandford Press, 1966) pp. 20, 101. Ted mentions using the vests and helmets for the first time on 17 January 1902. He offered the butterscotch and ginger round on 23 June 1902 when the crew celebrated Christmas on board.
13. MacInnes, Katherine, *Woman with the Iceberg Eyes: Oriana F. Wilson* (Cheltenham: The History Press, 2019) p. 47.
14. Seaver, George, *Edward Wilson of the Antarctic: naturalist and friend; with an introduction by Apsley Cherry-Garrard* (London: John Murray, 1933) p. 76.
15. Savours, Ann (ed.), *Edward Wilson: Diary of the 'Discovery' expedition to the Antarctic regions 1901-1904; edited from the original mss. in the Scott Polar Research Institute, Cambridge* (London: Blandford Press, 1966) p. 30.
16. *St James's Gazette*, Tuesday 6 August 1901.
17. The icon is in the collection of The Wilson Cheltenham Art Gallery & Museum. The story was told to be by Ann-Rachael Harwood.

18. Savours, Ann (ed.), *Edward Wilson: Diary of the 'Discovery' expedition to the Antarctic regions 1901-1904; edited from the original mss. in the Scott Polar Research Institute, Cambridge* (London: Blandford Press, 1966) p. 30-31.

Reunited

1. Savours, Ann, (ed.) *Edward Wilson: Diary of the 'Discovery' expedition to the Antarctic regions 1901-1904; edited from the original mss. in the Scott Polar Research Institute, Cambridge* (London: Blandford Press, 1966) p. 22.
2. Ibid for example p. 56 and 61.
3. Seaver, George, *Edward Wilson of the Antarctic: naturalist and friend; with an introduction by Apsley Cherry-Garrard* (London: John Murray, 1933) p. 2.
4. Oriana's letter to Cherry, 15 July 1913. MS 559/143/8; D. University of Cambridge, Scott Polar Research Institute.
5. Letter on *Discovery* headed notepaper, handwritten in ink, from Edward Adrian Wilson to his sister Polly, from Lyttelton, New Zealand. 29 November 1901. Cheltenham Borough Council and the Cheltenham Trust/The Wilson Family Collection object ref: 2015.29.6.
6. Letter on *Discovery* headed notepaper, handwritten in ink, from Edward Adrian Wilson to his sister Polly, 1 October 1901. Cheltenham Borough Council and the Cheltenham Trust/The Wilson Family Collection object ref: 2015.29.5.
7. Ibid.
8. Williams, Isobel, *With Scott in the Antarctic: Edward Wilson – explorer, naturalist, artist* (Stroud: History Press, 2008).
9. MacInnes, Katherine, *Woman with the Iceberg Eyes: Oriana F. Wilson* (Cheltenham: The History Press, 2019) p. 55.
10. Scott's letter to Ory quoted in Seaver, George, *Edward Wilson of the Antarctic: naturalist and friend; with an introduction by Apsley Cherry-Garrard* (London: John Murray, 1933).
11. Ory's letter to Jim Wilson, 24 April 1903. 1995.550.106 Cheltenham Borough Council and the Cheltenham Trust/The Wilson Family Collection.
12. MacInnes, Katherine, *Woman with the Iceberg Eyes: Oriana F. Wilson* (Cheltenham: The History Press, 2019) is a key source for how Oriana spent her time in New Zealand.
13. On 2 April 1904 the *Otago Daily Times* printed a report sent by their correspondent on 1 April saying, 'About 2 o'clock this morning the *Discovery*, the *Morning* and the *Terra Nova* sighted the light at Lyttelton Heads…'

14. Seaver, George, *Edward Wilson of the Antarctic: naturalist and friend; with an introduction by Apsley Cherry-Garrard* (London: John Murray, 1933) p. 141.
15. Ibid.
16. Savours, Ann (ed.), *Edward Wilson: Diary of the 'Discovery' expedition to the Antarctic regions 1901-1904; edited from the original mss. in the Scott Polar Research Institute, Cambridge* (London: Blandford Press, 1966) p. 357.
17. Ibid p. 357-359.
18. My interview with Isobel Williams 2 October 2019.
19. Seaver, George, *Edward Wilson of the Antarctic: naturalist and friend; with an introduction by Apsley Cherry-Garrard* (London: John Murray, 1933) p. 142.
20. Williams, Isobel, *With Scott in the Antarctic: Edward Wilson – explorer, naturalist, artist* (Stroud: History Press, 2008) p. 174.
21. MacInnes, Katherine, *Woman with the Iceberg Eyes: Oriana F. Wilson* (Cheltenham: The History Press, 2019) p. 73.
22. Savours, Ann (ed.), *Edward Wilson: Diary of the 'Discovery' expedition to the Antarctic regions 1901-1904; edited from the original mss. in the Scott Polar Research Institute, Cambridge* (London: Blandford Press, 1966) p. 374.
23. *The final tragedy: Remembering Hilda Evans* by Bill Conroy published in *Antarctic, The publication of the New Zealand Antarctic Society* Vol. 33, No. 3, 2015 Issue 233.
24. MacInnes, Katherine, *Woman with the Iceberg Eyes: Oriana F. Wilson* (Cheltenham: The History Press, 2019) p. 73.
25. Seaver, George, *Edward Wilson of the Antarctic: naturalist and friend; with an introduction by Apsley Cherry-Garrard* (London: John Murray, 1933) p. 143 and MacInnes, Katherine, *Woman with the Iceberg Eyes: Oriana F. Wilson* (Cheltenham: The History Press, 2019) p. 74.
26. Passenger list for the departure of *Tongariro* from Lyttelton, 11 June 1904.
27. Crow, Duncan, *The Edwardian Woman* (Routledge Library Editions: Women's History, 2012).
28. Seaver, George, *Edward Wilson of the Antarctic: naturalist and friend; with an introduction by Apsley Cherry-Garrard* (London: John Murray, 1933) p. 70-71.
29. MacInnes, Katherine, *Woman with the Iceberg Eyes: Oriana F. Wilson* (Cheltenham: The History Press, 2019) p. 83.
30. Seaver, George, *Edward Wilson of the Antarctic: naturalist and friend; with an introduction by Apsley Cherry-Garrard* (London: John Murray, 1933) p. 171.

Lois

1. Much of this background on Rhossili comes from Lucas, Robert, *Rhossili: A Village Background* (Cowbridge and Bridgend: D.Brown & Sons Ltd, 1989).
2. The census of 1861 lists William Beynon as a farmer of thirty acres and in the 1871 census he is a farmer of seven acres and publican.
3. Beynon, Leonard, *Rhossili: The Land, Landscape and People* (Swansea: West Glamorgan Archive Service, 2008.
4. *Gower, The Journal of The Gower Society*, 1 January 1993, vol. 44.
5. William Beynon is listed as green grocer in the 1881 census and also on Lois's birth certificate.
6. 1911 census for William and Jane Beynon.
7. This was part of the Church of England which was the established church in Wales until 1920. It was only after 1920 that The Church in Wales existed and became disestablished.
8. 1901 census.

Edgar

1. Rhossili School log book entry for 31 March 1882 says, 'Annie, Edgar and Arthur Evans left school this week, gone to Swansea to live.' Quoted in *Gower*, The Journal of The Gower Society 1 January 1998 vol.49. Gary Gregor and Isobel Williams believe the family moved in 1883.
2. Gregor, Gary C., *Swansea's Antarctic Explorer, Edgar Evans, 1876-1912* (Swansea: Swansea City Council, 1995).
3. *Worm* in Old English means serpent or dragon. Mutton detail comes from Beynon, Leonard, *Rhossili: The Land, Landscape and People* (Swansea: West Glamorgan Archive Service, 2008) p. 34.
4. Gregor, Gary, *Edgar Evans of Gower (1876-1912) From Rhossili to the South Pole* (Swansea: The Gower Society, 2008) p. 11.
5. Edgar's Service Certificate (No. 160225) National Archives Ref. ADM 188/235.
6. *South Wales Daily News*, 21 September 1904.
7. Interview with Edgar's niece, Sarah Owens, conducted by Stanley Richards and recorded in his letter to Raymond Pound on 18 June 1965 MS 761/16/4/1 University of Cambridge, Scott Polar Research Institute.
8. My conversation with John Evans 20 March 202. John remembers his nanny as being very pretty and a tiny, tiny woman.

9. From Edgar's Service Certificate (No. 160225) National Archives Ref. ADM 188/235. His height is given as 5 foot 10 inches. Frank Debenham's letter to Stanley Richards, 25 May 1962 estimates his height as 6 feet (MS 761/16/1/13) University of Cambridge, Scott Polar Research Institute.
10. Letter from Stanley Richards to Raymond Pound on 8 June 1965 (MS 761/16/4/1) University of Cambridge, Scott Polar Research Institute.
11. These descriptions of the landscape are drawn from those written by Edward Wilson and quoted in Seaver, George, *Edward Wilson of the Antarctic: naturalist and friend; with an introduction by Apsley Cherry-Garrard* (London: John Murray, 1933) p. 119 and p. 121.
12. Edgar's manhauling hours were listed by Sir Clements Markham on page 90 of his *Antarctic Obsession* as 173 days. My thanks to Michael Smith for pointing this out to me.
13. Letter from Edgar Evans to an unknown friend, 26 February 1903. Dundee Heritage Trust object number K 22.12.
14. Edgar's sledging journal has frequent mentions of food, its insufficiency and the lack of hot meals on occasion. MS 1487; BJ Journal, 27 January to 12 March 1911 [Western mountains sledge journey] University of Cambridge, Scott Polar Research Institute.
15. Edgar's Service Certificate (No. 160225) National Archives Ref. ADM 188/235.
16. Lucas, Robert, *Rhossili: A Village Background* (Cowbridge and Bridgend: D.Brown & Sons Ltd, 1989).
17. CADW listing for Church of St Mary, Rhossili reference number 11547. Accessed 26 June 2020.
18. *The Gower Church Magazine*, January 1905, LibraryLine, Swansea Council.
19. *South Wales Daily Post* 14 December 1904.
20. Dundee Heritage Trust. Letter from Edgar Evans to unknown friend, 26 February 1903 (K 22.12)
21. *The Gower Church Magazine*, January 1905, LibraryLine, Swansea Council.
22. Hughes, Wendy, *The story of Gower* (Capel Garmon: Gwasg Carreg Gwalch, 1992).
23. The crews of the expedition relief ships, *Morning* and *Terra Nova* also attended and were presented with bronze versions of the medal without a clasp. Hempleman-Adams, David, Gordon, Sophie and Stuart, Emma, *The Heart of the Great Alone: Scott, Shackleton and Antarctic Photography* (London: Royal Collection, 2011) p. 202.
24. My correspondence with the Royal Archives, Windsor Castle 29 January 2020. The Royal Archives do not have a record of the guest

list but because the investiture occurred just after their wedding and the couple did visit London, I think it is safe to assume that Lois accompanied Edgar.

25. Scott refers to the fact that he has never met Lois in a letter that he wrote to her in October 1911. West Glamorgan Archive Service GB 216 RISW/E3.

A Sailor's Wife

1. Kelly's Directory 1905 and 1906.
2. Walden Road first appears in the Kelly's directory in 1900. It was previously called Waldron Road and first appears in the 1896 Kelly's directory.
3. Edgar's Service Certificate (No. 160225) National Archives Ref. ADM 188/235.
4. *P.O. Edgar Evans*, Gower Society publication, 28 April 2015.
5. *Daily Telegraph*, 15 February 1913.
6. Men from *HMS Excellent* pulled the state gun carriage at the funerals of Edward VII, George V, George VI and Winston Churchill. From *Memorials and Monuments in Portsmouth – Field Gun Carriage* (memorialsinportsmouth.co.uk) by the curator of the museum at *HMS Excellent*, and Keeper of the State Gun-Carriage, Lt. Cdr. Brian Witts.
7. The 1901 census records that Lois, her family and all her neighbours in Rhossili were English speaking.
8. Barret-Ducrocq, Françoise, Love in the time of Victoria: sexuality, class and gender in nineteenth-century London. Translated by John Howe (London: Verso, 1991) p. 98.
9. From *Churches, Chapels and places of worship on Portsea Island* by John Offord (published by John Harman, 1989). Portsmouth was in the Diocese of Winchester until a diocese of its own was founded in 1927. The foundation stone for a permanent stone building for St Saviours was laid in 1913.
10. *Portsmouth Evening News*. 4 July 1904.
11. Weston, Agnes, *My Life among the Bluejackets* (London: James Nisbet & Co., 1909) p. 122.
12. Ibid p. 125-6. The reference to Indian clubs and battle axes comes from *Portsmouth Evening News*, 25 May 1903.
13. *Portsmouth Evening News*, 22 March 1939.
14. Francis Souper's involvement in the Temperance movement was frequently reported in the local press, for example, *The Susses Express*, 7 June 1888.

15. Weston, Agnes, *My Life among the Bluejackets* (London: James Nisbet & Co., 1909) p. 130.
16. Conley, Mary A., *"You Don't Make a Torpedo Gunner Out of a Drunkard:" Agnes Weston, Temperance, and the British Navy,* published in *The Northern Mariner/Le Marin du nord*, IX, No. 1 (January 1999), 1-22.
17. *Portsmouth Evening News*, 1 January 1904.
18. *Hampshire Telegraph*, 21 February 1913 reported that Mrs Evans is a member of Miss Weston's Wives meeting. Over 1,000 wives were involved in 1909 quoted in Weston, Agnes, *My Life among the Bluejackets* (London: James Nisbet & Co., 1909) p. 241.
19. Regular advertisements in the local press mention the HMS *Excellent* band including 17 September 1906, *Portsmouth Evening News*.
20. Weston, Agnes, *My Life among the Bluejackets* (London: James Nisbet & Co., 1909).
21. Lois is not listed in The Royal Sailors' Rest Books of Subscribers. The theory that this would not preclude her from benefits and that she would not have to sign the pledge to join the wives' meeting comes from my correspondence with Ros Black, author of *Scandal Salvation and Suffrage* (Troubadour: 2014)
22. Lucas, Robert, *Rhossili: A Village Background* (Cowbridge and Bridgend: D.Brown & Sons Ltd, 1989) p. 35.
23. Conley, Mary A., *"You Don't Make a Torpedo Gunner Out of a Drunkard:" Agnes Weston, Temperance, and the British Navy,* published in *The Northern Mariner/Le Marin du nord*, IX, No. 1 (January 1999), 1-22.
24. Ibid.
25. Royal Navy Service Record for Edgar Evans no.160225.
26. *The Times* 4, 9 and 14 July 1906.
27. Paper by Dr Steve Cobb (2010) *Testing Commerce Protection 'On the scale of twelve inches to the foot' The Royal Navy's 1906 'Grand Manoeuvres'* p. 7-9. Accessed via www.academia.edu.
28. Crane, David, *Scott of the Antarctic: A life of Courage and Tragedy in the Extreme South* (London: Harper Collins, 2005) p. 330.

Betrayal

1. Williams, Isobel, *Captain Scott's invaluable assistant – Edgar Evans* (Stroud: History Press, 2012) p. 104.
2. Herbert, Kari, *Polar Wives* (Vancouver: Greystone Books, 2012) p. 46.
3. Herbert, Kari, *Polar Wives* (Vancouver: Greystone Books, 2012) p. 238.
4. 1881 Census.

5. 1891 and 1901 Census. In 1901 Beatrice's mother is listed as a widow living on own means.
6. 1901 census shows Beatrice and her mother as resident at 246 Lake Road in Portsmouth and they are still there in 1905 according to Thomas's death certificate.
7. Royal Navy Service Record for Henry Thomas Glazier no.142087. UK, Naval Medal and Award Rolls, 1793-1972 (accessed via Ancestry) lists Glazier as having been awarded an Ashanti medal for services in Africa.
8. Death certificate for Thomas Henry Glazier. Death registered 7 April 1905.
9. The fact that Edgar had a family in Portsmouth was confirmed to me by the Evans family in a telephone conversation with Ants Ford (on behalf of John Evans) on 7 October 2020.
10. Birth certificate for Kathleen Lilian Evans, registered on 12 September 1906. Name of father is given as Edgar Evans and his occupation, Petty Officer RN.
11. *The poor child's nurse*, Briony Hudson wellcomecollection.org/articles/WckzzigAACe3DJPD.
12. Muriel's baptism record shows that the family were living in Walden Road when she was baptised.
13. Edgar is not listed as being resident in either Walden Road or Chapel Street in the 1907 or the 1908 Kelly's Directory or Electoral Roll. Muriel was baptised in March 1907 when the family lived in Walden Road and so they must have moved after that and before Ralph was born in December 1908.
14. Frost, Ginger S., *Living in sin: cohabiting as husband and wife in nineteenth-century England* (Manchester; New York: Manchester University Press; New York: Distributed exclusively in the USA by Palgrave Macmillan, 2008) p. 228.
15. Barret-Ducrocq, Françoise, *Love in the time of Victoria: sexuality, class and gender in nineteenth-century London*. Translated by John Howe (London: Verso, 1991) p. 169 and p. 172.
16. Kathleen Evans aged 4 is listed in the 1911 census as Beatrice's niece. Beatrice married Charles Amsden in 1914 (who'd been her lodger at Sultan Road) and in her marriage registration in 1928 Kathleen is recorded as Kathleen L. Amsden.
17. *Daily Telegraph*, 15 February 1913.
18. Norman was baptised in Rhossili in 1905 and Ralph in 1910 (he was born in 1908).
19. Crow, Duncan, *The Edwardian Woman* (Routledge Library Editions: Women's History, 2012).

Kathleen

1. The 'Heroic Age' of British polar exploration is usually defined as beginning with the Southern Cross expedition (1898–1900) and ending with the death of Ernest Shackleton on the Shackleton–Rowett expedition in 1922.
2. Smith, Michael, *I am just going outside: Captain Oates – Antarctic tragedy* (Cork: The Collins Press, 2002) p. 93.
3. Crow, Duncan, *The Edwardian Woman* (Routledge Library Editions: Women's History, 2012).
4. Ibid.
5. Young, Edith, Baroness Kennet, *Self-Portrait of an Artist. From the diaries and memoirs of Lady Kennet, Kathleen, Lady Scott* (London: John Murray, 1949) p. 76.
6. From a discussion with Kathleen's granddaughter, Louisa Young, 26 June 2020.
7. The principal sources for these sections on Kathleen's early life are her diary and the biography of her – Young, Louisa, *A great task of happiness: the life of Kathleen Scott* (London: Macmillan, 1995) and Young, Edith, Baroness Kennet, *Self-Portrait of an Artist. From the diaries and memoirs of Lady Kennet, Kathleen, Lady Scott* (London: John Murray, 1949).
8. Quoted in Young, Louisa, *A great task of happiness: the life of Kathleen Scott* (London: Macmillan, 1995) p. 3.
9. *Alumni Oxoniensis* (1715-1886) vol. 1.djvu/199.
10. Census 1881.
11. Quoted in Young, Louisa, *A great task of happiness: the life of Kathleen Scott* (London: Macmillan, 1995) p. 4.
12. Tasca, Cecilia et al. "Women and hysteria in the history of mental health." *Clinical practice and epidemiology in mental health: Clinical Practice & Epidemiology in Mental Health* vol. 8 (2012): 110-9. doi:10.2174/1745017901208010110.
13. Like Kathleen some of her siblings were not known by their first given name. I have referred to them as their family members did but their full names are: Robert Douglas, Grace Gwendolyn, Francis Rosslyn Courtney and Rosamund Hilda.
14. Young, Edith, Baroness Kennet, *Self-Portrait of an Artist. From the diaries and memoirs of Lady Kennet, Kathleen, Lady Scott* (London: John Murray, 1949) p. 17.
15. Marriage certificate for Lloyd Bruce and Ann Parker, St Mark's, Sheffield 31 May 1881.
16. Marriage certificate for Ann Wilson and Samuel Parker, York, 27 May 1850 and Obituary for Samuel Parker in the *Sheffield Telegraph* (Sheffield Libraries, Archives and Information).

17. Census entries 1861 and 1871. Ann is listed as an 'Annuitant' in the 1881 census.
18. Young, Edith, Baroness Kennet, *Self-Portrait of an Artist. From the diaries and memoirs of Lady Kennet, Kathleen, Lady Scott* (London: John Murray, 1949) p. 21.

Con

1. Young, Edith, Baroness Kennet, *Self-Portrait of an Artist. From the diaries and memoirs of Lady Kennet, Kathleen, Lady Scott* (London: John Murray, 1949) entry for 22 April 1938 p. 324.
2. Ibid p. 24.
3. Ibid p. 26.
4. Ibid p. 50.
5. Ibid p. 56.
6. Ibid p. 72.
7. Ibid entry for 4 November 1918 p. 168.
8. Ibid p. 70.
9. Ibid p. 83.
10. Ibid p. 83.
11. Ibid p. 85.
12. Parker, Sarah E., *Grace & favour: a handbook of who lived where in Hampton Court Palace, 1750 to 1950* (Surrey: Historic Royal Palaces, 2005) p. 14.
13. Mrs Zoe Thomson lived in Apartment 29 from 1900 to 1913 and Kathleen lived there for a time prior to her wedding. Parker, Sarah E., *Grace & favour: a handbook of who lived where in Hampton Court Palace, 1750 to 1950* (Surrey: Historic Royal Palaces, 2005) p. 80.
14. *Surrey Comet*, 5 September 1908.
15. Ibid.
16. Details from this section drawn from *Manchester Courier and Lancashire General Advertiser*, 4 September 1908, *Yorkshire Post and Leeds Intelligencer*, 3 September 1908.
17. *Manchester Courier and Lancashire General Advertiser*, 4 September 1908 and *Globe*, 2 September 1908,
18. *Halifax Evening Courier*, 3 September 1908.
19. Fiennes, Ranulph, *Captain Scott* (London: Coronet, 2004) p. 22-23.
20. Ettie Myers Scott married William Grey Ellison-Macartney in August 1897. Rose started her career in Nottingham Hospital in 1894 and then three years later became a nursing sister on the Gold Coast in Africa. She married Captain Eric Campbell of the Royal Irish Fusiliers in 1899.

21. Letter from Kathleen to Hannah Scott, date uncertain but 1906-8 (SPRI MS 1464/14/1) University of Cambridge, Scott Polar Research Institute.
22. Young, Louisa, *A great task of happiness: the life of Kathleen Scott* (London: Macmillan, 1995) p. 87.
23. Ibid p. 86.
24. Ibid p. 102.
25. Ibid p. 87.
26. Ibid p. 88.
27. Ibid p. 97.
28. Ibid p. 98.
29. Young, Edith, Baroness Kennet, *Self-Portrait of an Artist. From the diaries and memoirs of Lady Kennet, Kathleen, Lady Scott* (London: John Murray, 1949) p. 89.
30. Robert Peary's claim is still disputed as his fellow American Dr. Frederick Cook also claimed to have reached the North Pole.
31. Young, Louisa, *A great task of happiness: the life of Kathleen Scott* (London: Macmillan, 1995) p. 98.

A Hero's Wife

1. Extract of a letter from Ted to Ory from *Discovery* published in Seaver, George, *Edward Wilson of the Antarctic: naturalist and friend; with an introduction by Apsley Cherry-Garrard* (London: John Murray, 1933) p. 104.
2. Seaver, George, *Edward Wilson of the Antarctic: naturalist and friend; with an introduction by Apsley Cherry-Garrard* (London: John Murray, 1933) p. 137 footnote 1.
3. MacInnes, Katherine, *Woman with the Iceberg Eyes: Oriana F. Wilson* (Cheltenham: The History Press, 2019) p. 86.
4. The series of letters from Shackleton to Ted (but not Ted's replies) are published in Seaver, George, *Edward Wilson of the Antarctic: naturalist and friend; with an introduction by Apsley Cherry-Garrard* (London: John Murray, 1933) p. 174 onwards. This quote is from a letter written to Ted from Edinburgh on 15 February 1907.
5. Edward Wilson's letter to Scott, 31 March 1907 (MS 1453/188/4) University of Cambridge, Scott Polar Research Institute.
6. Seaver, George, *Edward Wilson of the Antarctic: naturalist and friend; with an introduction by Apsley Cherry-Garrard* (London: John Murray, 1933) p. 171.
7. Quoted in Herbert, Kari, *Polar Wives* (Vancouver: Greystone Books, 2012) p. 87.

8. Ibid.
9. Edward Wilson's letter to Scott, 8 March 1907 (MS 1453/188/3) University of Cambridge, Scott Polar Research Institute.
10. In January 2019 Stanfords completed its move from the store where it had been trading since 1901 and relocated to Mercer Walk. During the move a large number of antique text books, historic travel books, maps, atlases, artefacts and historical documents were uncovered, including this letter from Scott.
11. Herbert, Kari, *Polar Wives* (Vancouver: Greystone Books, 2012) p. 92.
12. Jones, Max, *The Last Great Quest: Captain Scott's Antarctic Sacrifice* (Oxford: Oxford University Press, 2003) p. 74-5.
13. Wheeler, Sara, *Cherry: a life of Apsley Cherry-Garrard* (London: Vintage, 2002) p. 64.
14. Sir Clements had, as a young man, been on one of the expeditions to rescue John Franklin and his men.
15. Jones, Max, *The Last Great Quest: Captain Scott's Antarctic Sacrifice* (Oxford: Oxford University Press, 2003) p. 118.
16. Herbert, Kari, *Polar Wives* (Vancouver: Greystone Books, 2012) p. 167.
17. Quoted in Herbert, Kari, *Polar Wives* (Vancouver: Greystone Books, 2012) p. 303.
18. Ibid p. 85.
19. Seaver, George, *Edward Wilson of the Antarctic: naturalist and friend; with an introduction by Apsley Cherry-Garrard* (London: John Murray, 1933) p. 182.
20. Ibid p. 242.
21. Recording of interviews between David Wilson and Evelyn Forbes (25 August 1995) and David Wilson and Michael Wilson (30 March 1995), Cheltenham Borough Council and the Cheltenham Trust/The Wilson Family Collection.
22. Wheeler, Sara, *Cherry: a life of Apsley Cherry-Garrard* (London: Jonathan Cape, 2001) p. 45.
23. Young, Edith, Baroness Kennet, *Self-Portrait of an Artist. From the diaries and memoirs of Lady Kennet, Kathleen, Lady Scott* (London: John Murray, 1949) p. 114.
24. Letter from Kathleen to Con, 18 Nov 1908 (MS 1453/3/223) University of Cambridge, Scott Polar Research Institute.
25. Young, Louisa, *A great task of happiness: the life of Kathleen Scott* (London: Macmillan, 1995) p. 113.
26. Oriana's letter to Caroline Oates quoted in Christie's London catalogue *The Polar Sale, 25 September 2001* (Lot 178) Page 235.

27. Edward Wilson's letter to Scott, 12 November 1908 (MS 1453/188/5) University of Cambridge, Scott Polar Research Institute.
28. Letter from Scott to Edgar written from expedition headquarters in Victoria Street, 23 March 1910. The letter was in the possession of Edgar's family until sold at auction at Sotheby's in December 1984 (Sotheby's auction catalogue, *English Literature and English History comprising Printed Books, Autograph Letters and Manuscripts*. 6-7 December 1984. Lot 512).
29. *Western Mail*, 12 February 1913. Lois said that his last letters were full of enthusiasm about reaching further south.
30. *Daily Telegraph*, 15 February 1913.
31. *Western Mail*, 12 February 1913.
32. Tryggve Gran wrote in his diary, 'Had Scott been first, Evans would have achieved financial independence…'
33. Royal Navy Service Record for Edgar Evans no.160225 shows that he was released to join the expedition on 19 April 1910.

The Departure of Terra Nova

1. Anthony M. Johnson *in Scott of the Antarctic and Cardiff* (Part 1). Published in *Morgannwg* transactions of the Glamorgan Local History Society vol.26 1 January 1982. Digital version created by The National Library of Wales.
2. Ibid.
3. Ibid.
4. Smith, Michael, *I am just going outside: Captain Oates – Antarctic tragedy* (Cork: The Collins Press, 2002) p. 62.
5. Ibid p. 85. Updated from original source to today's value.
6. Titus Oates was an English priest who became notorious in the 17th century by revealing a Catholic conspiracy to kill King Charles II called the Popish Plot. He was later found to have fabricated the entire story.
7. Wheeler, Sara, *Cherry: a life of Apsley Cherry-Garrard* (London: Jonathan Cape, 2001) p. 58-60.
8. The Captain Scott Society holds its annual dinner on this date every year in Cardiff.
9. The *Cambrian*, 17 June 1910.
10. The recollections of Edgar's niece Sarah Owens, quoted in Stanley Richards' letter to Raymond Pound, 18 June 1965 (MS 761/16/4/1) University of Cambridge, Scott Polar Research Institute.
11. *South Wales Daily News*, 15 June 1910.
12. This was published later in the *Western Mail* (12 February 1913).

13. *Daily Telegraph*, 15 February 1913.
14. Letter from Edgar to his mother written aboard *Terra Nova*, 21 June 1910. West Glamorgan Archive Service GB 216 RISW/E1. Edgar says that he was disappointed that Charley (who I presume to be his brother) and Will Thomas (who was the son of his sister Eliza Jane) weren't able to come to Cardiff.
15. A couple called the Bevans had taken over and held the licence until 1906. The village then petitioned against further letting of the house as a pub and the *Ship Inn* eventually become a farmhouse. *Gower*, The Journal of the Gower Society vol.44 1 January 1993.
16. *Western Mail*, 12 February 1913.
17. There were no trains in Gower and the first motor bus service only began in 1910.
18. Gregor, Gary C., *Swansea's Antarctic Explorer, Edgar Evans, 1876-1912* (Swansea: Swansea City Council, 1995).
19. *South Wales Evening Post*, 12 January 1994 obtained from collections at Swansea Council Library Service. John Faull is described as an Ironmonger in Wrights Swansea Directory, 1899 and in various South Wales trade directories from 1901 until 1923 as an Iron and Mineral Merchant and Ironmonger.
20. Letter from Edgar to his mother written aboard *Terra Nova*, 21 June 1910. West Glamorgan Archive Service GB 216 RISW/E1. Edgar says he saw Sarah and her sisters.
21. Williams, Isobel, *Captain Scott's invaluable assistant – Edgar Evans* (Stroud: History Press, 2012) p. 113.
22. As it sailed away, *Terra Nova* was kept close to the shore so that the people of Glamorgan could see the ship. (*Scott of the Antarctic and Cardiff* (Part 1) by Anthony M. Johnson. Published in *Morgannwg* transactions of the Glamorgan Local History Society vol.26 1 January 1982. Digital version created by The National Library of Wales. Gary Gregor says Edgar's family waved from the Rhossili cliffs in Gregor, Gary C., *Swansea's Antarctic Explorer, Edgar Evans, 1876-1912* (Swansea: Swansea City Council, 1995).

The Influence of the Petticoat

1. Young, Edith, Baroness Kennet, *Self-Portrait of an Artist. From the diaries and memoirs of Lady Kennet, Kathleen, Lady Scott* (London: John Murray, 1949) p. 89-90.
2. 1911 census and 1939 survey.

3. Letter from Kathleen to Hannah Scott, written in August 1910 from Admiralty House, Simons Bay, South Africa (MS 1464/14/4) University of Cambridge, Scott Polar Research Institute.
4. Letter from Kathleen to Con's sister Ettie Ellison-Macartney, written from Admiralty House, Simons Bay, South Africa, 3 August 1910 (MS 1464/14/2) University of Cambridge, Scott Polar Research Institute.
5. Letter from Kathleen to Hannah Scott, written in August 1910 from Admiralty House, Simons Bay, South Africa (MS 1464/14/4) University of Cambridge, Scott Polar Research Institute.
6. Letter (copy) from Henry Bowers to his mother, 31 July 1910 to 16 August 1910 (MS 783/1) University of Cambridge, Scott Polar Research Institute.
7. Letter from Kathleen to Scott's sister Rose Campbell, 29 August 1910 (MS 1464/14/3) University of Cambridge, Scott Polar Research Institute.
8. MacInnes, Katherine, *Woman with the Iceberg Eyes: Oriana F. Wilson* (Cheltenham: The History Press, 2019) p. 114.
9. Young, Louisa, *A great task of happiness: the life of Kathleen Scott* (London: Macmillan, 1995) p. 114.
10. Crane, David, *Scott of the Antarctic: A life of Courage and Tragedy in the Extreme South* (London: Harper Collins, 2005) p. 423.
11. The telegram was actually sent by his brother Leon who left *Fram* at Madeira.
12. Smith, Michael, *I am just going outside: Captain Oates – Antarctic tragedy* (Cork: The Collins Press, 2002) p. 115.
13. Scott, Robert, Falcon, *Scott's Last Expedition, Diaries 26 November 1910–29 March 1912* (Stroud: Amberley Publishing, 2012) p. 9.
14. Young, Edith, Baroness Kennet, *Self-Portrait of an Artist. From the diaries and memoirs of Lady Kennet, Kathleen, Lady Scott* (London: John Murray, 1949) p. 110.
15. Scott, Robert, Falcon, *Scott's Last Expedition, Diaries 26 November 1910- 29 March 1912* (Stroud: Amberley Publishing, 2012) p. 11.
16. Seaver, George, *Edward Wilson of the Antarctic: naturalist and friend; with an introduction by Apsley Cherry-Garrard* (London: John Murray, 1933) p. 205.
17. MacInnes, Katherine, *Woman with the Iceberg Eyes: Oriana F. Wilson* (Cheltenham: The History Press, 2019) p. 120.
18. Letter from Oates to his mother, Caroline written on 23 November 1910 (MS 1016/337) University of Cambridge, Scott Polar Research Institute.
19. Letter written by Henry Bowers, 7 December 1910 (MS 1505 1/1/3/103)) University of Cambridge, Scott Polar Research Institute.

20. Crow, Duncan, *The Edwardian Woman* (Routledge Library Editions: Women's History, 2012).
21. *The final tragedy: Remembering Hilda Evans* by Bill Conroy published in *Antarctic, The publication of the New Zealand Antarctic Society* Vol. 33, No. 3, 2015 Issue 233.
22. Young, Edith, Baroness Kennet, *Self-Portrait of an Artist. From the diaries and memoirs of Lady Kennet, Kathleen, Lady Scott* (London: John Murray, 1949) p. 190.
23. Crane, David, *Scott of the Antarctic: A life of Courage and Tragedy in the Extreme South* (London: Harper Collins, 2005) p. 436.
24. Letter written by Henry Bowers, 11 Sep. 1910 (MS 1505 1/1/3/95) University of Cambridge, Scott Polar Research Institute.
25. Letter from Henry Bowers to his siter May from Port, 28 November 1910 (MS 1505 1/1/3/100) University of Cambridge, Scott Polar Research Institute.
26. Letter written by Henry Bowers, 7 December 1910 (MS 1505 1/1/3/103)) University of Cambridge, Scott Polar Research Institute.
27. Crane, David, *Scott of the Antarctic: A life of Courage and Tragedy in the Extreme South* (London: Harper Collins, 2005) p. 436.
28. Ibid p. 439.
29. Mountevans, Admiral Lord, *South with Scott* (London and Glasgow: Collins, 1921) p. 29.
30. Young, Louisa, *A great task of happiness: the life of Kathleen Scott* (London: Macmillan, 1995) p. 117.

1910: The Penelopes

1. Quoted in MacInnes, Katherine, *Woman with the Iceberg Eyes: Oriana F. Wilson* (Cheltenham: The History Press, 2019) p. 100.
2. Herbert, Kari, *Polar Wives* (Vancouver: Greystone Books, 2012).
3. Ibid p. 206.
4. Ibid p. 275-276.
5. Spufford, Francis, *I may be some time: ice and the English imagination* (London: Faber, 1996) p. 123.
6. Jones, Max, *The Last Great Quest: Captain Scott's Antarctic Sacrifice* (Oxford: Oxford University Press, 2003) p. 19.
7. Herbert, Kari, *Polar Wives* (Vancouver: Greystone Books, 2012) p. 285-6.
8. From the preface of, Mill, H.R et al., *Rejoice my Heart: The Making of H.R. Mill's "The Life of Sir Ernest Shackleton" The Private Correspondence of Dr. Hugh Robert Mill and Lady Shackleton, 1922-33* (Santa Monica: Adélie Books, 2007).

9. Herbert, Kari, *Polar Wives* (Vancouver: Greystone Books, 2012) p. 190.
10. Koppel, Lily, *The astronaut wives club: a true story* (London: Headline, 2013).
11. Williams, Isobel, *Captain Scott's invaluable assistant – Edgar Evans* (Stroud: History Press, 2012) p. 119.
12. *Daily Telegraph*, 15 February 1913.
13. Rate Books for the property (Portsmouth History Centre) show that rent was approximately £12 a year in 1906. Modern equivalents on property are difficult to calculate, but it is approximately £1,450 a year.
14. Old Age Pensions Act 1908 (Standard Note: SN 4817) House of Commons Library.
15. Sarah Evans would certainly have qualified for a state pension, but the *Cambrian* reported on 13 February 1914 that she had been given an additional grant from the Treasury that meant she didn't need one. In either case it seems a pension of some kind reduced the financial responsibility for Lois after Edgar's death.
16. 1911 Census.
17. Letter from Kathleen to Hannah Scott, 1911? (SPRI MS 1464/14/7) University of Cambridge, Scott Polar Research Institute.
18. The story of the medal being sold was told to Isobel Williams by Lois's grandson John Evans and quoted in Williams, Isobel, *Captain Scott's invaluable assistant – Edgar Evans* (Stroud: History Press, 2012) p. 180. Edgar's decision to forego pay is mentioned here too, on p. 176.
19. Letter to Lois from Scott, October 1911 (West Glamorgan Archive Service GB 216 RISW/E3).
20. In a letter to his friend Sid, Edgar apologises for not writing on the way out on *Discovery*. He doesn't like writing and asks Sid to let their friend Dick have a look at this letter. Dundee Heritage Trust K 22.12.
21. A bundle of 50 of Edgar's letters, all written in 1911, were later returned to Lois and as Gary Gregor points out this represents at least one letter a week. The contents of these letters are unknown, and they have subsequently been lost or sold by the family. See note on sources.
22. Letter from Edgar to his mother written aboard *Terra Nova*, 3 Jan 1911 (West Glamorgan Archive Service GB 216 RISW/E2).

1911: The First Year Apart

1. Young, Edith, Baroness Kennet, *Self-Portrait of an Artist. From the diaries and memoirs of Lady Kennet, Kathleen, Lady Scott* (London: John Murray, 1949) p. 90.
2. Letter from Kathleen to Hanna Scott, 2 December 1910 (MS 1464/14/5) University of Cambridge, Scott Polar Research Institute.

3. Letter from Kathleen to Scott's sister Rose Campbell, 2 Dec 1910 (MS 1464/14/6) University of Cambridge, Scott Polar Research Institute.
4. Young, Louisa, *A great task of happiness: the life of Kathleen Scott* (London: Macmillan, 1995) p. 120-1.
5. Letter from Kathleen to Scott's sister Rose Campbell, 2 Dec 1910 (MS 1464/14/6) University of Cambridge, Scott Polar Research Institute.
6. Young, Louisa, *A great task of happiness: the life of Kathleen Scott* (London: Macmillan, 1995) p. 122.
7. The data base on the British Women Pilots' Assoc website states that Hilda B Hewlett, became the first British woman to pass her flying test on 18 August 1911. She received Pilot's Certificate no. 122 from the Royal Aero Club eleven days later on 29 August.
8. Young, Louisa, *A great task of happiness: the life of Kathleen Scott* (London: Macmillan, 1995) p. 127.
9. Young, Edith, Baroness Kennet, *Self-Portrait of an Artist. From the diaries and memoirs of Lady Kennet, Kathleen, Lady Scott* (London: John Murray, 1949) p. 102.
10. Young, Louisa, *A great task of happiness: the life of Kathleen Scott* (London: Macmillan, 1995) p. 128.
11. Young, Edith, Baroness Kennet, *Self-Portrait of an Artist. From the diaries and memoirs of Lady Kennet, Kathleen, Lady Scott* (London: John Murray, 1949) p. 100.
12. Ibid p. 99.
13. Herbert, Kari, *Polar Wives* (Vancouver: Greystone Books, 2012) p. 230-232.
14. Young, Edith, Baroness Kennet, *Self-Portrait of an Artist. From the diaries and memoirs of Lady Kennet, Kathleen, Lady Scott* (London: John Murray, 1949) p. 102.
15. Young, Louisa, *A great task of happiness: the life of Kathleen Scott* (London: Macmillan, 1995) p. 141.
16. Ibid p. 136-7.
17. Ibid p. 123.
18. Letter from Kathleen to Hannah Scott, 1911? (MS 1464/14/7) University of Cambridge, Scott Polar Research Institute.
19. Young, Louisa, *A great task of happiness: the life of Kathleen Scott* (London: Macmillan, 1995) p. 150.
20. This happened prior to a lecture by Nansen in November (Young, Edith, Baroness Kennet, *Self-Portrait of an Artist. From the diaries and memoirs of Lady Kennet, Kathleen, Lady Scott* (London: John Murray, 1949 p. 103.
21. Young, Louisa, *A great task of happiness: the life of Kathleen Scott* (London: Macmillan, 1995) p. 123-4.

22. Also in the *Daily Mirror*, 8 May 1911.
23. Letter from Kathleen to Keltie, 19 April 1913. RGS-IBG Archives CB8/Scott, R.F./File A-B 1911-1920.
24. Turney, Chris, *1912: the year the world discovered Antarctica* (London: Bodley Head, 2012) p. 216.
25. *Weekly Dispatch* (London), 14 May 1911.
26. Quoted by Isobel Williams in her talk for the Royal Geographical Society, *Sir Clements Markham President of the RGS: success of failure?* 10 May 2021.
27. Young, Edith, Baroness Kennet, *Self-Portrait of an Artist. From the diaries and memoirs of Lady Kennet, Kathleen, Lady Scott* (London: John Murray, 1949) p. 94.
28. Ibid p. 96.
29. MacInnes, Katherine, *Woman with the Iceberg Eyes: Oriana F. Wilson* (Cheltenham: The History Press, 2019) p. 134.
30. Ted's letter to John Fraser, 27 Nov 1910 quoted in Seaver, George, *Edward Wilson of the Antarctic: naturalist and friend; with an introduction by Apsley Cherry-Garrard* (London: John Murray, 1933) p. 205.
31. The film was released to the public in several episodes in 1911-12. It was reissued as a full-length silent version in 1924 and named *The Great White Silence*. In 1933 a sound version with music and commentary by Herbert Ponting was released and named *90 Degrees South*.
32. *The Bioscope*, 23 November 1911.
33. Young, Louisa, *A great task of happiness: the life of Kathleen Scott* (London: Macmillan, 1995) p. 137.
34. In her diary entry for 12 September 1911, Kathleen records that she had a meeting with the Gaumont company who told her that 'They have been through your films at last and say they have never seen anything so good.' It's not clear if Kathleen saw the films at this point (Young, Edith, Baroness Kennet, *Self-Portrait of an Artist. From the diaries and memoirs of Lady Kennet, Kathleen, Lady Scott* (London: John Murray, 1949 p. 99). However, *Kinematograph and Lantern Weekly* reported on 26 October 1911 that she had attended a private view on 19 October to which some key press were also invited.

1912: Losing the Pole

1. Smith, Michael, *I am just going outside: Captain Oates – Antarctic tragedy* (Cork: The Collins Press, 2002) p. 108.
2. *Yorkshire Evening Post*, 7 March 1912.
3. *The Globe*, *Yorkshire Evening Post* and the *Gloucester Citizen*.
4. *Pall Mall Gazette*, 8 March 1912.

5. Young, Edith, Baroness Kennet, *Self-Portrait of an Artist. From the diaries and memoirs of Lady Kennet, Kathleen, Lady Scott* (London: John Murray, 1949) p. 107-8.
6. *The Times*, 8 March 1912.
7. *Westminster Gazette*, 8 March 1912.
8. Young, Edith, Baroness Kennet, *Self-Portrait of an Artist. From the diaries and memoirs of Lady Kennet, Kathleen, Lady Scott* (London: John Murray, 1949) p. 108.
9. In a speech at the Royal Geographical Society Annual Meeting reported in *The Times* 21 May 1912.
10. Young, Edith, Baroness Kennet, *Self-Portrait of an Artist. From the diaries and memoirs of Lady Kennet, Kathleen, Lady Scott* (London: John Murray, 1949) p. 111.
11. Letter from Keltie to Kathleen, 21 November 1912, marked confidential. RGS-IBG Archives CB8/Scott, R.F./File A-B 1911-1920.
12. Young, Edith, Baroness Kennet, *Self-Portrait of an Artist. From the diaries and memoirs of Lady Kennet, Kathleen, Lady Scott* (London: John Murray, 1949) p. 115.
13. Letter from Keltie to Kathleen, 6 November 1913. RGS-IBG Archives CB8/Scott, R.F./File A-B 1911-1920.
14. *Daily Mirror*, 16 November 1912.
15. Amundsen referred to Curzon's comment in his autobiography as a 'thinly veiled insult'. His experience during his visit caused him to write '... I feel justified in saying that by and large the British are a race of very bad losers.' Amundsen, Roald, *My Life as an Explorer* (New York: 1927) pp. 71–2. My thanks to Liam Maloney for pointing this out.
16. Letter from Oriana Wilson to Mrs Cherry-Garrard 22 September 1912, MS 559/144/2; D, University of Cambridge, Scott Polar Research Institute.
17. Because of the problems with *Discovery* being frozen into the ice. Scott had planned for *Terra Nova* to sail home and over winter each year in New Zealand, before sailing back with supplies for the next year.
18. Letter from Ory to Reginald and Isabel Smith, written in Christchurch on 7 April 1912 (MS 1330/7) University of Cambridge, Scott Polar Research Institute.
19. Ibid.
20. Ibid.
21. Telegram sent from Oriana in New Zealand to the Wilson family at *Westal* (Cheltenham Borough Council and the Cheltenham Trust/The Wilson Family Collection object ref: 2010.36.
22. Tryggve Gran wrote in his diary, 'The fact that Amundsen was first at the Pole in a way meant more to Evans than the rest. Had Scott been

first, Evans would have achieved financial independence, but now the future must have seemed uncertain and unattractive.'

23. Letter from Lieut. Henry Pennell to Lois Evans written aboard *Terra Nova*, 1 April 1912. West Glamorgan Archive Service GB 216 RISW/E4.

1912: Messages from Antarctica

1. Letter from Ory to Reginald and Isabel Smith, written in Christchurch on 7 April 1912 (MS 1330/7) University of Cambridge, Scott Polar Research Institute.
2. Ted's letter to Ory dated 21 December 1911, quoted in Seaver, George, *Edward Wilson of the Antarctic: naturalist and friend; with an introduction by Apsley Cherry-Garrard* (London: John Murray, 1933) p. 275.
3. Sara Wheeler states that the theory was discredited at around the time that *Terra Nova* sailed and now it is thought that flightless birds evolved from birds with flight and not the other way around (*Cherry*, p. 107).
4. Ted's letter to Ory quoted in Seaver, George, *Edward Wilson of the Antarctic: naturalist and friend; with an introduction by Apsley Cherry-Garrard* (London: John Murray, 1933) p. 261.
5. Cherry-Garrard delivered the embryos and eggshells to the natural History Museum in the summer of 1913. One is on display in the Treasures gallery of the museum.
6. Letter from Ory to Reginald and Isabel Smith, written in Christchurch on 7 April 1912 (MS 1330/7) University of Cambridge, Scott Polar Research Institute.
7. Letter from Ted to Ory dated 24 Nov 1911, quoted in Seaver, George, *Edward Wilson of the Antarctic: naturalist and friend; with an introduction by Apsley Cherry-Garrard* (London: John Murray, 1933) p. 271.
8. Letter from Ory to Reginald and Isabel Smith, written in Christchurch on 7 April 1912 (MS 1330/7) University of Cambridge, Scott Polar Research Institute.
9. Letter from Oriana Wilson to Isabel Smith 2 May 1912 (MS 841/13;D), University of Cambridge, Scott Polar Research Institute.
10. Letter from Oriana Wilson to Mrs Cherry-Garrard 22 September 1912 (MS 559/144/2; D), University of Cambridge, Scott Polar Research Institute.
11. Letter from Ory to Reginald and Isabel Smith, written in Christchurch on 7 April 1912 (MS 1330/7) University of Cambridge, Scott Polar Research Institute.

12. From the New Zealand Dept of Conservation website entry for Scott's Cabin (www.doc.govt.nz/parks-and-recreation/places-to-go/canterbury/places/godley-head/scotts-cabin/). The hut was bought by Valerie and David Crichton in 1974 who built a house attached to it and used it as a study. After an earthquake in February 2011, their house and part of the cliff collapsed. The hut survived but was left in a hazard zone and facing demolition. The Crichtons gifted it to the Department of Culture and in 2013 the hut was rescued and moved to Godley Head. It is known as Scott's Cabin.
13. MacInnes, Katherine, *Woman with the Iceberg Eyes: Oriana F. Wilson* (Cheltenham: The History Press, 2019) p. 150.
14. Young, Edith, Baroness Kennet, *Self-Portrait of an Artist. From the diaries and memoirs of Lady Kennet, Kathleen, Lady Scott* (London: John Murray, 1949) p. 109-10.
15. *South West Daily Post*, 11 February 1913.
16. *Western Mail*, 12 February 1913.
17. Ibid.
18. *Daily Telegraph*, 14 and 15 February 1913.
19. *Western Mail*, 12 February 1913.

1912: Another Year of Waiting

1. Kathleen's bust of Asquith is now in the Tate's collection (N4467 The Earl of Oxford and Asquith).
2. Riddell, Fern, *Death in Ten Minutes- The Forgotten Life of Radical Suffragette Kitty Marion* (London: Hodder & Stoughton, 2019) p. 120.
3. Ibid p. 141.
4. Ibid p. 161.
5. Ibid p. 146.
6. From Lord Cromer's speech printed in *The Anti Suffrage Review*, March 1912, LSE Library.
7. *The Anti Suffrage Review*, February 1912, LSE Library.
8. Young, Edith, Baroness Kennet, *Self-Portrait of an Artist. From the diaries and memoirs of Lady Kennet, Kathleen, Lady Scott* (London: John Murray, 1949) p. 107.
9. *The Times*, 29 February 1912.
10. *Miss Violet Markham's Great Speech at the Albert Hall, February 28th, 1912*, The Women's Library, UDC 389.
11. Ibid.
12. Bush, Julia, *The anti-suffrage movement*, www.bl.uk/votes-for-women/articles/the-anti-suffrage-movement, 5 March 1918.

13. From A.B. Armitage, *Two Years in the Antarctic: Being a Narrative of the British National Antarctic Expedition* (London, 1905) p. 96. My thanks to Liam Maloney for drawing my attention to this.
14. Lord Curzon, *Fifteen Good Reasons Against the Grant of Female Suffrage*, 1912.
15. From Lord Curzon's speech printed in *The Anti Suffrage Review*, March 1912, LSE Library.
16. Lord Curzon, *Fifteen Good Reasons Against the Grant of Female Suffrage*, 1912.
17. Riddell, Fern, *Death in Ten Minutes- The Forgotten Life of Radical Suffragette Kitty Marion* (London: Hodder & Stoughton, 2019) p. 239.
18. Lord Curzon, *Fifteen Good Reasons Against the Grant of Female Suffrage*, 1912.
19. Young, Louisa, *A great task of happiness: the life of Kathleen Scott* (London: Macmillan, 1995) p. 150-151.
20. *The Times*, 29 February 1912.
21. Young, Edith, Baroness Kennet, *Self-Portrait of an Artist. From the diaries and memoirs of Lady Kennet, Kathleen, Lady Scott* (London: John Murray, 1949) p. 111.
22. Letter from Kathleen Scott to Lois Evans, 19 August 1912. Quoted in Gregor, Gary C., *Swansea's Antarctic Explorer, Edgar Evans, 1876-1912* (Swansea: Swansea City Council, 1995) p. 66.
23. There is a now empty envelope in Swansea Museum's collection, addressed to Edgar's mother which was sent from Portsmouth and postmarked 25 Oct 1912. I think this must have been a letter from Lois. If so then it shows that she was still there in October (collection item SM 2012.51.8).
24. Examples of aid given by Aggie and her organisation following numerous ship disasters in *Portsmouth Evening News*, 3 February 1912, 1 May 1912, 24 March 1902 and 27 April 1908.
25. Royal Navy Service Record for Stanley George Beynon no.204512.
26. Marriage certificate for Amelia Ann Andrews and Stanley Beynon, death certificate for Amelia Ann Andrews and birth certificate for Amelia Beatrice Beynon.
27. *South Wales Evening Post*, 12 January 1994 obtained from collections at Swansea Council Library Service.
28. *Daily Telegraph*, 15 February 1913.
29. *Western Mail*, 12 February 1913.
30. 1911 census shows that Sara Evans is living in the home of her widowed sister Anne Powell.
31. Lucas, Robert, *Rhossili: A Village Background* (Cowbridge and Bridgend: D.Brown & Sons Ltd, 1989).

32. Beynon, Leonard, *Rhossili: The Land, Landscape and People* (Swansea: West Glamorgan Archive Service, 2008) p. 75.
33. Hughes, W., *The Story of Gower*; Gwasg Carreg Gwalch, 1992 and Lloyd, D., 'The Penclawdd Cockle Industry', *Gower*, Volume XXXV, 1984.
34. The first batch came back with *Terra Nova* and the second was brought back by Ponting who was in London when it was shown (Anne Strathie).
35. Letter from Oriana Wilson to Mrs Cherry-Garrard, 22 September 1912, MS 559/144/2; D, University of Cambridge, Scott Polar Research Institute.
36. Letter from Oriana Wilson to Mrs Cherry-Garrard 1 January 1913, MS 559/144/3; D, University of Cambridge, Scott Polar Research Institute.
37. Young, Edith, Baroness Kennet, *Self-Portrait of an Artist. From the diaries and memoirs of Lady Kennet, Kathleen, Lady Scott* (London: John Murray, 1949) p. 116.
38. Letter from Oriana Wilson to Mrs Cherry-Garrard 1 January 1913, MS 559/144/3; D, University of Cambridge, Scott Polar Research Institute.

1912: Finding the Bodies

1. Wheeler, Sara, *Cherry: a life of Apsley Cherry-Garrard* (London: Jonathan Cape, 2001) p. 123.
2. The first support party sent home in December 1911 comprised Surgeon Edward Atkinson, Charles Wright, Apsley Cherry-Garrard and Petty Officer Patrick Keohane.
3. Wheeler, Sara, *Cherry: a life of Apsley Cherry-Garrard* (London: Vintage, 2002) p. 128.
4. Crean and Lashley had both been on *Discovery*, where Lashley had saved Scott by pulling him out of a crevasse. Teddy Evans fell dangerously ill with scurvy on the return journey, but they got him safely back to base and both men were awarded the Albert medal for bravery. Tom Crean walked the last thirty-five miles alone to summon help. He later joined Shackleton on his *Endurance* expedition and was one of the six men selected to join their leader on an epic mission to get help for their stranded crew mates.
5. Wheeler, Sara, *Cherry: a life of Apsley Cherry-Garrard* (London: Jonathan Cape, 2001) p. 96.
6. Ibid p. 132.
7. Scott, Robert, Falcon, *Scott's Last Expedition, Diaries 26 November 1910- 29 March 1912* (Stroud: Amberley Publishing, 2012) p. 283.
8. Ibid p. 284.

9. Ibid p. 283.
10. Scott's diary entry 7 January.
11. Scott, Robert, Falcon, *Scott's Last Expedition, Diaries 26 November 1910- 29 March 1912* (Stroud: Amberley Publishing, 2012) p. 291 and p. 292.
12. Ibid p. 293.
13. Wilson, D.M. and Elder, D.B., *Cheltenham in Antarctica: the life of Edward Wilson* (Cambridge: Cambridge University Press, 2002) p. 100.
14. Recent research by Susan Solomon has shown that the temperatures experienced by Scott in 1912 have been recorded only once on the Barrier since, in 1965. She has argued that this atypical weather was the main cause of the loss of the Polar Party. Solomon, Susan, *The coldest march: Scott's fatal Antarctic expedition* (New Haven; London: Yale University Press, 2001).
15. Scott, Robert, Falcon, *Scott's Last Expedition, Diaries 26 November 1910- 29 March 1912* (Stroud: Amberley Publishing, 2012) p. 307.
16. Ibid p. 308.
17. This detail was not made public at the time. Gran revealed it in an interview sixty years later. Jones, Max, *The Last Great Quest: Captain Scott's Antarctic Sacrifice* (Oxford: Oxford University Press, 2003) p. 126.
18. The account of finding the bodies and the records comes from Cherry-Garrard, Apsley, *The Worst Journey in the World* (London: Vintage Books, 2010) p. 497 onwards.
19. Mountevans, Admiral Edward Radcliffe Garth Russell Evans, 1st. baron, *South with Scott* (London and Glasgow: Collins, 1921) p. 279 and 281.
20. Wheeler, Sara, *Cherry: a life of Apsley Cherry-Garrard* (London: Jonathan Cape, 2001) p. 147.
21. Mountevans, Admiral Edward Radcliffe Garth Russell Evans, 1st. baron, *South with Scott* (London and Glasgow: Collins, 1921) p. 280-281.

If His Death Can Help People … I Can Be Happy in Giving Him Up

1. The account of the return of *Terra Nova* is drawn from Cherry-Garrard, Apsley, *The Worst Journey in the World* (London: Vintage Books, 2010) p. 592-3.
2. Jones, Max, *The Last Great Quest: Captain Scott's Antarctic Sacrifice* (Oxford: Oxford University Press, 2003) p. 99 note 8.
3. 10 February 1913 Post Office Telegraph from King George V to Lord Curzon, received 7.55pm. British Library, Asia, Pacific and Africa Collections, India Office Private Papers, MSS Eur F112/51.

4. Jones, Max, *The Last Great Quest: Captain Scott's Antarctic Sacrifice* (Oxford: Oxford University Press, 2003) p. 97-98.
5. Ibid p. 99.
6. *Auckland Star*, 11 February 1913, *Hawera & Normanby Star* 11 February 1913, *Gisborne Times* 12 February 1913 and many other New Zealand newspapers. See Papers Past.
7. MacInnes, Katherine, *Woman with the Iceberg Eyes: Oriana F. Wilson* (Cheltenham: The History Press, 2019) p. 155.
8. Ted Wilson's letter to Kinsey 10 February 1913. MacInnes, Katherine, *Woman with the Iceberg Eyes: Oriana F. Wilson* (Cheltenham: The History Press, 2019) p. 154.
9. Ted's father, quoted in Wilson, D.M. and Elder, D.B., *Cheltenham in Antarctica: the life of Edward Wilson* (Cambridge: Cambridge University Press, 2002) p. 107.
10. Lane, Heather, Boneham, Naomi and Smith, Robert D., (Editors) *The last letters: the British Antarctic Expedition 1910-13/the South Pole party: Captain Robert Falcon Scott, CVO, RN; Dr. Edward Adrian Wilson; Lt. Henry Robertson Bowers, RIM; Captain Lawrence Edward Grace Oates; Petty Officer Edgar Evans, RN* (Cambridge: Scott Polar Research Institute, 2012) p. 52-54. Ory did not keep Ted's letters and so this text has been assembled from extant sources in the Wilson Family Archive, the Scott Polar Research Institute and from George Seaver's book on Ted. Both letters were written in March 1912, the first probably on the 21st.
11. Scott, Robert, Falcon, *Scott's Last Expedition, Diaries 26 November 1910- 29 March 1912* (Stroud: Amberley Publishing, 2012) p. 309.
12. Wilson, D.M. and Elder, D.B., *Cheltenham in Antarctica: the life of Edward Wilson* (Cambridge: Cambridge University Press, 2002) p. 109.
13. Letter from Oriana Wilson to Tom Crean, 23 February 1913, Crean Collection, Kerry County Museum.
14. Wheeler, Sara, *Cherry: a life of Apsley Cherry-Garrard* (London: Jonathan Cape, 2001) p. 152-3.
15. Ibid p. 132-135.
16. Seaver, George, *Edward Wilson of the Antarctic: naturalist and friend; together with a memoir of Oriana Wilson; with an introduction by Apsley Cherry-Garrard* (London: John Murray, 1963) p. ix. Nicknames on board were common; Henry Bowers was called 'Birdie' because of his prominent nose, Ted Wilson was 'Uncle Bill' because he was the oldest and supported everybody on board, Oates was 'Soldier,' reflecting his army background or 'Titus' after the historical figure, Titus Oates and Scott was respectfully called, 'The Owner.'

17. Oriana's letters to Cherry on 22 May (MS 559/143/2; D) and 3 June 1913 (MS 559/143/3; D) University of Cambridge, Scott Polar Research Institute.
18. From Mrs Oriana F. Wilson to Mrs Sexton thanking her for her cable of sympathy on the news of her husband, Dr Edward A. Wilson's death, 20 February 1913. The Wilson Family Collection at Cheltenham Borough Council and The Cheltenham Trust (2004.123).

My Husband Died Bravely

1. *South Wales Evening Post*, 12 January 1994 obtained from collections at Swansea Council Library Service.
2. Letter from the Lord Mayor of London to Lord Curzon, 17 February 1913. British Library, Asia, Pacific and Africa Collections, India Office Private Papers, MSS Eur F112/51.
3. Jones, Max, *The Last Great Quest: Captain Scott's Antarctic Sacrifice* (Oxford: Oxford University Press, 2003) p. 164.
4. *Portsmouth Evening News*, 12 February 1913.
5. Jones, Max, *The Last Great Quest: Captain Scott's Antarctic Sacrifice* (Oxford: Oxford University Press, 2003) p. 99.
6. *Western Mail*, 12 February 1913.
7. *Daily Telegraph*, 15 February 1913.
8. The report published in the *Daily Telegraph* on 12 February 1913 confirms that the paper's correspondent arrived at Rhossili the day before, while the children were at school.
9. *Daily Telegraph*, 13 February 1913.
10. *Western Mail* 13 February 1913.
11. *Daily Telegraph*, 14 February and 15 February 1913.
12. *Western Mail*, 12 February 1913.
13. *Daily Telegraph*, 14 February 1913.
14. *South Wales Daily Post*, 11 February 1913.
15. Letter from Dr Atkinson to Lois written from the Ross Sea and dated 31 January 1912 [sic for 1913]. The letter was in the possession of Edgar's family until sold at auction at Sotheby's in December 1984 (Sotheby's auction catalogue, *English Literature and English History comprising Printed Books, Autograph Letters and Manuscripts*. 6-7 December 1984. Lot 518).
16. *Daily Telegraph*, 15 February 1913. Edgar thought Norman's eyesight was too poor to join the Navy.
17. *Cambrian*, 21 February 1913.
18. *Daily Telegraph*, 15 February 1913.
19. *Portsmouth Evening News*, 20 February 1913.

20. Letter from Teddy Evans to Lois written on board *Terra Nova*, 5 February 1913. The letter was in the possession of Edgar's family until sold at auction at Sotheby's in December 1984 (Sotheby's auction catalogue, *English Literature and English History comprising Printed Books, Autograph Letters and Manuscripts*. 6-7 December 1984. Lot 519). Also quoted in Gregor.
21. Interview with Edgar's niece, Sarah Owens, conducted by Stanley Richards and recorded in his letter to Raymond Pound in 1964 MS 761/16/3, University of Cambridge, Scott Polar Research Institute.
22. Letter from Frank Debenham to Stanley Richards MS 761/16/1/13, University of Cambridge, Scott Polar Research Institute.
23. *P.O. Edgar Evans* (Gower Society publication), 28 April 2015.
24. *Cambrian*, 21 February 1913.
25. *The final tragedy: Remembering Hilda Evans* by Bill Conroy published in *Antarctic, The publication of the New Zealand Antarctic Society* Vol. 33, No. 3, 2015 Issue 233.
26. Gregor, Gary C., *Swansea's Antarctic Explorer, Edgar Evans, 1876-1912* (Swansea: Swansea City Council, 1995) p. 73.

I Regret Nothing But His Suffering

1. Young, Louisa, *A great task of happiness: the life of Kathleen Scott* (London: Macmillan, 1995) p. 153-4.
2. MS 1464/23 University of Cambridge, Scott Polar Research Institute.
3. *Western Mail* 13 February 1913.
4. Kathleen's diary entry 25 February 1913 from Young, Edith, Baroness Kennet, *Self-Portrait of an Artist. From the diaries and memoirs of Lady Kennet, Kathleen, Lady Scott* (London: John Murray, 1949) p. 123.
5. Kathleen's diary entry 19 February 1913 from Ibid p. 121.
6. Kathleen's diary entry 21 February 1913 from Ibid p. 121.
7. Ibid p. 123.
8. Letter from Kathleen to Hannah Scott written on her voyage home from New Zealand on 5 March 1913. MS 1464/14/8 University of Cambridge, Scott Polar Research Institute.
9. Young, Edith, Baroness Kennet, *Self-Portrait of an Artist. From the diaries and memoirs of Lady Kennet, Kathleen, Lady Scott* (London: John Murray, 1949) entry for 6 March 1925 p. 232.
10. Scott's last letter to Kathleen (MS/1835/239) University of Cambridge, Scott Polar Research Institute.
11. Kathleen's diary entry 1 March 1913 from Young, Edith, Baroness Kennet, *Self-Portrait of an Artist. From the diaries and memoirs of*

Lady Kennet, Kathleen, Lady Scott (London: John Murray, 1949) p. 124.

12. *Evening Post*, 27 February 1913 (Wellington, New Zealand)
13. Published in various New Zealand newspapers, including the *Patea Mail* on 3 March 1913.
14. *Oamaru Mail*, 14 June 1913.
15. As early as 12 February 1913 Clements Markham was writing to Lord Curzon pressing for an honour for Kathleen as Scott's wife. On 19 February correspondence from Buckingham Palace enquired after a precedent and one was found in Henry Havelock, hero of the Indian Mutiny whose wife had been awarded a similar title after his death (12 February 1913 Clements Markham to Curzon and 19 February 1913 Stamfordham to Curzon BL MSSEUR F 112/51).
16. Passenger list for the *Remuera* (NZ passenger lists)
17. MacInnes, Katherine, *Woman with the Iceberg Eyes: Oriana F. Wilson* (Cheltenham: The History Press, 2019) p. 168.
18. Ponting's dark room in Antarctica had been used to develop the film that had been found next to Scott's body. From it emerged the images that Birdie had taken of the five men at the Pole in their moment of bitter sweet success before their fatal march home. Wheeler, Sara, *Cherry: a life of Apsley Cherry-Garrard* (London: Jonathan Cape, 2001) p. 147.

Our King upon His Knees

1. Jones, Max, *The Last Great Quest: Captain Scott's Antarctic Sacrifice* (Oxford: Oxford University Press, 2003) p. 103.
2. Barczewski, Stephanie L., *Antarctic destinies: Scott, Shackleton, and the changing face of heroism* (London: Continuum, 2007).
3. Jones, Max, *The Last Great Quest: Captain Scott's Antarctic Sacrifice* (Oxford: Oxford University Press, 2003) p. 230-232.
4. Barczewski, Stephanie L., *Heroic failure and the British* (New Haven: Yale University Press, 2016).
5. Jones, Max, *The Last Great Quest: Captain Scott's Antarctic Sacrifice* (Oxford: Oxford University Press, 2003) p. 99. Cherry's typing of the diary extracts is from Wheeler, Sara, *Cherry: a life of Apsley Cherry-Garrard* (London: Jonathan Cape, 2001) p. 147.
6. Ibid p. 101.
7. Scott, Robert, Falcon, *Scott's Last Expedition, Diaries 26 November 1910- 29 March 1912* (Stroud: Amberley Publishing, 2012) p. 314.
8. Langford, Paul, *Englishness Identified: manners and character, 1650-1850* (Oxford: Oxford University Press, 2000).

9. Barczewski, Stephanie L., *Heroic failure and the British* (New Haven: Yale University Press, 2016).
10. Heffer, Simon, *The age of decadence: Britain 1880 to 1914* (London: Cornerstone Digital, 2017) p. 188.
11. Riddell, Fern, *Death in Ten Minutes- The Forgotten Life of Radical Suffragette Kitty Marion* (London: Hodder & Stoughton, 2019) p. 181.
12. Daily Citizen (Manchester), 22 May 1913.
13. *Daily Mirror*, 8 May 1913.
14. Crow, Duncan, *The Edwardian Woman* (Routledge Library Editions: Women's History, 2012).
15. Letter from Clements Markham to Lord Curzon, 1 March 1913. British Library, Asia, Pacific and Africa Collections, India Office Private Papers, MSSEUR F 112/51.
16. Letter from Oriana Wilson to Lord Curzon, 19 May 1913. British Library, Asia, Pacific and Africa Collections, India Office Private Papers, MSS Eur F112/51.
17. Letter from Hannah Scott to Lord Curzon, 25 February 1913. British Library, Asia, Pacific and Africa Collections, India Office Private Papers, MSS Eur F112/51.
18. Barczewski, Stephanie L., *Heroic failure and the British* (New Haven: Yale University Press, 2016).
19. *The Scotsman* 15 February 1913.
20. Poem quoted in Jones, Max, *The Last Great Quest: Captain Scott's Antarctic Sacrifice* (Oxford: Oxford University Press, 2003) p. 136.
21. *Lakes Herald* 21 February 1913.
22. *The Scotsman* 15 February 1913.
23. *Lakes Herald* 21 February 1913.
24. *New York Times*. 14 January 1913.
25. Gregor, Gary C., *Swansea's Antarctic Explorer, Edgar Evans, 1876-1912* (Swansea: Swansea City Council, 1995) p. 72.
26. *Hampshire Telegrap*. 21 February 1913.
27. *Western Mail* 17 February 1913.
28. Jones, Max, *The Last Great Quest: Captain Scott's Antarctic Sacrifice* (Oxford: Oxford University Press, 2003)

For God's Sake Look after Our People

1. Scott's farewell letter to J.M. Barrie in Scott, Robert, Falcon, *Scott's Last Expedition, Diaries 26 November 1910- 29 March 1912* (Stroud: Amberley Publishing, 2012) p. 310.
2. *Feilding Star*, 19 May 1914 reported rumours of Kathleen's marriage to Barrie and a report from the United States that she had secretly

married Teddy Evans. The *New Zealand Times* printed Teddy's denial, issued via the Press Association, on 9 May 1914.

3. Con had named Kathleen and his brother in law William Grey Ellison-Macartney as joint Executors and Trustees of his estate but according to the probate record, William '...renounced probate thereof.'
4. Last Will & Testament of Edward Adrian Wilson, 25 July 1901. Probate granted in Gloucester on 1 May 1913.
5. My conversation with David Wilson, 25 September 2019.
6. MacInnes, Katherine, *Woman with the Iceberg Eyes: Oriana F. Wilson* (Cheltenham: The History Press, 2019) p. 172.
7. *Hansard*, House of Commons debate 11 February 1913, vol 48, c718.
8. Letter from Keltie to Lord Curzon, 11 February 1913. British Library, Asia, Pacific and Africa Collections, India Office Private Papers, MSS Eur F112/51.
9. Jones, Max, *The Last Great Quest: Captain Scott's Antarctic Sacrifice* (Oxford: Oxford University Press, 2003) p. 106.
10. Ibid p. 107. Updated from original source to today's value.
11. Letter from Kathleen Scott to Lord Curzon, 25 May 1913. British Library, Asia, Pacific and Africa Collections, India Office Private Papers, MSS Eur F112/51.
12. Letter from the Lord Mayor of London to Lord Curzon, 17 February 1913. British Library, Asia, Pacific and Africa Collections, India Office Private Papers, MSS Eur F112/51.
13. Letter from Sir Clements Markham to Lord Curzon, 23 February 1913. British Library, Asia, Pacific and Africa Collections, India Office Private Papers, MSS Eur F112/51.
14. Emily Bowers was granted funds and Caroline Oates, who came from a very wealthy family did not need them. Mrs Brissenden the widow of a sailor accidently drowned in New Zealand was also a beneficiary as was Mrs Abbott, the dependent mother of a Petty Officer driven insane by the privations endured on the expedition.
15. Parker, Sarah E., *Grace & favour: a handbook of who lived where in Hampton Court Palace, 1750 to 1950* (Surrey: Historic Royal Palaces, 2005) p. 115.
16. Letter from Kathleen to Keltie, ? 1914. RGS-IBG Archives CB7/Keltie.
17. *Weekly Dispatch* (London) 4 May 1913 and *Portsmouth Evening News* 30 April 1913.
18. Letter from Oriana Wilson to Kathleen Scott, 6 November 1913. MS 1453/190/5 University of Cambridge, Scott Polar Research Institute.
19. Letter from Oriana Wilson to Kathleen Scott, 10 May 1913. MS 1453/190/1 University of Cambridge, Scott Polar Research Institute.

20. Scott's farewell letter to J.M. Barrie in Scott, Robert, Falcon, *Scott's Last Expedition, Diaries 26 November 1910- 29 March 1912* (Stroud: Amberley Publishing, 2012) p. 310.
21. *Western Mail*, 12 February 1913.
22. Jones, Max, *The Last Great Quest: Captain Scott's Antarctic Sacrifice* (Oxford: Oxford University Press, 2003) p. 105.
23. *Gloucester Journal*, 15 February 1913.
24. *Western Mail* 13 February 1913.
25. *Hansard*, House of Commons debate 30 April 1913 vol. 52 cc. 1176-7.
26. *Western Mail*, 24 April 1913.
27. Ibid.
28. *Hampshire Telegraph*, 21 February 1913.
29. Gregor, Gary C., *Swansea's Antarctic Explorer, Edgar Evans, 1876-1912* (Swansea: Swansea City Council, 1995) p. 73–4.
30. Williams, Isobel, *Captain Scott's invaluable assistant – Edgar Evans* (Stroud: History Press, 2012) p. 74.
31. Told to me by Lois's grandson, John Evans, 20 March 2020.

Heroic Failures

1. Letter from Sir Clements Markham to Lord Curzon, 13 February 1913. British Library, Asia, Pacific and Africa Collections, India Office Private Papers, MSS Eur F112/51.
2. Letter from Keltie to Lord Curzon, 11 February 1913. British Library, Asia, Pacific and Africa Collections, India Office Private Papers, MSS Eur F112/51.
3. Jones, Max, *The Last Great Quest: Captain Scott's Antarctic Sacrifice* (Oxford: Oxford University Press, 2003) p. 110.
4. Quoted in Barczewski, Stephanie L., *Heroic failure and the British* (New Haven: Yale University Press, 2016).
5. Kathleen's letter to Lady Sandhurst c. 1913, National Maritime Museum AGC/S/28.
6. Notes of Lord Curzon's conversation with Kathleen Scott on 16 April 1913. British Library, Asia, Pacific and Africa Collections, India Office Private Papers, MSS Eur F112/51.
7. Letter from Sir Lewis Beaumont to Lord Curzon 17 April 1913. British Library, Asia, Pacific and Africa Collections, India Office Private Papers, MSS Eur F112/51.
8. Letter from Sir Lewis Beaumont to Lord Curzon 19 April 1913. British Library, Asia, Pacific and Africa Collections, India Office Private Papers, MSS Eur F112/51.
9. Curzon's post script about meeting Ory is not dated but it is likely that it was after 20 April 1913 as she wrote to him on that day from *Westal* thanking

him for his condolence letter and asking to meet him when she is up in London next to talk about Ted's work (British Library, Asia, Pacific and Africa Collections, India Office Private Papers, MSS Eur F112/51).

10. Turney, Chris, *1912: the year the world discovered Antarctica* (London: Bodley Head, 2012) p. 292.
11. Letter from Oriana to Cherry, 15 July 1913. MS 559/143/8; D University of Cambridge, Scott Polar Research Institute.
12. Letters from Sir Lewis Beaumont to Lord Curzon dated 17, 19 and 21 April 1913. British Library, Asia, Pacific and Africa Collections, India Office Private Papers, MSS Eur F112/51.
13. Smith, Michael, *I am just going outside: Captain Oates – Antarctic tragedy* (Cork: The Collins Press, 2002) p. 117.
14. Ibid p. 246-8.
15. Caroline Oates's notes of her meeting with Kathleen Scott reproduced in Christie's London catalogue *The Polar Sale, 25 September 2001* (Lot 178) Page 235.
16. According to Michael Smith, Scott ordered Wilson to hand out a lethal dose of opium to each man soon after 11 March (Smith, Michael, *I am just going outside: Captain Oates – Antarctic tragedy* (Cork: The Collins Press, 2002) p. 225). When Curzon and Kathleen discussed what had happened, they believed that 'Oates no doubt took opium and then killed himself.' (Notes of Lord Curzon's conversation with Kathleen Scott on 16 April 1913. British Library, Asia, Pacific and Africa Collections, India Office Private Papers, MSS Eur F112/51).
17. Caroline Oates's notes of her meeting with Oriana Wilson, 27 April 1913. Private collection.
18. Smith, Michael, *I am just going outside: Captain Oates – Antarctic tragedy* (Cork: The Collins Press, 2002) p. 247.
19. Ibid p. 251.
20. Letter from Oriana Wilson to Lord Curzon 20 April 1913. British Library, Asia, Pacific and Africa Collections, India Office Private Papers, MSS Eur F112/51.
21. Young, Edith, Baroness Kennet, *Self-Portrait of an Artist. From the diaries and memoirs of Lady Kennet, Kathleen, Lady Scott* (London: John Murray, 1949) p. 123.
22. Young, Louisa, *A great task of happiness: the life of Kathleen Scott* (London: Macmillan, 1995) p. 156-7.
23. Scott, Peter, *The Eye of the Wind* (revised edition) (London: Hodder & Stoughton, 1966) p. 19.
24. Young, Louisa, *A great task of happiness: the life of Kathleen Scott* (London: Macmillan, 1995) p. 161.

Gloriously Widowed

1. *Staffordshire Sentinel*, 22 May 1913 and *Irish Examiner*, 22 May 1913.
2. After Stanley, Nansen, Scott, Shackleton and Peary.
3. Letter from Keltie to Lord Curzon, 1 May 1913. British Library, Asia, Pacific and Africa Collections, India Office Private Papers, MSS Eur F112/51.
4. Letter from Keltie to Kathleen Scott, 24 February 1913. RGS-IBG Archives CB8/Scott, R.F./File A-B 1911-1920.
5. Ory's loyalty to her friend Pennell is shown as early as September 1912 when she writes that Evans must take over command of the ship of course because of his rank but it seems hard on Pennell who has navigated so well (22 September 1912 Letter from Oriana to Mrs Cherry-Garrard MS 559/144/2; D University of Cambridge, Scott Polar Research Institute.
6. Letter from Oriana Wilson to Lord Curzon, 19 May 1913. British Library, Asia, Pacific and Africa Collections, India Office Private Papers, MSS Eur F112/51.
7. Wheeler, Sara, *Cherry: a life of Apsley Cherry-Garrard* (London: Jonathan Cape, 2001) p. 138 and p. 150.
8. Ory's letter to Cherry, 19 October 1913. MS 559/143/12; D University of Cambridge, Scott Polar Research Institute.
9. Recording of interview between Evelyn Forbes and David Wilson, 11 August 1995, 10 Summerfield, Cambridge, Cheltenham Borough Council and the Cheltenham Trust/The Wilson Family Collection.
10. Wheeler, Sara, *Cherry: a life of Apsley Cherry-Garrard* (London: Jonathan Cape, 2001) p. 164.
11. Letter from Keltie to Lord Curzon, 1 May 1913. British Library, Asia, Pacific and Africa Collections, India Office Private Papers, MSS Eur F112/51.
12. Letter from Oriana Wilson to Kathleen Scott, 9 June 1913. MS 1453/190/4 University of Cambridge, Scott Polar Research Institute.
13. Letter from Oriana to Cherry, 13 Sep. 1913. MS 559/143/9; D. University of Cambridge, Scott Polar Research Institute.
14. MacInnes, Katherine, *Woman with the Iceberg Eyes: Oriana F. Wilson* (Cheltenham: The History Press, 2019) p. 197.
15. Relationships with Teddy Evans were souring in other quarters too. In the Autumn of 1913, there was a falling out with the Mansion House fund committee over what they regarded as an unauthorised issue of stamps for sale which Sir William Soulsby, Private Secretary to the Lord Mayor of London and secretary of the committee, described to Curzon as, 'very misleading and distasteful. I hope people will not connect our Fund with it.' (Sir William Soulsby to Lord Curzon,

27 September 1913. Curzon Correspondence, British Library, Asia, Pacific and Africa Collections, India Office Private Papers, MSS Eur F112/53).

16. *The final tragedy: Remembering Hilda Evans* by Bill Conroy published in *Antarctic, The publication of the New Zealand Antarctic Society* Vol. 33, No. 3, 2015 Issue 233.
17. Letter from Lewis Beaumont to Lord Curzon, 17 April 1913. British Library, Asia, Pacific and Africa Collections, India Office Private Papers, MSS Eur F112/51. He writes that Curzon now knows that Teddy Evans lost Scott's confidence and that he will be dependent on what Kathleen allows him from the diaries and journals to build up his paper.
18. Letter from Emily Shackleton to Dr. Mill, 26 January 1923 published in Mill, H.R et al., *Rejoice my Heart: The Making of H.R. Mill's "The Life of Sir Ernest Shackleton" The Private Correspondence of Dr. Hugh Robert Mill and Lady Shackleton, 1922-33* (Santa Monica: Adélie Books, 2007). Shackleton was able to give his own tribute to Scott at a later lecture by Teddy Evans, at the Queen's Hall on 9 June 1913.
19. Lord Curzon's correspondence at this time highlights the role of Ted Wilson. In a letter from the Lord Mayor to Lord Curzon on 17 February 1913, the suggestion is made that he was probably the most important member of the expedition after Scott. British Library Asia, Pacific and Africa Collections, India Office Private Papers, MSS Eur F112/51.
20. Letter from Oriana Wilson to Keltie, 26 April 1913. RGS-IBG Archives CB8/Scott,R.F./File D 1911-1920.
21. *Leeds Mercury*, 27 May, *Daily Mirror* 27 May and *Evening Mail* 28 May 1913.
22. *Cheltenham Chronicle*, 31 May 1913.
23. *Daily Mirror*, 27 May 1913.
24. Letter from Oriana Wilson to Kathleen Scott, 10 May 1913 MS 1453/190/1 University of Cambridge, Scott Polar Research Institute.
25. Letter from Edward Wilson (Ted's father) to Keltie, 17 March 1913. RGS-IBG Archives CB8/Scott, R.F./File D 1911-1920.
26. Letters from Oriana Wilson to Kathleen Scott, 20 May 1913 MS 1453/190/2 and 22 May 1913 MS 1453/190/3 both University of Cambridge, Scott Polar Research Institute.
27. Letter from Oriana Wilson to Cherry-Garrard, 10 June 1913 MS 559/143/5; D University of Cambridge, Scott Polar Research Institute.
28. Ory's letter to Cherry on 23 June 1913 confirms he was there and mentions that Mrs Bowers will sort out the things from the ship.

MS 559/143/6; D University of Cambridge, Scott Polar Research Institute.
29. *Western Mail*, 17 June 1913.
30. *Scott of the Antarctic and Cardiff* (Part 2) by Anthony M. Johnson. Published in *Morgannwg* transactions of the Glamorgan Local History Society vol.27 1 January 1983. Digital version created by The National Library of Wales.
31. *Western Mail*, 17 June 1913.
32. *Hampshire Telegraph*, 20 June 1913.
33. *Western Mail*, 17 June 1913.
34. Ibid 28 July 1913.
35. Diary of King George V in the Royal Archives, Windsor Castle.
36. *Western Mail*, 28 July 1913.
37. *Aberdeen Press & Journal* 28 July 1913.
38. Ibid.
39. Edgar's Polar Medal with two expedition clasps was sold at the family's request in November 1984 (Sotheby's auction catalogue *Orders, medals and decorations*, 1 November 1984). They had believed that the medal was the original until Sotheby's discovered that it was a replica, and the original was in the hands of a private collector. The replica was taken by Robert Swan on his expedition to the Antarctic in 1984-6 which followed Scott's route. *South Wales Evening Post*, 5 November 1984 obtained from collections at Swansea Council Library Service.
40. *Western Mail*, 12 February 1919.
41. *The Scotsman*, 12 February 1913.

The Strongest Man of the Party

1. Scott, Robert, Falcon, *Scott's Last Expedition, Diaries 26 November 1910- 29 March 1912* (Stroud: Amberley Publishing, 2012) p. 313.
2. Jones, Max, *The Last Great Quest: Captain Scott's Antarctic Sacrifice* (Oxford: Oxford University Press, 2003) p. 110.
3. Scott, Robert, Falcon, *Scott's Last Expedition, Diaries 26 November 1910- 29 March 1912* (Stroud: Amberley Publishing, 2012) p. 296.
4. Ibid entry for 19 January 1912 p. 298.
5. Quoted in Gregor, Gary C., *Swansea's Antarctic Explorer, Edgar Evans, 1876-1912* (Swansea: Swansea City Council, 1995) p. 85.
6. Scott, Robert, Falcon, *Scott's Last Expedition, Diaries 26 November 1910- 29 March 1912* (Stroud: Amberley Publishing, 2012) p. 287.
7. Smith, Michael, *I am just going outside: Captain Oates – Antarctic tragedy* (Cork: The Collins Press, 2002) p. 202. And Williams, Isobel,

Captain Scott's invaluable assistant – Edgar Evans (Stroud: History Press, 2012) p. 164. In 1985-6 when three men retraced the steps of Scott's expedition, they were advised by nutritionists that they required 8,000 calories a day to complete the arduous trek with that level of hard labour. When Sir Ranulph Fiennes and Dr Mike Stroud man-hauled for sixty-eight days across Antarctica they each lost forty four pounds in weight.

8. Williams, Isobel, *Captain Scott's invaluable assistant – Edgar Evans* (Stroud: History Press, 2012) p. 166.
9. Ibid p. 165.
10. Smith, Michael, *I am just going outside: Captain Oates – Antarctic tragedy* (Cork: The Collins Press, 2002) p. 202.
11. Mayberry, Jason Allen Mayberry, Scurvy and Vitamin C. Food and Drug Law. Winter 2004. Class and 3L Paper. April 27, 2004. Abstract. Harvard University (https://dash.harvard.edu/bitstream/handle/1/8852139/Mayberry.html).
12. For a more detailed discussion, see Williams, Isobel, *Captain Scott's invaluable assistant – Edgar Evans* (Stroud: History Press, 2012) p. 167.
13. Quoted in Solomon, Susan, *The coldest march: Scott's fatal Antarctic expedition* (New Haven; London: Yale University Press, 2001) p. 164.
14. Letter written by Thomas Griffith Taylor to Stanley Richards 11 June 1962 MS 761/16/4 University of Cambridge, Scott Polar Research Institute.
15. Edgar Evans' sledging journal MS 1487;BJ Journal, 27 January to 12 March 1911 [Western mountains sledge journey] University of Cambridge, Scott Polar Research Institute.
16. Frank Debenham's Diary, 15 February 1911 and 18 February 1911, MS 1654;D University of Cambridge, Scott Polar Research Institute.
17. Frank Debenham's, Diary, 20 February 1911, MS 1654;D University of Cambridge, Scott Polar Research Institute.
18. Letter written by Frank Debenham to Stanley Richards 25 May 1962 MS 761/16/1/13 University of Cambridge, Scott Polar Research Institute.
19. Scott, Robert, Falcon, *Scott's Last Expedition, Diaries 26 November 1910- 29 March 1912* (Stroud: Amberley Publishing, 2012) p. 287.
20. Ibid p. 291.
21. Ibid p. 292.
22. Ibid p. 297.
23. See Smith, Michael, *I am just going outside: Captain Oates – Antarctic tragedy* (Cork: The Collins Press, 2002).

24. Cherry-Garrard, Apsley, *The Worst Journey in the World* (London: Vintage Books, 2010) p. 544-545.
25. Jones, Max, *The Last Great Quest: Captain Scott's Antarctic Sacrifice* (Oxford: Oxford University Press, 2003) p. 99.
26. Scott, Robert, Falcon, *Scott's Last Expedition, Diaries 26 November 1910- 29 March 1912* (Stroud: Amberley Publishing, 2012) p. 307.
27. Quoted in Wheeler, Sara, *Cherry: a life of Apsley Cherry-Garrard* (London: Jonathan Cape, 2001) p. 49.
28. Ibid.
29. *The Mail*, 14 April 1913.
30. Crow, Duncan, *The Edwardian Woman* (Routledge Library Editions: Women's History, 2012).
31. Written in 1914 by his great friend J.M. Barrie as a biographical introduction to a book containing extracts of Scott's writings from *Discovery* and *Terra Nova*. Quoted in Jones, Max, *The Last Great Quest: Captain Scott's Antarctic Sacrifice* (Oxford: Oxford University Press, 2003) p. 245.
32. Jones, Max, *The Last Great Quest: Captain Scott's Antarctic Sacrifice* (Oxford: Oxford University Press, 2003) p. 111.
33. *Daily Express*, 12 February 1913.
34. Cherry's comment to George Seaver, quoted in Jones, Max, *The Last Great Quest: Captain Scott's Antarctic Sacrifice* (Oxford: Oxford University Press, 2003) p. 275.
35. *The Cambrian*, 21 February 1913 obtained from collections at Swansea Council Library Service.
36. Ibid.
37. Ibid.
38. *Daily Telegraph*, 15 February 1913.
39. Letter from Thomas Griffith Taylor to Stanley Richards, 11 June 1962 MS 761/16/4 University of Cambridge, Scott Polar Research Institute.
40. *P.O. Edgar Evans* (Gower Society publication) 28 April 2015.
41. Letter to Lois Evans from Scott, October 1911. West Glamorgan Archive Service GB 216 RISW/E3.
42. Solomon, Susan, *The coldest march: Scott's fatal Antarctic expedition* (New Haven; London: Yale University Press, 2001) p. 284. Edgar's grandson, John Evans told me that he believed they would not have made it to the pole without his ingenuity and skill.
43. *Western Mail*, 12 February 1913.
44. Ibid.

45. Quoted in Barczewski, Stephanie L., *Antarctic destinies: Scott, Shackleton, and the changing face of heroism* (London: Continuum, 2007) p. 130.
46. Letter written by Stanley Richards to Raymond Pound, 17 April 1964 MS 761/16/ University of Cambridge, Scott Polar Research Institute.
47. Jones, Max, *The Last Great Quest: Captain Scott's Antarctic Sacrifice* (Oxford: Oxford University Press, 2003) p. 112.
48. Quoted in Jones, Max, *The Last Great Quest: Captain Scott's Antarctic Sacrifice* (Oxford: Oxford University Press, 2003) p. 111-2.
49. Lois's grandson John Evans told me in a telephone conversation on 20 March 2020 that his father (Norman) had 'real stick about it' at school and only opened up about Edgar later in his life.
50. Jones, Max, *The Last Great Quest: Captain Scott's Antarctic Sacrifice* (Oxford: Oxford University Press, 2003) p. 127. Equivalent cost calculated via www.measuringworth.com.
51. Gregor, Gary C., *Swansea's Antarctic Explorer, Edgar Evans, 1876-1912* (Swansea: Swansea City Council, 1995) p. 82.
52. *Gower Church Magazine*, March 1914.
53. Williams, Isobel, *Captain Scott's invaluable assistant – Edgar Evans* (Stroud: History Press, 2012) p. 160.
54. Set of Player's cigarette cards commemorating 'Polar Exploration,' 1916. National Maritime Museum, Greenwich, London collection item ZBA2283.
55. February 1913. Mentioned in Gregor, Gary C., *Swansea's Antarctic Explorer, Edgar Evans, 1876-1912* (Swansea: Swansea City Council, 1995) p. 74.
56. Johnson, A.M., *Scott of the Antarctic and Cardiff*, published in *Morgannwg*, xxvi (1982) and xxvii (1983).

Men of Stone and Bronze

1. Cherry-Garrard, Apsley, *The Worst Journey in the World* (London: Vintage Books, 2010) p. 304-306.
2. Letter from Oriana to Cherry, 18 June 1914. MS 559/143/15; D University of Cambridge, Scott Polar Research Institute.
3. Letter from Oriana to Cherry, 5 June 1914. MS 559/143/14; D University of Cambridge, Scott Polar Research Institute.
4. Jones, Max, *The Last Great Quest: Captain Scott's Antarctic Sacrifice* (Oxford: Oxford University Press, 2003) p. 190.

5. Letter from Oriana to Cherry, 9 May 1914 MS 559/143/13; D. University of Cambridge, Scott Polar Research Institute.
6. Young, Louisa, *A great task of happiness: the life of Kathleen Scott* (London: Macmillan, 1995) p. 164.
7. Young, Edith, Baroness Kennet, *Self-Portrait of an Artist. From the diaries and memoirs of Lady Kennet, Kathleen, Lady Scott* (London: John Murray, 1949) p. 124-127 diary entries for July 1913 to February 1914.
8. The *Times*, 24 January 1914.
9. *The Times*, 23 February 1914.
10. *Daily Mirror*, 23 February 1914.
11. Warrior, Claire, (2016) *Rekindling Histories Families and British polar exploration* (PhD Thesis, University of Cambridge).
12. Jones, Max, *The Last Great Quest: Captain Scott's Antarctic Sacrifice* (Oxford: Oxford University Press, 2003) p. 156.
13. Oriana moved Ted's flag to the Scott Polar Research Institute so that it could be kept under museum conditions. Scott's is now in the collection at the National Maritime Museum.
14. The flag is still in the Royal Collection (RCIN 38032) and on display at Sandringham.
15. Barczewski, Stephanie L., *Antarctic destinies: Scott, Shackleton, and the changing face of heroism* (London: Continuum, 2007) p. 120. The ring is in the collection at The Wilson Cheltenham Art Gallery & Museum (collection item 2015.11.5).
16. The tiepin is now in the collection of the National Maritime Museum after it arrived unexpectedly at the museum sent through the post (ZBA7522). Kathleen's letter gifting the pin to Lady Sandhurst c. 1913 is in the archive (AGC/S/28).
17. Edward T. Wilson's letter to his daughter Lilian quoted in Christie's London catalogue *The Polar Sale, 25 September 2001* (Lot 178) Page 230.
18. MacInnes, Katherine, *Woman with the Iceberg Eyes: Oriana F. Wilson* (Cheltenham: The History Press, 2019) p. 201.
19. Recording of interview between Evelyn Forbes and David Wilson, 11 August 1995, 10 Summerfield, Cambridge, Cheltenham Borough Council and the Cheltenham Trust/The Wilson Family Collection.
20. David Wilson told me in an email on 26 July 2021 that because many of that generation died without issue, the two halves eventually came back into single ownership and formed the backbone of his father's donation to the Wilson Gallery in Cheltenham in 1994/5. The two halves were recently conserved, and the family had to fight hard to keep them separate and not have them restored into a single book.

21. Reference to Ory's visit to the studio and the wake is in MacInnes, Katherine, *Woman with the Iceberg Eyes: Oriana F. Wilson* (Cheltenham: The History Press, 2019) p. 205-6. Letter from Oriana to Cherry, 5 June 1914 says that Kathleen and Sir Clements are planning to stay the night at *Westal*. MS 559/143/14; D. University of Cambridge, Scott Polar Research Institute.
22. Letter from the Assistant Secretary of the Royal Geographical Society to Grace Scott, 10 October 1913. RGS-IBG Archives CB8/Scott,R.F./ File A-B 1911-1920.
23. Letters from the Scott family to Lord Curzon between March and December 1913, Curzon Correspondence, British Library, Asia, Pacific and Africa Collections, India Office Private Papers, MSS Eur F112/52.
24. Undated note of a conversation with Lady Scott, presumably by Curzon, in the Curzon Correspondence files in the British Library, Asia, Pacific and Africa Collections, India Office Private Papers, MSS Eur F112/53.
25. Lewis Beaumont to Lord Curzon, 2 August 1913. Curzon Correspondence, British Library, Asia, Pacific and Africa Collections, India Office Private Papers, MSS Eur F112/53.
26. Sir William Soulsby to Lord Curzon, 11 August 1913. Curzon Correspondence, British Library
27. Sir William Soulsby to Lord Curzon, 3 November 1913. Curzon Correspondence, British Library, Asia, Pacific and Africa Collections, India Office Private Papers, MSS Eur F112/53.
28. Sir William Soulsby to Lord Curzon, 13 January 1914. Curzon Correspondence, British Library, Asia, Pacific and Africa Collections, India Office Private Papers, MSS Eur F112/53.
29. Jones, Max, *The Last Great Quest: Captain Scott's Antarctic Sacrifice* (Oxford: Oxford University Press, 2003) p. 155.
30. Recording of interview between Evelyn Forbes and David Wilson, 11 August 1995, 10 Summerfield, Cambridge, Cheltenham Borough Council and the Cheltenham Trust/The Wilson Family Collection.
31. From Seaver, George, *Edward Wilson of the Antarctic: naturalist and friend; with an introduction by Apsley Cherry-Garrard* (London: John Murray, 1933) p. 123-4. It was Ted's great friend John Fraser who thought he would have taken up medical research.
32. Recording of interview between Evelyn Forbes and David Wilson, 11 August 1995, 10 Summerfield, Cambridge, Cheltenham Borough Council and the Cheltenham Trust/The Wilson Family Collection.

Knitting for Victory

1. Jones, Max, *The Last Great Quest: Captain Scott's Antarctic Sacrifice* (Oxford: Oxford University Press, 2003)
2. Ibid p. 200-1.
3. Ibid p. 259.
4. Jones, Max, *The Last Great Quest: Captain Scott's Antarctic Sacrifice* (Oxford: Oxford University Press, 2003) p. 257.
5. Beynon, Leonard, *Rhossili: The Land, Landscape and People* (Swansea: West Glamorgan Archive Service, 2008) p. 154-5.
6. *The Formation of the Swansea Battalion 1914-15*, J.R. Alban in *Gower*, the Journal of the Gower Society, Vol. 25, The National Library of Wales.
7. John Wilfred Joseph Faull, Royal Field Artillery. Territorial Force (Driver). World War I Service Medal and Award Rolls, 1914-1920.
8. Gosling, Lucinda, *Knitting for Tommy: keeping the Great War soldier warm* (Stroud: The History Press, 2014).
9. www.scarletfinders.co.uk list of local work depots.
10. Women's Archive Wales, *Women, Wales and War.*
11. Website of the Women's Land Army (womenslandarmy.co.uk).
12. Extracts from the Rhossili School Log Books for 1882 and 1883, quoted in Beynon, Leonard, *Rhossili: The Land, Landscape and People* (Swansea: West Glamorgan Archive Service, 2008.

Sculpting Beauty from Horror

1. Letter from Kathleen to Keltie, 1 August 1914, RGS-IBG Archives/Keltie.
2. Young, Louisa, *A great task of happiness: the life of Kathleen Scott* (London: Macmillan, 1995) p. 164-5.
3. Young, Edith, Baroness Kennet, *Self-Portrait of an Artist. From the diaries and memoirs of Lady Kennet, Kathleen, Lady Scott* (London: John Murray, 1949) entry for 1 November 1916 p. 147.
4. Ibid p. 147.
5. Wheeler, Sara, *Cherry: a life of Apsley Cherry-Garrard* (London: Jonathan Cape, 2001) p. 174.
6. Young, Edith, Baroness Kennet, *Self-Portrait of an Artist. From the diaries and memoirs of Lady Kennet, Kathleen, Lady Scott* (London: John Murray, 1949) entries for 6 May and 10 June 1917.
7. Wheeler, Sara, *Cherry: a life of Apsley Cherry-Garrard* (London: Jonathan Cape, 2001) p. 195.
8. Ibid p. 191.

9. Young, Edith, Baroness Kennet, *Self-Portrait of an Artist. From the diaries and memoirs of Lady Kennet, Kathleen, Lady Scott* (London: John Murray, 1949) entry for 4 November 1918 p. 168.
10. *The Times*, 24 January 1916.
11. Herbert, Kari, *Polar Wives* (Vancouver: Greystone Books, 2012) p. 242.
12. Young, Edith, Baroness Kennet, *Self-Portrait of an Artist. From the diaries and memoirs of Lady Kennet, Kathleen, Lady Scott* (London: John Murray, 1949) entry for June – 1916 p. 144.
13. Jones, Max, *The Last Great Quest: Captain Scott's Antarctic Sacrifice* (Oxford: Oxford University Press, 2003) p. 258.
14. Young, Edith, Baroness Kennet, *Self-Portrait of an Artist. From the diaries and memoirs of Lady Kennet, Kathleen, Lady Scott* (London: John Murray, 1949) entry for 19 September 1929 p. 270.

Casualties of War

1. From Anne Strathie's talk for the Gilbert White's House Online Antarctic series, *From Ice Floes to Battlefields: Terra Nova expedition members in World War I*, 18 March 2021.
2. www.nzhistory.govt.nz/war/first-world-war-nurses.
3. *Evening Mail*, 2 August 1915.
4. *Leeds Mercury*, 21 September 1915.
5. Letter from Ory to Cherry, 13 April 1916. MS 559/143/19; D. University of Cambridge, Scott Polar Research Institute.
6. *Otago Daily Times*, 31 October 2016.
7. MacInnes, Katherine, *Woman with the Iceberg Eyes: Oriana F. Wilson* (Cheltenham: The History Press, 2019) p. 208-209.
8. Letter from Ory to Cherry, 3 May 1918. MS 559/143/21; D. University of Cambridge, Scott Polar Research Institute.
9. MacInnes, Katherine, *Woman with the Iceberg Eyes: Oriana F. Wilson* (Cheltenham: The History Press, 2019) p. 212.
10. Letter from Ory to Cherry, 3 May 1918. MS 559/143/21; D. University of Cambridge, Scott Polar Research Institute.
11. MacInnes, Katherine, *Woman with the Iceberg Eyes: Oriana F. Wilson* (Cheltenham: The History Press, 2019) p. 221. Greenstreet was not the same man who was First Officer on *Endurance*
12. Letter from Ory to Cherry, 3 May 1918. MS 559/143/21; D. University of Cambridge, Scott Polar Research Institute.
13. Letter from Ory to Cherry, 4 September 1915. MS 559/143/16; D. University of Cambridge, Scott Polar Research Institute.
14. Constance Mary Souper in the *Westminster, London, England, Church of England Marriages and Banns, 1754-1935* accessed via Ancestry.

The marriage took place at St Peter's which was within the ecclesiastical boundary of St George Hanover Square where it was registered.

15. Letter from Ory to Cherry, 4 September 1915. MS 559/143/16; D. University of Cambridge, Scott Polar Research Institute.
16. Letter from Ory to Cherry, 29 February 1916. MS 559/143/17; D. University of Cambridge, Scott Polar Research Institute.
17. Ibid.
18. Find A Grave, database and images (https://www.findagrave.com: accessed 07 January 2019), memorial page for Second Lieutenant Noel Beaumont Souper (unknown–1 Jul 1916), Find A Grave Memorial no. 12568202, citing Thiepval Memorial, Thiepval, Departement de la Somme, Picardie, France; Maintained by IWPP Custodial Account (contributor 48586138).
19. Wheeler, Sara, *Cherry: a life of Apsley Cherry-Garrard* (London: Jonathan Cape, 2001) p. 193.
20. Kathleen's diary entry, 9 November 1916.
21. Kathleen's diary entry, 29 Dec 1916 (Kennet Papers).
22. Seaver, George, *Edward Wilson of the Antarctic: naturalist and friend; together with a memoir of Oriana Wilson; with an introduction by Apsley Cherry-Garrard* (London: John Murray, 1963) p. 223.
23. MacInnes, Katherine, *Woman with the Iceberg Eyes: Oriana F. Wilson* (Cheltenham: The History Press, 2019) p. 214.
24. Electoral Register for 1918 shows that Rosalie is living with Ory.
25. From Anne Strathie's talk for the Gilbert White's House Online Antarctic series, *From Ice Floes to Battlefields: Terra Nova expedition members in World War I*, 18 March 2021.
26. Ibid.
27. Ibid.
28. Seaver, George, *Edward Wilson of the Antarctic: naturalist and friend; with an introduction by Apsley Cherry-Garrard* (London: John Murray, 1933) p. 68.
29. My interview with David Wilson, 25 September 2019.
30. Young, Edith, Baroness Kennet, *Self-Portrait of an Artist. From the diaries and memoirs of Lady Kennet, Kathleen, Lady Scott* (London: John Murray, 1949) entry for 17 November 1918 p. 169.

A New Family

1. Kathleen's diary entries for 19 July 1917 and 16 Sep. 1918.
2. Young, Edith, Baroness Kennet, *Self-Portrait of an Artist. From the diaries and memoirs of Lady Kennet, Kathleen, Lady Scott* (London: John Murray, 1949) p. 178.

3. Ibid p. 186.
4. Herbert, Kari, *Polar Wives* (Vancouver: Greystone Books, 2012) p. 317.
5. Young, Edith, Baroness Kennet, *Self-Portrait of an Artist. From the diaries and memoirs of Lady Kennet, Kathleen, Lady Scott* (London: John Murray, 1949) p. 248.
6. Ibid p. 203.
7. Ibid p. 213.
8. Kathleen's diary entries for 1933 and 1934.
9. Young, Edith, Baroness Kennet, *Self-Portrait of an Artist. From the diaries and memoirs of Lady Kennet, Kathleen, Lady Scott* (London: John Murray, 1949) entry for 12 March 1937 p. 316.
10. Ibid p. 233.
11. Ibid, entry for 20 March 1935 p. 302.
12. The Polar Sale including The Neil Silverman Collection, Christie's 25 September 2002. https://www.christies.com/en/auction/the-polar-sale-including-the-neil-silverman-collection-17902/
13. From the preface of Mill, H.R et al., *Rejoice my Heart: The Making of H.R. Mill's "The Life of Sir Ernest Shackleton" The Private Correspondence of Dr. Hugh Robert Mill and Lady Shackleton, 1922-33* (Santa Monica: Adélie Books, 2007).
14. Parker, Sarah E., *Grace & favour: a handbook of who lived where in Hampton Court Palace, 1750 to 1950* (Surrey: Historic Royal Palaces, 2005) p. 115.
15. Letter from Emily Shackleton to Hugh Robert Mill, 12 August 1924 published in Mill, H.R et al., *Rejoice my Heart: The Making of H.R. Mill's "The Life of Sir Ernest Shackleton" The Private Correspondence of Dr. Hugh Robert Mill and Lady Shackleton, 1922-33* (Santa Monica: Adélie Books, 2007) p. 114-5.
16. Letter from Emily Shackleton to Hugh Robert Mill, 6 November 1924, published in Ibid, p. 117-8.
17. Wheeler, Sara, *Cherry: a life of Apsley Cherry-Garrard* (London: Jonathan Cape, 2001) p. 213.
18. Max Jones lists the changes that were made on p. 123 of his *The Last Great Quest: Captain Scott's Antarctic Sacrifice* (Oxford: Oxford University Press, 2003). Only sixty-eight words were altered or cut from Scott's sixty page account of the march back.
19. Wheeler, Sara, *Cherry: a life of Apsley Cherry-Garrard* (London: Jonathan Cape, 2001) p. 161.
20. Excerpts from *The Worst Journey in the World* by Apsley Cherry-Garrard appear by permission of the Scott Polar Research Institute, University of Cambridge.

21. Young, Edith, Baroness Kennet, *Self-Portrait of an Artist. From the diaries and memoirs of Lady Kennet, Kathleen, Lady Scott* (London: John Murray, 1949) entry for 16 February 1927 p. 253.
22. Wheeler, Sara, *Cherry: a life of Apsley Cherry-Garrard* (London: Jonathan Cape, 2001) p. 219.
23. Young, Edith, Baroness Kennet, *Self-Portrait of an Artist. From the diaries and memoirs of Lady Kennet, Kathleen, Lady Scott* (London: John Murray, 1949) entry for 5 September 1929 p. 269.
24. Letter from Kathleen to George Seaver quoted in MacInnes, Katherine, *Woman with the Iceberg Eyes: Oriana F. Wilson* (Cheltenham: The History Press, 2019) p. 267.
25. Young, Edith, Baroness Kennet, *Self-Portrait of an Artist. From the diaries and memoirs of Lady Kennet, Kathleen, Lady Scott* (London: John Murray, 1949) entry for 26 March 1939 p. 329.
26. Ibid, entry for 5 September 1929 p. 269.

Family Tensions

1. MacInnes, Katherine, *Woman with the Iceberg Eyes: Oriana F. Wilson* (Cheltenham: The History Press, 2019) p. 224.
2. Ibid p. 242.
3. Oriana's letter to Cherry, 22 February 1929. MS 559/143/25; D. University of Cambridge, Scott Polar Research Institute.
4. Recording of interviews between David Wilson and Evelyn Forbes (25 August 1995) and David Wilson and Michael Wilson (30 March 1995), Cheltenham Borough Council and the Cheltenham Trust/The Wilson Family Collection.
5. Seaver, George, *Edward Wilson of the Antarctic: naturalist and friend; together with a memoir of Oriana Wilson; with an introduction by Apsley Cherry-Garrard* (London: John Murray, 1963) p. 221.
6. Recording of interviews between David Wilson and Evelyn Forbes (25 August 1995) and David Wilson and Michael Wilson (30 March 1995), Cheltenham Borough Council and the Cheltenham Trust/The Wilson Family Collection.
7. Oriana's letter to Isabel Smith, 9 January 1935. MS 559/145/1; D. University of Cambridge, Scott Polar Research Institute.
8. Seaver, George, *Edward Wilson of the Antarctic: naturalist and friend; together with a memoir of Oriana Wilson; with an introduction by Apsley Cherry-Garrard* (London: John Murray, 1963) p. 220.
9. MacInnes, Katherine, *Woman with the Iceberg Eyes: Oriana F. Wilson* (Cheltenham: The History Press, 2019) p. 227-8 and p. 232. It is

Katherine MacInnes that points out the irony that it was Ory who had a new species named after her and not Ted.

10. MacInnes, Katherine, *Woman with the Iceberg Eyes: Oriana F. Wilson* (Cheltenham: The History Press, 2019)
11. Recording of interviews between David Wilson and Evelyn Forbes (25 August 1995) and David Wilson and Michael Wilson (30 March 1995), Cheltenham Borough Council and the Cheltenham Trust/The Wilson Family Collection.
12. Oriana's letter to Isabel Smith, 9 January 1935. MS 559/145/1; D. University of Cambridge, Scott Polar Research Institute.
13. Recording of interviews between David Wilson and Evelyn Forbes (25 August 1995) and David Wilson and Michael Wilson (30 March 1995), Cheltenham Borough Council and the Cheltenham Trust/The Wilson Family Collection.
14. MacInnes, Katherine, *Woman with the Iceberg Eyes: Oriana F. Wilson* (Cheltenham: The History Press, 2019) p. 241.
15. The 1921 census shows that Ory was staying with Connie at her home in Brixham in June, shortly after the birth of her second child Eleanor. Elizabeth (Betty) was four years old.
16. Letter from Ory to Cherry, 13 December 1916. MS 559/143/20; D. University of Cambridge, Scott Polar Research Institute.
17. MacInnes, Katherine, *Woman with the Iceberg Eyes: Oriana F. Wilson* (Cheltenham: The History Press, 2019) p. 250-252.
18. Her youngest sibling Adrian died in 1961.
19. Told to me by David Wilson in our email exchange, 26 July 2021.
20. Seaver, George, *Edward Wilson of the Antarctic: naturalist and friend; together with a memoir of Oriana Wilson; with an introduction by Apsley Cherry-Garrard* (London: John Murray, 1963) p. 220.
21. Recording of interviews between David Wilson and Evelyn Forbes (25 August 1995) and David Wilson and Michael Wilson (30 March 1995), Cheltenham Borough Council and the Cheltenham Trust/The Wilson Family Collection.
22. Seaver, George, *Edward Wilson of the Antarctic: naturalist and friend; together with a memoir of Oriana Wilson; with an introduction by Apsley Cherry-Garrard* (London: John Murray, 1963) 221.
23. Seaver, George, *Edward Wilson of the Antarctic: naturalist and friend; together with a memoir of Oriana Wilson; with an introduction by Apsley Cherry-Garrard* (London: John Murray, 1963) p. 221.
24. MacInnes, Katherine, *Woman with the Iceberg Eyes: Oriana F. Wilson* (Cheltenham: The History Press, 2019) p. 243-245.
25. Recording of interviews between David Wilson and Evelyn Forbes (25 August 1995) and David Wilson and Michael Wilson (30 March

1995), Cheltenham Borough Council and the Cheltenham Trust/The Wilson Family Collection.

26. Ibid.
27. Ibid.
28. Ibid.
29. Ory's letter to Isabel Smith, 21 February 1935 (MS 559/145/3;D) University of Cambridge, Scott Polar Research Institute.
30. Recording of interviews between David Wilson and Evelyn Forbes (25 August 1995) and David Wilson and Michael Wilson (30 March 1995), Cheltenham Borough Council and the Cheltenham Trust/The Wilson Family Collection.
31. Last Will and Testament of Oriana Wilson, 11 January 1930.
32. Codicil to the Last Will and Testament of Oriana Wilson dated 11 January 1934.

A Family Home

1. Spufford, Francis, *I may be some time: ice and the English imagination* (London: Faber, 1996) p. 238 and Solomon, Susan, *The coldest march: Scott's fatal Antarctic expedition* (New Haven; London: Yale University Press, 2001) p. 283.
2. *Daily Telegraph*, 14 February 1913.
3. John Faull is recorded as having Ironmongers premises in Clydach Road in *Wright's Swansea Directory*, 1899 and this is shown as his address in various trade directories as well as censuses up to the 1920s.
4. Their older sister Jane had died in 1901.
5. Marjory Ellen was born in 1902 and Margaret Eileen in 1909.
6. *The Morris Family and Swansea*, J.M. Davies in *Gower*, the Journal of the Gower Society, Vol. 5, The National Library of Wales.
7. Electoral Registers, 1839–1966. She is still there in the 1921 census.
8. 1921 census.
9. Anne died in 1919 and the 1921 census shows Sarah now living with her sister Elizabeth.
10. 1921 census and Gregor, Gary C., *Swansea's Antarctic Explorer, Edgar Evans, 1876-1912* (Swansea: Swansea City Council, 1995) p. 3.
11. The 1921 census records that Lois's eighteen-year-old niece Marjorie Faull was helping her grandparents at their home.
12. These pensions included 2 shillings a week for each child from the Navy, ending when Ralph and Norman were fourteen and Muriel sixteen, and 3 shillings each from the government until they reached the age of eighteen.
13. The 1921 census records the family living at 5 Slate Street and Norman as an out-of-work apprentice electrician at the steelworks.

He is fifteen at this point and so must have begun his apprenticeship earlier to be recorded as being temporarily out of work.

14. *Kelly's Directory* of 1910 lists Lewis Yelland as a manager of a butcher's shop on Woodfield Street. The electoral registers from 1923 to 1927/8 show that he has business premises at 4 Pentrepoeth with a 'Lois Evans' in occupation (he is living at No. 30). Lois would have been qualified to vote for the first time because the Representation of the People Act 1918 enfranchised women over thirty who were occupiers in their own right.
15. The Rate Books held by the West Glamorgan Archive Service show that Lois was paying rent at 62 *Heol Fedw* in 1929. Unfortunately, there is a gap in their records between 1923 (when Heol Fedw) did not exist) and 1929.
16. The Rate Books held by West Glamorgan Archive Service; TR 3/14/90 April 1929 and TR/3/14/94 October 1929 show that when Lois first moved in she paid £5 1s 3d twice a year, the equivalent of approximately £390 a year today.
17. Lois's grandson John Evans told me about the name of the house and Ants Ford told me about the portrait.
18. Beatrice was widowed in 1923 and Electoral Registers 1839-1966 show that she moved soon after to 27 Ernald Place
19. 1939 Register. Most of the women are listed as housewives.
20. Electoral Registers, 1839-1966 show that from 1928 to 1930 Norman was living at 12 Waun Road with Edward and Lizzie Rogers.
21. Electoral Registers.
22. Recommendation of Award (1944 Birthday Honours) for John Wilfred Joseph Faull, The National Archives WO/373/156/653.
23. Electoral Registers, 1839-1966 show Norman and Lydia living with Lois in 1945 and 1946 and at 9 Fendrod Walk from 1947.
24. Elisabeth Blanchet and Sonia Zhuravlyova, *Prefabs: A Social and Architectural History* (published by Historic England).
25. 1939 Register.
26. Told to me by John Evans in a telephone conversation on 20 March 2020.
27. 1939 Register. Ralph is described as 'Plater Constructional Engineering.' Electoral Registers, 1839-1966 show that he and Sheila lived with Lois until she died in 1952.
28. *South Wales Evening Post*, 24 April 1952.

Forgotten Widows

1. Gladys' sister Mabel was Hilda Russell's best friend and Teddy Evans is said to have broken her heart by falling in love with Hilda instead of her (my telephone conversation with Susanna Ferrar, 19 June 2020).

2. MacInnes, Katherine, *Woman with the Iceberg Eyes: Oriana F. Wilson* (Cheltenham: The History Press, 2019) p. 269 -270.
3. My interview with David Wilson, 25 September 2019, and his recorded interview with Evelyn Forbes.
4. Young, Edith, Baroness Kennet, *Self-Portrait of an Artist. From the diaries and memoirs of Lady Kennet, Kathleen, Lady Scott* (London: John Murray, 1949) p. 340.
5. Elizabeth Jane Howard married Peter in 1942 when she was nineteen. She left him in 1946 to become a writer. Her series of novels, the *Cazalet Chronicles*, drew heavily on her memories of this time and includes a fictionalised portrayal of her mother-in-law Kathleen.
6. Young, Edith, Baroness Kennet, *Self-Portrait of an Artist. From the diaries and memoirs of Lady Kennet, Kathleen, Lady Scott* (London: John Murray, 1949) p. 361.
7. *South Wales Evening Post*, 24 April 1952.
8. Lois's grandson John told me that he had seen her lying in her coffin and was terrified. He was only a young boy.
9. *South Wales Evening Post*, 24 April 1952.
10. Scott, Peter, *The Eye of the Wind: An Autobiography* (London: Hodder & Stoughton, 1961) p. 19-22.
11. Lois's grandson John Evans told me in a telephone conversation on 20 March 2020 that his father (Norman) had 'real stick about it' at school and only opened up about Edgar later in his life.
12. Gregor, Gary C., *Swansea's Antarctic Explorer, Edgar Evans, 1876-1912* (Swansea: Swansea City Council, 1995) p. 84.
13. Ibid.
14. Ibid p. 82.
15. *Horowhenua Chronicle*, 7 July 1938.
16. Young, Edith, Baroness Kennet, *Self-Portrait of an Artist. From the diaries and memoirs of Lady Kennet, Kathleen, Lady Scott* (London: John Murray, 1949) p. 274.
17. Barczewski, Stephanie L., *Antarctic destinies: Scott, Shackleton, and the changing face of heroism* (London: Continuum, 2007) p. 226 and p. 230.
18. This comes from *Scott of the Antarctic*, a book about the film written by its polar advisor David James (p. 36) which Michael Smith drew my attention to.
19. *South Wales Evening Post*, 24 April 1952.
20. David Wilson told me he had asked the producers why the wives were depicted as they were and this is the answer he was given (our telephone conversation 25 September 2019).

Index

Anne Fletcher is an historian and writer. She has a career in heritage and has worked at some of the most exciting historic sites in the country including Hampton Court Palace, St Paul's Cathedral, Westminster Abbey, Bletchley Park and Tower Bridge. She previously wrote *From the Mill to Monte Carlo* (2018), which was widely covered in the national press.